Border Towns and Border Crossings

Border Towns and Border Crossings

A History of the U.S.-Mexico Divide

Roger Bruns

GREENWOOD™

An Imprint of ABC-CLIO, LLC
Santa Barbara, California • Denver, Colorado

Library of Congress Cataloging-in-Publication Data

Names: Bruns, Roger A., 1941– author.
Title: Border towns and border crossings : a history of the U.S.-Mexico divide / Roger Bruns.
Description: Santa Barbara, California : Greenwood, an imprint of ABC-CLIO, LLC, [2019] | Includes bibliographical references and index.
Identifiers: LCCN 2019013034 (print) | LCCN 2019017318 (ebook) | ISBN 9781440863530 (ebook) | ISBN 9781440863523 (hardback : alk. paper)
Subjects: LCSH: Mexican-American Border Region—History. | Mexican-American Border Region—History—Sources. | Mexican-American Border Region—Social conditions. | Mexican-American Border Region—Economic conditions. | Borderlands—United States. | Borderlands—Mexico. | Border patrols—United States. | Immigration enforcement—United States. | United States—Emigration and immigration.
Classification: LCC F786 (ebook) | LCC F786 .B88 2019 (print) | DDC 972/.1—dc23
LC record available at https://lccn.loc.gov/2019013034

ISBN: 978-1-4408-6352-3 (print)
978-1-4408-6353-0 (ebook)

23 22 21 20 19   1 2 3 4 5

This book is also available as an eBook.

Greenwood
An Imprint of ABC-CLIO, LLC

ABC-CLIO, LLC
147 Castilian Drive
Santa Barbara, California 93117
www.abc-clio.com

This book is printed on acid-free paper ∞

Manufactured in the United States of America

Contents

Introduction

The U.S.-Mexican border, *la frontera*, is far more than a line or markers or fences that separate two countries. It is history and commerce and culture, as well as a minefield of political tension, fear, violence, and exploitation. It is binational cooperation as well as competition. Along its winding path of nearly 2,000 miles from the Pacific Ocean to the Gulf of Mexico, it is a landscape of desert and waterway that has been traversed for centuries and coveted by many.

But most of all the border is its people, great numbers of whom, carrying their required legal documents, cross each day: the Mexican commercial truck driver in Nuevo Laredo who begins his work day at about 8 a.m. and typically returns home around 11 p.m. after crossing the border several times through long processing and customs lines; the young woman student from Juárez, Chihuahua, who crosses the border to go to school at the University of Texas-El Paso; the elderly woman who manages to secure a ride from Tucson, Arizona, to cross the border in Nogales where she can fill a medical prescription at far less cost than she can in the United States; the couple from Brownsville, Texas, who cross the Gateway Bridge to have lunch at Garcia's, a popular restaurant and bar in Matamoros, Tamaulipas; the Mexican American auto mechanic who lives in Ciudad Acuña, Coahuila, because he can afford a house there and crosses the river to work in Del Rio, Texas; the man from San Luis Río, Colorado, who wakes up most mornings at 4 a.m., walks downtown to the parking lot near Del Sol supermarket where buses await to take him and many other workers across the border, and then boards another bus that takes him to lettuce fields near Yuma, Arizona, where he often works for ten hours before making the return trip home; the man from Douglas, Arizona, who crosses the border to volunteer at the Migrant Resource Center in Agua Prieta, Sonora, to help recently deported men, women, and children with basic needs such as food and medical attention, as well as advice on how to reach their next destinations.

At border ports of entry across four states, over 350 million crossings occur each year. But through the years, and especially into the twenty-first century, the image of the border has taken on an increasingly sinister image. If the border can be seen as a metaphor for cross-cultural and bilingual melding, it is also a source of growing anxiety over national security and safety.

The life of the border and its sister cities involves a long history of conflict and interaction and evolving interrelationships between people and cultures. For over a century and a half, the U.S.-Mexican border has been the scene of violence, racial and cultural animosity, and conflicting visions of what the United States should embrace—an "America First" ideology promoting strict border control and cultural stability or the respect for changing cultural norms and increasing diversity that values the contributions of individuals from various backgrounds and nations.

The painful and shameful spectacle in 2018 of children from Central America being separated from their parents and held in detention centers did not occur in a historical vacuum; it is the culmination of conflict and struggle over policy, values, and economic forces throughout the history of the border—from the marking of the lines after the Treaty of Guadalupe Hidalgo and the Gadsden Purchase in the middle of the nineteenth century to today's demands for a border wall to be erected from Tijuana/San Diego to Matamoras/Brownsville.

This book explores the history of the border, from a time when there were no fences, when settlers and the government were more concerned about Apache depredations than with drug enforcement and contentious debate over immigration policies.

It will look at the challenges of marking the border lines, the melding of cultures, the developing industries and cross-border workers, the violence in times both of war and peace, the advent of agencies to contend with myriad issues from immigration to warring cartels, the social and economic exchanges between countries, the shared visions, and the relationships between the "sister cities" that face each other across the border.

Because, for all of the conflict, violence, and tension throughout the years, the border remains a gathering place where individuals with disparate heritages mold an ever-evolving cultural mix, one where the words of the Arizona poet laureate, Alberto Ríos, we forever hope will always be true:

The border is what joins us,
Not what separates us.

1

Creating the Line

In 1848 in a small village named La Villa de Guadalupe Hidalgo just outside Mexico City, the United States and Mexico signed a treaty that among settlers of different heritages has reverberated with resentment and animus for generations after. The Treaty of Guadalupe Hidalgo, ending the Mexican War, ceded to the United States vast territories of California, Arizona, and New Mexico, as well as portions of Colorado, Utah, and Nevada, for the paltry sum of $15 million. Although the terms of the treaty did not precisely define the rights of Mexicans remaining in the lands taken over by the United States, it did offer a guarantee that they would be granted the same rights as U.S. citizens. Those guarantees would wither away as economic, social, and political power was soon dominated by the onrush of newly arrived citizens from the United States.

MANIFEST DESTINY OR CONQUEST?

On January 12, 1848, Abraham Lincoln, a young freshman Whig congressman from Illinois, delivered a speech to the U.S. House of Representatives questioning the motives and the constitutional right of the U.S. government to prosecute the ongoing war against Mexico. The previous December, Lincoln had introduced what became known as the "Spot Resolutions," an audacious political statement that challenged the president of the United States, James K. Polk, to show to the American people that the first spot of blood of the conflict had, indeed, been spilled on U.S. soil, a claim that supporters used to justify the war itself.

Lincoln, along with others, was in fact issuing a challenge not only to the prosecution of the war, a conflict that an inferior Mexican army had no chance of winning, but to the whole idea of so-called "Manifest Destiny," a concept sweeping throughout much of the country, fueled by an eager press, that the United States, superior in virtue and morality, was preordained by God to advance its Anglo-Saxon, white race government, motivated by Protestant Christian ideals, to expand and civilize the territory across to the Pacific Coast, driving aside all those who stood in its way—whatever their own historical and cultural claims to the lands.

This was God's plan to bring enlightenment and prosperity to a savage wilderness. Lincoln was thus challenging the notion that Manifest Destiny and is the impetus for war with Mexico was directed by the Deity and was suggesting instead that it was merely another instance of a nation on a mission of bloody conquest.

By the time Lincoln made his speech on the floor of the House of Representatives, the war had dragged on for nearly two years. Given the fact that the end result of the war would be the conquest of a massive amount of land by the United States and the drawing of what is now the U.S.-Mexican border, it is notable that the beginning of the conflict was itself rooted in a boundary dispute that involved Texas.

In 1921 Mexico won independence in a revolutionary war against Spain. The country of Mexico at that time extended northward into areas that are now Texas, New Mexico, Utah, Nevada, Arizona, California, and part of Colorado. As settlers from the eastern United States moved into areas in northern Mexico, tensions escalated into violence. By 1835 approximately 30,000 Americans lived in Texas and outnumbered native Mexicans by six to one. Many of the new settlers brought their slaves with them.

As the hostilities grew more heated, the new residents became determined throw off Mexican rule and establish their own government and declared their independence in 1836, an action that culminated in the iconic slaughter by Mexican troops of 187 defenders of a mission in San Antonio called the Alamo, a subsequent massacre of more than 300 captives at the city of Goliad, and the decisive battle at San Jacinto, which resulted in the rout of a large Mexican force and the capture of the Mexican commander, Antonio López de Santa Anna.

The Texans had won their independence. It was now the Republic of Texas or, as many called it, the "Lone Star Republic."

Nine years later, the U.S. Congress annexed Texas as a state, an action that was fiercely opposed by politicians representing non-slaveholding states, who were angered that the political balance of power in the country would be shifted to states that allowed slavery. It was a balance of power that slaveholding and non-slaveholding states had fought over for decades.

The annexation of Texas as a state was also provocative in the eyes of the Mexican government and involved a disputed area of land. The traditional border that separated Mexico and Texas had been the Nueces River. Nevertheless, President Polk encouraged settlers to uphold claims to the land to the Rio Grande River, about 150 miles south of the Nueces, and assured them that the U.S. government would stand by their claims to that land.

In a further provocation, in March 1846, the president ordered General Zachary Taylor to lead an armed force into the disputed territory, an action that on its surface seemed to many specifically designed to trigger an aggressive response. In the eyes of Lincoln and others opposed to a confrontation with Mexico, the move was an overt ploy conceived to produce war, near-certain U.S. victory, and a conquering of western land that would fulfill the dreams of Manifest Destiny.

When a force of Mexican troops did engage Taylor's force in an area of thatched huts occupied by Mexican residents in the town of Matamoras in the disputed area of land and several U.S. troops lost their lives, the war was on, The Polk administration claimed that the Mexicans had first spilled U.S. blood in the exchange of fire; war opponents questioned whether that first "spot" of blood had been spilled on American soil. Polk used the news of the loss of life in the skirmishes to gain congressional support for a declaration of war against Mexico on May 13, 1846.

In his speech on the House floor in 1848, Lincoln said of President Polk:

> I more than suspect already, that he is deeply conscious of being in the wrong; that he feels the blood of this war, like the blood of Abel, is crying to Heaven against him; that he ordered General Taylor into the midst of a peaceful Mexican settlement, purposely to bring on a war; that originally having some strong motive—what I will not stop now to give my opinion concerning—to involve the two countries in a war, and trusting to escape scrutiny by fixing the public gaze upon the exceeding brightness of military glory—that attractive rainbow that rises in showers of blood—that serpent's eye that charms to destroy-he plunged into it, and has swept on and on, till disappointed in his calculation of the ease with which Mexico might be subdued, he now finds himself he knows not where.

At the time Lincoln delivered his speech, the carnage and death suffered on both sides of the warring armies, along with civilian casualties, had been far more serious than supporters of the war could have imagined when hostilities began. The romance of the recruiting notices and the promised glory at the onset of the war for Manifest Destiny had devolved into the gore, atrocities, disease, and agony of battlefields.

The names of small Mexican villages and towns now became known for the skirmishes and pillaging for which they became reluctant hosts—Burrita, Camargo, Chihuahua, Churubusco, Huamantla, Buena Vista, Contreras, Molino del Rey, and many others.

The U.S. military began its attack on Mexican forces with a strategy designed to take control of northern Mexico and force an early surrender. Two U.S. armies moved south from Texas, and a third, under the leadership of Colonel Stephen Kearny, moved west to what is now New Mexico and California. Armed with superior weaponry, U.S. forces began to inflict devastating casualties in a number of battles, including Palo Alto and Resaca de Palma. By the summer of 1846, Mexican forces had been routed in crippling fights south of Texas and in California. Following General Taylor's capture of the northern Mexican city of Monterey, a bloody, dispiriting affair, the Mexicans finally surrendered but bargained for a temporary truce that allowed both sides to recover. The Mexicans left the city with their arms and ammunition, a condition of the truce that infuriated President Polk, who wanted complete surrender and a hastened end to the war.

In the parched deserts of northern Mexico the hostilities continued long past the U.S. government's original expectations. An overland expedition to Mexico City to force a peace settlement seemed daunting. At this stage, General Winfield Scott concocted a strategy that would not only surprise the Mexican resisters but would result in fewer casualties on both sides: an amphibious landing on the beaches near the Mexican eastern port city of Vera Cruz. In March 1847 over 12,000 U.S. soldiers successfully landed and indiscriminately bombarded the town with mortar shells, leaving scores of women and children dead. The army then began its march to Mexico City.

In September 1847, on the outskirts of Mexico City, Scott's army engaged in a gruesome confrontation that left the battlefield littered with thousands of dead

Mexican and U.S. soldiers and scores of mangled mules and horses. As the U.S. forces began the occupation of the city, it would signify the end of serious Mexican military resistance.

Many of those who participated in the war, remembering the horrors that some soldiers inflicted on the Mexican population, expressed shame and remorse over the scenes they witnessed. One of those soldiers was Ulysses Grant, a lieutenant in the U.S. Army's Fourth Infantry, whose name would later become inextricably linked with Congressman Lincoln from Illinois. Grant later remembered the Mexican War in his last years as a cruel and wicked exercise in wanton power and wasted lives.

THE TREATY OF GUADALUPE HIDALGO

On February 2, 1848, with the signing of the Treaty of Guadalupe Hidalgo and the creation of the border between the United States and Mexico, the futures of the two countries were profoundly marked. North of the Rio Grande would be the state of Texas. To the west would be California and, after subsequent treaty negotiations, the lands in between that would eventually include Nevada, Arizona, New Mexico, and Utah, as well as parts of Oklahoma, Wyoming, and Colorado. The war cost the country of Mexico half of its land.

The treaty negotiations featured an unlikely character: a man named Nicholas Trist. A lawyer born into the aristocracy in Virginia and married to Thomas Jefferson's granddaughter, Trist became a clerk in the State Department in 1828 and then served as President Andrew Jackson's private secretary. Later, he was U.S. Consul in Cuba for eight years before returning to Washington as President Polk's chief clerk of the State Department.

At the urging of Secretary of State James Buchanan, Polk sent Trist as an agent to join General Scott in Mexico with the mission to negotiate an end to the war. As the military hostilities ended, Polk had second thoughts about the treaty negotiations, becoming convinced that Trist would not be aggressive enough in the talks to reach an agreement that would bring the maximum spoils of war—the greatest amount of land that would be possible to secure from the Mexican negotiators. He sent a recall message to Trist to call off the negotiations; Polk would rather they take place in Washington under his watchful eye.

The message took six weeks to reach Trist in Mexico City, and the chief State Department clerk and now peace negotiator was not only taken aback by the instruction but reluctant to call off the talks that had proceeded. A rebellious Trist, personally opposed to insisting on an agreement that would largely swallow up most of the country of Mexico, decided to ignore the order.

Much to the later fury of the president, Trist concluded the treaty on February 2, 1848, personally signing the document along with three Mexican negotiators. When Trist returned to Washington he was summarily fired by the president for his insubordination. Leaving the nation's capital, Trist managed to find office jobs for the Philadelphia, Wilmington, and Baltimore Railroad and later accepted a job as postmaster of Alexandria, Virginia.

Although his work for the U.S. government had ended, Trist's action in Mexico City became one of the many "what-ifs" of American history. Although Trist had lost his job by the time he returned to Washington, the Treaty of Guadalupe Hidalgo did survive. And although Mexico did indeed lose its entire northern holdings in the disastrous war, it could have been worse if not for Trist, Many government officials in Washington and a large amount of public opinion seemed to crave even greater aggrandizement after the victory—an even greater land grab than the treaty provided, Indeed, many had called for the United States to take most, if not all, of Mexico. If it had not been for Trist's insubordination, the border between the United States and Mexico might very well have been much farther south than it is today.

THE GADSDEN PURCHASE

Although the Treaty of Guadalupe Hidalgo had defined nearly all of the U.S.-Mexico border, there would be other disputes and negotiations over the years between the two countries that would alter the contours. The most significant became known as the Gadsden Purchase, a treaty signed on December 30, 1853, in which Mexico sold to the United States for $10 million approximately 30,000 square miles of territory establishing the southern borders of what would become the states of Arizona and New Mexico. The treaty not only had enormous impact on the eventual border but also reflected the tensions over the ever-worsening conflict between northern and southern states over the issue of slavery.

Simmering tensions between the United States and Mexico over jurisdiction of the border and a number of financial claims led President Franklin Pierce to send an ambassador to Mexico to negotiate a purchase of land not included in the Treaty of Guadalupe Hidalgo. He was James Gadsden, a former military officer and president of a South Carolina railroad company, an ardent champion of slavery interests, and a close friend of Secretary of War Jefferson Davis.

Davis, a leading political figure from Mississippi, and other prominent Southern leaders hoped to steer through Congress legislation that would lead to the construction of a transcontinental railroad connecting the American South with California. In order to establish a route that could lead to such a venture, Davis and the others eyed the Mesilla Valley, a fertile agricultural area fed by the waters of the Rio Grande and centered in what is now Las Cruces, New Mexico, as a missing area necessary to build the railroad. As Gadsden headed to Mexico, the Mesilla Valley was a hotbed of contention, with both countries claiming the rights to the area.

In 1853 Mexican officials had actually evicted Americans from their property in the disputed land. Governor William Lane of New Mexico responded by declaring the Mesilla Valley part of the U.S. territory of New Mexico—an action that prompted Mexican president Antonio de Santa Anna to send troops into the valley. It was now up to Gadsden not only to diffuse this particular diplomatic standoff, as well as other financial claims that had arisen between the two countries, but also to seek the purchase of land that would move the U.S. border farther south.

Gadsden met with Santa Anna on September 25, 1853. Although Santa Anna refused to sell a large portion of Mexico, he needed money to fund an army to contend with an ever-growing problem in northern Mexico—raids by Apache Indians on towns and villages. On December 30, 1853, he and Gadsden signed a treaty.

When Gadsden had first left Washington on his mission to structure a deal, President Pierce had given instructions to buy as much land as he could. The administration viewed the deal as an opportunity to open up as much land as possible for the future expansion of slavery. The treaty he brought back to the United States was for 38,000 square miles in exchange for $15 million. When the treaty was handed over to the Senate for ratification, it immediately became the target of northern Senators determined to thwart any future efforts by the South to add new slave states.

After heated debate, the treaty was not approved. Pierce then asked the Senate to approve a possible modified deal for nearly 30,000 square miles at a cost of $10 million. The compromise was approved, Gadsden returned to Mexico, and Santa Anna agreed to the terms.

As for the dreams of a federally funded transcontinental railroad through the South to California, they died amidst the feverish, internecine political war in the Congress over the slavery issue. Years later, after the Civil War, Collis P. Huntington and other railroad entrepreneurs pulled together the resources to build the railway line that Jefferson Davis and others had dreamed about at the time he sent James Gadsden to Mexico. The railroad would run from Los Angeles east through the desert country of Arizona and New Mexico and on to San Antonio and New Orleans. It would be called the Southern Pacific.

As the River Shifts, So Does the Border: The Chamizal Convention Treaty of 1963

When borders are delineated by rivers, boundaries change with river movement. Most of the time the change is relatively imperceptible and not a source of contention. In 1963, however, the Chamizal Convention resolved a boundary dispute between the United States and Mexico at a point in the Rio Grande near El Paso, Texas-Juárez, and Chihuahua called the Chamizal tract. For over a hundred years, the river's naturally shifting contour, as well as a major nineteenth-century flood, resulted in approximately 600 acres that had essentially been moved north of the border.

In 1962, on a trip to Mexico City, President John F. Kennedy and President Adolfo López Mateos began to discuss a possible resolution of the problem. Through diplomatic efforts between the two countries, U.S. Ambassador Thomas Mann and Mexican Foreign Minister Manuel Tello signed the Chamizal Convention treaty in Mexico City in July 1963. The following year, President Lyndon Johnson signed the treaty and through U.S. congressional action the "Chamizal Convention Act" became law. In addition to the relocation of the border, the countries agreed to build a cement structure at that location in the river to make the border between the two cities permanent and unchanging.

On a day in September 1964, as a gesture of friendship and goodwill, President Johnson and President Mateos shook hands on the international bridge between the two cities. Thousands of onlookers cheered.

MARKING THE LINE

To carry the surveying and mapping obligations of the Treaty of Guadalupe into effect, a joint United States and Mexican Boundary Commission began its work in 1849. Many Americans had heard the historical tales about the most celebrated marking of a boundary in U.S. history—the harrowing adventures of the team of Jeremiah Dixon and Charles Mason in marking the Mason-Dixon line prior to the American Revolution to resolve a border dispute between British colonies in Colonial America. Those stories of traversing rough terrain, encountering exhausting conditions imposed by weather, sickness, and the fears of slaughter by Iroquois Indians in many ways presaged the challenges that faced those with the daunting task of establishing and marking the nearly 2,000-mile U.S.-Mexican border from the Pacific Ocean to the Gulf of Mexico.

According to the Treaty of Guadalupe Hidalgo, the line would extend from the mouth of the deepest channel of the Río Bravo del Norte (the Rio Grande), up the river to "the town called Paso" (Ciudad Juárez), then to the first branch of the Gila River, and "thence down the middle of the said branch and of the said river, until it empties into the Rio Colorado; thence across the Rio Colorado, following the division line between Upper and Lower California, to the Pacific Ocean."

The work began on July 6, 1849, near San Diego. U.S. and Mexican survey teams crisscrossed the borderlands, meeting regularly to confirm each other's work. The tasks were manifold: to survey, map, and demarcate the boundary line; to place physical markers at locations along the border; to gather information about the flora and fauna in the regions; and to attempt to mark constructive and amicable relations with various Native American tribes.

The massive boundary project would last more than seven years involving several separate boundary commissions, all of which faced not only the treacherous physical demands of the work but also various political machinations; personal disputes; financial difficulties; inaccurate information; confusing work assignments; and the challenge of coordinating the work with separate U.S. and Mexican teams of surveyors, engineers, botanists, scientists, cartographers, and military personnel.

A number of political appointees who served as U.S. commissioners on the project left for various reasons before the fifth commissioner, William Emory, an experienced military engineer, took the lead. Emory was able to gain the confidence and cooperation of the Mexican team led by José Salazar y Larregui. Over time the two forged an alliance that kept the work progressing with steady efficiency.

Working in conditions that ranged from the hellfire heat of the desert that saw temperatures as high as 120 degrees to snow-clogged mountain peaks, the work dragged on. At one point in the Sonora Desert, Emory reported that the team had managed to traverse only seventeen miles in three days as they faced massive rock formations with precipices and steep ravines that would challenge any outdoorsman. They trudged along a stretch of over a hundred miles in which they found no new sources of water.

Throughout the arduous work, the teams were cutting across ancient lands occupied by Native American tribes: the Pimas, Maricopas, Tohono O'odhams, and

Cocopahs. Many of the Native Americans served as guides and provided food and water to the surveyors. The Apache raiders, however, were another story. Their aggression was a constant concern, and a number of altercations hindered the surveying work.

In addition to creating topographical maps and illustrations, the teams marked the boundary with stone mounds and obelisks. Some were built without mortar; others were constructed with marble or cast iron. They became the fundamental reference points for a number of boundary disputes that would arise over the years.

In 1851 the team completed the California survey extending from San Diego to the Colorado River. Work in the eastern section of the border was a halting process until the Gadsden Purchase clarified areas that had formally been in dispute. In October 1855 Emory reported that the land survey between Paso and the Colorado River—the monumental effort to mark the U.S.-Mexico border—was now finished.

Nevertheless, with increasing growth in the borderlands during the second half of the nineteenth century, disputes erupted over the exact location of the boundary line in a number of locations. In 1891 Mexican and U.S. officials launched a new Boundary Resurvey project to analyze conditions of the new communities occupying the border region, assess the condition of the markers that were placed three decades earlier and repair or replace them as necessary, and clarify the boundary further with additional markers.

Border survey team posing at La Sierra del Tule, Hermosillo, Sonora, ca. 1892. Along the nearly 2,000-mile length of the border, surveying teams faced myriad climates and terrain—from scorching desert heat to rugged mountains. (National Archives)

The resurvey team increased the number of boundary monuments from 52 to 258. Six-feet high and 12 inches square at the base, the obelisks sat in concrete and featured attached plaques identifying the border in both English and Spanish. In the years following, the number of markers would increase to nearly 500, as city officials in growing towns and cities felt it necessary to mark clearly the border line.

Many of the original fifty-two monuments still stand. The first one erected, a block of polished marble, stands a few hundred feet from the Pacific Ocean between Tijuana and San Diego. It rests in an area dedicated in 1972 by First Lady Pat Nixon as "Friendship Park."

In the letters, memoirs, and other later writings of the intrepid surveyors and their teams that participated in the massive undertaking of marking the boundary are many musings about the landscape through which they passed—about the rugged, sometimes almost impassable terrain; about the unforgiving desert heat; about the lack of lush vegetation; and about the dangers that seemed a constant, from Indians to snakes and strange insects, to unknown diseases that might lurk in the surroundings. What they did not see in these environs, in this the American Southwest, was the future, one that soon would be characterized in terms of cattle, agriculture, and minerals, especially copper and silver. In what some saw as wasteland there would be a bonanza of riches.

DOCUMENTS

Speech of Representative Abraham Lincoln (Whig-IL) on Mexican War, January 12, 1848

In his first and only term in the U.S. House of Representatives, Abraham Lincoln did not, as so many other newcomers, take a back seat. Although his opposition to the Mexican War made him unpopular with many politicians, as well as the public caught up in patriotic fervor, he echoed the call for restraint that had distinguished his esteemed Whig colleague from Kentucky, Henry Clay. Lincoln's "Spot Resolutions" questioning President Polk's assertion that American blood had been spilled in U.S. territory, brought much notice and contention. In his speech to the House on January 12, 1848, Lincoln, far from backing down, pressed the issue. The war would soon end, but Lincoln's challenge to its legitimacy and U.S. aggression never wavered. This is an excerpt from that speech.

Mr. Chairman:

. . . When the war began, it was my opinion that all those who, because of knowing too *little*, or because of knowing too *much*, could not conscientiously approve the conduct of the President, (in the beginning of it,) should, nevertheless, as good citizens and patriots, remain silent on that point, at least till the war should be ended. Some leading Democrats, including ex-President Van Buren, have taken this same view, as I understand them; and I adhered to it, and acted upon it, until since I took my seat here; and I think I should still adhere to it, were it not that the President and his friends will not allow it to be so. Besides, the continual effort of the President to argue every silent vote given for supplies into an endorsement of the justice and wisdom of his conduct; besides that singularly candid paragraph in his late message, in which he tells us that Congress, with great unanimity, (only two in the Senate and fourteen in the House dissenting,) had declared that, "by the act of the Republic of Mexico, a state of war exists between that Government and the United States;" when the same journals that informed him of this, also informed him, that when that declaration stood disconnected from the question of supplies, sixty-seven in the House, and not fourteen merely, voted against it; besides this open attempt to prove by telling the *truth,* what he could not prove by telling the *whole truth,* demanding of all who will not submit to be misrepresented, in justice to themselves, to speak out; besides all this, one of my colleagues, [Mr. Richardson,] at a very early day in the session, brought in a set of resolutions, expressly endorsing the original justice of the war on the part of the President. Upon these resolutions, when they shall be put on their passage, I shall be *compelled* to vote; so that I can not be silent if I would. Seeing this, I went about preparing myself to give the vote understandingly, when it should come. I carefully examined the President's messages, to ascertain what he himself had said and proved upon the point. The result of this examination was to make the impression, that, taking for true all the President states as facts, he falls far short of proving his justification; and that the President would have gone farther with his proof, if it had not been for the small matter that the *truth* would not permit him. . . .

It is a singular fact, that if anyone should declare the President sent the army into the midst of a settlement of Mexican people, who had never submitted, by consent or by force to the authority of Texas or of the United States, and that *there,* and thereby, the first blood of the war was shed, there is not one word in all the President has said which would either admit or deny the declaration. In this strange omission chiefly consists the deception of the President's evidence-an omission which, it does seem to me, could scarcely have occurred but by design. My way of living leads me to be about the courts of justice; and there I have sometimes seen a good lawyer, struggling for his client's neck, in a desperate case, employing every artifice to work round, befog, and cover up with many words some point arising in the case, which he *dared* not admit, and yet *could* not deny. Party bias may help to make it appear so; but, with all the allowance I can make for such bias, it still does appear to me that just such, and from just such necessity, is the President's struggle in this case.

Some time after my colleague [Mr. Richardson] introduced the resolutions I have mentioned, I introduced a preamble, resolution, and interrogatories, intended to draw the President out, if possible, on this hitherto untrodden ground. To show their relevancy, I propose to state my understanding of the true rule for ascertaining the boundary between Texas and Mexico. It is, that *wherever* Texas was *exercising* jurisdiction was hers; and *wherever* Mexico was exercising jurisdiction, was hers; and that *whatever* separated the actual exercise of jurisdiction of the one from that of the other, was the true boundary between them. If, as is probably true, Texas was exercising jurisdiction along the western bank of the Nueces, and Mexico was exercising it along the eastern bank of the Rio Grande, then *neither* river was the boundary; but the uninhabited country between the two was.

The extent of our territory in that region depended, not on any *treaty-fixed* boundary, (for no treaty had attempted it,) but on revolution. Any people anywhere, being inclined and having the power, have the *right* to rise up and shake off the existing government, and form a new one that suits them better. This is a most valuable, a most sacred right—a right which, we hope and believe, is to liberate the world. Nor is this right confined to cases in which the whole people of an existing government may choose to exercise it. Any portion of such people that can *may* revolutionize, and make their *own* of so much of the territory as they inhabit.

More than this, a *majority* of any portion of such people may revolutionize, putting down a *minority*, intermingled with, or near about them, who may oppose their movement. Such minority was precisely the case of the Tories of our own Revolution. It is a quality of revolutions not to go by *old* lines, or *old* laws; but to break up both, and make new ones. As to the country now in question, we bought it of France in 1803, and sold it to Spain in 1819, according to the President's statements. After this, all Mexico, including Texas, revolutionized against Spain; and still later, Texas revolutionized against Mexico. In my view, just so far as she carried her revolution, by obtaining the *actual*, willing or unwilling, submission of the people, so *far* the country was hers, and no farther.

Now, sir, for the purpose of obtaining the very best evidence as to whether Texas had actually carried her revolution to the place where the hostilities of the present war commenced, let the President answer the interrogatories I proposed, as before mentioned, or some other similar ones. Let him answer fully, fairly, and candidly. Let him answer with *facts*, and not with arguments. Let him remember he sits where Washington sat; and, so remembering, let him answer as Washington would answer.

As a nation *should* not, and the Almighty *will* not, be evaded, so let him attempt no evasion, no equivocation. And if, so answering, he can show that the soil was ours where the first blood of the war was shed—that it was not within an inhabited country, or, if within such, that the inhabitants had submitted themselves to the civil authority of Texas, or of the United States, and that the same is true of the site of Fort Brown-then I am with him for his justification. In that case I, shall be most happy to reverse the vote I gave the other day. I have a selfish motive for desiring that the President may do this; I expect to give some votes, in connection with the war, which, without his so doing, will be of doubtful propriety in my own judgment, but which will be free from the doubt, if he does so. But if he *cannot*, or *will not* do this—if, on any pretence , or no pretence, he shall refuse or omit it, then I shall be fully convinced, of what I more than suspect already, that he is deeply conscious of being in the wrong; that he feels the blood of this war, like the blood of Abel, is crying to Heaven against him; that he ordered General Taylor into the midst of a peaceful Mexican settlement, purposely to bring on a war; that originally having some strong motive—what I will not stop now to give my opinion concerning—to involve the two countries in a war, and trusting to escape scrutiny by fixing the public gaze upon the exceeding brightness of military glory—that attractive rainbow that rises in showers of blood—that serpent's eye that charms to destroy-he plunged into it, and has swept *on* and *on*, till disappointed in his calculation of the ease with which Mexico might be subdued, he now finds himself he knows not where.

How like the half insane mumbling of a fever-dream is the whole war part of his late message! At one time telling us that Mexico has nothing whatever that we can get but territory; at another, showing us how we can support the war by levying contributions on Mexico. At one time urging the national honor, the security of the future, the prevention of foreign interference, and even the good of Mexico herself, as among the objects of the war; at another, telling us that, "to reject indemnity, by refusing to accept a cession of territory, would be to abandon all our just demands, and to wage the war, bearing all its expenses, *without a purpose or definite object*."

So, then, the national honor, security of the future, and everything but territorial indemnity, may be considered the *no-purposes* and *indefinite* objects of the war! But, having it now settled that territorial indemnity is the only object, we are urged to seize, by legislation here, all that he was content to take a few months ago, and the whole province of Lower California to boot, and to still carry on the war—to take *all* we are fighting for, and *still* fight on. Again, the President is resolved, under all circumstances, to have full territorial indemnity for the expenses of the war; but he forgets to tell us how we are to get the *excess* after those expenses shall have surpassed the value of the *whole* of the Mexican territory. So, again, he insists that the separate national existence of Mexico, shall be maintained; but he does not tell us how this can be done after we shall have taken *all* her territory. Lest the questions I here suggest be considered speculative merely, let me be indulged a moment in trying to show they are not.

The war has gone on some twenty months; for the expenses of which, together with an inconsiderable old score, the President now claims about one half of the Mexican territory, and that by far the better half, so far as concerns our ability to make anything out of it. It *is* comparatively uninhabited; so that we could establish land offices in it, and raise some money in that way. But the other half is already inhabited, as I understand it, tolerably densely for the nature of the country; and all its lands, or all that are valuable, already appropriated as private property. How, then, are we to make anything out of these lands with this encumbrance on them, or how remove the encumbrance? I suppose no one will say we should kill the people, or drive them out, or make slaves of them, or even confiscate their property? How, then, can we make much out of this part of the territory? If the prosecution of the war has, in expenses, already equaled the *better* half of the country, how long its future prosecution will be in equaling the less valuable half is not a *speculative*, but a *practical* question, pressing closely upon us; And yet it is a question which the President seems to never have thought of.

As to the mode of terminating the war and securing peace, the President is equally wandering and indefinite. First, it is to be done by a more vigorous prosecution of the war in the vital parts of the enemies country; and, after apparently talking himself tired on this point, the President drops down into a half despairing tone, and tells us, that "with a people distracted and divided by contending factions, and a government subject to constant changes, by successive revolutions, *the continued success of our arms may fail to secure a satisfactory peace*." Then he suggests the propriety of wheedling the Mexican people to desert the counsels of their own leaders, and trusting in our protection, to set up a government from which we can secure a satisfactory peace telling us that "*this may become the only mode of obtaining such a peace*." But soon he falls into doubt of this too, and then drops back on to the already half abandoned ground of "more vigorous prosecution." All this shows that the President is in no wise satisfied with his own positions. First, he takes up one, and, in attempting to argue us *into* it, he argues himself *out* of it; then seizes another, and goes through the same process; and then, confused at being able to think of nothing new, he snatches up the old one again, which he has some time before cast off. His mind, tasked beyond its power, is running hither and thither, like some tortured creature on a burning surface, finding no position on which it can settle down and be at ease.

Again, it is a singular omission in this message, that it no where intimates when the President expects the war to terminate. At its beginning, General Scott was, by this same President, driven into disfavor, if not disgrace, for intimating that peace could not be conquered in less than three or four months. But now, at the end of about twenty months, during which time our arms have given us the most splendid successes—every department, and every part, land and water, officers and privates, regulars and volunteers, doing all that men *could* do, and hundreds of things which it had ever before been thought men *could not* do; after all this, this same President gives us a long message, without showing us that, as to the end, he himself has even an imaginary conception. As I have before said, he knows not where he is. He is a bewildered, confounded, and miserably perplexed man. God grant he may be able to show there is not something about his conscious more painful than all his mental perplexity!

Source: *Congressional Globe*, Thirtieth Congress, First Session, New Series, No. 10, 154–56. Available at http://teachingamericanhistory.org/library/document/the-war-with-mexico-speech-in-the-united-states-house-of-representatives.

Treaty of Guadalupe Hidalgo, 1848

The signing of the Treaty of Guadalupe Hidalgo on February 2, 1848, represented the signal historical moment that defined the border between the United States and Mexico. Under its terms Mexico ceded to the United States the northern half of its country, the result of a war that, however questionable its origins and purpose, opened the way for an onrush of settlement that signaled the beginning of borderlands relations between the two countries and all of their concomitant ramifications. The following is an extract of this iconic document.

TREATY OF PEACE, FRIENDSHIP, LIMITS, AND SETTLEMENT BETWEEN THE UNITED STATES OF AMERICA AND THE UNITED MEXICAN STATES CONCLUDED AT GUADALUPE HIDALGO, FEBRUARY 2, 1848; RATIFICATION

ADVISED BY SENATE, WITH AMENDMENTS, MARCH 10, 1848; RATIFIED BY PRESIDENT, MARCH 16, 1848; RATIFICATIONS EXCHANGED AT QUERETARO, MAY 30, 1848; PROCLAIMED, JULY 4, 1848. . . .

In the Name of Almighty God

The United States of America and the United Mexican States animated by a sincere desire to put an end to the calamities of the war which unhappily exists between the two Republics and to establish Upon a solid basis relations of peace and friendship, which shall confer reciprocal benefits upon the citizens of both, and assure the concord, harmony, and mutual confidence wherein the two people should live, as good neighbors have for that purpose appointed their respective plenipotentiaries, that is to say: The President of the United States has appointed Nicholas P. Trist, a citizen of the United States, and the President of the Mexican Republic has appointed Don Luis Gonzaga Cuevas, Don Bernardo Couto, and Don Miguel Atristain, citizens of the said Republic; Who, after a reciprocal communication of their respective full powers, have, under the protection of Almighty God, the author of peace, arranged, agreed upon, and signed the following: Treaty of Peace, Friendship, Limits, and Settlement between the United States of America and the Mexican Republic.

Article I

There shall be firm and universal peace between the United States of America and the Mexican Republic, and between their respective countries, territories, cities, towns, and people, without exception of places or persons.

Article II

Immediately upon the signature of this treaty, a convention shall be entered into between a commissioner or commissioners appointed by the General-in-chief of the forces of the United States, and such as may be appointed by the Mexican Government, to the end that a provisional suspension of hostilities shall take place, and that, in the places occupied by the said forces, constitutional order may be reestablished, as regards the political, administrative, and judicial branches, so far as this shall be permitted by the circumstances of military occupation . . .

Article V

The boundary line between the two Republics shall commence in the Gulf of Mexico, three leagues from land, opposite the mouth of the Rio Grande, otherwise called Rio Bravo del Norte, or Opposite the mouth of its deepest branch, if it should have more than one branch emptying directly into the sea; from thence up the middle of that river, following the deepest channel, where it has more than one, to the point where it strikes the southern boundary of New Mexico; thence, westwardly, along the whole southern boundary of New Mexico (which runs north of the town called Paso) to its western termination; thence, northward, along the western line of New Mexico, until it intersects the first branch of the river Gila; (or if it should not intersect any branch of that river, then to the point on the said line nearest to such branch, and thence in a direct line to the same); thence down the middle of the said branch and of the said river, until it empties into the Rio Colorado; thence across the Rio Colorado, following the division line between Upper and Lower California, to the Pacific Ocean.

The southern and western limits of New Mexico, mentioned in the article, are those laid down in the map entitled "Map of the United Mexican States, as organized and defined by various acts of the Congress of said republic, and constructed according to the best authorities. Revised edition. Published at New York, in 1847, by J. Disturnell," of which map a copy is added to this treaty, bearing the signatures and seals of the undersigned Plenipotentiaries. And, in order to preclude all difficulty in tracing upon the ground the limit separating Upper from Lower California, it is agreed that the said limit shall consist of a straight line drawn from the middle of the Rio Gila, where it unites with the Colorado, to a point on the coast of the Pacific Ocean, distant one marine league due south of the southernmost point of the port of San Diego, according to the plan of said port made in the year 1782 by Don Juan Pantoja, second sailing-master of the Spanish fleet, and published at Madrid in the year 1802, in the atlas to the voyage of the schooners Sutil and Mexicana; of which plan a copy is hereunto added, signed and sealed by the respective Plenipotentiaries.

In order to designate the boundary line with due precision, upon authoritative maps, and to establish upon the ground land-marks which shall show the limits of both republics, as described in the present article, the two Governments shall each appoint a commissioner and a surveyor, who, before the expiration of one year from the date of the exchange of ratifications of this treaty, shall meet at the port of San Diego, and proceed to run and mark the said boundary in its whole course to the mouth of the Rio Bravo del Norte. They shall keep journals and make out plans of their operations; and the result agreed upon by them shall be deemed a part of this treaty, and shall have the same force as if it were inserted therein. The two Governments will amicably agree regarding what may be necessary to these persons, and also as to their respective escorts, should such be necessary.

The boundary line established by this article shall be religiously respected by each of the two republics, and no change shall ever be made therein, except by the express and free consent of both nations, lawfully given by the General Government of each, in conformity with its own constitution. . . .

Article VIII

Mexicans now established in territories previously belonging to Mexico, and which remain for the future within the limits of the United States, as defined by the present treaty, shall be free to continue where they now reside, or to remove at any time to the Mexican Republic, retaining the property which they possess in the said territories, or disposing thereof, and removing the proceeds wherever they please, without their being subjected, on this account, to any contribution, tax, or charge whatever.

Those who shall prefer to remain in the said territories may either retain the title and rights of Mexican citizens, or acquire those of citizens of the United States. But they shall be under the obligation to make their election within one year from the date of the exchange of ratifications of this treaty; and those who shall remain in the said territories after the expiration of that year, without having declared their intention to retain the character of Mexicans, shall be considered to have elected to become citizens of the United States.

In the said territories, property of every kind, now belonging to Mexicans not established there, shall be inviolably respected. The present owners, the heirs of these, and all Mexicans who may hereafter acquire said property by contract, shall enjoy with respect to it guarantees equally ample as if the same belonged to citizens of the United States.

Article IX

The Mexicans who, in the territories aforesaid, shall not preserve the character of citizens of the Mexican Republic, conformably with what is stipulated in the preceding article, shall be incorporated into the Union of the United States. and be admitted at the proper time (to be judged of by the Congress of the United States) to the enjoyment of all the rights of citizens of the United States, according to the principles of the Constitution; and in the mean time, shall be maintained and protected in the free enjoyment of their liberty and property, and secured in the free exercise of their religion without; restriction . . .

Article XII

In consideration of the extension acquired by the boundaries of the United States, as defined in the fifth article of the present treaty, the Government of the United States engages to pay to that of the Mexican Republic the sum of fifteen millions of dollars.

Immediately after the treaty shall have been duly ratified by the Government of the Mexican Republic, the sum of three millions of dollars shall be paid to the said Government by that of the United States, at the city of Mexico, in the gold or silver coin of Mexico The remaining twelve millions of dollars shall be paid at the same place, and in the same coin, in annual installments of three millions of dollars each, together with interest on the same at the rate of six per centum per annum. This interest shall begin to run upon the whole sum of twelve millions from the day of the ratification of the present treaty by—the Mexican Government, and the first of the installments shall be paid—at the expiration of one year from the same day. Together with each annual installment, as it falls due, the whole interest accruing on such installment from the beginning shall also be paid . . .

Article XXIII

This treaty shall be ratified by the President of the United States of America, by and with the advice and consent of the Senate thereof; and by the President of the Mexican Republic, with the previous approbation of its general Congress; and the ratifications shall be exchanged in the City of Washington, or at the seat of Government of Mexico, in four months from the date of the signature hereof, or sooner if practicable. In faith whereof we, the respective Plenipotentiaries, have signed this treaty of peace, friendship, limits, and settlement, and have hereunto affixed our seals respectively. Done in quintuplicate, at the city of Guadalupe Hidalgo, on the second day of February, in the year of our Lord one thousand eight hundred and forty-eight.

N. P. TRIST
LUIS P. CUEVAS
BERNARDO COUTO
MIGL. ATRISTAIN

Source: National Archives and Records Administration, Washington, D.C.; RG 11, General Records of the United States, National Archives identifier #299809; transcription on numerous online sites. Available at http://avalon.law.yale.edu/19th_century/guadhida.asp.

Gadsden Purchase Treaty, 1853–1854

Through negotiations between U.S. and Mexican officials in Mexico City in December 1853, a region of approximately 30,000 square miles of present-day Arizona and southwestern New Mexico became part of U.S. territory. The purchase of land from Mexico for $10 million was concluded with a treaty signed by American ambassador to Mexico James Gadsden and Mexican officials and ratified by Congress and signed by President Franklin Pierce in June 1854.

By the President of the United States of America A Proclamation.

WHEREAS a treaty between the United States of America and the Mexican Republic was concluded and signed at the City of Mexico on the thirtieth day of December, one thousand eight hundred and fifty-three; which treaty, as amended by the Senate of the United States, and being in the English and Spanish languages, is word for word as follows:

IN THE NAME OF ALMIGHTY GOD: The Republic of Mexico and the United States of America desiring to remove every cause of disagreement which might interfere in any manner with the better friendship and intercourse between the two countries, and especially in respect to the true limits which should be established, when, notwithstanding what was covenanted in the treaty of Guadalupe Hidalgo in the year 1848, opposite interpretations have been urged, which might give occasion to questions of serious moment: to avoid these, and to strengthen and more firmly maintain the peace which happily prevails between the two republics, the President of the United States has, for this purpose, appointed James Gadsden, Envoy Extraordinary and Minister Plenipotentiary of the same, near the Mexican government, and the President of Mexico has appointed as Plenipotentiary "ad hoc" his excellency Don Manuel Diez de Bonilla, cavalier grand cross of the national and distinguished order of Guadalupe, and Secretary of State, and of the office of Foreign Relations, and Don Jose Salazar Ylarregui and General Mariano Monterde as scientific commissioners, invested with full powers for this negotiation, who, having communicated their respective full powers, and finding them in due and proper form, have agreed upon the articles following:

ARTICLE I The Mexican Republic agrees to designate the following as her true limits with the United States for the future: retaining the same dividing line between the two Californias as already defined and established, according to the 5th article of the treaty of Guadalupe Hidalgo, the limits between the two republics shall be as follows: Beginning in the Gulf of Mexico, three leagues from land, opposite the mouth of the Rio Grande, as provided in the 5th article of the treaty of Guadalupe Hidalgo; thence, as defined in the said article, up the middle of that river to the point where the parallel of 31° 47′ north latitude crosses the same; thence due west one hundred miles; thence south to the parallel of 31° 20′ north latitude; thence along the said parallel of 31° 20′ to the 111th meridian of longitude west of Greenwich; thence in a straight line to a point on the Colorado River twenty English miles below the junction of the Gila and Colorado rivers; thence up the middle of the said river Colorado until it intersects the present line between the United States and Mexico.

For the performance of this portion of the treaty, each of the two governments shall nominate one commissioner, to the end that, by common consent the two thus nominated, having met in the city of Paso del Norte, three months after the exchange of the ratifications of this treaty, may proceed to survey and mark out upon the land the dividing line stipulated by this article, where it shall not have already been surveyed and established by the mixed commission, according to the treaty of Guadalupe, keeping a journal and making proper plans of their operations. For this purpose, if they should judge it necessary, the contracting parties shall be at liberty each to unite to its respective commissioner, scientific or other assistants, such as astronomers and surveyors, whose concurrence shall not be considered necessary for the settlement and of a true line of division between the two Republics; that line shall be alone established upon which the commissioners may fix, their consent in this particular being considered decisive and an integral part of this treaty, without necessity of ulterior ratification or approval, and without room for interpretation of any kind by either of the parties contracting.

The dividing line thus established shall, in all time, be faithfully respected by the two governments, without any variation therein, unless of the express and free consent of the two, given in conformity to the principles of the law of nations, and in accordance with the constitution of each country respectively.

In consequence, the stipulation in the 5th article of the treaty of Guadalupe upon the boundary line therein described is no longer of any force, wherein it may conflict with that here established, the said line being considered annulled and abolished wherever it may not coincide with the present, and in the same manner remaining in full force where in accordance with the same.

ARTICLE II. The government of Mexico hereby releases the United States from all liability on account of the obligations contained in the eleventh article of the treaty of Guadalupe Hidalgo; and the said article and the thirty-third article of the treaty of amity, commerce, and navigation between the United States of America and the United Mexican States concluded at Mexico, on the fifth day of April, 1831, are hereby abrogated.

ARTICLE III. In consideration of the foregoing stipulations, the Government of the United States agrees to pay to the government of Mexico, in the city of New York, the sum of ten millions of dollars, of which seven millions shall be paid immediately upon the exchange of the ratifications of this treaty, and the remaining three millions as soon as the boundary line shall be surveyed, marked, and established.

ARTICLE IV. The provisions of the 6th and 7th articles of the treaty of Guadalupe Hidalgo having been rendered nugatory, for the most part, by the cession of territory granted in the first article of this treaty, the said articles are hereby abrogated and annulled, and the provisions as herein expressed substituted therefor. The vessels, and citizens of the United States shall, in all time, have free and uninterrupted passage through the Gulf of California, to and from their possessions situated north of the boundary line of the two countries. It being understood that this passage is to be by navigating the Gulf of California and the river Colorado, and not by land, without the express consent of the Mexican government; and precisely the same provisions, stipulations, and restrictions, in all respects, are hereby agreed upon and adopted, and shall be scrupulously observed and enforced by the two contracting governments in reference to the Rio Colorado, so far and for such distance as the middle of that river is made their common boundary line by the first article of this treaty.

The several provisions, stipulations, and restrictions contained in the 7th article of the treaty of Guadalupe Hidalgo shall remain in force only so far as regards the Rio Bravo del Forte, below the initial of the said boundary provided in the first article of this treaty; that is to say, below the intersection of the 31° 47′30′/parallel of latitude, with the boundary line established by the late treaty dividing said river from its mouth upwards, according to the fifth article of the treaty of Guadalupe.

ARTICLE V. All the provisions of the eighth and ninth, sixteenth and seventeenth articles of the treaty of Guadalupe Hidalgo, shall apply to the territory ceded by the Mexican Republic in the first article of the present treaty, and to all the rights of persons and property, both civil and ecclesiastical, within the same, as fully and as effectually as if the said articles were herein again recited and set forth.

ARTICLE VI. No grants of land within the territory ceded by the first article of this treaty bearing date subsequent to the day-twenty-fifth of September-when the minister and subscriber to this treaty on the part of the United States, proposed to the Government of Mexico to terminate the question of boundary, will be considered valid or be recognized by the United States, or will any grants made previously be respected or be considered as obligatory which have not been located and duly recorded in the archives of Mexico.

ARTICLE VII. Should there at any future period (which God forbid) occur any disagreement between the two nations which might lead to a rupture of their relations and reciprocal peace, they bind themselves in like manner to procure by every possible method the adjustment of every difference; and should they still in this manner not succeed, never will they proceed to a declaration of war, without having previously paid attention to what has been set forth in article twenty-one of the treaty of Guadalupe for similar cases; which article, as well as the twenty-second is here reaffirmed.

ARTICLE VIII. The Mexican Government having on the 5th of February, 1853, authorized the early construction of a plank and railroad across the Isthmus of Tehuantepec, and, to secure the stable benefits of said transit way to the persons and merchandise of the citizens of Mexico and the United States, it is stipulated that neither government will interpose any obstacle to the transit of persons and merchandise of both nations; and at no time shall higher charges be made on the transit of persons and property of citizens of the United States, than may be made on the persons and property of other foreign nations, nor shall any interest in said transit way, nor in the proceeds thereof, be transferred to any foreign government.

The United States, by its agents, shall have the right to transport across the isthmus, in closed bags, the mails of the United States not intended for distribution along the line of communication; also the effects of the United States government and its citizens, which may be intended for transit, and not for distribution on the isthmus, free of custom-house or other charges by the Mexican government. Neither passports nor letters of security will be required of persons crossing the isthmus and not remaining in the country.

When the construction of the railroad shall be completed, the Mexican government agrees to open a port of entry in addition to the port of Vera Cruz, at or near the terminus of said road on the Gulf of Mexico.

The two governments will enter into arrangements for the prompt transit of troops and munitions of the United States, which that government may have occasion to send from one part of its territory to another, lying on opposite sides of the continent.

The Mexican government having agreed to protect with its whole power the prosecution, preservation, and security of the work, the United States may extend its protection as it shall judge wise to it when it may feel sanctioned and warranted by the public or international law.

ARTICLE IX. This treaty shall be ratified, and the respective ratifications shall be exchanged at the city of Washington within the exact period of six months from the date of its signature, or sooner, if possible.

In testimony whereof, we, the plenipotentiaries of the contracting parties, have hereunto affixed our hands and seals at Mexico, the thirtieth (30th) day of December, in the year of our Lord one thousand eight hundred and fifty-three, in the thirty-third year of the independence of the Mexican republic, and the seventy-eighth of that of the United States.

JAMES GADSDEN,
MANUEL DIEZ DE BONILLA
JOSE SALAZAR YLARBEGUI
J. MARIANO MONTERDE,

And whereas the said treaty, as amended, has been duly ratified on both parts, and the respective ratifications of the same have this day been exchanged at Washington, by WILLIAM L. MARCY, Secretary of State of the United States, and SENOR

GENERAL DON JUAN N. ALMONTE, Envoy Extraordinary and Minister Plenipotentiary of the Mexican Republic, on the part of their respective Governments:

Now, therefore, be it known that I, FRANKLIN PIERCE, President of the United States of America, have caused the said treaty to be made public, to the end that the same, and every clause and article thereof, may be observed and fulfilled with good faith by the United States and the citizens thereof

In witness whereof I have hereunto set my hand and caused the seal of the United States to be affixed.

Done at the city of Washington, this thirtieth day of June, in the year of our Lord one thousand eight hundred and fifty-four, and of the Independence of the United States the seventy-eighth.

BY THE PRESIDENT:
FRANKLIN PIERCE
W. L. MARCY, Secretary of State

Source: National Archives and Records Administration, Washington, D.C.; RG 46, Records of the U.S. Senate; transcription on numerous online sites. Available at http://utminers.utep.edu/edhamlyn/Gadsden%20Purchase%20Treaty%201853.pdf.

Early Newspaper Report on the Potential Riches in the Mines of Southern Arizona Near the Mexican Border, 1879

More than a hundred years before the U.S. and Mexican teams of surveyors and scientists began marking the border directed by the Treaty of Guadalupe Hidalgo, Yaqui Indians had discovered balls of silver on land that is near present-day Nogales. The discovery attracted prospectors and miners who rushed to the area. After miners removed the most easily unearthed silver, the area was idle until additional silver veins were discovered in the 1870s. One of the prospectors drawn to the territory was Ed Schieffelin, who wandered through an area east of Nogales in 1877 between the San Pedro River and the Dragoon Mountains. Soldiers from Fort Huachuca in Arizona Territory allegedly told Schieffelin that among the rattlesnakes and roaming Apaches in the area about the only thing he would find would be his tombstone. Instead, Schieffelin found one of the richest silver lodes in the history of the borderlands. Remembering the words of the soldiers, he called the discovery the Tombstone Mining District. A certain boom town would soon follow. This is an extract from an early Arizona Territory newspaper about the quest for the silver riches of the Sonora Desert lands.

The Mines.

Great as is the wealth of Sonora in agricultural and pastoral resources, her chief glory lies in her mines. The low mountain ranges abound in minerals, but the mines which are . . . worked are but few in number compared with those whose wealth has been explored and definitely known, but whose development has been prevented or retarded by the incursions of the murderous Apaches that have, until a few years past, infested and laid waste the outlying districts.

A Romantic Story.

It is not the purpose of this general article on the resources of this little known country to describe the mines of Sonora, but there attaches to one section of the State near the American border, a history so romantic that a condensed account of it must prove generally interesting, particularly as it is the only place in Mexico where placers of silver were ever known to exist. The "Planchas de Plata" (literally slabs of silver enticing name), is the name given to a locality in the Arizona Mountains, a dozen miles south of the border, 75 miles south of Tucson and 45 miles due north of Magdalena, where, 121 years ago, according to the archives of Spain and Mexico, Spanish explorers discovered large masses of pure silver on the surface of the ground, and at a depth of a few feet in the form of slabs, balls and grains, some of them very large one weighing as much as 140 arrobas (3,500 pounds), which had to be melted to be weighed and transported. All these discoveries were claimed by the crown, and no encouragement being given to miners to remain in presence of hostile Indians, the mines were speedily abandoned and the records locked up by the Jesuit Fathers, so that they could not be readily traced. Later, in 1817 Don Dionisio Robles . . . with a force of 200 men, penetrated the district and found what they believed to be the old placers, and obtained a quantity of silver in pure masses, he was compelled to return on account of the Indians after a stay of only eight days. About the year 1850, in an expedition made by parties in Hermosillo, a large lump of native silver was found, which was taken to the City of Mexico and caused considerable excitement there. About this time also, the great banking house of Jecker, Torre & Co., obtained from the Mexican government a grant of all the mines in the Sierra de Arizona . . . for the purpose of colonization. By their orders and at their expense, an expedition was organized in San Francisco in 1852, under the command of the unfortunate Count Gaston Raousset-Boulbon, 400 thoroughly disciplined men old French soldiers. They landed at Guaymas, and after considerable delay marched to Sáric, a town on the north bank of the Magdalena river . . . the Count marched to Hermosillo, where he met the government troops and defeated them. He was subsequently taken sick, some say poisoned, and . . . under an arrangement with the authorities embarked for San Francisco. In 1854, Raousset organized another expedition in San Francisco; and landed at Guaymas. Again encountering the opposition of the authorities, and an engagement ensued, in which he was defeated, captured, tried by court-martial and shot.

The Expedition of 1871.

In 1870–71, Gen Serna, (then Vice-Governor of Sonora) obtaining some information regarding this district, organized an expedition to discover it. The hostile Apaches, through the efforts of Gen. Crook, in Arizona, and the Mexican authorities in Sonora, had now been subdued and removed to distant reservations. Gen. Serna had no difficulty in finding the spot from which these large masses had been taken, and he himself found a lump weighing 45 pounds. No less than 40 tons of pure silver has been taken out of the spot. Under his protection, quite a number of prospect ores and miners went to work on the old and to search for new placers. The district prospected by them seems quite small not over two or three miles square. No other placer was found, but in the veins which were discovered and opened, considerable quantities of chlorides of silver were found. A few feet below the surface this became more diffused, the veins widened, and though apparently filled with good ores, not native silver nor rich chlorides were found in sufficient quantities to repay the search. As these men were unprepared to work ores of any sort, the object of the expedition being alone for native or placer silver, after a few months the place was again abandoned, one man only being left, who kept up the search a few months longer, meantime sinking a shaft on a vein which he called "Mejai," to a depth of . . . 125 feet, and reducing the ores obtained . . . but finding no masses of pure silver as expected, and encountering more water than his rude appliances could handle, he, too, gave up. That the sliver in its pure state and in enormous masses, was actually found is a matter too fully established by history and official records to admit of a doubt.

Description of the Mixes.

The . . . country is granite and porphyry. This is generally overlaid with a porphyritic conglomerate to varying depths in the summits of the ridges. The general direction of all the veins or ledges disclosed is nearly magnetic northeast and southwest. The ore of the Raousset . . . is found in the conglomerate and appears to be in a series of parallel veins, each from two to five feet in width, lying close together and covering the whole surface of the hill. The openings are mostly open cuts; seven of them cover a length on the veins of 25 feet and a width of 75 feet, their greatest depth being only 20 feet! "El Hilo" is half a mile south and at an elevation of 4,100 feet above tide. The ore is very rich in chlorides, and from a cut 30 feet long, two feet wide, and four or five feet deep, Gen. Serna, in 1872, is said to have taken $12,600 from the chloride ores and 50 pounds of silver from a single lot of 400 pounds of rock. The mine is now being worked by Mexicans. There are a great number of mines in this district, whose average assays reach from $50 to $100 per ton. The district lies upon a series of high ridges, separated by small gulches which converge toward the spot occupied by the hamlet, lying between Serna's and Borquer's haciendas. . . . All the gulches contain running streams of water. Such is the description of the famous Planchas de Plata, a district famous in the last and destined to be more famous in the future, though we trust that it will not cost the blood and treasure to garner its wealth that has been expended in the past. The Sonora railway will greatly aid in the development of the Planchas do Plata, as it will of Southern Arizona for which it will afford the shortest and most direct route to the sea, but whether that be built or not, the district will be made to yield its treasures, and the secrets of the earth be made to unfold.

Source: *The Phoenix Herald*, Arizona Territory, Phoenix, June 11, 1879.

2

Civil War Border Strategy

CLASHES IN THE BORDERLANDS

Bull Run, Shiloh, Fredericksburg, Chickamauga, Spotsylvania, Cold Harbor, Nashville, Gettysburg—these are the names of towns and battles central to the fate of the Civil War. None are on the Mexican border. Nevertheless, in the minds of Confederate and Union leaders alike, the borderlands were pivotal in their strategic plans. Could the South find a way to exert control along the Rio Grande and the desert mountain lands that led to California and gain new territory and, with it, new slave states? Could the North mobilize enough forces in California and along the border to repulse any such southern ambitions?

Along the border, from Texas to California, individuals and groups began to take sides. Texas soon became an ardent supporter of the Confederacy, although pockets of Union supporters, particularly Hispanics, remained loyal to the Union; California remained uneasily part of the Union. The ultimate support of settlers in the territories of New Mexico and Arizona appeared uncertain.

At the same time commanders of the two sides struggled to gain control of the regions, there loomed another factor weighing on the tactical equations that war planners on both sides had to make—an invasion by French forces to take control in Mexico. For the South, the French invasion could mean fresh supplies and a new ally; for the Union, French ambitions were an obvious threat that needed adept diplomatic skill as well as potential military containment.

Following the outbreak of the war and its early battles, including Bull Run in Manassas, Virginia, three European countries—Great Britain, France, and Spain—decided forcefully to press claims against Mexico in connection with defaulted loans. Mexican President Benito Juárez, with his country strapped for cash, had imposed a two-year moratorium on payment of his foreign debt, and the three countries decided to act. On October 21, 1861, representatives from the three countries agreed to a joint intervention in Mexico and prepared to send troops.

The action by the three European powers placed President Lincoln and his Secretary of State William Seward in a gnarling diplomatic bind. On the one hand, the action of sending troops would be in direct violation of the Monroe Doctrine, a policy that opposed foreign colonization in the Americas; on the other hand, an aggressive posture by the Lincoln administration might trigger a backlash in which one or all three European countries might recognize the Confederacy and even provide direct assistance in the Confederate war effort. In walking this thin diplomatic tightrope, Seward began an exchange of notes to the European states encouraging their neutrality and expressing U.S. concern about their overt action in Mexico.

It was not only the appearance of foreign troops in Mexico that appeared as a dire threat to Union fortunes. Throughout the war, despite the efforts of a U.S. naval blockade of Confederate ports, it was English-made guns and ammunition that kept the South's armies equipped—a trade of guns for cotton, the South's so-called "White Gold." At the time the South seceded in early 1861, it had perhaps 10 percent of the industrial base of the North. It was British factories and arsenals that kept the South in arms. Two years into the war, for example, General Ulysses Grant in his assault on Vicksburg found that the enemy was using new British Enfield Rifles. At the Siege of Petersburg, Union troops found ammunition boxes stamped "Royal Arsenal Woolwich."

At the eastern edge of the Mexican border was Matamoras, across from Brownsville, Texas. It became a hub of this trade. If the South had not been able to export its cotton on a large scale to British companies in return for rifles and other weapons, it could not have sustained its war effort. Here in Matamoros, as in some other Mexican ports, merchant ships could dock, unload weapons, load cotton, and return to England. Preventing blockade-running cargo ships from unloading weapons of war for the South was a critical challenge for President Lincoln and his wartime advisors.

1861

It did not take long for military operations to begin along the borderlands. The Confederates struck first. Shortly after Fort Sumter and the beginning of hostilities in the East, Henry Hopkins Sibley a twenty-two-year antebellum veteran military leader who had served on the frontier in numerous battles against Indians and in the Mexican War, joined the Confederate cause. Sibley soon met with Confederate President Jefferson Davis and presented an audacious plan outlining what amounted to a Confederate takeover of the West. He would lead a mounted force of soldiers, live off the land, drive away any federal troops, and bring under Confederate control the entire Southwest. Confederate leaders gave Sibley a brigadier's commission, approved the plan, gave him the authority necessary to form a brigade of Texans, and charged him to clear the border area in New Mexico and Arizona as a prelude to a final push into California.

Meanwhile, in July 1861, Lieutenant Colonel John R. Baylor led the 2nd Texas Mounted Rifles into New Mexico, battled Union troops from Fort Fillmore, occupied the town of Mesilla, and took over the fort. On August 1, 1861, Baylor made a declaration: the southern portion of New Mexico would now become the "Confederate Territory of Arizona." Mesilla would be its capitol and he its military governor.

Beginning what became known as the New Mexico Campaign, Sibley formed what he called the Army of New Mexico, composed of over 3,000 men, and set off from San Antonio in November. He assured his troops and anyone who would listen that they would be greeted as liberators along the border.

1862

In January 1862, British, Spanish, and French troops landed in Mexico to meet with President Benito Juárez to force the Mexicans to repay loans. The British and Spanish forces returned to Europe after striking a deal with the Mexican government. The French remained. It was becoming clear that the French were in Mexico not just to reclaim unpaid debt; they were there as a conquering force. Their goal would be to take over Mexico and establish a permanent presence in North America. War in Mexico was imminent.

By February, Henry Sibley was marshalling forces to make his New Mexico Campaign a rousing success, one that he trusted would establish himself as a heroic Confederate military commander. His immediate goal was to lay siege to the federal stronghold of Fort Craig on the Rio Grande, commanded by Union Colonel Edward Canby.

Jockeying for position, the two forces met at a site on the Rio Grande north of Fort Craig near the town of Valverde. After both sides suffered extensive losses, Sibley made a foolish effort to complete the grand plan he had laid out to President Davis. With his forces depleted and running low on supplies, he decided to continue up the Rio Grande.

Arriving in Albuquerque on March 2, Sibley and his men found that Union forces had left the town and destroyed most of the military supplies. If Sibley had hoped to reinforce his troops in Albuquerque, those hopes were dashed. Nevertheless, in the town square, Sibley's men raised the Confederate flag, and Sibley himself established a temporary headquarters.

The immediate goal for Sibley and his Texas force was now to overrun Fort Union, the largest U.S. military post in the region, a fortress that protected the Santa Fe Trail and its overland trading traffic against Indian attacks. While Sibley and some of his men remained in Albuquerque with troops to protect supplies, a large contingent pressed on through the town of Santa Fe and toward Fort Union. Unfortunately for Sibley's men, Union commanders, anticipating an attack, were now reinforced by troops from Colorado. The Confederates were trudging in the winter cold toward a Union enemy far greater in numbers than they believed awaited them.

But it would not be at Fort Union that the Confederates would face off against the enemy; Union commanders decided to surprise the invaders and intercept their advance. The two forces met at a location called Glorieta Pass at the southern tip of the Sangre de Cristo Mountains, southeast of Santa Fe on the Santa Fe Trail.

After fierce fighting, the Confederates abandoned any hopes of continuing on to Fort Union. With many of their supply wagons and supplies destroyed, they headed south, back to Albuquerque. Low on food and other supplies, with many of their horses lost in the warfare, Sibley's weary and overextended troops managed to make it back to El Paso and relative safety. His grand plan—the one eagerly embraced by President Davis—was in ruin. There would be no Confederate West or even an additional military front in which the Confederates could assert their power. Sibley's vision of his conquering army marching onward to California had been dashed at this hitherto unknown spot in New Mexico. Many writers later called the battle at Glorieta Pass "The Gettysburg of the West."

In addition to thwarting Sibley's plan, Union power along the Mexican border in 1862 further asserted itself in the form of a force of soldiers that became known as "The California Column." Led by Colonel James H. Carleton, the 5,000-man group of volunteers, including Hispanic scouts familiar with the dangers of the desert landscape and the location of water sources, set off in the spring of 1862 to fortify Union control of the border from the West Coast to El Paso. They captured Tucson, sixty miles from the border in Arizona; engaged in a skirmish north of Tucson at a jagged rock formation called Picacho Peak on April 15; established Fort Bowie in southeastern Arizona; moved across New Mexico, meeting up with General Canby's troops who had driven Sibley's army to El Paso; and pressed farther into the interior of Texas. The North now held a distinct, if tenuous, military advantage along the U.S.-Mexican border.

Meanwhile, 1,200 miles east from El Paso at Pittsburg Landing, Tennessee, General Ulysses S. Grant led his Army of the Tennessee to a decisive victory against Confederate General Albert Sidney Johnston's troops at the Battle of Shiloh, a bloody and decisive affair that helped consolidate the Union's control of the Mississippi River.

And 1,200 miles south from El Paso, the French army moved confidently toward Mexico City and an expected triumph over undermanned Mexican troops loyal to President Juárez. French confidence was soon shattered, however. At a small town called Puebla, Mexican defenders led by General Ignacio Zaragoza and Porfirio Diaz surprisingly and soundly turned back the French advance on May 5, 1862. The French would have to wait for reinforcements to continue their quest to take over Mexico. The defeat of the French at that battle would be celebrated by Mexicans and Mexican Americans for generations to come. The celebration would be known as Cinco de Mayo.

War blazed across North America.

1863

When Emperor Napoleon III of France sent troops to Mexico in early 1862, along with British and Spanish forces, it was ostensibly to collect debts owed to the respective governments. Following negotiations and a settlement, the British and Spanish returned to Europe. France remained, and it was clear that France's leader had much more in mind than a repayment of debts. The French attack on Puebla in 1862 that had been repulsed by Mexican troops left no doubt of the ultimate objective of Napoleon III—a "Grand Scheme" to replace the democratically elected government of Benito Juárez with French leadership. France had launched a campaign to take over Mexico and establish a powerful French presence in North America.

In May 1863, newly fortified French troops marched again on Mexico City. This time there would be no Cinco de Mayo, no iconic victory by besieged Mexicans against the invader. This time the French overran Mexican forces in a second battle at Puebla and marched into Mexico City and established a new government. The Juárez administration fled north into exile.

About the same time that the French marched into Mexico City, General Grant's Union Army began a nearly two-month siege of the city of Vicksburg, Mississippi, that would finally eliminate the last Confederate stronghold in Mississippi. The simultaneous events in Mexico and in Mississippi presaged an ultimate showdown on the U.S.-Mexican border that would decide the fate of France as a power in North America.

In July 1863, French leaders voted to invite Archduke Maximilian of Austria, to accept the throne of this new French puppet government. Maximilian eventually agreed and would arrive in Mexico the following year.

Southern leaders eagerly embraced the French adventures in Mexico, hoping that Napoleon III would officially grant diplomatic recognition to the Confederate government and thus fulfill a long-held hope that Rebel fortunes would be wildly enhanced by a powerful European ally.

In July 1863, Napoleon III refused officially to recognize the Confederacy but approved the shipment of munitions and rifles across the border from Mexico into Texas. The Confederates now had a ready supply of arms not only from British company blockade runners but also supplies from the French. Cities such as Matamoros, Brownsville, and Laredo were vital to the continued Confederate ability to prosecute the war effort.

The French lack of formal recognition of the Confederacy coincided with the North's strategically crucial victory in Gettysburg, Pennsylvania, a battle that dashed Confederate General Robert E. Lee's hopes for a successful invasion of northern territory. Yet even with this conclusive battle, the Union's final victory and the conclusion of the seemingly endless conflict remained elusive. Realizing the enormous sieve that the U.S.-Mexican border represented in the guns-for-cotton resupply of the enemy, President Lincoln decided to turn additional war resources to the area.

In November 1863, 6,000 troops from the Army's 13th Corps arrived on the barrier islands near the mouth of the Rio Grande. Once again, the Union was in Brownsville, Texas. The order was to clear the area of supply and infiltration along the Rio Grande. Setting up a base in Brownsville, the troops planned to travel along the Rio Grande and destroy enemy equipment, supplies, and especially cotton stores that awaited foreign traders of military equipment. Their first target was Laredo.

1864

The Union effort throughout the war to tighten cotton-smuggling routes along the Rio Grande had been sporadic at best. The town of Brownsville, for example, changed hands from Confederate to Union forces a number of times during the war. The South continued to resupply its troops as steamboats hauled cotton along Rio Grande valley towns to such places as the Port of Bagdad in Matamoras, across from Brownsville, where ships offloaded weapons and supplies and took on bales of cotton that would reach textile mills in England and France.

Laredo was one of those towns with large stores of cotton that fed the Confederate economic lifeline that the Union was determined to overrun. On March 19, 1864, with Union troops approaching the town, Confederate defenders, led by Colonel Santos Benavides who had received information that the attack was imminent, were able to send for reinforcements. Benavides ordered his troops to stack hundreds of bales of cotton to be used as barricades. The Union assault faltered. Once again, Union troops had not extinguished the guns-for-cotton trade that had kept the southern armies supplied.

In June 1864, Archduke Maximilian entered Mexico City to be crowned Emperor of the Imperial Throne of Mexico. The thirty-one-year old emperor settled in Chapultepec Castle on a hill where Aztec rulers had long ago resided. As the French army continued to drive a weaker Mexican army farther to the north of the country, Maximilian, much to the surprise of many of his backers, took a more progressive stance over the growing area of Mexico controlled by his troops. He saw himself as something of a protector of much of the Mexican peasantry and even decided to abolish serfdom and child labor.

By early 1965, the French had taken control of most of the country. The future of the French reign in Mexico, nevertheless, would not rest on its ability to defeat the Mexican army, now scattered in northern regions of the country. The fate of the French in Mexico would instead rest on the events north and east of the Rio Grande.

1865

On April 9, 1865, in Appomattox Court House, Virginia, General Robert E. Lee surrendered the Confederate Army of Northern Virginia to Lieutenant General Ulysses S. Grant. The Civil War—four years of fierce combat that took the lives of over 600,000 individuals—had at last come to an end.

Palmito Ranch, Texas: The Last Battle of the Civil War, 1865

The windswept plain at the southernmost tip of Texas, midway between Brazos Island and Brownsville, Texas, dotted with chaparral, marsh plants, and small palmetto trees, did not resemble the terrain of any major battle of the Civil War. Yet at a place called Palmito Ranch, a few hundred Union and Confederate forces faced off in what became known as the last battle of the war. It began on the afternoon of May 13, 1865, slightly a month after General Robert E. Lee had surrendered his army to General Ulysses S. Grant at Appomattox Court House, Virginia, and almost exactly a month after President Abraham Lincoln had been assassinated. Although the Trans-Mississippi department of the Confederate Army had yet formally to surrender, an informal truce had been arranged so that both sides along the Rio Grande had ceased fighting. In violation of this truce, for no apparent reason, a Union force attacked this Confederate outpost. The Union force was repulsed, losing as many as 100 casualties. Union leaders attempting to explain the ignominious act blamed artillery said to have been supplied by the French army occupying the nearby Mexican town of Matamoros. Union Private John J. Williams of the 34th Indiana Infantry Regiment was one of those who would not return home after this meaningless fight. He is believed to be the last man killed in combat in the Civil War.

Depiction of Confederate troops in Brownsville, Texas, May 1865. At the eastern edge of the border across from the port city of Matamoras, Brownsville was the hub of Confederate trade in weapons from Europe that helped sustain its war effort. It was also the scene of many skirmishes throughout the war. (Library of Congress)

Nevertheless, at a small garrison near the mouth of the Rio Grande at Palmito Ranch, near Brownsville, Texas, Union and Confederate soldiers would fight the last battle of the Civil War. A Union commander at Brazos Island decided to make one last foray at the enemy near Brownsville. Innumerable such attacks had marked the last several years as the two sides had thrown thousands of young men into the slaughter. This skirmish, over a month after the Confederate surrender, however, was in its own unique way unnecessary and superfluous. For as many as one hundred men, nevertheless, it was far more than that. They lost their lives.

PROTECTING THE BORDER: SHERIDAN HEADS WEST

Major General Phillip H. Sheridan was at the surrender meeting at Appomattox. Indeed, Sheridan's forces had played a pivotal role in forcing Lee's Army of Northern Virginia into a hazardous strategic position, one without an escape route, and one that finally convinced Lee that his only option was surrender. He was highly respected by General Grant.

Grant believed early on after the war that the U.S.-Mexican border needed immediate protection and that to allow further French aggression in the region would be to jeopardize seriously U.S. interests in North America. The French and their imperialist threat in North America, Grant realized, had to be driven out, either through diplomacy or, most likely, through military intimidation or direct action.

On April 14, 1865, the nation lost President Lincoln to assassination. His death came little more than a week after the surrender at Appomattox. Approximately a month later, Grant asked Sheridan to take on a mission to control the border.

When Sheridan's forces of 25,000 men arrived in Texas, the Mexican army was in a near hopeless condition: exhausted, demoralized troops; lack of guns, ammunition, horses, food, and medical and other supplies; and a tightening noose of French forces closing in. Sheridan quickly moved into action. He sent scouts across the border and had troops line portions of the Rio Grande in a threatening posture designed to let the French know that they might soon enter the conflict in Mexico.

Sheridan's maneuvers on the Rio Grande, restoring U.S. control of the border, were effective. "These reports and demonstrations resulted in alarming the Imperialists so much that they withdrew the French and Austrian soldiers from Matamoras, and practically abandoned the whole of northern Mexico," Sheridan later wrote in his memoirs.

At the same time, Sheridan ordered his men to leave large quantities of guns and other military supplies at various locations on the American side of the Rio Grande. It was an invitation to the Mexican troops to cross the river, gather up the arms, and rebuild their forces. The Mexicans readily accepted the invitation. Sheridan had thus begun to reinforce Mexican troops without the United States formally joining an armed conflict with the French. A reenergized and reinforced army under Benito Juárez thus became the aggressor and began to force the French south.

In December 1865, Secretary Seward sent France an ultimatum. The friendship between the two countries, Seward wrote, would be in jeopardy unless France abandoned its armed intervention in Mexico and its efforts to establish its own government. Napoleon decided not to go to war with the United States. In early 1866, Napoleon III made a critical decision to abandon the entire Mexican enterprise and to pull troops out of Mexico.

For Maximilian, the decision amounted to a death sentence. In May 1867, Mexican troops captured Maximilian, and on June 19, 1867, he was executed by a firing squad on a hillside outside the city of Querétaro. Benito Juárez resumed his presidency.

The lines of the U.S.-Mexican border had survived not only the Civil War but also European intervention.

DOCUMENT

General Grant Orders General Sheridan to Protect Border, 1865, Memoirs of General Philip Sheridan

Although Philip Sheridan, the most celebrated Union cavalry commander in the Civil War, was best known for his exploits in a number of pivotal battles—Perryville, Chickamauga, the Wilderness, Cold Harbor, Richmond, the Shenandoah Valley campaign, and Appomattox—he also became something of a legend in the West. He began his army career defending frontier posts. Following the war, after General Ulysses S. Grant sent him on a successful mission to defend the U.S. border against possible French attacks, he became military governor of Louisiana and Texas and later succeeded William T. Sherman as commander in chief of the U.S. Army. As did Grant, Sheridan wrote his memoirs. They were published in the year of his death: 1888. The following is an extract from those memoirs dealing with his strategies along the border following the Civil War.

The surrender at Appomattox put a stop to all military operations on the part of General Grant's forces, and the morning of April 10 my cavalry began its march to Petersburg, the men anticipating that they would soon be mustered out and returned to their homes. At Nottoway Court House I heard of the assassination of the President. The first news came to us the night after the dastardly deed, the telegraph operator having taken it from the wires while in transmission to General Meade. The dispatch ran that Mr. Lincoln had been, shot at 10 o'clock that morning at Willard's Hotel, but as I could conceive of nothing to take the President there I set the story down as a canard, and went to bed without giving it further thought. Next morning, however, an official telegram confirmed the fact of the assassination, though eliminating the distorted circumstances that had been communicated the night before.

When we reached Petersburg my column was halted, and instructions given me to march the cavalry and the Sixth Corps to Greensboro', North Carolina, for the purpose of aiding General Sherman (the surrender of General Johnston having not yet been effected), so I made the necessary preparations and moved on the 24th of April, arriving at South Boston, on the Dan River, the 28th, the Sixth Corps having reached Danville meanwhile. At South Boston I received a dispatch from General Halleck, who immediately after Lee's surrender had been assigned to command at Richmond, informing me that General Johnston had been brought to terms. The necessity for going farther south being thus obviated we retraced our steps to Petersburg, from which place I proceeded by steamer to Washington, leaving, the cavalry to be marched thither by easy stages.

The day after my arrival in Washington an important order was sent me, accompanied by the following letter of instructions, transferring me to a new field of operations:

"HEADQUARTERS ARMIES OF THE UNITED STATES.
"Washington, D. C., May 17, 1865.

"GENERAL: Under the orders relieving you from the command of the Middle Military Division and assigning you to command west of the Mississippi, you will proceed without delay to the West to arrange all preliminaries for your new field of duties.

"Your duty is to restore Texas, and that part of Louisiana held by the enemy, to the Union in the shortest practicable time, in a way most effectual for securing permanent peace.

"To do this, you will be given all the troops that can be spared by Major-General Canby, probably twenty-five thousand men of all arms; the troops with Major-General J. J. Reynolds, in Arkansas, say twelve thousand, Reynolds to command;

the Fourth Army Corps, now at Nashville, Tennessee, awaiting orders; and the Twenty-Fifth Army Corps, now at City Point, Virginia, ready to embark.

"I do not wish to trammel you with instructions; I will state, however, that if Smith holds out, without even an ostensible government to receive orders from or to report to, he and his men are not entitled to the considerations due to an acknowledged belligerent. Theirs are the conditions of outlaws, making war against the only Government having an existence over the territory where war is now being waged.

"You may notify the rebel commander west of the Mississippi—holding intercourse with him in person, or through such officers of the rank of major-general as you may select—that he will be allowed to surrender all his forces on the same terms as were accorded to Lee and Johnston. If he accedes, proceed to garrison the Red River as high up as Shreveport, the seaboard at Galveston, Malagorda Bay, Corpus Christi, and mouth of the Rio Grande.

"Place a strong force on the Rio Grande, holding it at least to a point opposite Camargo, and above that if supplies can be procured.

"In case of an active campaign (a hostile one) I think a heavy force should be put on the Rio Grande as a first preliminary. Troops for this might be started at once. The Twenty-Fifth Corps is now available, and to it should be added a force of white troops, say those now under Major-General Steele.

"To be clear on this last point, I think the Rio Grande should be strongly held, whether the forces in Texas surrender or not, and that no time should be lost in getting troops there. If war is to be made, they will be in the right place; if Kirby Smith surrenders, they will be on the line which is to be strongly garrisoned.

"Should any force be necessary other than those designated, they can be had by calling for them on Army Headquarters.

"U. S. GRANT,
"Lieutenant-General."

On receipt of these instructions I called at once on General Grant, to see if they were to be considered so pressing as to preclude my remaining in Washington till after the Grand Review, which was fixed for the 23d and 24th of May, for naturally I had a strong desire to head my command on that great occasion. But the General told me that it was absolutely necessary to go at once to force the surrender of the Confederates under Kirby Smith. He also told me that the States lately in rebellion would be embraced in two or three military departments, the commanders of which would control civil affairs until Congress took action about restoring them to the Union, since that course would not only be economical and simple, but would give the Southern people confidence, and encourage them to go to work, instead of distracting them with politics.

At this same interview he informed me that there was an additional motive in sending me to the new command, a motive not explained by the instructions themselves, and went on to say that, as a matter of fact, he looked upon the invasion of Mexico by Maximilian as a part of the rebellion itself, because of the encouragement that invasion had received from the Confederacy, and that our success in putting down secession would never be complete till the French and Austrian invaders were compelled to quit the territory of our sister republic. With regard to this matter, though, he said it would be necessary for me to act with great circumspection, since the Secretary of State, Mr. Seward, was much opposed to the use of our troops along the border in any active way that would be likely to involve us in a war with European powers.

Under the circumstances, my disappointment at not being permitted to participate in the review had to be submitted to, and I left Washington without an opportunity of seeing again in a body the men who, while under my command, had gone through so many trials and unremittingly pursued and, assailed the enemy, from the beginning of the campaign of 1864 till the white flag came into their hands at Appomattox Court House.

I went first to St. Louis, and there took the steamboat for New Orleans, and when near the mouth of the Red River received word from General Canby that Kirby Smith had surrendered under terms similar to those accorded Lee and Johnston. But the surrender was not carried out in good faith, particularly by the Texas troops, though this I did not learn till some little time afterward when I was informed that they had marched off to the interior of the State in several organized bodies, carrying with them their camp equipage, arms, ammunition, and even some artillery, with the ultimate purpose of going to Mexico. In consequence of this, and also because of the desire of the Government to make a strong showing of force in Texas, I decided to traverse the State with two columns of cavalry, directing one to San Antonio under Merritt, the other to Houston under Custer. Both commands were to start from the Red River—Shreveport and Alexandria—being the respective initial points—and in organizing the columns, to the mounted force already on the Red River were added several regiments of cavalry from the east bank of the Mississippi, and in a singular way one of these fell upon the trail of my old antagonist, General Early. While crossing the river somewhere below Vicksburg some of the men noticed a suspicious looking party being ferried over in a rowboat, behind which two horses were swimming in tow. Chase was given, and the horses, being abandoned by the party, fell into the hands of our troopers, who, however, failed to capture or identify the people in the boat. As subsequently ascertained, the men were companions of Early, who was already across the Mississippi, hidden in the woods, on his way with two or three of these followers to join the Confederates in Texas, not having heard of Kirby Smith's surrender. A week or two later I received a letter from Early describing the affair, and the capture of the horses, for which he claimed pay, on the ground that they were private property, because he had taken them in battle. The letter also said that any further pursuit of Early would be useless, as he "expected to be on the deep blue sea" by the time his communication reached me. The unfortunate man was fleeing from imaginary dangers, however, for striking his trail was purely accidental, and no effort whatever was being made to arrest him personally. Had this been especially desired it might have been accomplished very readily just after Lee's surrender, for it was an open secret that Early was then not far away, pretty badly disabled with rheumatism.

By the time the two columns were ready to set out for San Antonio and Houston, General Frank Herron,—with one division of the Thirteenth Corps, occupied Galveston, and another division under General Fred Steele had gone to Brazos Santiago, to hold Brownsville and the line of the Rio Grande, the object being to prevent, as far as possible, the escaping Confederates from joining Maximilian. With this purpose in view, and not forgetting Grant's conviction that the French invasion of Mexico was linked with the rebellion, I asked for an increase of force to send troops into Texas in fact, to concentrate at available points in the State an army strong enough to move against the invaders of Mexico if occasion demanded. The Fourth and Twenty-fifth army corps being ordered to report to me, accordingly, I sent the Fourth Corps to Victoria and San Antonio, and the bulk of the Twenty-fifth to Brownsville. Then came the feeding and caring for all these troops—a difficult matter—for those at Victoria and San Antonio had to be provisioned overland from Indianola across the "hog-wallow prairie," while the supplies for the forces at Brownsville and along the Rio Grande must come by way of Brazos Santiago, from which point I was obliged to construct, with the labor of the men, a railroad to Clarksville, a distance of about eighteen miles.

The latter part of June I repaired to Brownsville myself to impress the Imperialists, as much as possible, with the idea that we intended hostilities, and took along my chief of scouts—Major Young—and four of his most trusty men, whom I had had sent from Washington. From Brownsville I dispatched all these men to important points in northern Mexico, to glean information regarding the movements of the Imperial forces, and also to gather intelligence about the ex-Confederates who had crossed the Rio Grande. On information furnished by these scouts, I caused General Steele to make demonstrations all along the lower Rio Grande, and at the same time demanded the return of certain munitions of war that had been turned over by ex-Confederates to the Imperial General (Mejia) commanding at Matamoras. These demands, backed up as they were by such a formidable show of force created much agitation and demoralization among the Imperial troops, and measures looking to the abandonment of northern Mexico were forthwith adopted by those in authority—a policy that would have resulted in the speedy evacuation of the entire country by Maximilian, had not our Government weakened; contenting itself with a few pieces of the contraband artillery varnished over with the Imperial apologies. A golden opportunity was lost, for we had ample excuse for crossing the boundary, but Mr. Seward being, as I have already stated, unalterably opposed to any act likely to involve us in war, insisted on his course of negotiation with Napoleon.

As the summer wore away, Maximilian, under Mr. Seward's policy, gained in strength till finally all the accessible sections of Mexico were in his possession, and the Republic under President Juárez almost succumbed. Growing impatient at this, in the latter part of September I decided to try again what virtue there might be in a hostile demonstration, and selected the upper Rio Grande for the scene of my attempt. Merritt's cavalry and the Fourth Corps still being at San Antonio, I went to that place and reviewed these troops, and having prepared them with some ostentation for a campaign, of course it was bruited about that we were going to invade Mexico. Then, escorted by a regiment of horse I proceeded hastily to Fort Duncan, on the Rio Grande just opposite the Mexican town of Piedras Negras. Here I opened communication with President Juárez, through one of his staff, taking care not to do this in the dark, and the news, spreading like wildfire, the greatest significance was ascribed to my action, it being reported most positively and with many specific details that I was only awaiting the arrival of the troops, then under marching orders at San Antonio, to cross the Rio Grande in behalf of the Liberal cause.

Ample corroboration of the reports then circulated was found in my inquiries regarding the quantity of forage we could depend upon getting in Mexico, our arrangements for its purchase, and my sending a pontoon train to Brownsville, together with which was cited the renewed activity of the troops along the lower Rio Grande. These reports and demonstrations resulted in alarming the Imperialists so much that they withdrew the French and Austrian soldiers from Matamoras, and practically abandoned the whole of northern Mexico as far down as Monterey, with the exception of Matamoras, where General Mejia continued to hang on with a garrison of renegade Mexicans.

The abandonment of so much territory in northern Mexico encouraged General Escobedo and other Liberal leaders to such a degree that they collected a considerable army of their followers at Comargo, Mier, and other points. At the same time that unknown quantity, Cortinas, suspended his free-booting for the nonce, and stoutly harassing Matamoras, succeeded in keeping its Imperial garrison within the fortifications. Thus countenanced and stimulated, and largely supplied with arms and ammunition, which we left at convenient places on our side of the river to fall into their hands, the Liberals, under General Escobedo—a man of much force of character—were enabled in northern Mexico to place the affairs of the Republic on a substantial basis.

Source: Sheridan, Philip. *Personal Memoirs of P. H. Sheridan, Vol. 2, Chapter 8.* New York: Charles L. Webster & Company, 1888; The letter of. U.S. Grant to Philip Sheridan, May 17, 1865, Library of Congress, Manuscript Division, Philip Henry Sheridan Papers.

3

Border Unrest

There is solitude along the expanse of the border. Along the winding, slow-moving Rio Grande; through the parched, sandy, windblown desert lands where vegetation stoically withstands a need for water; and through the stony ravines to the towering, jagged crests of the mountains where each slow earth's turn reveals new layers of shadows and definition of the vast ranges, the borderlands exude a sense of lonely power, inhospitable yet alluring.

Especially in the mid-1850s, a time when the border line had only small towns along its length from the Pacific to the Gulf, most times there was little to rupture the natural tranquility. Nevertheless, there were always the adventurers, Apache warriors, cattle rustlers, and bandits, along with sheriffs, posses, and army troops with whom they battled. There was always a vulnerability to the quietness and repose of the land.

Perhaps the best exemplar of this border unrest in the mid-nineteenth century can be seen in the exploits of Juan Cortina. To Anglos, he was nothing more than a notorious bandit; to many of his Mexican admirers, however, he was "The Robin Hood of the Rio Grande."

Born at Camargo, Tamaulipas, just south of the Rio Grande to a wealthy cattle rancher, by the late 1850s Cortina was living north of the border and became a rancher, like his father. In the summer of 1859, in Brownsville's Market Square, Cortina witnessed a scene that seared his senses: here was an Anglo marshal pistol-whipping a Mexican worker who had once labored on his family's farm. The outraged Cortina shot the marshal in the shoulder, helped the Mexican on his horse, and rode off. Cortina had seen too much of this Anglo arrogance and harsh treatment of Mexicans in his life. The incident in Brownsville was like an emotional trigger.

Two months later, Cortina led an armed group of Mexicans into Brownsville on a raid to release Mexican prisoners who, he felt, had been unfairly jailed by Anglos. In the course of the raid, Cortina's men killed four men. But to Cortina, the raid was only the beginning of a crusade. With his followers shouting, "Death to the gringos!" Cortina planted the Mexican flag and declared the town the Republic of the Rio Grande. At a nearby ranch, he issued a proclamation denouncing the

Illustration from 1864 of Juan Cortina, known to his followers as "The Robin Hood of the Rio Grande." A patriot to his admirers and a bandit to his enemies, Cortina and his small peasant and lower-class army fought a series of battles against the Texas Rangers and U.S. Army forces in protest of unfair land seizures from Mexican landowners by U.S. courts and political leaders. (Library of Congress)

horrors that had been inflicted on the Mexican people in the border regions by invading Anglos—"vampires" he called them—who had stolen property that was supposedly protected by treaty. They had, he declared, treated his people not only with humiliation but also with violence. "A society is organized in the State of Texas," he declared in the proclamation, "which devotes itself sleeplessly until the work is crowned with success, to the improvement of the unhappy condition of those Mexicans resident therein; extermination [of] their tyrants, to which end those which compose it are ready to shed their blood and suffer the death of martyrs."

Juan Cortina's quixotic movement would not be long-lived. The Texas Rangers were quick to strike back, along with support from the U.S. Army. But with the backing of several hundred supporters from both sides of the border—Tejanos who were willing to take up arms—Cortina and his force became a formidable nemesis to border stability.

Cortina's small army finally retreated to Mexico after a stinging defeat in Rio Grande City in December 1859. Cortina's defiance and those of his supporters never wavered. Months after the retreat, the border saw sporadic fighting and raiding, with much property destroyed along a one-hundred-mile stretch of the border. Nevertheless, "Cortina's War," as it became known in history and folklore, was over.

Cortina later fought with Benito Juárez against French intervention in the 1860s and was made a general in the Mexican army. He later became acting governor of Tamaulipas.

Juan Cortina would not be a lone adventurer along the border. The relatively unsecured land and the possibilities it offered lured others.

SEEKERS OF GLORY: THE FILIBUSTERERS

The word filibuster comes from the Dutch *vribuiter*, meaning freebooter or fortune hunter. In the mid-nineteenth century, northern Mexico was particularly inviting to a number of such privateers or filibusterers. From small groups of bandits who were content with plundering small towns to individuals intent on conquering territory and setting up their own private fiefdoms, the adventurers were, to the Mexican government, a direct threat to the sovereignty of the country.

In October 1855, a captain of the Texas Rangers named James Callahan, accompanied by a band of other Rangers and some mercenary soldiers, crossed the Rio Grande on what amounted to an expedition to recover runaway slaves who had fled to northern Mexico. During the invasion, Callahan and his men managed to take possession of the town of Piedras Negras and then set fire to houses to cover their retreat when faced with Mexican troops. Captain Callahan's nefarious and singularly inglorious effort led to a U.S. Claims Commission financial settlement to over one hundred Mexican citizens for damages incurred in the escapade.

In 1857, Henry A. Crabb, a former California state senator who had been defeated in a bid for reelection, decided on his own path that he imagined would lead to a grander destiny than a seat in the state legislature. He decided to embark on a mission to colonize a portion of Sonora. Managing to enlist over one hundred men for what he called the Gadsden Colonization Company, he met fierce resistance from Mexican soldiers, who had no use for Anglo adventures. After a six-day siege, the soldiers of fortune were defeated, and all of the men, including Crabb, were executed.

The most renowned, or at least notorious, of the filibusterers was William Walker. Born in Nashville, Tennessee, Walker proved himself something of a prodigy at an early age. He graduated *summa cum laude* from the University of Nashville at the age of fourteen and studied medicine at the University of Edinburgh and the University of Heidelberg before achieving a medical degree from the University of Pennsylvania at the age of nineteen. But medicine was not to be his calling. He, like other filibusterers had more visionary and lofty ambitions.

His vision was to cross the border with an armed force and establish an independent Republic of Sonora, a colony that could someday become another state of the United States. He formed a company, sold scrip that could be redeemed for lands in Sonora, and in October 1853 set out with forty-five men on his audacious expedition.

Landing in La Paz, the capital of Baja California, Walker and his men stormed the government offices, brazenly declared the town the capital of a new Republic of Lower California, announced that he was president, and even proudly displayed a new flag. Soon realizing his precarious position with regard to possible retaliation by Mexican troops, Walker moved his operation to Ensenada, where he issued a new proclamation establishing the Republic of Sonora. Once again his announcement was complemented by the hoisting of yet another new flag.

Walker's empire in Sonora, teetering from lack of supplies and too few soldiers, was soon over. He abandoned this adventure but not his ambition to take over as a leader somehow, somewhere.

The somewhere became Nicaragua a year later, where Walker joined a revolutionary faction, helped them take over the country, and managed to become president in 1856, a position he held for about a year.

The foreign migrations of Walker would come to an end in 1860. On another expedition, he was taken prisoner by the British navy, turned over to authorities in

Honduras, and was summarily executed. Like Henry Crabb and other filibusterers of the mid-1900s, William Walker met an ignominious end.

The filibuster expeditions would not be the most serious threats to the stability of the U.S.-Mexican border. Those threats would require the intervention of the U.S. military.

U.S. TROOPS AND THE APACHE WARS

For generations, Apaches had roamed the Southwest living off the land, fighting the encroaching Spanish, raiding, and rustling. To these and other Indian tribes, the creation of the U.S.-Mexican border meant nothing. To them there was no line, no ownership, no property rights, and no defined nation-states. It was all just land, sacred land, on which they and their elders had lived their lives.

As the U.S. Army conducted its massive military campaign across the West to defeat the various Indian tribes that stood in the way of new settlements, and as those tribes were herded into reservations, it was the Apaches that most fiercely resisted the encroachment. And of the various tribes of Apaches in the Southwest, it was the Chiricahuas that gained the most notoriety. Their homelands extended throughout southwestern New Mexico, southeastern Arizona, and into northern Mexico. When Anglo settlers began to arrive and take possession of an increasing area of this land, bitter and deadly conflict was inevitable.

Indians called the mountains in southeast Arizona "Huachuca," meaning "place of thunder." Here, where legions of desert clouds, marshaling explosions of light and sound, can assault the landscape with startling and sudden ferocity, the U.S. Army in 1877 built a key fort deep in the heart of Apache country. Nestled against the base of the mountains in an area of hidden caves and failed mines and overgrown with cottonwood and ponderosa pine, Fort Huachuca was home to soldiers who marched on Brown's Parade Field, kept their guns and artillery in wartime order, and prepared to take on the warrior bands that harassed small towns and ranches. Here, about fifteen miles from the U.S.-Mexican border, scouts and lookouts could see clearly in three directions over the San Pedro and Sana Cruz Valleys, could see the trail dust churned up by Apache raiding parties, and could see the smoke and fire left in the aftermath of skirmishes and plunder. Fort Huachuca became a central location for troops to wage war against the Apaches.

As early as 1848 and the signing of the Treaty of Guadalupe Hidalgo, the Chiricahuas had served notice to the military that they would not meekly surrender. When a group of Apaches raided several towns near El Paso and stole a large number of mules, a military contingent followed the raiders and destroyed their camp. It was this continual raiding by Apaches across the new border that drove the U.S. Army to establish a number of posts, like that of Fort Huachuca, from Texas to Arizona. By the early 1870s, eight posts had been constructed along the Rio Grande, and an additional five forts were established along the border of Arizona and New Mexico.

During the 1860s, the fiercest Apache raids were led by warriors under the command of Cochise. Parrying military efforts to corral the Apache fighters on numerous occasions, Cochise, using well-honed guerilla techniques, continued to harass and plunder settlements. Although Cochise and his band wreaked havoc on both settlers and the military alike and killed hundreds, they eventually retreated into a stronghold in the Dragoon Mountains, where amidst ancient, jagged rock formations they could outmaneuver any attempts to locate and destroy them.

By 1872, an aging Cochise agreed to a peace settlement offered by the United States that allowed for a large reservation in southeast Arizona for his people, tired of the constant threat of annihilation. He died two years later.

In the early 1970s, the army's military efforts against the Apaches were led by General George Crook. A veteran of the Civil War and of a two-year campaign in the Pacific Northwest to subdue the Paiute tribe, Crook was sent to Arizona Territory by President Ulysses S. Grant to bring an end to the hostilities with the Apaches. It was Crook who managed to convince Cochise to accept the reservation in southeast Arizona. Unlike most of the Indian fighters of his day, Crook grasped the cultural divides separating the Indians and whites and did his best to encourage amicable and humane solutions. In 1875 Crook left Arizona to take command of the Department of the Platte in its ultimately successful fight against the Cheyenne.

Shortly after Crook's departure, the Chiricahua Apache reservation was disbanded; the Chiricahuas were now to reside in a reservation farther north in the White Mountains. The dislocation of the Chiricahuas and the further disruption of their people brought further turmoil and defiance in Arizona. A new leader emerged who epitomized that defiance—Geronimo.

For over three decades, he had led bands of warriors over an astonishing area of land, ranging from western Arizona to New Mexico and deep into northern Sonora and Chihuahua, Mexico. Many of those charged with apprehending Geronimo on his various raids seemed certain that he had some kind of supernatural instinct to evade and bewilder his enemies, all the time making off with much bounty for his tribe. And now, angered over various humiliations against and broken promises made to his people, Geronimo defied the new reservation and went on the attack, his guerilla raids once again terrifying both Mexicans and U.S. citizens on both sides of border.

In 1882, George Crook was ordered back to the Arizona Territory to deal with the mounting problems posed by the intrepid Apache leader. In May 1882, working with Apache scouts who knew some of the territory of Geronimo's sanctuary hideouts in the mountains along the Arizona–New Mexico border, Crook's soldiers managed to overtake the canny leader and convince him to return with his people to the reservation.

During the next four years, Geronimo fled the reservation on a number of occasions, only to be tracked down by Crook once again. After another escape by Geronimo from the reservation, the War Department reprimanded Crook for his failure. He resigned, replaced by Brigadier General Nelson Miles, a military leader with far less concern for the future integration of the Apaches in society and with far more determination to rid the Southwest of the menace the tribe posed.

Geronimo, leader of the Chiricahua Apache tribe, along with his son and two braves, ca. 1866. Led by the tactical brilliance of Geronimo, the Chiricahua Apaches, entrenched in the mountainous regions of northern Mexico and southern Arizona, proved to be a formidable foe for General George Crook and other U.S. Army soldiers. (Library of Congress)

It would take several thousand regular army soldiers, along with hundreds of Apache and Navajo scouts, to bring an end to the murderous raids of Geronimo and his band. The Apaches darted back and forth across the border and into and out of the multitudes of rock formations they knew so well, all the while occasionally raiding farms and killing unsuspecting ranchers and their families. When approached by regiments high in numbers but often stymied by the guerilla ambushes, Geronimo and his men managed to hold their own, at least for several months. At one point one of the cavalry units seemed to have the Apache band totally surrounded. After charging into the location, the officer in charge would later report, as so many others had done, that they had captured everything there except Indians.

After a long summer of eluding the overwhelming U.S. military force, his band exhausted, hungry, and longing to see their family members on the reservation, Geronimo surrendered in the fall of 1886. Soon, all of the Chiricahua Apaches were placed on trains and sent as prisoners of war to Florida. They were later removed to Fort Sill in Oklahoma.

Along the border after 1886, there would be few raids of Indians. Yet there had been other forces at play in the borderlands that wreaked havoc. For all its rugged beauty and natural solitude, the border seemed always a source of unrest.

The El Paso Salt War of 1877

Yes, it was a war over salt. One hundred miles east of El Paso, the Salt Flats of Guadalupe, the remnants of an ancient shallow lake from millions of years past, had been the place where Mexicans and Mexican Americans over the years had been able to extract free salt, a precious resource not only for seasoning but also for its use in silver smelting. In 1877, some Anglos grandly announced that the salt beds were on their property and no longer would the salt be free, but rather would be available only for a price. The sudden announcement sparked resentment, to say the least. What followed can only be described as a chaotic clash of national pride, political power, rank greed, and human folly writ large. The clashes involved fistfights, gunfights, pillaging mobs, killings, and a diplomatic skirmish between the United States and Mexico that actually sparked talk of war between the two countries. The resolution of the conflict required not only the services of the Texas Rangers but also the intervention of the U.S. Ninth Cavalry. The Salt Flats was opened for privatization, much to the lasting resentment of the Tejano population.

OUTLAWS

Bandits, rustlers, highwaymen, gunslingers, cowboys, desperados, and other assorted violators of the law—the border had them all. From Brownsville, Texas, to California, they crossed the border with relative impunity robbing stagecoaches, stealing horses and cattle, and waylaying unsuspecting victims, all the time with law enforcement—federal, territorial, and local—usually ill equipped and underfunded to stamp out the marauding.

Ranchers along the border had to deal with the constant threat of losing their livestock. Back and forth across the border, gangs cut fences, hustled cattle, fought off enemy gangs as well as the law, and protected their ill-gotten herds, all the time trying to establish ways to feed, water, and market the animals.

Unfortunately for law-abiding cattle ranchers, many of whom were just beginning to establish their business, rustling could come from all directions—Mexican invaders crossing the Rio Grande to steal cattle from U.S. ranches and rustlers from the United States crossing the border to steal from Mexican herds. Outlaws became familiar with the marshy thickets along the Rio Grande, where they managed to carve out trails to drive stolen cattle and elude pursuers.

At the request of the governor of Texas, Harvey McNelly, a former Confederate officer in the Civil War and a captain in the Texas Rangers, formed his own raiding party to counterattack the rustlers. With a force of about forty tough frontier veterans, McNelly crossed the Mexican border on several occasions and attacked several Mexican gangs and brought back to the United States much stolen cattle, some of which had belonged to the wealthy cattleman, Richard King.

At one point in 1875, McNelly ordered his men to stack the corpses of several Mexican bandits in the Brownsville town square as a symbol of his determination. McNelly's raids nevertheless created something of a foreign diplomatic entanglement, one for which he was reprimanded by his own government. To cattlemen along the border, however, McNelly is remembered not as a foreign invader violating the sovereignty of another country, but as a hero righting wrongs.

The name of John Kinney occupies a special place in rustling fame. After a stint in the army, Kinney joined up with a notable group of desperadoes that included such killers such as Jessie Evans and Charles Ray (alias "Pony Diehl"). The group, working both sides of the border, roamed from the border to the Great Plains, encountering numerous other outlaws. Kinney himself earned the distinction of being shot in the face in an altercation with Billy the Kid, an injury from which he recovered and, unlike the Kid, Kinney lived to an old age.

Eventually, Kinney set up his own lucrative rustling enterprise, enlisting the cooperation of a number of local law enforcement gentlemen and business leaders, who profited handsomely from his burgeoning empire. For a time he worked out of El Paso and then, in 1879, in Mesilla, New Mexico. Some historians have credited Kinney with nothing less than constructing the Southwest's most organized criminal empire of its day.

Managing to employ a network of rustling gangs, the operation ranged from New Mexico into Chihuahua, Mexico, and from El Paso west into Sonora, Mexico. He set up a ranch south of Rincon, New Mexico, that included its own slaughterhouse, an establishment that enabled the enterprising Kinney to ship beef by rail either in live form or in choice cuts. A Santa Fe newspaper dubbed Kinney "King of the Rustlers."

He was eventually brought down in 1883 by federal agents and volunteer militia and spent a short time in Leavenworth Prison. Nevertheless, he lived to 1919, the owner of a couple of mines.

In southern Arizona the term "cowboys" in the 1880s had little to do with the professions of ranchers and ranch hands. The term had more to do with a group of cattle thieves and their control of money and power. From ranches in the San Pedro and San Simon Valleys, they stole cattle, especially in northern Mexico, ran them back across the border, rebranded them, fought off intruders, and invaded towns and outposts in northern Sonora and southern Arizona.

There was also the matter of stagecoach robbery. In many instances, the bandits not only stole strongboxes but also killed the drivers and passengers. So dangerous became some routes in the 1880s that Wells Fargo & Company had to temporarily suspend service to some towns.

Many of the bandits were gunslingers and misfit cowhands; many of them were on the run from the law in other states. They began to have almost free rein as marauders. Through intimidation and reward, these bandits often enlisted the support of law enforcement officials and began to exercise such increasing control that federal officials in Washington worried whether Arizona Territory would degenerate into anarchy. Although the Department of Justice began to provide funds to organize groups of deputies to track down the bandits, the thugs and toughs fought for control relatively unscathed. Federal posses chased the gangs back and forth across the border, arrested some, killed others, and obtained a few convictions, but the violence continued.

According to some estimates by deputies early in 1881, more than one hundred outlaws were operating near the border in Arizona. John Cooper, acting governor of Arizona in 1881, lamented that men of every shade of character had begun to overwhelm and prey upon the more industrious and honorable classes of citizens.

The most infamous of the cowboys was led by Newman Clanton, better known as "Old Man Clanton." Tennessee born and a Confederate Army veteran, Newman lived for a time in California before moving to Arizona Territory in 1873. It was along the San Pedro River that the family would build a ranch that would become not just a location for raising and branding cattle but also a center for a larger enterprise that would involve rustling, stagecoach robbing, and other nefarious activities. The Clanton enterprise, led by Old Man Clanton, also involved sons Ike, Phin, and Billy, as well as such infamous outlaw figures as Curly Bill Brocius, Tom and Frank McLaury, Billy Claiborne, and John Ringo.

In July 1881 Old Man Clanton and several of his boys ambushed and killed a group of Mexican smugglers carrying silver in Guadalupe Canyon, an area that straddles the border of what is now Arizona and New Mexico.

It would take only a month for Mexicans to get revenge. In that same canyon, Old Man Clanton and several of his men were killed in retaliation as they bedded down for the night with a herd of cattle. The event became known in Western lore as the Guadalupe Canyon Massacre.

On October 26, 1881, the Clanton family enterprise would suffer another devastating blow. In the silver mining town of Tombstone, Arizona, thirty miles from the border, Marshal Virgil Earp, along with his brothers Wyatt and Morgan and friend Doc Holliday, faced off against Ike and Billy Clanton, the McLaury brothers, and Billy Claiborne. Billy Clanton and the McLaury brothers did not survive. Neither did the story—at least in its true form—but was rather spun through the years in various versions in dime novels, books, magazines, television shows, movies, and so on. The fight occurred on Allen Street, just west of the house of photographer Cornelius Fly and down the street from a corral. But one of the most celebrated and myth-producing fights in the history of the West and the border would not conjure up quite the same image if it had been called "The Gunfight West of Fly's House." For chroniclers of the event, "The Gunfight at the O.K. Corral" was much better.

NATIVISM'S NEWEST TARGET: THE CHINESE

Almost as soon as the California gold rush began in 1849, Chinese workers, especially from the poverty-racked coastal province of Canton, began to arrive in California, a place they called Gam-San ("Gold Mountain" in Cantonese). They fanned out across California—many to the U.S.-Mexican border—willing to work for wages well below those paid to other workers.

At the end of the U.S. Civil War, Chinese workers took jobs in construction of the transcontinental railroad. The men received ten to twenty dollars per month, as well as food and quarters. In 1880, by the time the Southern Pacific Railroad reached Tucson, Arizona, about sixty miles from the border, it had been largely responsible for employing large numbers of Chinese laborers in Arizona Territory, especially Pima County. As word of the effectiveness of Chinese laborers spread, the owners of Arizona's copper mines near the border also began to use them extensively. It was profitable. They were cheap and reliable.

Nevertheless if Chinese workers were good for management, they were not good for other workers unwilling to do backbreaking work for a pittance. And as the numbers of Chinese workers grew, so did the vicious animus toward their manners, culture, appearance, and language. Soon, the racial epithets swelled, not only among the white population but also in newspaper reporting. Of the many offensive sobriquets aimed at the Chinese, the word "Celestials" (from Celestial Empire, or an empire ruled in accord with Heaven) was perhaps the most common and least derisive.

Many of the mine owners walked a fine line in their defense of hiring "Coolie labor." One owner assured the press and the world that if he hired any Chinese workers, it would be for tasks that neither white men nor Mexicans would be willing to undertake. After all, he, along with others, would not want to be responsible for starting a "Mongolian invasion."

Despite facing growing and often bitter discrimination and hostility, the Chinese managed to settle and find work not only in mines but also in other occupations such as woodcutters, cooks, and servants. Some began farming; others started doing laundry work. A few opened opium dens in places such as Tombstone, Arizona.

Yet as early as 1880, a group of Tombstone residents, led by the town's newspaper editor, began to hold meetings to demand the exclusion of the Chinese. Like other nativist and racist groups throughout U.S. history, the anti-Chinese element in Tombstone and in towns across the borderlands found sport in taunting the foreign element in their midst, in some cases even starting bonfires in the streets and holding mass protests. Somehow, many came to believe that ridding the borderlands of the Chinese would in some way bring more peace and prosperity.

Although the Chinese composed a tiny number of the nation's total inhabitants, the U.S. Congress, reacting to the xenophobia in 1882, not only in Arizona but also in other parts of the country, passed the Chinese Exclusion Act, the first significant law restricting immigration into the United States. The statute suspended Chinese immigration for ten years and declared the Chinese ineligible for naturalization.

Nativism was not a new phenomenon in American history. Well before the attacks on the Chinese, other immigrant groups had been targeted, most recently Irish Roman Catholics. Somehow, numbers of Americans believed, the nation was going to be taken over by a foreign invasion of Irish Catholics and by the Pope. In some parts of the country, groups hung the Pope in effigy. Nativists even formed political organizations based almost entirely on anti-Catholic bigotry.

Yet despite the nativist impulse alive in the country for many years, there had been no federal limitations on immigration prior to 1882. But over 300,000 Chinese had come to the United States since 1850. And now, especially along the border, with all its unrest, with its unfulfilled promises to so many who had not cashed in on the riches of gold and silver and copper, and with families coping to earn a living in new boom towns that seemed to offer less than had been promised, many found scapegoats—the Chinese. Yes, the unrest would continue and marshals, sheriffs, and the public would have to continue to deal with robbery, rustling, and other assorted crimes and vices. But at least, many naively thought, with the passage of the Chinese Exclusion Act, one of the principal causes of the unrest had been eradicated.

DOCUMENTS

Juan Cortina and the Case against Texas, 1859

When Juan Cortina led his armed group of Mexicans on a raid in Brownsville, Texas, in 1859, it was an attack of rage and resentment against Anglo treatment of his fellow Mexicans. He had seen enough of the arrogant racial and cultural humiliation, of the unfair treatment in the courts and by law enforcement, and of the overt disrespect by Anglos of his people in seemingly every aspect of their interactions. His audacious actions have been seen in Mexican American popular culture as symbolic of militant resistance and a revolt against racism. Well beyond his own lifetime Mexicans in Texas and across the border would speak of Cortina in somewhat reverent terms; Anglos would continue to vilify him and his life. When he wrote a proclamation in 1859 describing his crusade, it would presage the kind of militant, aggressive resistance to Anglo domination and contempt that inspired the Chicano movement a century later.

PROCLAMATION

County of Cameron,
Camp in the Rancho del Carmen,
November 23, 1859

Compatriots: A sentiment of profound indignation, the love and esteem which I profess for you, the desire which you have for that tranquility and those guarantees which are denied you, thus violating the most sacred laws, is that which moves me to address you these words, hoping that they may prove some consolation in the midst of your adversity, which heretofore has borne the appearance of predestination.

The history of great human actions teaches us that in certain instances the principal motive which gives them impulse is the natural right to resist and conquer our enemies with a firm spirit and lively will; to persist in and to reach the consummation of this object, opening a path through the obstacles which step by step are encountered, however imposing or terrible they may be.

In the series of such actions, events present themselves which public opinion, influenced by popular sentiment, calls for deliberation upon their effects, to form an exact and just conception of the interests which they promote; and this same public opinion should be considered as the best judge, which, with coolness and impartiality, does not fail to recognize some principle as the cause for the existence of open force and immutable firmness, which impart the noble desire of cooperating with true philanthropy to remedy the state of despair of him who, in his turn, becomes the victim of ambition, satisfied at the cost of justice.

There are, doubtless, persons so overcome by strange prejudices, men without confidence or courage to face danger in an undertaking in sisterhood with the love of liberty, who, examining the merit of acts by a false light, and preferring that of the same opinion contrary to their own, prepare no other reward than that pronounced for the "bandit," for him who, with complete abnegation of self, dedicates himself to constant labor for the happiness of those who suffering under the weight of misfortunes, eat their bread, mingled with tears, on the earth which they rated.

If, my dear compatriots, I am honored with that name, I am ready for the combat.

The Mexicans who inhabit this wide region, some because they were born therein, others because since the treaty Guadalupe Hidalgo, they have been attracted to its soil by the soft influence of wise laws and the advantages of a free government, paying little attention to the reasoning of politics, are honorably and exclusively dedicated to the exercise of industry, guided by that instinct which leads the good man to comprehend, as uncontradictory truth, that only in the reign of peace can he enjoy, without inquietude, the fruit of his labor. These, under an unjust imputation of selfishness and churlishness, which do not exist, are not devoid of those sincere and expressive evidences of such friendliness and tenderness as should gain for them that confidence with which they have inspired those who have met them in social intercourse. This genial affability seems as the foundation of that proverbial prudence which, as an oracle, is consulted in all their actions and undertakings. Their humility, simplicity, and docility, directed with dignity, it may be that with excess of goodness, can, if it be desired, lead them beyond the common class of men, but causes them to excel in an irresistible inclination towards ideas of equality, a proof of their simple manners, so well adapted to that which is styled the classic land of liberty. A man, a family, and a people, possessed of qualities so eminent, with their heart in their hand and purity on their lips, encounter every day renewed reasons to know that they are surrounded by malicious and crafty monsters, who rob them in the tranquil interior of home, or with open hatred and pursuit; it necessarily follows, however great may be their pain, if not abased by humiliation and ignominy, their groans suffocated and hushed by a pain which renders them insensible, they become resigned to suffering before an abyss of misfortunes.

Mexicans! When the State of Texas began to receive the new organization which its sovereignty required as an integrate part of the Union, flocks of vampires, in the guise of men came and scattered themselves in the settlements, without any capital except the corrupt heart and the most perverse intentions. Some, brimful of laws, pledged to us their protection against the attacks of the rest; others assembled in shadowy councils, attempted and excited the robbery and burning of the houses of our relatives on the other side of the river Bravo; while others, to the abusing of our unlimited confidence, when we entrusted them with our titles, which secured the future of our families, refused to return them under false and frivolous pretexts; all, in short, with a smile on their faces, giving the lie to that which their black entrails were meditating. Many of you have been robbed of your property, incarcerated, chased, murdered, and hunted like wild beasts, because your labor was fruitful, and because your industry excited the vile avarice which led them. A voice infernal said, from the bottom of their soul, "kill them; the greater will be our gain!" Ah! This does not finish the sketch of your situation. It would appear that justice had fled from this world, leaving you to the caprice of your oppressors, who become each day more furious towards you; that, through witnesses and false charges, although the grounds may be insufficient, you may be interred in the penitentiaries, if you are not previously deprived of life by some keeper who covers himself from responsibility by the pretense of your flight. There are to be found criminals covered with frightful crimes, but they appear to have impunity until opportunity furnish them a victim; to these monsters indulgence is shown, because they are not of our race, which is unworthy, as they say, to belong to the human species. But this race, which the Anglo-American, so ostentatious of its own qualities, tries so much to blacken depreciate, and load with insults, in a spirit of blindness, which goes to the full extent of such things so common on this frontier, does not fear, placed even in the midst of its very faults, those subtle inquisitions which are so frequently made as to its manners, habits, and sentiments; nor that its deeds should be put to the test of examination in the land of reason, of justice, and of honor. This race has never humbled itself before the conqueror, though the reverse has happened, and can be established; for his is not humbled who uses among his fellow-men those courtesies which humanity prescribes; charity being the root whence springs the rule of his actions. But this race, which you see filled with gentleness and inward sweetness, gives now the cry of alarm throughout the entire extend of the land which it occupies, against all the artifice interposed by those who have become chargeable with their division and discord. This race, adorned with the most lovely disposition towards all that is good and useful in the line of progress, omits no act of diligence which might correct its many imperfections, and lift its grand edifice among the ruins of the past, respecting the ancient traditions and the maxims bequeathed by their ancestors, without being dazzled by brilliant and false appearances, nor crawling to that exaggeration of institution which, like a sublime statue, is offered for their worship and adoration.

Mexicans! Is there no remedy for you? Inviolable laws, yet useless, serve, it is true, certain judges and hypocritical authorities, cemented in evil and injustice, to do whatever suits them, and to satisfy their vile avarice at the cost of your patience and suffering; rising in their frenzy, even to the taking of life, through the treacherous hands of their bailiffs. The wicket way in which many of you have been oftentimes involved in persecution, accompanied by circumstances making it the more bitter, is now well known; these crimes being hid from society under the shadow of a horrid night, those implacable people, with the haughty spirit which suggests impunity for a life of criminality, have pronounced, doubt ye not, your sentence, which is, with accustomed insensibility, as you have seen, on the point of execution.

Mexicans! My part is taken; the voice of revelation whispers to me that to me is entrusted the work of breaking the chains of your slavery, and that the Lord will enable me, with powerful arm, to fight against our enemies, in compliance with the requirements of that Sovereign Majesty, who, from this day forward, will hold us under His protection. On my part, I am ready to offer myself as a sacrifice for your happiness; and counting upon the means necessary for the discharge of my ministry, you may count upon my cooperation, should no cowardly attempt put an end to my days. This undertaking will be sustained on the following bases:

First. A society is organized in the State of Texas, which devotes itself sleeplessly until the work is crowned with success, to the improvement of the unhappy condition of those Mexicans resident therein; extermination their tyrants, to which end those which compose it are ready to shed their blood and suffer the death of martyrs.

Second. As this society contains within itself the elements necessary to accomplish the great end of its labors, the veil of impenetrable secrecy covers "The Great Book" in which the articles of its constitution are written; while so delicate are the difficulties which must be overcome that no honorable man can have cause for alarm, if imperious exigencies require them to act without reserve.

Third. The Mexicans of Texas repose their lot under the good sentiments of the governor elect of the State, General Houston, and trust that upon his elevation to power he will begin with care to give us legal protection within the limits of his powers.

Mexicans! Peace be with you! Good inhabitants of the State of Texas, look on them as brothers, and keep in mind that which the Holy Spirit saith: "Thou shalt not be the friend of the passionate man; nor join thyself to the madman, lest thou learn his mode of work and scandalize thy soul."

Juan N. Cortina

Source: U.S. Congress, House of Representatives, "Difficulties on the Southwestern Frontier," 36th Congress; 1st Session, 1860, H. Exec. Doc. 52, April 2, 1860, 790–782.

Letter of Territorial Governor of Arizona to Attorney General of the United States on Border Violence in Arizona Territory, 1881

As the depredations of outlaws and thieves on the Arizona territorial border became increasingly violent, it became clear to U.S. marshals and other law enforcement officials that additional reinforcements were needed. From his office in the territorial capitol of Prescott, Acting Governor John Gosper apprised U.S. Attorney General Wayne MacVeagh of the murder and mayhem taking place.

Executive Department
Territory of Arizona
Prescott, August 18–81

Sir:

Referring to the spirit of lawlessness prevailing along the line between the United States and Mexico in the Territory of Arizona the result of which is the frequent taking of life and property and the almost constant disturbance of the peace, permit me to suggest and even to urge that the Department of Justice over which you have the honor to preside shall make a reasonable appropriation of its funds to be used by the U.S. Marshal of this Territory in the employment of discreet and courageous persons to operate in conjunction with the local civil authorities in those sections where this spirit of lawlessness most prevails.

The "Cowboys" (so-called) are many of the fugitives from justice from eastern states and when banded together in small companies bent upon murder and robbing they become very dangerous and are a terror to any civilized community.

This spirit of recklessness and utter disregard for the life and rights of the peaceful citizen must be put down by some judicious procedure no matter at what the cost.

The military forces commanded by Colonel Wilcox are tied hand and foot by a foolish law of Congress, and come under the civil authorities and can aid only in cases where attempts at arrest are forcibly resisted.

A small sum of money only is at the disposal of the Executive of this Territory which he can use in the direction of suppressing crime but of that sum a liberal amount shall be used in aiding the local authorities in enforcing the law and bringing these outlaws to speedy justice.

The local peace and good will of both governments, the protection of the lives and property of citizens of both governments demand energetic action, and I would be glad to hear from you on this subject.

John J. Gosper
Acting Governor
To Hon. Attorney General of the United States

Source: National Archives and Records Administration, RG 60, Records of the Department of Justice, Source-Chronological Files, Arizona, Letters of Marshal Crowley P. Dake, 1881, Microfilm M2028.

Chinese Exclusion Act, 1882

The Chinese Exclusion Act of 1882 represented the first time in U.S. history that the government targeted immigrants based solely on their national origin and race. The irony, of course, is that border hostilities and tensions over the years have been between individuals of Spanish descent and Anglos. Yet it was the Chinese, with their distinguishing appearance, manners, culture, and habits, who became a focal point of stereotypical labeling and increasing prejudice, not only on the border but also in other parts of the country, that convinced U.S. leaders that the Chinese were a menace and had to be contained. The irony of this treatment of the Chinese is especially stark considering the fact that, in a number of cases, Chinese workers dressed up in Mexican clothes and learned to speak some Spanish in order to pass themselves off when looking for employment. The Chinese Exclusion Act was not repealed until 1943. In 2012, the U.S. Congress officially apologized for this egregiously racial piece of legislation.

Forty-Seventh Congress. Sess. 1. Chap. 126. 1882

May 6, 1882. An Act to execute certain treaty stipulations relating to Chinese.

Whereas in the opinion of the Government of the United States the coming of Chinese laborers to this country endangers the good order of certain localities within the territory thereof: Therefore,

Be it enacted by the Senate and House of Representatives of the United States of America in Congress assembled, That from and after the expiration of ninety days next after the passage of this act, and until the expiration of ten years next after the passage of this act, the coming of Chinese laborers to the United States be, and the same is hereby, suspended; and during such suspension it shall not be lawful for any Chinese laborer to come, or having so come after the expiration of said ninety days to remain within the United States.

SEC. 2. That the master of any vessel who shall knowingly bring within the United States on such vessel, and land or permit to be landed, any Chinese laborer, from any foreign port or place, shall be deemed guilty of a misdemeanor, and on conviction thereof shall be punished by a fine of not more than five hundred dollars for each and every such Chinese laborer so brought, and maybe also imprisoned for a term not exceeding one year.

SEC. 3. That the two foregoing sections shall not apply to Chinese laborers who were in the United States on the seventeenth day of November, eighteen hundred and eighty, or who shall have come into the same before the expiration of ninety days next after the passage of this act, and who shall produce to such master before going on board such vessel, and shall produce to the collector of the port in the United States at which such vessel shall arrive, the evidence hereinafter in this act required of his being one of the laborers in this section mentioned; nor shall the two foregoing sections apply to the case of any master whose vessel, being bound to a port not within the United States, shall come within the jurisdiction of the United States by reason of being in distress or in stress of weather, or touching at any port of the United States on its voyage to any foreign port or place: Provided, That all Chinese laborers brought on such vessel shall depart with the vessel on leaving port.

SEC. 4. That for the purpose of properly identifying Chinese laborers who were in the United States on the seventeenth day of November eighteen hundred and eighty, or who shall have come into the same before the expiration of ninety days next after the passage of this act, and in order to furnish them with the proper evidence of their right to go from and come to the United States of their free will and accord, as provided by the treaty between the United States and China dated November seventeenth, eighteen hundred and eighty, the collector of customs of the district from which any such Chinese laborer shall depart from the United States shall, in person or by deputy, go on board each vessel having on board any such Chinese laborers and cleared or about to sail from his district for a foreign port, and on such vessel make a list of all such Chinese laborers, which shall be entered in registry-books to be kept for that purpose, in which shall be stated the name, age, occupation, last place of residence, physical marks of peculiarities, and all facts necessary for the identification of each of such Chinese laborers, which books shall be safely kept in the custom-house; and every such Chinese laborer so departing from the United States shall be entitled to, and shall receive, free of any charge or cost upon application therefor, from the collector or his deputy, at the time such list is taken, a certificate, signed by the collector or his deputy and attested by his seal of office, in such form as the Secretary of the Treasury shall prescribe, which certificate shall contain a statement of the name, age, occupation, last place of residence, persona description, and facts of identification of the Chinese laborer to whom the certificate is issued, corresponding with the said list and registry in all particulars. In case any Chinese laborer after having received such certificate shall leave such vessel before her departure he shall deliver his certificate to the master of the vessel, and if such Chinese laborer shall fail to return to such vessel before her departure from port the certificate shall be delivered by the master to the collector of customs for cancellation. The certificate herein provided for shall entitle the Chinese laborer to whom the same is issued to return to and re-enter the United States upon producing and delivering the same to the collector of customs of the district at which such Chinese laborer shall seek to re-enter; and upon delivery of such certificate by such Chinese laborer to the collector of customs at the time of re-entry in the United States said collector shall cause the same to be filed in the custom-house anti duly canceled.

SEC. 5. That any Chinese laborer mentioned in section four of this act being in the United States, and desiring to depart from the United States by land, shall have the right to demand and receive, free of charge or cost, a certificate of identification similar to that provided for in section four of this act to be issued to such Chinese laborers as may desire to leave the United States by water; and it is hereby made the duty of the collector of customs of the district next adjoining the foreign country to which said Chinese laborer desires to go to issue such certificate, free of charge or cost, upon application by such Chinese laborer, and to enter the same upon registry-books to be kept by him for the purpose, as provided for in section four of this act.

SEC. 6. That in order to the faithful execution of articles one and two of the treaty in this act before mentioned, every Chinese person other than a laborer who may be entitled by said treaty and this act to come within the United States, and who shall be about to come to the United States, shall be identified as so entitled by the Chinese Government in each case, such identity to be evidenced by a certificate issued under the authority of said government, which certificate shall be in the English language or (if not in the English language) accompanied by a translation into English, stating such right to come, and which certificate shall state the name, title or official rank, if any, the age, height, and all physical peculiarities, former and present occupation or profession, and place of residence in China of the person to whom the certificate is issued and that such person is entitled, conformably to the treaty in this act mentioned to come within the United States. Such certificate shall be prima-facie evidence of the fact set forth therein, and shall be produced to the collector of customs, or his deputy, of the port in the district in the United States at which the person named therein shall arrive.

SEC. 7. That any person who shall knowingly and falsely alter or substitute any name for the name written in such certificate or forge any such certificate, or knowingly utter any forged or fraudulent certificate, or falsely personate any person named in any such certificate, shall be deemed guilty of a misdemeanor; and upon conviction thereof shall be fined in a sum not exceeding one thousand dollars, and imprisoned in a penitentiary for a term of not more than five years.

SEC. 8. That the master of any vessel arriving in the United States from any foreign port or place shall, at the same time he delivers a manifest of the cargo, and if there be no cargo, then at the time of making a report of the entry of the vessel pursuant to law, in addition to the other matter required to be reported, and before landing, or permitting to land, any Chinese passengers, deliver and report to the collector of customs of the district in which such vessels shall have arrived a separate list of all Chinese passengers taken on board his vessel at any foreign port or place, and all such passengers on board the vessel at that time. Such list shall show the names of such passengers (and if accredited officers of the Chinese Government traveling on the business of that government, or their servants, with a note of such facts), and the names and other particulars, as shown by their respective certificates; and such list shall be sworn to by the master in the manner required by law in relation to the manifest of the cargo. Any willful refusal or neglect of any such master to comply with the provisions of this section shall incur the same penalties and forfeiture as are provided for a refusal or neglect to report and deliver a manifest of the cargo.

SEC. 9. That before any Chinese passengers are landed from any such line vessel, the collector, or his deputy, shall proceed to examine such passenger, comparing the certificate with the list and with the passengers; and no passenger shall be allowed to land in the United States from such vessel in violation of law.

SEC. 10. That every vessel whose master shall knowingly violate any of the provisions of this act shall be deemed forfeited to the United States, and shall be liable to seizure and condemnation in any district of the United States into which such vessel may enter or in which she may be found.

SEC. 11. That any person who shall knowingly bring into or cause to be brought into the United States by land, or who shall knowingly aid or abet the same, or aid or abet the landing in the United States from any vessel of any Chinese person not lawfully entitled to enter the United States, shall be deemed guilty of a misdemeanor, and shall, on conviction thereof, be fined in a sum not exceeding one thousand dollars, and imprisoned for a term not exceeding one year.

SEC. 12. That no Chinese person shall be permitted to enter the United States by land without producing to the proper officer of customs the certificate in this act required of Chinese persons seeking to land from a vessel. And any Chinese person found unlawfully within the United States shall be caused to be removed therefrom to the country from whence he came, by direction of the President of the United States, and at the cost of the United States, after being brought before some justice, judge, or commissioner of a court of the United States and found to be one not lawfully entitled to be or remain in the United States.

SEC. 13. That this act shall not apply to diplomatic and other officers of the Chinese Government traveling upon the business of that government, whose credentials shall be taken as equivalent to the certificate in this act mentioned, and shall exempt them and their body and house-hold servants from the provisions of this act as to other Chinese persons.

SEC. 14. That hereafter no State court or court of the United States shall admit Chinese to citizenship; and all laws in conflict with this act are hereby repealed.

SEC. 15. That the words "Chinese laborers", wherever used in this act shall be construed to mean both skilled and unskilled laborers and Chinese employed in mining.

Approved, May 6, 1882.

Source: U.S. Statutes at Large, 47th Congress, 1st Session, CH. 117–120,126. 1882. https://www.loc.gov/law/help/statutes-at-large/47th-congress/session-1/c47s1ch126.pdf.

Report of Brigadier General George Crook, 1883

Generally regarded as one of most successful U.S. Army leaders in the so-called "Indian Wars," George Crook, unlike many other army commanders who fought various tribes, tried to find ways to help integrate Native Americans into an emerging U.S. society in the West. Inclined to use Indian scouts as allies, to negotiate rather than to conquer, and to seek a less aggressive approach than annihilation of Indians and their culture, Crook found himself in his most challenging role as commander at a time when the elusive Geronimo was terrorizing the border. The following report illustrates both Crook's strategy in waging war against the Indians and his thoughts about future reconciliation.

HEADQUARTERS DEPARTMENT OF ARIZONA,
Whipple Barracks, Prescott, July 23, 1883.

To the
Assistant Adjutant General,
Military Division of the Pacific,
Presidio of San Francisco, Cal.

Sir:

I have the honor to report that, upon assuming command of this Department in September last, I made a careful investigation of the Indian question and the results of the inquiry were embodied in letters to the Division Commander.

I was convinced that the return of raiding parties of Chiricahuas might be looked for at any time, and to be prepared for such an irruption. I made such disposition of my troops and scouts as would be most likely to prevent extended and general depredations. . . .

To pursue a raiding party of Apaches in southern Arizona, with any hope of overtaking or destroying them is one of the most hopeless tasks that could be delegated to officers and soldiers. The Indians on such occasions travel without impedimenta of any kind, and move across the country at the rate of seventy-five miles a day, abandoning and killing their horses as fast as they play out, and helping themselves to remounts at every ranch they pass; while the troops must follow the trail with but one mount.

But while the hostiles were making a trail of blood through Arizona and New Mexico, they were unconsciously sowing the seed for their own destruction. One of their number, Pe-nal-tishn, deserted, made his way into the San Carlos Agency, was seized by Lieutenant Britton Davis, Third Cavalry, and turned over to me at Willcox, where I had proceeded on the 2nd of April.

After a severe examination Pe-nal-tishn, generally called by his sobriquet 'Peaches,' 1 agreed to conduct me to the stronghold of the hostiles in the Sierra Madre, on the boundary line between Sonora and Chihuahua. I concluded to trust him and accepted his services. . . .

While these matters were pending, I proceeded by railroad to Guaymas and Hermosillo, Sonora, and to the city of Chihuahua, Chihuahua, to meet and consult with the Mexican officials—civil and military—and arrange, if possible, for a harmonious understanding of the International questions involved, and mutual cooperation.

The reception extended me was of the most hospitable and cordial character; Generals Carbo and Topete, and their staff, in Sonora, and Governor Torres and other prominent functionaries in that State; and Governors Samaniego and Terrasses, of the State of Chihuahua, and Mayor Zubriah of the city of Chihuahua and other gentlemen received me most cordially and gave assurances that they would in every possible way aid in the subjugation of the Chiricahuas, who had for so many years murdered and plundered their people as well as our own. Consuls Willard at Guaymas and Scott at Chihuahua rendered me valuable assistance, for which I desire to express most grateful recognition.

To pass over minor details I reached San Bernardino Springs, on the International boundary line, on the 29th of April . . . By the 8th of May we had entered the Sierra Madre, making the movement at night to avoid detection. The signs of the presence of hostile Chiricahuas became abundant. There were abandoned camps of fifteen, twenty, thirty and forty families; cattle, homes and ponies, living and dead.

The country was the roughest imaginable but well suited as a place of refuge for the Chiricahuas, who, unless taken by sudden surprise, could, from their points of vantage, withstand an army. We found at all times an abundance of the purest water and plenty of fuel, the mountains being covered with forests of pine and oak. We made our way cautiously, and with considerable difficulty, farther and farther into the recesses of the Sierra Madre, the trail becoming very precipitous. A number of mules were lost by slipping over precipices, but in each case the contents of their packs, when not too much damaged, were saved with much trouble.

On the 12th, the guide "Peaches" conducted us to the stronghold of the enemy, a formidable place, impregnable to attack, had such been dreamed of. To be explicit, the whole Sierra Madre is a natural fortress, and to drive the Chiricahuas from which, by any method other than those we employed, would have cost hundreds of lives. The enemy was not to be found in this particular fortress. The nature of the Apaches impels them to change their camps every few days, and thus avoid as much as possible anything like a surprise. Indeed, they never have anything like a permanent camp. Their temporary abodes are merely brush "wick-a-ups," which can be built in half an hour and destroyed in a few moments, so as to leave to the unpracticed eye hardly a trace of their presence . . .

We could never hope to catch them in the rugged peaks, and the effort would surely cost the lives of many men, each rock being a fortress from behind which the Chiricahuas could fight to the death with their breech-loading guns. Two alternatives seemed presented; we must either return, let the excitement quiet down, and then if permitted, steal back again and take the chances of another surprise, during which period the Chiricahuas would be continuing their depredations in Mexico and our own country; or, we must accept their surrender.

To continue the narrative: The next day (May 17,) the Chiricahuas made a signal smoke, and six squaws came in. With these I declined to talk, telling them that their representative men must come in if they desired to discuss the situation with me. Early on the 18th, Chihuahua entered my camp. He is not a chief, but is one of the most prominent men of his tribe, noted for intelligence and bravery. He said that the country to which we had penetrated, was looked upon as impregnable; that the Mexican troops had never succeeded in getting into it, but had always been met and driven back with rocks as well as bullets, as soon as they had passed the foot-hills. He explained that the sense of security was so great that a large number of the men were then absent on raids in Sonora and Chihuahua. He told me where the different chiefs were raiding. He spoke bitterly of the Mexicans, but said the Chiricahuas would be glad to make peace; that a large element in the band was getting tired of constant war, and would gladly settle down if allowed to do so. The reason given for their hatred of the Mexicans, was the treachery of which they had been guilty, the Chiricahuas alleging that they had made it a point to kill their women and children, and run away from their men. He further said that on a recent occasion they had invited a delegation of Chiricahuas to visit one of their small towns near Casas Grandes, and while receiving them with outward manifestations of good will, had gotten them all under the influence of liquor, and then murdered a number and taken others prisoners. . . .

From that on, the Chiricahuas came in rapidly from all points of the compass—men, women and children. All the chiefs surrendered, gave themselves up.

Jeronimo, Chato, Bonito, Loco, Natchez (the son of Cochise,) and one named Ka-e-te-na, who was not recognized as ever having been on the reservation. He said that he had never been on the reservation, and had always lived in the Sierra Madre.

The only Indian of prominence whom I did not meet was Juh. The Indians stated that there had been a tribal difference, and in consequence of bad blood, Juh, with one man and two or three squaws, had gone off into the country near the sources of the Yaqui River, some distance to the south.

These chiefs said that they wanted to make peace and return to the San Carlos reservation. I replied that they had been committing atrocities and depredations upon our people and the Mexicans, and that we had become tired of such a condition of affairs and intended to wipe them out; that I had not taken all this trouble for the purpose of making them prisoners; that they had been bad Indians, and that I was unwilling to return without punishing them as they deserved; that if they wanted a fight, they could have one any time they pleased. I told them that the Mexican troops were moving in from both sides, and it was only a matter of a few days until the last of them should be under the ground . . .

Jeronimo and all the chiefs at last fairly begged me to be taken back to San Carlos. I replied that they were asking a great deal, that I had no power to put them on the reservation, and that I could not close my eyes to the atrocities of which they had been guilty; many of the Americans wanted their band rooted out, and that if I took them to San Carlos, no doubt a cry would be raised for their blood.

They had not only to face the Americans, but the Mexicans also, whose people they had murdered in so cruel a manner. They could not expect me to fight their battles or palliate their villainous conduct. Jeronimo and the others then said: "We give ourselves up, do with us as you please." They begged me to remain where I was for a few days longer, and explained what scarcely needed explanation, that the country was so fearfully rough, they could not gather up all their people at once, as they were so much scattered. To this I could not assent, the supply of rations for the command making such delay impossible. We had by this time 384 Chiricahua Indians and six Mexican captives to feed, and it was about as much as we could do to get back to our base without danger of starvation.

Jeronimo then said that if we would go along slowly towards the boundary, they could send their runners out to warn all those who had not yet come in, and they would try and overtake us at San Bernardino; or, if not successful in that, would move along the mountains until they reached San Carlos.

I assented to their sending after the remainder of their people, still hiding in the mountains, but refused to give them any written passes, telling them that if they could not catch up with the troops, they must take their chances of being killed by any Mexicans or Americans they might encounter.

In dealing with this question I could not lose sight of the fact that the Apache Indian represents generations of warfare and bloodshed. From his earliest infancy he has had to defend himself against enemies as cruel as the beast of the mountain and forest. His own nature differs but little from that of the wolf or coyote; in his brief moments of peace he constantly looks for attack or ambuscade, and in his almost constant warfare, no act of bloodshed is too cruel or unnatural.

It is, therefore, unjust to punish him for violations of a code of war which he has never learned, and which he can with difficulty understand. He has in almost all his combats with white men found that his women and children are the first to suffer, that neither age or sex are spared. In the surprise and attack of camps, women and children are killed in spite of every precaution; nor can this loss of life be prevented by any orders or foresight of the commander, any more than the shells fired into a beleaguered city can be prevented from killing innocent citizens, or burning private property. Nor does this fact surprise him, since it is in accordance with his own custom of fighting, but with this fact before we can understand why he should be ignorant of the rules of civilized warfare. All that we can reasonably do is to keep him under such supervision that he cannot plan new outbreaks without running the risk of immediate detection; for these new acts of rascality punish him so severely that he will know we mean no nonsense.

As rapidly as possible make a distinction between those who mean to do good and those who secretly desire to remain as they are. Encourage the former and punish the latter. Let the Apache see that he has something to gain by proper behavior, and something to lose by not falling in with the new order of things. Vengeance is just as much to be deprecated as a silly sentimentalism . . .

It is not advisable to let an Indian think that you are afraid of him even when fully armed. Show him that at his best he is powerless in your hands, he will become your best friend and cheerfully obey all that he may be instructed to do. It is unfair too, to deprive him of means of protecting his home and property against the white scoundrels, who, armed to the teeth, infest the border, and would consider nothing so worthy of their prowess, as the plunder of ponies or other property from unarmed Indians just beginning to plant or raise stock. So long as white horse and cattle thieves roam the country, so long should the Indians at San Carlos be allowed to carry arms for their own protection . . .

Very respectfully,
Your obedient servant,
GEORGE CROOK,
Brigadier General, Commanding

Source: Annual Report of Brigadier General George Crook, U.S. Army; Crook to Assistant Adjutant General, Military Division of the Pacific, Presidio of San Francisco, California, July 23, 1883. https://archive.org/stream/GR_928/GR_928_djvu.txt.

4

Boom Towns along the Border

Lured by the potential riches from mining and other ventures, settlers, boosters, and capitalists turned border areas into boom towns. Some developed and thrived; others became ghost towns.

The growth in the last half of the nineteenth century along the border was spurred by an expanding railroad network that began to connect areas in northern Mexico and new towns in the United States to major population and commercial centers in each country. The transcontinental Southern Pacific spurred the growth of other railroad lines near the border that served to deliver to hungry markets the copper, silver, lead, agricultural products, and livestock that new mine owners, ranchers, and other entrepreneurs could now deliver at much greater speed and efficiency.

The Santa Fe railroad—the Atchison, Topeka and Santa Fe—and other rail outlets soon became available for the boom towns that sprung up along the border from the Gulf of Mexico to the Pacific Ocean. They could now reach the processing plants and distribution centers that heretofore had been impossible.

With the ever-growing number of rail links, mine owners in Arizona and Sonora, for example, could ship their ores east with less difficulty. With improved irrigation techniques and links to the rail lines, new agricultural ventures could capitalize, turning what had been barren areas into profitable crop production.

And with the new towns came not only the fortune seekers but also new settlers looking for a new life in the West as bankers, store owners, blacksmiths, tailors, entertainers, family farmers, doctors, lawyers, and ministers along with hosts of other individuals that make up the life of new towns.

From Tijuana and San Diego in the west to Matamoras and Brownsville at the Gulf, boom towns sprung to life almost overnight. Cananea, Sonora, for example, grew from a village of approximately one hundred individuals in 1891 to a center of mining of some 25,000 people and soon was producing 10 percent of Mexico's mineral output.

A few boom towns such as San Diego/Tijuana, Ambos Nogales, El Paso/Juárez, and Laredo/Nuevo Laredo became major metropolitan areas; others grew quickly and faded just as quickly into obscurity; some remain as small towns with a rich historical legacy. One is Douglas, Arizona.

DOUGLAS, ARIZONA

One of the most learned entrepreneurs to make a significant mark in border history was Dr. James Douglas. Born in Quebec, Canada, in 1837, Douglas graduated from Queen's College, Kingston, Canada, in 1858, continued his studies in medicine and theology at the University of Edinburgh, and then entered an entirely different field—he studied chemistry and was for a time a professor at Morrin College, Quebec. Working with Dr. Thomas Sterry Hunt at Université Laval, a research university in Quebec City, Canada, Douglas discovered a method of extracting copper from its ore. He also invented a number of other methods that refined work in the mining industry. In 1864, he became managing director of the Harvey Hill Copper Company in Quebec and a decade later moved to Phoenixville, Pennsylvania, northwest of Philadelphia, to become superintendent of a copper smelter and refinery complex. As his reputation spread, Douglas's work led him to southern Arizona.

In 1881, the Phelps, Dodge, & Co. of New York asked Douglas to evaluate several possible mining areas in Arizona. One of his most enthusiastic suggestions was to explore the copper mining possibilities in the Mule Mountains in an area just north of the border and a small town called Bisbee. A small mining venture was already underway in the area, and his research of the quality of the ore prompted Douglas to advise Phelps, Dodge to purchase the claim and make an extensive investment in exploration.

The ensuing negotiations led to the creation of the Copper Queen Consolidated Mining Company in 1885. This venture, as well as others in the area, made fortunes for both the company and for Douglas, who became not only president and

Gambling at the Orient Saloon in Bisbee, Arizona, ca. 1900. Such establishments were popular among the miners, ranch hands, and other workers on the borderlands frontier. (National Archives)

general manager of the Copper Queen but also head of other mines both in Arizona and in Sonora, Mexico, most notably in Nacozari, a small town nestled in the foothills of the Western Sierra Madre Mountains.

Under the leadership of James Douglas, the Copper Queen became one of the top copper-producing mines in the world. But the success of the Copper Queen depended, as so many other mining ventures in the West, on the ability to move copper ore efficiently and relatively inexpensively to smelters; in other words, it depended on railroads. Thus, Douglas and Phelps, Dodge entered the railroad business.

First, they constructed lines that linked Bisbee to the Southern Pacific junction at Benson, Arizona. Then they searched for a new area of land as near to Bisbee as possible where they could build a new smelter. Douglas selected an area along the Mexican border just across from a small town called Agua Prieta that had an abundant water supply and adequate space for its workers. Phelps, Dodge would begin work on the construction of this new smelter and a railroad line to service it. The town would be called Douglas.

In the early 1900s, railroad lines continued to proliferate. Small lines from various mining sites merged with other lines. They often changed names, and, especially in southern Arizona and Sonora, Mexico, a lacework connected mining sites with the transportation necessary to make the mining industry increasingly profitable. James Douglas was instrumental in working to help Phelps, Dodge expand its operations all the way to El Paso through construction of the El Paso and Southwestern Railroad. For the town of Douglas itself, this meant that it could boast of having the only smelter site in Arizona that had railroad tracks leading in four directions—north to areas in the Sulphur Springs Valley, east to El Paso, south to Nacozari, and west to Bisbee and Tucson.

Phelps, Dodge was not the only mining company to build a smelter in Douglas; its main rival, the Calumet and Arizona Mining Company, also located in the town to take advantage of what was quickly becoming a transportation hub for the industry.

By the second decade of their operation, the two smelters in Douglas were producing over 10 percent of the copper in the United States. Meanwhile, the town, incorporated in 1905, was growing. In 1914, it had a population of around 5,000.

Unlike a number of other mining towns in which Phelps, Dodge had set up operations and which almost always disappeared after the mines were depleted, Bisbee was never meant to be entirely a company town. Because of its promising location in relation to the railroads, water supply, border commerce, and its general surroundings in relatively flat land, Douglas became an attractive location for other business and investment growth.

From its early conglomeration of shacks built of railroad ties and tents that characterized the town in 1901 and 1902, Douglas was soon transformed within a few years into a bustling community of around 7,000 residents who had started businesses of various kinds and had constructed tree-lined streets, parks, and attractive residences. There were now all the elements of a thriving town—businesses of all kinds, a library, churches, a hospital, doctors and dentists, schools, a newspaper, restaurants, a post office, and an elegant hotel called the Gadsden that featured an ornate lobby, marble staircases, gold leaf–topped pillars, and a Tiffany stained glass mural. Douglas now had a community center, a YMCA, an art gallery, entertainment venues, and the usual areas of bars and red light enterprises. One newspaper called Douglas the "Wonder City of the West."

In 1910, with the beginning of a revolution in Mexico, an influx of U.S. military personnel arrived in the area to protect against border incursions. The section of Douglas predominantly occupied by Mexican Americans began to grow in the coming years with increasing numbers of refugees from the war. After a number of skirmishes near Agua Prieta and as battles in northern Mexico increased in ferocity, by 1915 the U.S. Army had stationed some 6,000 troops of the Ninth Cavalry in Douglas and had even built a number of protective trenches along the border. Although the military clashes did not cross into Douglas, Mexican and U.S. cross-border business interests suffered from the mistrust and anxiety brought on by the chaos of the war.

By 1917, the nation's attention was not on hostilities in Mexico but on the beginnings of what would be World War I. For U.S. manufacturing for any war effort, the copper industry was vital. And now, Bisbee, Douglas, and the mining industries in Cochise County became national news because of a labor confrontation that exploded into violence and chaos.

The Industrial Workers of the World (IWW) had largely been born in the mining camps of the West and had responded to the needs of the frontier working class, a class largely powerless, exploited, and excluded from craft-union membership. From its first convention in 1905, the so-called Wobblies, with its tough rhetoric and anticapitalist militancy, had first made inroads among low-paid factory workers of the industrial East. Later they joined strikes across the West for lumberjacks, harvest workers, railroad gandy dancers, miners, and other migratory workers. And now they were in southwest Arizona.

In addition to some of the Wobbly tactics of advocating work stoppage and sabotage, the IWW was proficient at recruiting miners from minority and immigrant groups who were routinely paid lower wages not only in the mining industry but also in various jobs and trades in mining towns.

By June 1917, the IWW had successfully recruited enough workers to join in presenting the Bisbee mining companies with a list of strike demands. They included improvements in safety and working conditions, an end to unequal treatment of foreign and minority workers, and an improved wage scale. All the copper companies quickly refused the demands, and the labor war was on in southwest Arizona.

Rumors abounded about unions being infiltrated by pro-Germans and about caches of dynamite and weapons about to be unleashed on the population of Bisbee and surrounding towns, Soon, an anti-union Citizens' Protective League, organized under the control of Sheriff Harry Wheeler and various vigilante groups, began to plot ways to fight off the oncoming disaster.

On the night of July 11 various local leaders met and agreed that although the strikers and their allies had not up to that point instigated violence, they should be removed by force from the area. The heavily armed vigilante organization would round up the strikers, load them into boxcars, and haul them like cattle to New Mexico, where they would be dropped off.

Lines of workers herded out of Arizona to New Mexico after a copper mine strike in Bisbee, July 1917. Later known as the "Bisbee Deportation," over 1,000 striking miners, some of them members of the Industrial Workers of the World (IWW), were apprehended by a well-organized and well-armed vigilante army and forced out of the state on foot and in cattle cars. (Library of Congress)

The following day, they pulled it off. At 2:00 a.m., calls were made to the vigilante groups, some of them in Douglas. By 5:00 a.m. about 2,000 so-called "special sheriffs" gathered for their assault. Wearing white handkerchiefs on their arms, they rounded up strikers and alleged sympathizers in the Bisbee and Douglas areas, many of whom had no connection with the strike, corralled them in the town's ballpark, loaded them in cattle cars, and deported them out of the state. It was an unprecedented vigilante action that would go down in American history as "The Bisbee Deportation." No state or federal government entities had been notified or given authority. The Western Union telegraph office had been seized to prevent communication. Essentially, the action was a mass kidnapping.

Soon, the governor of New Mexico provided temporary housing for the deportees. Later, a presidential mediation commission investigated the actions of the vigilante groups and found its actions totally illegal and without authority. Nevertheless, no company or individual, through subsequent trials in both federal and state courts, was ever convicted.

A list of those individuals rounded up in the deportation said much about the ethnic makeup of the miners and others caught up in the raid and about the diversity of workers in the southwestern Arizona copper mines. The largest number were Mexicans, followed by "Americans," Irish, Finns, Serbians, Croatians, Germans, Austrians, British, and others. The mining community was a veritable melting pot of nationalities.

Despite the labor unrest and fierce national condemnation of the illegal tactics used by vigilantes in Cochise County to violate the civil rights of the strikers, the city of Douglas in 1917 was in the midst of a fabulous boom period. The onset of World War I and the need for copper indispensable to industrial production of the war effort made the town a hub of activity—railroad cars furiously coming and going from Douglas carrying copper bars in record numbers, and the population increasing to over 20,000 as extra miners and troops stationed at Camp Harry J. Jones arrived.

By 1918, the two smelters in Douglas employed 2,300 men and the El Paso & Southwestern Railroad increased its labor force to keep up with the demands for extra service.

As the population increased, so did other businesses necessary to bring goods and services, from the importation of cattle to the advent of new roads and buildings. For three years until the end of the war effort in 1921, Douglas enjoyed glory days of growth and national importance.

As the war ended, so did the intense demand for copper and so did the boom days of Douglas. Soon, smelters were inactive, miners were out of work, and other businesses in the town slumped. For a time the Salvation Army helped those out of work; many others left the area for good.

There would be other times of mining resurgence in the Douglas area over the years, but the prosperity and growth of the town had been forever stemmed. Nevertheless, Douglas survived.

Today, Douglas, with its rich cultural and economic heritage, bills itself as a "Gateway to Mexico" and its Rio Sonora region. A hundred years after its boom days, Douglas, with a population of approximately 17,000, is no longer a vital U.S. mining area but with its nearby scenic attractions, historical landmarks, and educational opportunities through Cochise College and affiliated University of Arizona course offerings, the town has kept pace with twenty-first-century changes.

Not far from Douglas, a few abandoned buildings tell another story of a mining town called Ruby.

RUBY, ARIZONA

Slightly north of the border about thirty miles in the mountains and valleys northwest of Nogales, Arizona, is an area known as *Oro Blanco* (White Gold), a place where early Spanish explorers had found a type of gold ore that had a relatively high concentration of silver, giving it a white appearance. Although the ore was difficult to process because of its amalgam form that made extraction difficult, a company called the Montana Gold and Silver Mine opened in 1877 with expectations that it could find ways of turning that silver and gold concentration into a fortune.

Despite a rugged terrain, lack of good roads and little water, as well as the still-remaining danger of bandit attacks and the threat of renegade Apaches, the new mine got off to a fitful but determined start and began producing some gold and silver that made their way to markets. Plagued by the high cost of processing the ore and with elementary extraction methods, the mine owners built a dam to collect water runoff, enabling a number of small operators to work the ore in several locations. Nevertheless, it was a slow-going operation.

In 1912, when Arizona became a state, the small town took the first name of the wife of the new postmaster—Ruby. But despite the best efforts of the Montana Company, the fortunes of the town of Ruby would not rest on the production of gold and silver; it would rest on the production of lead and zinc.

In 1917, some new speculators, familiar with growing markets and the composition of the kind of ore being mined in Ruby, began a new company that turned the fortunes of this tiny hamlet and middling mining operation. By the mid-1920s Ruby, Arizona, was a genuine boom town.

Soon, there was the influx not only of working miners but also the bare necessities of the town—a hospital, mercantile stores, a school that accommodated over 150 children, assorted wood frame houses, hostels, tents, law enforcement, jail, one telephone, a gas station to service a few automobiles owned in the town and others that visited, a pool hall that also showed movies, and even a baseball team. But indoor plumbing was scarce, the noise from the mine and its facilities was deafening, and the townspeople constantly had to deal with the talcum powder–like mine dust that covered everything.

Ruby also produced its own unfortunate historical episode of infamy. When bandits from Mexico killed two proprietors of a store in Ruby and made off with its money along with money from the post office, it sparked a full-fledged manhunt for the killers who were finally brought to justice.

Instead of the surface mining of the past, in Ruby, the shafts now dropped to 750 feet below the surface, with lateral bores heading out some 2,000 feet. To compensate for the lack of available water, the company built two dams to gather rain and runoff that in turn formed two lakes. When that project was not sufficient, the company built a fifteen-mile-long pipe to the Santa Cruz Valley to lift water some 1,500 feet into two storage tanks. Soon, the company was able to provide electricity through the use of diesel engines. In the 1930s the mine was producing more lead and zinc than any other mine in the state of Arizona, and the town could boast a population of 1,200 individuals covering over 400 acres.

But the life of Ruby would depend only on the available supply of useable ore that could be extracted from its surroundings. Unlike Douglas, it did not have the enormous advantage of rail lines that connected it to other enterprises or that placed it in the path of other industrial and commercial enterprises.

By 1940, the main company responsible for the lead and zinc production realized that the end had come; it dynamited the main shaft entrances and left the area. Its demise was the demise of the town of Ruby.

Over the years, a number of individuals have made aborted efforts to bring the area back to life. An essayer took over the property for nearly two decades and tried unsuccessfully to mine the ore tailings that piled nearby and to explore the abandoned shafts. In the late 1960s he sold the land, amounting to over 300 acres, to some private interests in Tucson, Arizona.

Various discarded visions for the property included turning it into a movie set, making the ghost town into an historical attraction, turning the area into a private club or an RV park, and so on. For a time, the area became a haven for counterculture squatters, who saw the place as the perfect embodiment of a lifestyle far removed from the rumblings of organized society. Eventually, they were evicted from the private property.

Remains of some of the old buildings are still there. But more importantly, as some who have been to the site devoutly claim, there are ghosts.

LAREDO, TEXAS/NEUVO LARREDO, TAMAULIPAS

Douglas was a boom town that survived; Ruby was a boom town that did not. A select few on the border were boom towns that not only survived but became major commercial and cultural cities. The sister cities of Laredo, Texas, and Nuevo Laredo, Tamaulipas, exemplify another evolutionary development of the borderlands.

Unlike Douglas and Ruby, boom towns that sprung from the mining industry, Laredo has a long Spanish history dating from the eighteenth century—it was founded in 1755 in an area along the Rio Grande northwest of what is now the eastern terminus of the U.S.-Mexican border. San Agustín de Laredo was a colonial city of New Spain named for a town on the north coast of Spain. It was one of the last provinces of New Spain designed to colonize northern Mexico.

Its first settlers raised cattle, mules, sheep, and goats, and the small town became a frontier outpost. During the early 1800s, ranchers traded cattle hides and wool in exchange for food and other necessities, all the while trying to fight off attacks by Indian raiders.

When the Treaty of Guadalupe Hidalgo was signed in 1848, the new border, designated by the treaty as the Rio Grande River, resulted in a division of the town. Those families who wished to remain in Mexico crossed the river and kept their Mexican citizenship. Some were so attached to their Mexican heritage that they excavated the bones of ancestors and took them across the river as well.

Thus, in May 1755, a new town was formally founded in Mexico and, after several name iterations, was called Nuevo Laredo. The sister town across the river became known simply as Laredo.

In both towns, adobe houses and buildings dotted the landscape. Ranchers stocked sheep, cattle, and goats; a few farmers raised some crops; and residents were forced to deal with depredations of notorious bandit gangs and Indian raids, even with the presence of U.S. Army at Fort McIntosh.

During the Civil War, a Confederate regiment took over the area under the command of Colonel Santos Benavides and helped facilitate the flow of cotton from the South as it engaged in its wartime trade for weapons. Following the war the U.S. once again occupied Fort McIntosh.

Unlike many other boom towns along the U.S.-Mexican border, the evolution of Nuevo Laredo/Laredo from a relatively insignificant ranching and farming community into a major center of commercial activity—its period of explosive growth and importance (its "boom" period)—had nothing to do with the discovery of mineral wealth. It had everything to do with railroads and their power to make the sister cities a hub of international trade.

In the 1880s railroad building affecting the border had begun to reach a feverish level. The Texas-Mexican Railway provided a direct route from Corpus Christi, Texas, to Mexico City. It ran through Laredo via a newly completed bridge, thereby making it the first major railway to serve both countries.

Other connecting lines increased the flow of goods. Soon, Nuevo Laredo/Laredo was a true "Gateway to Mexico," an oft-used expression of other towns along the border but, in this case, appropriate. Boom times were on.

Within eight years, the population of the sister cities increased from approximately 3,500 to well over 11,000. No longer was this a sleepy area along the Rio Grande but a new bustling hub, powered by international trade. By 1895, imports into Mexico through Nuevo Laredo were greater than those of Nogales, Piedras Negras, and Matamoras combined. The Mexican consulate in Laredo, Texas, became the second largest consulate from that country outside of New York City.

Soon, there was an electric railway system connecting the sister cities, a telephone exchange, brick and ice plants, new public schools and churches, bustling new businesses on both sides of the river, and efficient water systems. The National Lines of Mexico built a large machine shop in Laredo to help keep up with the shipping boom, and a 1,700-foot, 7-span railroad bridge across the Rio Grande was soon considered a magnificent nineteenth-century architectural accomplishment. In an area that for many decades had seen only modest adobe and brick structures there was now an elegant hotel called the Hamilton in Laredo and three-story buildings. There was a baseball park and a racetrack and a bridge for pedestrians to cross the river.

Before the boom there had been very few Anglo citizens on either side of the river except for the troops at Fort McIntosh. Now, there were several thousand in Laredo laying the groundwork for a cultural melding of the people, one that would be halting and difficult, with misunderstanding and conflict but, over time, fulfilling in many ways for many people.

The violence of the Mexican Revolution that began in 1910 and lasted for almost a decade brought many across the border to Laredo, including a number of prominent families of Mexico who sought sanctuary from the tumult. Many of those families invested in businesses and ranching.

Workers found jobs in new industries that had emerged in the city, such as brick manufacturing and onion agriculture. New barrios appeared that would help define the city for generations to come.

Soon, natural gas was discovered in an area east of Laredo, a development that in many ways fostered yet another boom for the region. A number of fields yielded new jobs and brought an influx of new arrivals from other parts of the United States as well as from Mexico.

In 1942, an area normally used for some of the cattle ranges that surround the Laredo area, became a military site. The U.S. Air Force built the Laredo Army Airfield, a facility that instructed recruits in aerial gunnery during World War II. Later, it acted as a base for pilot training as part of the Air Training Command.

Over the years Nuevo Laredo, like many other border towns, became a hub for *maquiladoras*, factories built by multinational companies to take advantage of lower wages paid to workers in Mexico. As the city reached the new millennium, it could boast over sixty *maquiladoras* that employed over 20,000 people.

Today, the two cities represent a major land port of entry. Laredo/Nuevo Laredo is the largest U.S.-Mexican truck crossing. Nearly half of international trade headed for Mexico and nearly 40 percent of Mexican international trade crosses through Laredo/Nuevo Laredo.

Five bridges now service the sister cities, including four vehicular bridges and a railroad bridge. The World Trade Bridge itself is the busiest U.S.-Mexican crossing point, processing more than 12,000 cargo vehicles per day.

Laredo/Nuevo Laredo is, overall, the largest commercial crossing from Mexico into Texas, with more than 3,600 train crossings each year, as well as more than 2 million trucks, served by Interstate Highway 35/Mexican Federal Highway 85.

Millions of pedestrian crossings increase the retail trade in both cities. In the Laredo area alone, the U.S. Customs and Border Patrol employs about 2,000 Customs field officers and nearly 2,000 Border Patrol agents.

All of this has made Laredo/Nuevo Laredo a major metropolis. The population of Nuevo Laredo is approximately 375,000 and that of Laredo is approximately 260,000.

Nevertheless, in recent years, Nueva Laredo has unfortunately attracted groups who have not been a boon to the progress that the area has shown in so many other ways; it has had to deal with the influx of drug cartel violence. In 2012, the city was the scene of a series of murder attacks involving rival gangs known as Sinaloa Cartel, Gulf Cartel, and Los Zetas. Fighting a turf war over control of the drug smuggling routes, the cartel thugs left a trail of bodies of rival gang members that so alarmed the Mexican national government that it sent forces to northern Mexico to attempt to prevent the violence.

But the war between the gangs has not abated. Splinter groups emerged, fighting each other for control. The violence, which had formerly been mostly against competing cartel thugs, has spilled over into a spate of murders against journalists attempting to cover the bloodshed. The U.S. State Department has issued tourist warnings that the organized criminal elements might target public and private passenger vehicles.

Despite the warring cartel violence in Nuevo Laredo, the growing commerce of the region continues. And, most importantly, as with most other sister cities along the border, the close-knit relationships between the people living on both sides of the river is enduring.

In January 2018, Laredo/Nuevo Laredo continued a yearly celebration that began in 1898—a month-long festival with carnivals, concerts, and other events honoring the birthday of George Washington. At the Juárez-Lincoln Bridge, dignitaries from both cities and nations gathered to open the celebration, emphasizing cultural ties, lasting friendship between the two cities and the two nations, and the continuing need to foster a richer understanding between the peoples of the Americas.

DOCUMENTS

James Douglas and Railroad Construction: Extract from His Unpublished Autobiography

He was a renaissance man on the frontier. Educated in both theology and medicine, Dr. James Douglas had also been a professor of chemistry and a director of copper companies in both Canada and the United States when he arrived in

Cochise County to evaluate the mining prospects in the area for Phelps, Dodge & Co. It was through his research in the Bisbee area that the company purchased land claims that led to the growth of the Copper Queen Consolidated Mining Co. In his career, Douglas not only managed mining companies but, as a chemist, also invented a number of processes for ore extraction and other improvements in mining processes. Douglas also became heavily involved in the planning, development, and negotiation for the construction of new railroads to improve the ability of the mines to ship their products more expeditiously to markets. Late in his life, Douglas wrote an autobiography. The following is an excerpt that reveals some of the inside considerations relating to his efforts in railroad building.

When the Queen Mine was opened in 1880, timber for mining purposes was cut on the Chiricahua Mountains at an elevation of about 9,000 feet, by a contractor, Ross, and hauled some thirty miles, the contract price being some thirty-two dollars. The profits on store goods sold to the teamsters somewhat reduces that price. This continued for years after the consolidation, and till 1890 when the Government is said to have been instigated by the Southern Pacific—commenced a criminal suit against Ross for cutting on mineral lands, and a civil suit against the Copper Queen Company for buying illegally cut lumber.

The suit dragged on for years, till finally decided against the government by the Supreme Court of the United States. It was a hopeless case, but a Government suit once commenced, must drag on to its consummation in the highest court, for no official likes to take the responsibility of stopping it. Whether the Southern Pacific instigated it, or not, the Southern Pacific at once offered to deliver Oregon pine to us at Benson at about $20.00.

Then for each contract commenced a contest between the Southern Pacific, through the Blinn Lumber Co., for northern pine delivered through San Pedro and the Santa Fe for the same lumber delivered through Guaymas over the Sonora RR.

The bids seldom differed more than 25 or 30 cents. Sometimes we got the contract and sometimes the other. One day I was surprised by getting from Mr. Hanley, the traffic manager of the Santa Fe, a message to the effect that he had withdrawn the special rates on lumber, etc., between Fairbank (our Junction Point) and Benson, and would charge us full locals, as he was not running the Sonora Branch for our special benefit. He had lost his contract by 25 cents, and lost his temper. He would not regard as sincere our threat to parallel his road for those 18 miles, even though we withdrew all our freight, and hauled at the price he demanded, the local maximum tariff of 15 cents per ton mile.

The Southern Pacific was willing to receive us hospitably at Benson, and to Benson therefore we built during the summer of 1894. This was the first addition to the Arizona & Southeastern R.R., and no thought of extension was suggested till we had bought the Moctezuma Copper Co. mines, seventy miles south of the frontier in Mexico, from the Guggenheims, and had developed them to the point where Railroad communication was necessary. The teaming road crossed the frontier, and the American and United States Custom houses were situated not far from the present town of Naco, and from that point railway surveys started, and a line was projected through a difficult broken country flanking the Magellan Mountains.

We built a spur from Deer Point on our Arizona & Southeastern to the frontier, and called the town which began to grow up at that point Naco, and were collecting building material for our Mexican Railroad when one day driving along Snake Ridge on my way to Nacozari, the thought suddenly struck me that we were building eastward some 20 miles in Mexico and traversing a very difficult country, when probably there was a better route by following a line due east north of the border and following a north and south water grade south of the border.

Building was suspended while new surveys were made, which induced us to change all our plans and had a most momentous influence on the future operations of the Company. Mr. Wambugh laid out a line to the Sulphur Spring Valley in United States Territory. It was the only poor piece of locating of which he was guilty, and which we have had to change for a better, which for reasons we quite understood was not at first adopted.

The Sulphur Spring Valley, the dry bed of the Agua Prieta (Black Water) gave us a much better route southward than any of the lines run from Naco. Having decided to build thus far eastward, two suggestions rapidly followed: first, to move our Bisbee Works from their cramped location to the spacious valley, with its ample underflow of water, then to extend our railroad eastward and reach a competitive point, such as El Paso, where we would have as competitors for out freight from four trunk lines of railroad instead of being at the mercy of one. But before proceeding to build further feast than Douglas, our Mexican junction, we entered into negotiations with the Southern Pacific for trackage rights which would have enabled us to handle our own freight between Douglas and El Paso in our own trains by merely linking up our line with some nearby station of the Southern Pacific, thus avoiding the building of 200 miles of parallel track.

Just at this crisis Mr. C.P. Huntington, the originator of the Central Pacific and the inspiring and controlling spirit of the whole Southern Pacific system, died. Mr. Edwin Hawley, his Eastern Agent, and closest and confidential friend, told me that the last instructions C.P. gave him before taking the train for his Adirondack retreat, where he died that night, was to write and ascertain from me our intention with regard to eastern extension.

Mr. Hayes succeeded him as President, but was in office for but a short time till Mr. E. H. Harriman secured control of the Southern Pacific, and having already become master of the Union Pacific, made it possible to unite into one system the two disjointed members of the Central Rocky Mountain road with the complete transcontinental system which his masterful predecessor had built up without state aid.

The Southern Pacific proposed to allow us to use Southern Pacific tracks on paying half the bonded interest on the section used, and half the cost of maintenance, and would have been remarkable had we been a road of the same standard and carrying the same volume of business as the Southern Pacific; but would have cost us more in fixed charges than if we owned our own road into El Paso, and far more for maintenance of way than to keep our own road, with its light traffic and repair. We therefore decided to build to the Rio Grande . . .

Source: Dr. James Douglas Collection, MS 1031, Autobiography Manuscript, Arizona Historical Society-Tucson.

Oral History with Martha Jane Guthrie Bruemmer, Gadsden, Arizona, 2011

Yuma, Arizona, with its border crossing at San Luis, is one of the richest agricultural regions of the Southwest and has become known as the winter vegetable capital of the world. The sun shines relentlessly in the area, often with an intensity seen almost nowhere else. The desert landscape, dotted with mesquite scrub, creosote bush, and sand hills, seems hardly the place where lettuce and other agricultural industries could thrive. When Martha Jane Bruemmer's grandparents arrived in 1919 in Gadsden, Arizona, a few miles from Yuma, as sharecroppers, it was little more than a dusty outpost. She grew up in the area and later reflected on life on the Arizona border during the first half of the twentieth century. The following is an extract of her recollections.

Laurie Boone: Hello, this is Laurie Boone. I'm at the San Luis Library Branch of the Yuma County Library District in San Luis, Arizona, on April 19, 2011. Today I'm interviewing Martha Jane Bruemmer. Thank you very much for being here. Where are you from originally, where is your family from, and what prompted your family to come to this area of Yuma?

Martha Jane Bruemmer: Well, I was born in 1936, and my parents lived in Gadsden, Arizona at that time. My grandparents, both my paternal and my maternal grandparents, had arrived here in the 1920s. Actually, my grandparents Guthrie, my father's parents, came here in 1917. They had left Arkansas in 1912 and had gone to Calexico, California, because the Yuma area was not as developed at that time. So they spent four years in Calexico or Los Angeles, and came to the Yuma Valley in 1917 in February. The reason for their coming here was the opening of the Laguna Dam, which opened irrigation to the Yuma Valley, and there was wonderful, prosperous farming area here. They sharecropped farming with a German farmer, Mr. Hans Holing, and then after two years of being here—so in 1919—they were able to buy forty acres in Gadsden. My father and his three sisters attended Gadsden Grammar School.

My mother's parents then came here in 1920 from Texas. She was a few years younger than my father. They ultimately married in 1930, and as I said, I was born in 1936. So my family has been here continuously since 1917 and 1920 . . .

Boone: Okay, so you went to school in Gadsden the first grades. . . .

Bruemmer: Eight years.

Boone: The first eight years. Can you tell me what that school was like, and what the students were like, and how your experience in that school was?

Bruemmer: Well, I'd like to go back to the experience of my father and my aunts from the Guthrie side. When they first came here, the Gadsden School was not in existence. They went to a school, the Alameda School, and I believe it was around 1921 that the grammar school in Gadsden was built. And my Aunt Imer [phonetic]—this is an experience she had when she was in first grade—and she describes that in school there were all different nationalities of children living here. Some of the family names that I remember—Segula, Metika, Vomisol, Nelson [all phonetic spellings]—these were Yugoslavian, Czechoslovakian, Russian, Swedish—plus there were Cocopah Indians as well as a number of Hispanic families. Some of the early Hispanic families that I remember were Gonzalez, Comache—I forget some of the others.

But my aunt describes that there were different nationalities of children in the Gadsden School. The teacher would have ten nationalities at a time stand up in front and show something to the rest of the class—an early show-and-tell—speaking in their own languages. It was very interesting to me. The main languages in our school, though, were Indian, Mexican, and American.

I went to the Gadsden Grammar School then in 1941 and graduated in 1948. . . .

Boone: And was it, at the time, as many people living in Gadsden? Or it had been a booming town and now it was kind of in its decline?

Bruemmer: Well originally the town of Gadsden was quite prominent. In 1905, I believe, when the town was established as a town, there were two churches, the Catholic church and the Methodist church. There were six cotton gins within the vicinity. There was a meat market, there was a drugstore, a couple of saloons, a couple of gasoline stations . . . There were several things that caused the decline of the area. Cotton, the boll weevil became a very terrible blight on the crop. And so cotton could no longer be raised, and that caused the decline.

I should talk a little bit about the cotton itself. That was a crop that many people came from Mexico and from other areas to pick the cotton. Other crops pretty much could be managed—the alfalfa and the grains—by the farmer himself. But these needed further labor for us to pick those crops . . .

Boone: What has it been like for you to grow up in a border town, and can you describe some of the changes and experiences that you've seen over the years with the border here at San Luis?

Bruemmer: My own impression from my childhood was that San Luis, Mexico, was really only about a ten-block area. Possibly there was more, but that's all I ever saw of it. It was not a large town. And comparing now, when I sit in my little ranch home in Gadsden and I look to the south, the border town extends extensively. I mean, there are two hundred some odd thousand people. It is just amazing. The lights go on forever to the east. That is really a tremendous exponential growth over that period of time.

Formerly I don't remember there being very much of a problem in crossing the border: Simply give the place of birth, and that was it. But I do remember during the

Second World War there were a number of draft dodgers, as we called them, who passed over into Mexico. Maybe this has been forgotten. It seems that during the Vietnam War we heard more of passing into Canada. But at that point in the Second World War, there were people who did cross over, and I knew a couple of families whose sons went to Mexico, across the San Luis border. During the Second World War, servicemen were not permitted to go across the border. That was forbidden. I presume that they felt that they might not come back, they might go AWOL.

As far as growing up on the border, I think it's been an enriching experience to know people from other cultures. The early immigrants that I mentioned during my grandparents' early arrival here, they were all assimilated. Their children became English speakers, and so there was nothing foreign about their culture. Being so close to the Mexican border, there was still the influence of Mexico, which I've appreciated through the years.

Boone: During your time in Gadsden, you have seen San Luis, Arizona, go from virtually nothing, a no place, to a pretty large city for this area. And for what we can tell, it's going to just keep growing. Why do you think this has happened, and how do you feel about it, being a neighbor in Gadsden?

Bruemmer: Certainly my earliest memories of San Luis, Arizona, there was just a small block of houses I remember. I remember the Sanchez family quite well. In fact, one of my classmates married into that family. I remember the little market, the Verdugo Market, and I remember there was a small post office. Whether it was part of the market, I'm not sure. But I always remember the Catholic church up on the hill, and the customs house, but beyond that, there really was nothing. As time went on—and of course I left the area after I went away to college, and never returned until I came as a winter visitor to spend the winters here fourteen years ago—the Bracero Program brought many immigrants into the area. I'm not sure exactly how the program allowed these people to become citizens, but certainly that had a tremendous impact upon the region. It's a wonder to see that San Luis, Arizona has developed into such a beautiful city. I think it's a very positive influence to have this large healthy city right on the border.

Source: Yuma County Library District, San Luis Branch, Martha Jane Bruemmer, Interview Number 1, Interviewed by Laurie Boone, April 19, 2011; also available at Arizona Memory Project, http://azmemory.azlibrary.gov/cdm/compoundobject/collection/ycldsan/id/34.

5

Mexico's Revolution and Violence on the Border

In 1910 Mexico became engulfed in a violent revolution that would last a decade, and it would profoundly influence the history and character of the border.

Since 1876, military leader Porfirio Diaz had ruled Mexico as its president with such centralized power and authority that he became, for all intents and purposes, a dictator. Political aspirants who challenged Diaz were either intimidated to drop such aspirations or faced a rigged election system.

It is true that the Diaz regime had modernized Mexico with the assistance of foreign investment and new industry, especially in the northern part of the country. Through a powerful centralized government, Diaz paved the way for capitalist development that saw extensive railroad construction; increased exports; and burgeoning economic growth in mining, banking, and textiles.

New professional classes of lawyers, small commercial farmers, and merchants emerged in this age of economic prosperity. Yet the prosperity—the national wealth—was firmly entrenched in the upper classes. At the same time the United States was in the grip of enormous industrial expansion and the age of the so-called "robber barons" who reaped an enormous financial share of that prosperity. Under Diaz, Mexico was also gripped by a consolidation of wealth and power that left the lower classes in abject poverty and an aspiring professional class saw far less economic advantage than they had hoped for and deserved.

In addition to the accumulated wealth among the privileged elite, the political system under Diaz had degenerated into a sink of corruption. Diaz controlled the press; audaciously intimidated the few politicians who had the courage to oppose him and played one against another through cunning tactics of rumor-mongering; jailed many opponents without trial, especially journalists who dared challenge his policies and integrity and accuse him of abuse of power; rigged elections, both nationally and at the local level through ballot fraud and even terror tactics using mounted police; and appointed to run state governments only those politicians he trusted and who had pledged their loyalty to him.

In addition, the nature of the centralized power under the rule of Diaz meant that local governmental institutions had less control over their own affairs. This was a system that had eroded the autonomy many individuals and groups across the country had enjoyed for decades. As the centralized government increasingly assumed greater and greater power, a growing sense of resentment and bitterness generated a nascent resistance that would grow ominously for the regime.

As the dictator himself reached eighty years of age, many citizens and rising political resistance groups saw him as a relic whose system not only deserved to be overturned but was more and more vulnerable. In 1906 the resistance to the political repression of the system and its tentacles exploded in a labor strike in the town of Cananea near the U.S. border, the site of a major copper mine operation owned by U.S. business leaders. Now, suddenly, a labor uprising overtly challenged the status quo. During the strike, the manager of the company's store fired shots at striking miners gathered at the site. In retaliation, the crowd erupted, killing store officials and burning down the building. The violence grew so sustained that the Diaz administration managed to recruit several hundred Arizona Rangers to help quell the violence.

Other labor strikes ensued in the following years. A railroad strike in 1906 was followed a year later by an uprising by textile workers at the French-owned Rio Blanco Mill near Orizaba in the Mexican state of Veracruz. When Diaz ordered federal troops to put down the strike, a number of labor organizers were executed, and accounts of railroad cars carrying away the bodies of many dead workers became, for the enemies of Diaz, the kind of political ammunition that presaged revolution.

By 1910 the country was in turmoil. Led by zealous reformers, armed farm workers and other groups left behind in the so-called "prosperity" of the Diaz regime began to attack haciendas and other estates, driving many landlords from the countryside. Enraged by the loss of their lands through the years by government corruption and deceit, a number of fledgling peasant revolutionist groups began to form, threatening Diaz and his cohorts as never before.

In 1910 Díaz, who had long ago promised never to run for reelection, once again ignored his pledge and refused to step aside. He was opposed by Francisco Madero, a wealthy landowner with reformist ideas to help the lower classes rise out of poverty and for a government free of corruption and unlimited power. Although voters flocked to vote Diaz out of office, he declared himself the winner and threw Madero in jail. When released, Madero crossed the border into Texas and briefly settled in San Antonio. It was here that he would plot to overthrow the dictator who had stolen the election; it was here that he made plans that would ignite revolution.

After Madero made an open call to overthrow the dictator, Diaz's forces began to round up and kill dissidents. The call for revolution and the violent reaction of Diaz sparked a number of Mexican military men and reformers to action.

Emiliano Zapata, the son of a *mestizo* peasant who trained horses, had already been arrested over a decade earlier for stirring peasants to protest the appropriation of their lands. He had briefly served in the army, and now, sensing the real time had come for change, he formed a small army made up of peasants who immediately began stirring up trouble for wealthy landowners. An idealist, his vision was a Mexico where the poor could own and farm a piece of land.

In the state of Chihuahua, the names of Pascual Orozco and Pancho Villa now spread through the revolutionary ranks. Orozco, a muleteer by trade, and Villa, a well-known bandit, began to capture towns.

In February 1911 Madero, who had recruited over a hundred men while holed up in Texas, crossed the border into Mexico and began to raise additional forces. After growing his numbers to about 600 men, Madero decided to attack one of the country's federal garrisons in Casas Grandes. Although the attack proved to be foolish, given the strength of the fort, and although Madero himself suffered injuries, he retreated to safety. His audacious attack earned him the respect of other rebel armies led by Orozco, Villa, and others.

Soon, the three rebels united their armies and began a drive toward Mexico City. Meanwhile, Zapata's troops blitzed southern Mexico, capturing towns and forcing Diaz to keep part of the federal army in place, rather than concentrating his forces to protect Mexico City. As the scattered and divided federal army began to suffer a series of defeats, especially in a bloody encounter with Zapata's army in the town of Cuautla, Diaz began to realize that his reign was ending.

On April 7, 1911, rebel forces, led by Pancho Villa and Pascual Orozco with over 2,000 men, assaulted Mexican federal army troops at Ciudad Juárez, located just across the border from El Paso, Texas, at the foot of the Franklin Mountains. It was the first major battle of the Mexican Revolution.

Pancho Villa and members of his small army photographed at Hacienda de Bastillos, Chihuahua, 1911. Of all the military figures vying for power during the Mexican Revolution, it was the flamboyant Villa who carried out many of his raids along the border, including an attack on Columbus, New Mexico, in 1916. (Library of Congress)

Although General Juan Navarro, commanding 700 federal troops, heavily barricaded Juárez and set up machine-gun emplacements, his forces were no match for the overwhelming peasant army that effectively blasted their way into the city using dynamite to blow up buildings and concealing themselves in others.

In some ways the Battle of Juárez was reminiscent of the first days of the first major battle of the U.S. Civil War seven decades earlier. At Manassas, Virginia, in the first Battle of Bull Run, civilians riding horses and driving carriages and carrying picnic lunches traveled to the battle site as if it were an entertainment venue. But when the fighting began, with the slaughter of war in full view before them, most of the civilians, frightened by the horror, soon fled en masse.

And now, at the beginning of revolution in Mexico, across the Rio Grande from Juárez in El Paso, an almost carnival atmosphere pervaded the area before the actual fighting began. Newspaper reporters converged on the scene; photographers and a few men set up the latest motion picture equipment; and citizens anticipating the action gathered, some paying a quarter a head to sit on such favorable viewing sites as the top of the Mills Building and the Sheldon Hotel. In the vicious fighting and utter destruction of much of the infrastructure of the city of Juárez, a few U.S. citizens got too close to the action and were killed or wounded.

Eventually, the federal troops, outnumbered and lacking water and supplies, surrendered on May 10, 1911. The Battle of Ciudad Juárez essentially ended Díaz's rule and brought Francisco Madero to power.

Diaz resigned from power and managed to escape the country with his life, going into exile in France. He issued a statement saying that Madero had unleashed a tiger. The revolution was under way.

THE REVOLUTIONISTS: THEIR RISE AND FALL

The thirty-five-year reign of power of Diaz had come to an end. The struggle for power that followed would involve Madero, Zapata, Villa, Victoriano Huerta (a veteran military leader), Venustiano Carranza (a well-known political figure), Álvaro Obregón (a former chickpea farmer who became both a military and political leader), and others.

It would become a decade-long violent quest for power, with shifting alliances and betrayals, assassinations, nationwide horrific violence, and an imposing threat to relations with the U.S. government and the preservation of order and stability on the border. It would be a struggle for power that took thousands of lives and ruined many thousands of others, a debilitating and dizzying array of skirmishes, attacks, and slaughters led by numerous military and political figures, all jockeying for advantage and willing to plot and plunder their way to achieve it.

Madero was the first to take power, calling for a new election, which he won handily. He hardly fit the profile of the others hungering for power. A former student at a business school in Paris and at the University of California, Berkeley, he was physically unimposing, a vegetarian, and a spiritualist who had only recently moved into the arena of politics, idealistically preaching a more democratic Mexico to replace the moneyed crowd who had run the country under Diaz.

After Madero took office in October 1911, the hopes of a peaceful transfer of power under a more democratic government soon were swept aside. On the one side there were the competing interests and political jousting by the various military leaders who had, along with Madero, driven Diaz from power. On the other side, there were the prosperous merchant and entrepreneurial classes and conservative faithful fearful of losing fortunes and influence.

Shortly after Madero took office, he was confronted by Zapata, the leader of the peasant guerrilla army, who was eager to have land reforms—a return of property to those who had lost their holdings through corruption and fraud. Zapata presented Madero and the country with a document called "The Plan of Ayala," a revolutionary press for action by the government to return the stolen land by expropriation and nationalization. The call was for "Tierra y Libertad" ("Land and Liberty").

A dashing figure with a prominent moustache and huge sombrero, Zapata and his small army, in their military campaign to oust Diaz, had already taken land from wealthy hacienda owners and redistributed to it to their peasant followers. Now he wanted Madero to follow his example nationwide.

With a shaky political alliance behind him, Madero could not agree either to Zapata's demands or to the conservative faction still holding much economic power and ambition. Attempting to straddle a middle ground in a time of strident revolutionary demands and conservative backlash, Madero faced a certain doomed political position. His loyal forces repelled a number of small uprisings, but Madero faced a looming disaster.

It came when a military revolt erupted in Mexico City in February 1913. Madero had trusted the powerful military general, Victoriano Huerta, to remain committed to his leadership; the trust was misplaced. Madero was arrested and assassinated on his way to prison. Huerta took over, and the revolutionary battle for power gathered even more hostility and brutality.

Huerta's position atop Mexico's government was just as fragile as it had been under Madero. As word of Madero's assassination spread, other revolutionists openly chafed at his assumption of power. Among many, Huerta became known as "The Usurper."

Huerta's greatest threat came from Venustiano Carranza, a former governor of Coahuila who had supported Madero's presidency. When Madero was overthrown, Carranza drafted the so-called Plan de Guadalupe, a call for Mexico to return to the values of the Constitution of 1857, which had defined Mexico as a representative, democratic republic and from which, Carranza maintained, the country had seriously abandoned its precepts through corruption. Carranza's followers became known as Constitutionalists.

Although a revolutionist, Carranza was far more moderate than others who sought to overthrow Huerta, such as Zapata, the leader of the peasant army in the south, and Villa, the bandit leader in the north who would constantly raise havoc along the border. Mexico had thus entered a phase where roaming armies, largely unaffiliated with each other, carried on their individual campaigns to gain power. And along the border violence became commonplace.

In March 1913, in the city of Nogales, Sonora, at the Arizona border, a Constitutionalist force assembled by General Obregón attacked a Mexican federal garrison under General Emilio Kosterlitzky, an immigrant to Mexico from Russia who had once served in the tsar's navy.

In military terms, it was a minor affair. Nevertheless, the First Battle of Nogales (there would be two more in the coming years) presaged a protracted period of violent clashes along the border. Indeed, shortly after the Nogales clash, Obregón's troops would drive federal forces out of the Sonoran states of Cananea, Naco, and Guaymas.

By April 1913 revolutionaries under Carranza had secured positions along the border between Texas and the Mexican state of Coahuila. In October 1913 Villa and his men took control of the city of Juárez.

Although the U.S. government appeared uncertain how to respond to the events in Mexico, President Wilson opposed Huerta, whom he regarded as a corrupt dictator, and threw his support to his opposition. In April 1914 the United States sent troops to Veracruz to prevent Huerta's forces from receiving shipments of arms from Germany. Indeed, U.S. sailors and marines for a time gained control of the city after bombarding Mexican soldiers from warships. The action by U.S. military forces enraged not only Hueristas but also the Mexican citizenry and its government for this outright violation of Mexican sovereignty. In a number of Mexican cities, protestors attacked U.S.-owned businesses and held demonstrations in which they burned the U.S. flag. The incident in Veracruz left bitter resentment between the two governments.

In July 1914 Huerta decided to flee the country. He escaped to Jamaica, then briefly lived in Spain, but still harbored a deep-seated desire for revenge and planned once again to take over power. Huerta traveled to the United States, where he was arrested on charges of fomenting rebellion in Mexico. He died in El Paso, Texas. There was strong evidence that he had been poisoned. Another domino had fallen.

For the next several years, the fight for power would center on the four aspirants to the presidency who had troops in the field ready to do battle—Carranza, Villa, Zapata, and Obregón. In 1914, Carranza seized the reins of government. Among the four vying for power, Carranza, who had been a senator under the Diaz regime, was the only one who had actual experience in governmental leadership. The others were military figures whom he not only distrusted but also despised. To Carranza, they were entirely unfit to lead the country.

For the three military leaders, Carranza represented the ultimate political animal, a man with no vision or deeply held principles, an opportunist with no ideals on which to guide the country to a brighter future. The struggle between these men and their followers would be long and violent.

RACIAL HATRED AND BORDER SECURITY

As the violence in Mexico escalated, U.S. Army troops mobilized along the border. Its mission was to prevent the battles in northern Mexico and the border towns from spilling over into U.S. territory. Given the length of the border and the relative shortage of troops, the task was daunting. Because of national sovereignty concerns, U.S. troops were under orders not to cross the border or to fire shots at Mexicans unless they intentionally attacked U.S. troops or citizens.

Meanwhile, the racial and cultural aspects of border life during these tumultuous years of political struggle in Mexico were becoming increasingly evident. In the 1880s an English visitor in Texas left the country convinced that it was nearly impossible to convince Anglos that Mexicans were human. After all, he said, they treated them like dogs or perhaps not as well.

Through the second half of the nineteenth century, as Anglos, spurred by the growth of railroads, moved into towns and cities along the border and began to seize political and economic power from Mexicans who had remained in the United States after the Treaty of Guadalupe Hidalgo, a searing racial hatred that had always been present steadily grew more intense. National prejudice and ethnic identification increasingly began to dictate relations between Mexicans and Anglos. The Mexican War was half a century past, but the lingering animosities and bitterness were deep and abiding.

Through both legal and illegal machinations, Mexican families in Texas had been largely dispossessed of their land, robbed by such wealthy land barons as the King family, whose holdings grew to more than 500,000 acres. Mexican Americans had little recourse in the courts or to law enforcement. Resentment and hatred on both sides escalated.

In January 1915, burning antipathy of Mexican Americans toward their treatment by what they saw as Anglo enemies exploded in print on a document discovered by a deputy sheriff in Texas. The document, found in the possession of a man who had been arrested, called for nothing less than an insurrection along the border to take back the land that had been stolen by Anglos. It was "The Plan de San Diego."

The call was for a revolution to begin in February 1915. The army of revolutionists would "arise in arms against the Government and Country of the United States of North America, one as all and all as one, proclaiming the liberty of the individuals of the black race and its independence of Yankee tyranny which has held us in iniquitous slavery since remote times; and at the same time and in the same manner we will proclaim the independence and segregation of the states bordering upon the Mexican Nation, which are: TEXAS, NEW MEXICO, ARIZONA, COLORADO, and UPPER CALIFORNIA, of which states the REPUBLIC OF MEXICO was robbed in a most perfidious manner by North American imperialism."

Aligning the movement with grievances of both African Americans and Native Americans, who had been robbed of their freedoms and property as had the Mexicans, the authors of the manifesto were announcing the beginning of violent retribution against their oppressors and the establishment of a new government along the border.

Although U.S. government officials and state and local law enforcement were skeptical about the fanciful document, word spread about an impending race war. When Anglo ranchers and others clamored for additional border security, the Texas Rangers increased their presence in the lower Rio Grande and the U.S. Army added patrols, especially in Texas.

Soon it became clear that there were enough adherents to the promised crusade against Anglo domination that a group of guerillas, sometimes numbering at most one hundred men, began what they hoped would bring a reign of terror that would drive Anglos away from the border.

Crossing into the United States, they attacked farms, robbing them of livestock, food, equipment, and rifles. The bandit gangs sabotaged railroads and irrigation pumping stations. They focused their fury on some of the wealthiest land holdings, especially the King ranch.

Although few Anglos were killed in the raids, the violence, not surprisingly, provoked panic and fury among the population. Their retaliation was brutal and deadly.

Soon, vigilante groups organized. Also, the Texas Rangers and local police officers began a ferocious systematic manhunt for any Mexican they suspected of being a bandit. In August 1915 the Rangers killed scores of Mexicans, with some estimates as high as 300. In addition, there were numerous lynchings.

In October, after bandits derailed a train near Brownsville, Rangers and vigilantes shot and hung ten Mexicans. Many Mexican Americans fled across the border, refugees from the vigilantes and law enforcement officials who zealously tracked down anyone who, because they looked to be Mexican, could be a bandit. Several Mexican American landowners gave up small parcels of land that were soon confiscated.

Bodies of Mexicans were found along the roads. In some cases, there were mass graves. In 1915 and well into the following year, estimates of the numbers of Mexicans killed ranged into the thousands. The discovery of bodies of Mexicans who had been "evaporated," a euphemism of the period, was so commonplace that newspapers barely commented on it at all. Mexicans would later look back on the slaughter and refer to it as simply "La Matanza" (The Killing).

PANCHO VILLA RAIDS COLUMBUS, NEW MEXICO

He became known as El Centauro del Norte (The Centaur of the North). It was a sobriquet Pancho Villa embraced.

Born Doroteo Arango in 1878, in San Juan del Rio, Durango, to a small farmer, Pancho Villa became a fugitive in his early teens after shooting a man who was harassing one of his sisters. For several years, he joined a group of bandits operating from mountain hideouts. He changed his name while on the run, became a skilled horseman, and for a time worked in Chihuahua as a miner, a profession which it did not take long for him to abandon. Robbing banks and wealthy owners of haciendas, he gained a following among the peasantry of northern Mexico, as well as growing fame and admiration for his audacious and daring escapades.

At the beginning of the Mexican Revolution, he joined Francisco Madero's uprising that drove Porfirio Diaz from power. Villa's forces, known as Division del Norte, scored major victories in the northern areas of Mexico, especially near the border. Soon, the cavalry army of peasants led by the daring Villa became celebrity news to reporters and the residents in the United States as photographs and stories began to bring to public attention the events of battles near the border. Usually wearing a wide-brimmed sombrero and ammunition belts crisscrossed on his chest, Villa absorbed and reveled in the spotlight, at one point even signing a contract with the Mutual Film Company of Hollywood, an early producer of silent films. Although the resulting film was of middling quality and was rarely shown in public, the access accorded the film producers by Villa to his life and battles was extraordinary.

Villa traveled back and forth across the border, buying weapons and supplies. When he made a visit to Deming, New Mexico, in 1914, admiring onlookers stood along the streets to glimpse the famous bandit warrior. The legends and lore would grow through the years of the U.S.-Mexican border bandit hero.

However, by 1915, as the U.S. government began to accord the government of Victoriana Carranza an increasing measure of support, Villa, who was a staunch enemy of the current federal Mexican regime, took great offense. The charismatic rebel general was especially infuriated that the United States was now allowing Carranza's troops to travel on U.S. railroads, a factor that led to Villa's troops suffering a major loss at a battle in Agua Prieta, Sonora. He now looked across the border with much greater suspicion and anger.

In early 1916 the city of El Paso, Texas, became a hotbed of racial hysteria. On January 12, a group of *Villista* soldiers at Santa Ysabel, Chihuahua, stopped a train carrying eighteen Anglo miners and executed them on the spot. The following morning, the train carrying the bodies of the dead U.S. miners arrived at the El Paso railway freight depot, where citizens unloaded the corpses and took them to undertakers. The realization by El Paso leaders and citizens of the horrific slaughter of innocent U.S. citizens fueled what would later be called "The El Paso Race Riot of 1916."

Hundreds of Anglos and Mexican Americans battled in the streets, mostly in the Chihuahuita section of the city. Soldiers from Fort Bliss, along with hastily organized vigilante groups, fought for hours before the troops were able to round up large numbers of Mexicans suspected somehow of being connected to the Villa army and the incident in Mexico. At times during the riot, the melee involved over 1,000 individuals. Many women and children were injured. The riot was finally quelled by additional infantry from Fort Bliss that were called to the scene because local law enforcement could not handle the violence.

In early March 1916, less than two months after the riots, El Paso became the scene of another incident of horror. During the Mexican Revolution U.S. Customs agents had begun a mandatory delousing of Mexicans crossing the border, not only a humiliating process that involved bathing in a combination of kerosene and vinegar but also a dangerous one. At an El Paso jail someone struck a match near a disinfection tub and over twenty detainees were burned alive.

Although the horrendous incident in El Paso had nothing directly to do with Villa or his troops, on March 9, 1916, the rebel leader struck across the border with an unprecedented assault on a U.S. town. Estimates of 1,000 or more *Villistas,* led by General Ramón Banda Quesada, raided Columbus, New Mexico, in the early morning hours, attacking a detachment of the 13th U.S. Cavalry at Camp Furlong, seizing horses, mules, and ammunition; looting and torching parts of the town; and killing eighteen soldiers and civilians.

During the siege of Columbus, soldiers from Camp Furlong managed to maneuver two machine guns in the downtown area across from each other, where they unleashed a withering fusillade of fire that ripped through the invaders and finally drove them from the scene. Nearly one hundred of Villa's men died in the attack, and others perished as U.S. troops chased them back into Mexico.

U.S. government leaders and military experts searched for answers as to why Villa had turned so violently against the United States. Some suspected that Columbus had been targeted specifically because of Villa's association with one of the prominent U.S. merchants in the town who in the past had supplied arms and ammunition to Villa. Whatever the specific motive behind the Columbus raid, there is no question that the guerilla leader deeply resented President Wilson's efforts to prop up the Carranza regime.

Across the nation, news of the attack against a U.S. town by a foreign invader made headlines, and many political and military advisors called for retaliation. President Wilson quickly responded, directing Secretary of War Newton Baker to organize a punitive expedition into Mexico to capture or kill the notorious Villa. The expedition would be led by General John J. Pershing.

PERSHING'S PUNITIVE EXPEDITION

A highly respected military veteran of the Indian Wars and the Spanish-American War, and with service in a number of countries abroad, including China and the Philippines, General John J. "Black Jack" Pershing brought much experience as well as gravitas as the leader of an expedition that would lead troops into Mexico, an action that would not only be provocative to U.S.-Mexican relations but also unprecedented since the Treaty of Guadalupe Hidalgo. Mexico was a sovereign nation, and Pershing and his men were tasked to cross its border, all in the pursuit of one bandit and his followers.

Men of Company A of General John Pershing's army during the Mexican campaign at San Geronimo, Mexico, 1916. In retaliation against Pancho Villa's raid on Columbus, New Mexico, the so-called "Punitive Expedition" conducted by the U.S. Army in Mexico was the most overt across-the-border military action taken by U.S. troops during the Mexican Revolution. (National Archives)

In March 1916 Pershing began the extraordinary venture, one that would in time involve some 10,000 soldiers; include such equipment as automobiles, trucks, and even airplanes; and last nearly a year.

The U.S. Army established its base command for the operation in Columbus, New Mexico, shortly after the raid. U.S. Secretary of State Robert Lansing conducted negotiations with the Carranza government to enter Mexico, a proposition that was grudgingly granted only with the condition that U.S. troops would not venture farther south than the northern state of Chihuahua.

Meanwhile, President Wilson ordered National Guard units from states across the country to travel to the Mexican border in case Carranza decided to retaliate against the Pershing expedition. Over 100,000 Guardsmen made the trek from as far away as the northern states. Wisconsin, for example, mustered approximately 4,000 soldiers who traveled to Texas.

From the beginning of the operation Pershing and his men faced intimidating challenges, especially keeping supply and communication lines operating and in tracking their elusive prey through terrain that they knew little about and which Villa knew in detail. Mexican citizens as well as government officials offered little assistance to this unwanted incursion into their country, and, in some instances, Pershing's men met with military resistance, not only from Villa's men but also from forces of Carranza.

Soon, Pershing realized that many of Carranza's forces were now openly joining forces with Villa. The U.S. general now concluded that his men could possibly be cut off from the U.S.-Mexican border if the Carranza government decided to order all of its forces to expel the U.S. expedition. Pershing moved his troops back toward the north.

Although the U.S. Army still had not captured or killed Villa himself, the rebel leader's army suffered substantial losses during the expedition and was severely depleted. Satisfied that the mission had at least removed the immediate threat of Villa's presence on the border and realizing that diplomatic tensions between Mexico and the United States were reaching a crisis not seen since the Mexican War a half-century earlier, the U.S. government officially ended the expedition in February 1917.

While Pershing's army chased Villa in Mexico, the border area still remained volatile. On several occasions, Mexican bandits were able to mount attacks, especially in Texas. Nevertheless, none of the incursions resembled anything like the orchestrated attack by Villa on Columbus, New Mexico.

THE ZIMMERMAN TELEGRAM, WORLD WAR I, AND BORDER CONCERNS

In addition to the concerns about continuing border depredations committed by bandits during the late stages of the Mexican Revolution, the United States was suddenly faced with another factor that fed fears about lax control of the border—the possibility that Mexico might consider allying itself with Germany in World War I.

Since the beginning of the war in Europe in 1914, President Wilson had been determined to keep the United States out of the conflict. Nevertheless, a number of depredations committed on the high seas by German ships that took the lives of some Americans and the escalating possibility that Great Britain, a staunch ally, might succumb to the German onslaught had greatly influenced not only President Wilson but also the American public that perhaps the United States should abandon its policy of neutrality. In late February 1917 a dramatic revelation helped break whatever patience and reluctance for war that still remained. It would be known as "The Zimmerman Telegram."

In January 1917 German Foreign Secretary Arthur Zimmerman sent a coded telegram to Heinrich von Eckardt, the German ambassador to Mexico. The telegram contained two vital pieces of information. First, it announced that Kaiser Wilhelm's government had decided to unleash unrestricted submarine warfare against merchant ships, a decision that would greatly affect U.S. commerce. Second, it proposed that Mexico enter the war on the side of Germany with the prospect that victory would enable the Mexicans to "reconquer" the territory in the border states of Texas, New Mexico, and Arizona it had lost over a half-century earlier in the Mexican War.

British naval intelligence operators intercepted and decoded the message shortly after it arrived in Mexico City. At first, British officials were wary of sharing the information with the U.S. government, fearing that the Germans would now be privy to the fact that British cryptographers had broken the German code. However, realizing that Germany's unrestricted submarine warfare would seriously undermine their own war effort, British leaders decided to use the telegram to help sway Wilson and other U.S. policy makers to join the war on the side of the Allies. President Wilson received the contents of the Zimmerman telegram in late February 1917 and released its contents to the American press.

On April 2, 1917, President Wilson appeared before a joint session of Congress requesting a declaration of war against Germany. One of the principal factors cited by Wilson in his appeal was the attempts by German leaders to encourage Mexico to attack the United States. On April 4, 1917, the U.S. Senate voted to declare war on Germany; the House concurred two days later.

The Carranza government did consider the German offer. Nevertheless, given the political uncertainty in Mexico, along with its lack of sufficient military strength to challenge seriously the U.S. forces in another U.S.-Mexican war, Carranza decided against entering the war. Although an alliance between Germany and Mexico did not materialize, it is true that a number of German "agents provocateurs" traveled to Mexico and joined a few bandit gangs to stir trouble on the border and to encourage Mexican diversionary attacks on the United States.

Indeed, in the summer of 1918, the U.S. Army intelligence unit at Fort Huachuca, Arizona, learned of a German presence in Sonora, Mexico, and ordered additional troops to begin surveillance operations. The intelligence report proved to be accurate.

In late August a skirmish between a U.S. Customs agent in Nogales, Arizona, and a Mexican who refused to stop for questioning escalated into a small-scale fight between 10th Cavalry soldiers allied with troops from the 35th Infantry against a force of Mexican troops accompanied by German "advisors." It would be known as the Battle of Ambos Nogales (Both Nogales).

George S. Patton in Pershing's Punitive Expedition

When John J. Pershing launched his punitive expedition into Mexico attempting to capture Pancho Villa in the spring of 1916, he filled his ranks with many highly regarded subordinates. One of those was a thirty-two-year-old second lieutenant named George S. Patton. During the expedition, Patton, a graduate from the U.S. Military Academy in 1909 who had served on border patrol in Texas and New Mexico, saw his first action in battle.

With Pershing's forces headquartered in Dublán, about a hundred miles south of Columbus, New Mexico, where Villa had conducted his raid, Patton led troops on a mission to attack a group of *Villistas*. When he returned from the skirmish, Pershing began calling him "Bandit."

Patton later accompanied Pershing to Europe during World War I, where he commanded the first U.S. Automobile Cavalry Unit in France. Later, George S. Patton would become one of the most celebrated generals of the United States during World War II with service in North Africa, Sicily, and Europe. By then he was called "Old Blood and Guts."

The battle took the lives of several Mexican soldiers and citizens, as well as a few U.S. soldiers. When a white flag of surrender appeared on the Mexican side, the cross-border fight was over. In its aftermath, the sister cities agreed to erect a fence along International Street.

THE PORVENIR MASSACRE AND HEARINGS ON THE TEXAS RANGERS, 1918

The clashes between Anglos and Mexicans along the U.S.-Mexican border during these years cemented further the deep racial hostility that had always existed. The later ramifications would be profound. Soon, the casual crossing by citizens on both sides of the border would be far less congenial. Soon, there would be such signs as "No Mexicans or Dogs" on the front of some restaurants and other establishments along the border.

In late January 1918 the small town of Porvenir, Texas, on the banks of the Rio Grande in Presidio County was essentially wiped off the map by a massacre. A small farming community of 140 people of Mexican descent, Porvenir became an unlikely and tragic epicenter for pent-up rage directed toward Mexicans and Mexican Americans because of continued bandit raids across the border.

U.S. troops, Texas Rangers, and local law enforcement all continued to patrol the border with some success, but isolated incursions continued to plague U.S. businesses and farmers, especially in West Texas. When a number of raiders attacked a ranch in Presidio County, law enforcement officials believed some of the culprits had come from Porvenir, although later evidence suggested that the belief was unfounded.

On the night of January 28, a group of men, mostly Texas Rangers and perhaps a few U.S. Cavalry and local ranchers, marched into the small village; separated old men, women, and young children; and shot dead fifteen men and boys between the ages of sixteen and seventy-two. As the fifteen were being executed, survivors fled, crossing the river into Mexico. The next morning a group of women returned across the Rio Grande with horse carts to retrieve the bodies. A local schoolmaster who survived later said that the Rangers and the others had made forty-two orphans that night.

The execution atrocities were not enough for the invaders. Within the next few days, the buildings and houses of the small village were knocked down and burned. By the time the work was finished, Porvenir ceased to exist.

The Texas Rangers faced no criminal charges in the massacre. The event nevertheless brought such notoriety that Texas Governor William P. Hobby disbanded Company B of the Rangers and dismissed five men for their actions.

In 1919 Representative José T. "J. T." Canales, the only Mexican American in the Texas legislature, filed nineteen charges against the Texas Rangers after his own research on the violence on the Texas border, including the Porvenir massacre., A select committee with members from both the Texas House and the Senate formed to conduct a formal investigation of Texas Ranger violence. Although many legislators were leery or outright hostile to the investigation, Canales persisted, despite threats on his life. Some of his enemies called him "the greaser from Brownsville."

The select committee heard weeks of testimony from people who witnessed the events at Porvenir and elsewhere or who had been victims of violence. Witnesses, both of Mexican descent and Anglos, recounted episodes of the violence by the Rangers that exhibited egregious cruelty against Mexicans. In his own testimony Canales charged that violence had so overtaken the Texas border in these years that arrests meant instant death. "The Rangers," he said, "had established a precedent that is, whenever a suspect was arrested they would unceremoniously execute him on the road to Brownsville or to the jail, without giving him any opportunity. Frequently we would find dead bodies, and the ranches burned. Relatives were intimidated to the extent that they would not even bury their own relatives. That condition existed until it was nauseating, nauseating. It was terrible."

The investigation found evidence that the Rangers were in violation of both civil and criminal laws but did not sanction those violators. Indeed, many of the men who were named in hearings later took positions in various agencies of Texas law enforcement.

In February 1919 a final report did recommend a slight reorganization of the Rangers. Later that session, the legislature passed a bill, authored by Canales, that made some changes in the Ranger force and established procedures for citizen complaints.

As the Canales investigation demonstrated so clearly, the U.S.-Mexican boundary was far more than just a line; it was a hardened racial boundary.

Representative Canales left the legislature soon after the investigation. No Mexican American would again serve in the Texas legislature until 1956.

THE LAST MAN STANDING

As the Mexican Revolution dragged on into its ninth year, Venustiano Carranza maintained a shaky hold on power. Following the withdrawal of Pershing's punitive expedition, the fight for control in Mexico continued in full force. Although both Zapata and Villa continued to mount some pressure on the regime of Carranza, his forces prevailed. Zapata was assassinated in April 1917, and Carranza called together a constitutional convention that paved the way for his election as president.

His main rival for power was Álvaro Obregón, who sensed that Carranza had lost touch with not only leaders in the various state government establishment but had disillusioned much of the Mexican people. In June 1919 Obregón announced that he would campaign for the presidency.

Obregón had been a supporter of Carranza during the overthrow of the Huerta regime and had remained steadfast as a military leader in opposition to both Pancho Villa and Emiliano Zapata, who had fought to depose the Carranza regime. Obregón had even lost his right arm in battle in 1915.

After serving for a short period in the Carranza government, Obregón retired to a farm in Sonora. During those two years, as he watched from outside the government, he became disenchanted with Carranza's leadership. Because he had stayed away from the levers of governmental power, he had also gained a certain respect not only from the populace but also from political insiders, who saw him as less grasping for leadership than other prominent Mexican leaders who had been deeply involved in the revolution.

In April 1920, nevertheless, Obregón reemerged, enraged that Carranza had attempted to impose his own puppet successor on the country. Suddenly, Obregón was no longer content to remain on the sidelines, his agricultural pursuits now giving way once again to political ambition.

He announced that he would run for president, a declaration that outraged Carranza and led to a vengeful encounter between forces loyal to Carranza and those of Obregón. The encounter proved fatal to Carranza, who was assassinated later in the summer. By the end of 1920 Obregón was Mexico's president.

He proved able in the job, attempting to make peace with military leaders still in opposition, instituted some land reform, and took several measures to improve an impoverished education system. He also made efforts to strengthen ties with the United States.

Although the next decade would continue to see some jockeying for power, including the assassination of Obregón after he was elected president again in 1927, the Mexican Revolution, as far as the turbulence on the U.S.-Mexican border was concerned, had essentially burned itself out.

The savage violence of the Mexican Revolution can be epitomized by the fate of those men who fought with such ambition, treachery, and zeal to gain the ultimate of power in a nation buffeted by profound division and unrest: Francisco Madero, assassinated February 1913; Victoriano Huerta, possible cirrhosis of the liver, probable poisoning, January 1916; Emiliano Zapata, assassinated April 1919; Venustiano Carranza, possible suicide, probable assassination, May 1920; Pancho Villa, assassinated, July 1923; and Álvaro Obregón, assassinated July 1928.

The revolution had created a major population shift of Mexicans into the United States as they sought refuge from violence and searched for jobs. For large agricultural interests in the United States, that shift presented not a danger but an opportunity advantageous to their interests—cheap labor. Soon, however, the ramifications of the border unrest of the decade of the revolution would lead to major efforts by the U.S. government to control the influx of immigrants and to create a permanent force to protect the border itself.

DOCUMENTS

Report from American Consulate in Nogales, Sonora, on Conditions along the Border, 1915

As small armies skirmished along the border during the Mexican Revolution, U.S. diplomatic and military leaders close to the action provided a constant supply of information to the Wilson administration in Washington. The area around Nogales, Sonora, was especially active with military forays at various times. The following dispatch from the American consul in Nogales to the State Department in December 1915 is one such communication.

AMERICAN CONSULATE
Nogales, Mexico, Dec. 14, 1915

Subject: Political and Economic Conditions in North Sonora

The Honorable
The Secretary of State, Washington

Sir:

I have the honor to report that north Sonora is practically free of Villa troops; 80 miles west of Nogales 150 raided El Plomo Mine, American owned, one day last week; this band is still active in the Altar District.

Gen. Rodriguez was defeated at Fronteras, below Agua Prieta, December 10 and 11, the Carranza troops under Gen. Calles taking and executing prisoners variously reported at from 100 to 400. The Villa forces retired eastward, via Colonia Oaxaca, Calles making a pretense of following them.

With the departure of Villa troops from the community, Americans are returning in large numbers to Sonora. The Cananea Consolidated Copper Co. and other industries at Cananea are resuming operations; the Moctezuma Copper Co. will re-open at Nacozari as soon as railway communications can be established. El Tigre will also re-open soon, and likewise the Creston Company at La Colorado.

The S. P. de M. railway is now running trains through from Nogales to Guaymas. The line is also open from Naco to Cananea and is being repaired between Nogales and Cananea.

Telegraph lines are open, but tolls excessive; it costs 10 cents gold a word to telegraph to Guaymas.

The money muddle seems the greatest resistance to early economic order. Bank notes are gradually weakening, Carranza fiat currency is slow at 5cents, and all Mexican workmen clamor for pay in American money. I am told Senor Luis Cabrera is expected in Mexico City in January, from Spain, with a plan to rehabilitate the country's finances and that General Carranza will await his arrival before taking any steps to straighten out the money tangle.

American ranchers in Sonora are having no little trouble still with military authorities over seizure of horses, cattle, and hay. The authorities take such property at will, usually giving a receipt, or else offering payment at a price lower than seems fair to the owners. It is hoped this practice can be stopped.

Numerous Chinese were killed by Villistas; 5 or 6, at Fronteras; 10 to 20 (reported) at La Colorado; a few at other points, including Magdalena. Four were killed at Santa Barbara, supposedly by Calles' troops.

The usual number of wounded and prisoners were executed when Nogales was occupied, the customary seizure of the property of absentees was made, and a number of Mexicans and Americans of Sonora who happened to be on the American side of the line were not allowed to return to Mexico. Certain Mexicans, who have taken out their first American naturalization papers appealed here for help in saving their property. Little can be done for such, as the Mexicans do not recognize them as Americans.

Gen. Calles, it is understood, will be left in charge by Obregon as acting Governor of Sonora. This is generally regarded as an unfortunate selection, owing to Calles' notoriously unfair attitude to American interests in territory formerly controlled by Maytorana.

The opening of railway traffic with Guaymas and the Yaqui Valley is relieving the food situation through central and north Sonora—which had become almost critical in remote villages.

But prices of food, wood, and other necessities are higher than ever known here.

Sonora is now a "dry" state. By military order all saloons are closed, and the sale of liquors forbidden. This has helped keep order.

Oppression, abuse of authority, and dishonesty continues, of course; but, broadly speaking, conditions are much better than for many months past, and are improving daily.

It would be too much to expect that these people, after four years of license and lawlessness, should settle down—over night—to lives of order and respect for law.

I have the honor to be,
Sir, Your obedient servant,
Frederick Simpich
American Consul

Source: American Consul Frederick Simpich to Secretary of State Robert Lansing, December 14, 1915, National Archives and Records Administration, RG 59, Records of the Department of State, Internal Affairs of Mexico, 1910–29, File #812.00/17031; Microfilm M274, roll 50.

Plan de San Diego, 1915

The "Plan de San Diego," written by Mexican revolutionaries and named for a small Texas town, called for a revolt against the United States to begin in February 1915. Its charge was for the recovery of lands seized by the United States from Mexicans after the Treaty of Guadalupe Hidalgo and for an uprising of an army of Mexican Americans and other minorities to retaliate against violent Anglo racial suppression. In many ways the document echoed the same bitter resentment and hostility voiced by Juan Cortina in 1859, when his band of supporters raided the Texas town of Brownsville. Over fifty years had passed since Cortina passionately called for rebellion and liberation against Anglo domination. Now, the numbers of Anglo settlers on the border had dramatically increased, Anglo economic and political dominance prevailed, and racial animosity had turned especially violent during the Mexican Revolution, with lynchings and murders almost commonplace.

In late January 1915, when federal and state officials discovered a copy of the plan in McAllen, Texas, they arrested Basilio Ramos Jr., one of the leaders of the plot. The document provoked much panic, especially after bandits launched a series of raids, sabotaging irrigation pumping stations and railroad trestles and attacking farms. The promised revolution never materialized; instead, it gave sanction to even more violent reprisals against Mexicans. Like the manifesto issued by Cortina in 1859, the grievances aired in Plan de San Diego would again find voice in another half-century from various leaders of what would be known as the Chicano movement.

PROVISIONAL DIRECTORATE OF THE PLAN OF SAN DIEGO, TEX . . .

JANUARY 6TH, 1915

We who in turn sign our names, assembled in the REVOLUTIONARY PLOT OF SAN DIEGO, TEXAS, solemnly promise each other, on our word of honor, that we will fulfill, and cause to be fulfilled and complied with, all the clauses and provisions stipulated in this document, and execute the orders and the wishes emanating from the PROVISIONAL DIRECTORATE of this movement, and recognize as military Chief of the same, MR. AGUSTIN S. GARZA, guaranteeing with our lives the faithful accomplishment of what is here agreed upon.

1. On the 20th day of February, 1915, at two o'clock in the morning, we will arise in arms against the Government and Country of the United States of North America, one as all and all as one, proclaiming the liberty of the individuals of the black race and its independence of Yankee tyranny which has held us in iniquitous slavery since remote times; and at the same time and in the same manner we will proclaim the independence and segregation of the states bordering upon the Mexican Nation, which are: TEXAS, NEW MEXICO, ARIZONA, COLORADO, and UPPER CALIFORNIA, of which states the REPUBLIC OF MEXICO was robbed in a most perfidious manner by North American imperialism.

2. In order to render the foregoing clause effective, the necessary army corps will be formed, under the immediate command of military leaders named by the supreme revolutionary congress of San Diego, Texas, which shall have full power to designate a supreme chief, who shall be at the head of said army. The banner which shall guide us in this enterprise shall be red, with a white diagonal fringe, and bearing the following inscription: "equality and independence," and none of the subordinate leaders or subalterns shall use any other flag (except only the white flag for signals). The aforesaid army shall be known by the name of: "liberating army for races and peoples."

3. Each one of the chiefs will do his utmost, by whatever means possible to get possession of the arms and funds of the cities which he has beforehand been designated to capture, in order that our cause may be provided with resources to continue the fight with better success, the said leaders each being required to render an account of everything to his superiors, in order that the latter may dispose of it in the proper manner.

4. The leader who may take a city must immediately name and appoint municipal authorities, in order that they may preserve order and assist in every way possible the revolutionary movement. In case the Capital of any State which we are endeavoring to liberate be captured, there will be named in the same manner superior municipal authorities, for the same purpose.

5. It is strictly forbidden to hold prisoners, either special prisoners (civilians) or soldiers; and the only time that should be spent in dealing with them is that which is absolutely necessary to demand funds (loans) of them; and whether these demands be successful or not, they shall be shot immediately, without any pretext.

6. Every stranger who shall be found armed and who cannot prove his right to carry arms, shall be summarily executed, regardless of his race or nationality.

7. Every North American over sixteen years of age shall be put to death; and only the aged men, the women, and the children shall be respected; and on no account shall the traitors to our race be spared or respected.

8. The Apaches of Arizona, as well as the Indians (Redskins) of the territory, shall be given every guarantee; and their lands which have been taken from them shall be returned to them, to the end that they may assist us in the cause which we defend.

9. All appointments and grades in our army which are exercised by subordinate officers (subalterns) shall be examined (recognized) by the superior officers. There shall likewise be recognized the grades of leaders of other complots which may not be connected with this, and who may wish to co-operate with us; also those who may affiliate with us later.

10. The movement having gathered force, and once having possessed ourselves of the States above alluded to, we shall proclaim them an independent republic, later requesting (if it be thought expedient) annexation to Mexico, without concerning ourselves at that time about the form of government which may control the destinies of the common mother country.

11. When we shall have obtained independence for the negroes, we shall grant them a banner, which they themselves shall be permitted to select, and we shall aid them in obtaining six States of the American union, which states border upon those already mentioned, and they may form from these six States a republic, and they may be, therefore, independent.

12. None of the leaders shall have power to make terms with the enemy without first communicating with the superior officers of the army, bearing in mind that this is a war without quarter; nor shall any leader enroll in his ranks any stranger, unless said stranger belong to the Latin, the Negro, or the Japanese race.

13. It is understood that none of the members of this complot (or anyone who may come in later), shall, upon the definite triumph of the cause which we defend, fail to recognize their superiors, nor shall they aid others who, with bastard designs, may endeavor to destroy what has been accomplished by such great work.

14. As soon as possible, each local society (junta) shall nominate delegates who shall meet at a time and place beforehand designated, for the purpose of nominating a permanent directorate of the revolutionary movement. At this meeting shall be determined and worked out in detail the powers and duties of the permanent directorate, and this revolutionary plan may be revised or amended.

15. It is understood among those who may follow this movement that we will carry as a singing voice the independence of the negroes, placing obligations upon both races; and that, on no account will we accept aid either moral or pecuniary, from the Government of Mexico; and it need not consider itself under any obligations in this, our movement.

"equality and independence" San Diego, Texas, Jan. 6, 1915

President. [Signed] L. Ferrigno. Secretary. [Signed] A. González. [Signed] A. S. Garza [Signed] A. A. Saenz [Signed] Manuel Flores [Signed] F. Cisneros [Signed] B. Ramos, Jr. [Signed] Porfirio Santos [Signed] A. G. Almaraz

Source: Translated copy of "Plan de San Diego," National Archives and Records Administration, RG 59, Records of the Department of State, Internal Affairs of Mexico, 1910–1929, 812.00/1583; available on National Archives Microfilm M-274, 145–8.

Arizona Governor Offers Protection to Mexican Refugees, 1916

Throughout the course of the Mexican Revolution, Mexican refugees arrived in the United States seeking protection from the battlefield horrors and destruction of the war. The chaos forced the border states to make crucial decisions regarding the arrival of these individuals in the immediacy of the moment. Were they a danger to the U.S. population? What kinds of specific protections should they be accorded, if any?

In Arizona the refugees found a governor inclined to provide protection. His name was George Hunt, a man who had in his own past faced an uncertain future when he arrived in Arizona with two burros and no job. He worked as a waiter, a mucker in a mine, a ranch hand, and a clerk at the general store. Eventually he became a successful businessman, and in 1912, the year that Arizona became the last contiguous state to be admitted to the Union, he became its first governor in the early years of the Mexican Revolution. One of the most popular political figures in the history of the state, Hunt served as Arizona's first governor, its third, its fifth, and its seventh.

A Democrat, Hunt fought for passage of legislation restricting child labor and other progressive measures. In the case of Mexican refugees, he chose for his state a posture of sanctuary. On June 25, 1916, the Bisbee Daily Review *ran the following story.*

MEXICANS TO ENJOY STATE PROTECTION

Assurances Given That Law-abiding Residents Will Not Be Disturbed.

Sheriff Harry C. Wheeler has received from Governor Hunt the following announcement insuring to law-abiding Mexicans the same protection from the State authorities as prevails in times of undisturbed peace:

"Whereas, recent developments in Mexico, whereby the United States has come to assume a new and important relation toward all elements of the Mexican people, may reasonably be assumed to have given rise to the uncertainty as to the attitude that would be observed by the State Government of Arizona in the event of further complications however serious, toward all foreign people of whatever class or faction, residing permanently or temporarily within this state:

"Now, therefore, I, Geo. W. P. Hunt, Governor of Arizona, by virtue of the authority vested in me by law, do give assurance of the intent and purpose of the State of Arizona to maintain toward every Mexican and other foreign resident not a fugitive from justice or otherwise directly answerable to the lawful authority of another State, or to the Government of the United States, such an attitude of guardianship, protection, and justice as ordinarily characterizes the State's demeanor in time of peace toward the acknowledged individual residents; according them all usual and reasonable privileges and every safeguard of security compatible with the public peace and safety."

Source: *Bisbee Daily Review* (Bisbee, Arizona), June 25, 1916, Serial and Government Publications Division, Library of Congress, Washington, D.C.

Testimony of Texas Representative J. T. Canales on Depredations by Texas Rangers on Mexican Border, 1919

Landowner, lawyer, legislator, and, later, one of the founders of the League of United Latin American Citizens (LULAC), José Tomás Canales was one of the most respected and successful men of Mexican American heritage in Texas. Nevertheless, his accomplishments and positions of authority had not insulated him from the biting racism so prevalent in the early 1900s, and he understood well the underlying tensions and bitterness on both sides of the racial and cultural divide. During the Mexican border raids in 1915 and 1916, Canales assembled a company of Mexican American scouts to gather intelligence for the U.S. Army. Nevertheless, as a member of the Texas House of Representatives beginning in 1917, he became one of the few legislators to call to account the depredations of Texas Rangers on the border during the Mexican Revolution.

Through his efforts, the Texas legislature formed the Joint Committee of the House and Senate in the Investigation of the Texas State Ranger Force. The committee began its hearings on January 31, 1919, and heard testimony for two weeks. The most damning testimony came from Canales himself, who had personally investigated the many instances of cruelty and lawlessness committed by the Rangers. Challenged at every point during the two weeks of testimony, Canales and a few allies were able to demonstrate that, contrary to the mission and culture demanded in the ranks of the Rangers, the violence had been real and the behavior repugnant to everything the Texas Rangers were supposed to represent. Later that session, his colleagues did pass legislation that put into place some modest reforms.

For Canales, he had enough politics. The enmity and rancor he had stirred up among the ardent supporters of the Texas Rangers continued, with various legislators, hostile reporters, and others continuing to criticize his stand against the Rangers. He decided not to run for reelection. Instead, he was active in several infant Mexican American civil rights groups and other civic organizations in South Texas. He also authored a number of books, including two that touched on the life of his great uncle—Juan Cortina.

Testimony of J. T. Canales, February 8, 1919

My name is J. T. Canales. I was born in the old County of Nueces, State of Texas, very near to the present town of Kingsville. I am forty-two years old, will be next month. I went to the public schools of my county, came to Austin and attended business college, from here I went to Kansas City and graduated in the public schools of Kansas City, Kansas, and from there I went to Michigan and graduated from the University of Michigan in 1899, and have been practicing law in the State of Texas ever since then as a general practitioner, criminal as well as civil law. I was first elected Representative in 1904 and represented my district in the Twenty-Ninth Legislature, 1905, and was re-elected in 1907 and was re-elected for 1909, and then I did not run again until 1916, when I represented my district. I represented my district in the previous Legislature, Thirty-Fifth Legislature, and then ran for re-election to the present Legislature.

I have lived in Brownsville and its vicinity since 1904. I am well acquainted with the conditions there. I was born and raised on a ranch and am thoroughly acquainted with the Rangers. I have known the Rangers ever since I was born; in fact my home, La Cabra Ranch that belonged to my father, has been a haven for the Rangers. They stayed there, were stationed there, came there at all hours, got our horses or meals there, and they got our services. I have known among the Ranger forces some of the noblest and best men that I know, Captain Hughes, Captain Rogers, who is now United States Marshal, Captain Wright, who used to be Sergeant under Captain Hughes, and various other individuals. At that time they gave us protection. They were a capable set of men, and did not need any restriction because their own conscience was a self-restraint and law. In 1915, so far as my recollection goes, is when the first general outrages perpetrated by Rangers began. The service began to degenerate since that time. I will describe the condition of my town and my country about that time . . .

There was a great deal of dissatisfaction in wages. Some of those Mexicans were not paid by men who employed them. Some of those Mexicans were beaten and mistreated by what I supposed, or who were reputed to be, good men in my country, who took advantage of the conditions so as not to pay them, and in that manner agitated the friction between the two races. However, all of this went on, there was nothing but a general stealing . . . they stole saddles, arms, ammunition, and horses, but no life of an American in any way was threatened . . .

It was about the latter part of June or the first part of July that the first trouble commenced. It was the incident related here by several witnesses, and Daniel Hinojosa, who is now in the Ranger Service, and Frank Carr, a deputy sheriff of Captain Vann, starting with the prisoner by the name of Rodolpho Munoz form San Benito, only nineteen or twenty miles from Brownsville, at eleven o' clock at night, when they could have taken him in the morning, they could have taken him on an afternoon, they could have taken him safely in an automobile but they started with him about eleven o' clock, and it was generally known that he was in concert with certain citizens, among them some leading citizens not only of San Benito but of Harlingen. They arrested this man about a mile and a half from San Benito where the road turns to the right, met a band that took this prisoner from them and after torturing him, because the effects of the torture were seen in the dead body, they hung him there. That incident immediately had this effect: that every person who was charged with crime refused to be arrested, because they did not believe that the officers of the law would give them the protection guaranteed to them by the Constitution and the laws of this State. The immediate effect, then, was that all men who were charged with crime would refuse to submit to arrest . . .

The incident that followed was related by captain Vann at Paso Real, wherein these people were killed in their own house. Following this, the killing of the Austins at Sebastian, for which two Mexicans were convicted and hung . . . this Norias fight . . . no Ranger participated. They were there, but they were out on a scout . . . five Mexicans were killed and not a single American was killed at that time, one was slightly wounded. The Rangers arrived about an hour after the incident . . . Now Captain Ransom was sent there . . . and they began to kill Mexicans without giving them absolutely no chance, and those persons proved themselves innocent. On the mere dicta or information being given by any man then they would go over there and unceremoniously kill him. The effect was that immediately every relative of that Mexican would go to Mexico with his tale of woe and it aroused a strong feeling between them and the bandits instead of being minimized. That feeling increased at an alarming extent, to the extent that practically the Mexican border on the other side was at war with us, sympathizing with the relatives of these men that had been wrongfully killed, taken out of their homes at night after they had said, "if you surrender your arms we can protect you," yet after they surrendered their arms these men would go into their homes afterwards and shoot them at night . . .

The Rangers had established a precedent, that is, whenever a suspect was arrested they would unceremoniously execute him on the road to Brownsville or to the jail, without giving him any opportunity. Frequently we would find dead bodies, and the ranches burned. Relatives were intimidated to the extent that they would not even bury their own relatives. That condition existed until it was nauseating, nauseating. It was terrible.

Source: Proceedings of the Joint Committee of the Senate and House in the Investigation of the Texas State Ranger Force (Austin: Texas State Archives, 1919), 856–69. https://www.tsl.texas.gov/sites/default/files/public/tslac/treasures/images/law/1919rangerVolume2.pdf.

6

Patrolling the Border

Throughout its history, the United States, as other nations, has always struggled to come to grips with the arrival to its country of "others"—groups of people of different colors, cultures, religions, and practices. In the late 1880s and early twentieth century, the United States formally prohibited by law the immigration of Chinese and other Asians, except Japanese and Filipinos, as well as other categories of individuals deemed unworthy or undesirable. They included paupers, prostitutes, those afflicted with disease, illiterates, those considered insane, and others considered extreme political radicals such as anarchists.

Along the U.S.-Mexico border in the late 1890s, however, the arrival of Mexican workers was a boon to new business interests in agriculture and mining. There was little regulation of immigration at the border and no laws that would turn migrant workers from Mexico into "illegal aliens." Those Mexican laborers, after all, were breaking no laws and they were contributing to the growth of the country.

During the Mexican Revolution many from Mexico fled to the United States to escape violence and regions devastated by war in search of employment and a better future. Immigration numbers from Mexico rose sharply during these years. During the same period, immigrants were also arriving in large numbers from Asia and eastern and southern Europe.

At the same time, other forces were at work, and much of it had to do with the fear of too many "others." Was this rapid influx of foreigners compromising the Anglo-Saxon culture? Could these new arrivals portend an increase in crime? Would the newcomers, willing to work for lower wages, dramatically affect Anglo workers already in the United States?

LIMITING IMMIGRATION

Around the turn of the century the U.S. Congress, responding to economic and xenophobic concerns, attempted on several occasions to pass laws restricting the numbers of immigrants from Europe. One of the restrictions proposed was to introduce a literacy test designed to weed out less educated foreigners. Presidents Grover Cleveland and William Howard Taft both vetoed such legislation.

A U.S. Immigration Commission, composed of members of Congress and presidential appointees, released a report in 1911 that concluded that "degenerate" stock from southern and eastern Europe was not capable of satisfactory assimilation and that their continued migration to the United States could cause a host of social problems. Along with labor leaders who feared that the new arrivals would compromise labor negotiations and nativist groups who lamented Catholic and Jewish immigration, the push for restrictive immigration was formidable.

When President Woodrow Wilson took office, he soon faced legislation passed by both houses of Congress that, like the earlier bills vetoed by Cleveland and Taft, required immigrants to pass literacy tests. In January 1915 Wilson vetoed similar legislation, concluding that it was a "radical departure from the traditional and long-established policy of the country" to be an open gate to those from other countries seeking asylum and the even more radical change of a literacy test that turns "away from tests of character and of quality" and excludes those who come to seek the opportunity for education and a richer life.

Wilson's veto in 1915 only staved off what seemed to be the inevitable. In 1917 Congress overrode another Wilson veto and passed an immigration law that instituted the literacy test, expanded the list of reasons why individuals could be denied entry into the United States, increased the amount of a head tax imposed on those accepted into the country, and provided for greater enforcement procedures.

Subsequent legislation in 1921 and 1924 took an even more draconian step; they began a quota system based on race and nationality. The legislation heavily favored immigrants from western Europe and heavily reduced the influx of foreigners from southern and eastern European countries. In an attempt to increase protection against incursions at the border by foreigners not given formal immigration status, the United States also established the U.S. Border Patrol in 1924.

The laws did not put numerical limits on those from the Western Hemisphere. Lobbying efforts by southwestern ranchers and farmers proved crucial in exempting Mexico from the quotas.

Not restricting immigration from Mexico, however, did not sit easily with many who focused on the racial and cultural baggage they believed Mexicans brought to the United States, and many carried on a sustained campaign to demonize and dehumanize the immigrants. One of the most zealous detractors of the Mexican people happened to be in Congress. His name was John C. Box from East Texas.

Congressman Box rose on the House floor on a day in 1928 and delivered perhaps the most vile and poisonous remarks about a nation's people as any speech ever given in the history of the House. Mexicans, he ranted, were largely illiterate, diseased, an inferior racial stock, a blend that results when "low-grade Spaniard, peonized Indian, and Negro slave mixes with Negroes, mulattoes, and other mongrels, and some sorry whites. . . ."

Congressman Box introduced legislation to restrict Mexican immigration. It was defeated. At least for the moment, Mexicans were welcome to cross the border.

CROSS-BORDER WORKERS

How did these Mexicans who crossed the border searching for jobs fit into the U.S. labor force? By the 1920s the U.S. Southwest grew nearly 40 percent of the vegetable and fruit production in the country; the farm labor to pick the crops came largely from Mexican laborers. For U.S. farmers, Mexican labor was not merely convenient—it was essential. The *campesinos* who stooped in those fields hour after hour and day after day took on jobs that farmers found difficult to fill among Anglo workers.

Mexican labor also enabled mine workers and railroad operators to fill their necessary workforces. When nativist groups and others who harbored deep-seated fears and repulsion about the influx of brown-skinned workers from Mexico, it was the farmers, mine operators, and railroad officials who were quite aware of these workers' abilities and willingness to take on rigorous labor and who fought mightily against attempts to keep Mexicans on the other side of the border.

These workers came from all parts of Mexico. Their travel to the border was helped greatly by the railroad networks in Mexico that connected with U.S. rail systems. Farm laborers in isolated parts of Mexico now realized that if they could find their way to a rail line that headed north, they could take the chance to change their lives in the United States. Not only could they reach the border but could possibly move their families farther north and east to large industrial urban areas.

The city of Juárez and the Mexican Central Railroad were major contributors to this mobility. Along the railroad tracks from places such as Zacatecas, Guadalajara, and Guanajuato men, women, and children arrived at Juárez, across from El Paso, seeking new opportunities. Also, the Mexican National Railway ran from Mexico City to Nuevo Laredo, Tamaulipas, across the border from Laredo, Texas. It was these two lines that connected to U.S. rail systems and produced ever-increasing mobility not only for immigrants but also for commerce.

By the 1920s El Paso became something like the Ellis Island of the U.S.-Mexican border, a gateway to opportunity. Located at the westernmost part of Texas where it meets New Mexico, El Paso was approximately at the midpoint of the entire stretch of the border from Brownsville to San Diego. It its two neighborhoods of El Segundo Barrio and Barrio Chihuahuita, generations of Mexicans formed communities that would live on. The two barrios became the starting point for thousands of families who crossed the border and made new lives in the United States.

During the Mexican Revolution, the two barrios grew large with refugees from the violence, and many of them stayed. Francisco Madero lived in El Segundo Barrio for a time as he plotted to overthrow the Diaz regime. These two barrios that edged up against the Rio Grande were also the scene of battles between U.S. Border agents and liquor smugglers during the years of Prohibition.

Not only *campesinos* began to cross the border in search of a new life. Although a large percentage of the migrants were unskilled, the new arrivals did include teachers, lawyers, architects, doctors, and other professionals. Many of those individuals stayed in El Paso; others moved on to such cities as Tucson, San Antonio, and, especially, Los Angeles.

U.S. border agents inspecting a freight train from Mexico for smuggled immigrants, El Paso, Texas, June 1938. During the so-called "repatriation" of Mexicans from the United States during the Great Depression, as many as two million individuals were forced to leave the country. U.S. customs officials were determined to apprehend those who tried to return to the United States, along with any others seeking to cross the border. (Library of Congress)

The largest number of Mexican immigrants in the 1920s and 1930s were male and young. Many left their homes with the intention of returning after earning enough money to have made the trek worthwhile; others left family members behind and tried to gain a foothold in the United States before seeking to have the family rejoined. Some families could easily visit relatives on the other side of the border, although increased border regulation over the years made such movement more arduous. Some new arrivals formed *mutualistas* (mutual aid societies)—social clubs—and began to assert themselves aggressively into community life.

MEXICAN AMERICAN "REPATRIATION"

Beginning in 1929, as industrial production in the United States fell by 50 percent and job losses increased sharply, the Great Depression took a horrendous toll on citizens across the country. It would take an especially sharp toll on Mexicans and Mexican Americans. As the Depression sank the economy to greater and greater depths and workers became more desperate, animosity toward Mexican immigrants intensified.

In 1930 President Herbert Hoover sharply denounced the presence of Mexicans as one factor contributing to the nation's economic catastrophe. In his 1930 State of the Union Address he urged Congress to strengthen the deportation laws to more fully rid the nation of "alien criminals." His adjective "criminal" appeared to include not only those Mexicans in the country who had committed criminal behavior but also those who had entered the country without authorization.

The Hoover administration had powerful allies in their push to move those individuals of Mexican heritage to Mexico. Organized labor, led by the American Federation of Labor, approved of the move, convinced that new jobs would now be available for union members. Chambers of commerce, the American Legion, and the Veterans of Foreign Wars were all behind the move, with pronouncements that American jobs should be for American workers. Social agencies and other civic groups pushed for removal on the grounds that their limited resources should be mainly to benefit Anglo citizens. Powerful newspapers such as the Hearst network, and magazines such as the *Saturday Evening Post* lauded the move. Make America for Americans again.

Thus, U.S. leaders decided that one of the solutions to the economic disaster plaguing the nation was to send as many in the "Mexican" communities in the United States back to Mexico. The argument was simple. If Mexicans were sent out of the country, the job market would not only be better for Anglos, but there would also be fewer government benefits to pay out because of the exodus.

Thus, law enforcement agencies, businesses, civic organizations, and the media launched a concerted campaign to deport Mexicans and Mexican Americans convicted of crimes and to persuade, threaten, and intimidate others of Mexican ancestry, many of them U.S. citizens, to head to Mexico. The towering irony in all of this was that prior to the Great Depression, those same Mexican Americans had been recruited to work in the United States by businesses because they offered a source of cheap labor in railroad construction, ranching, mining, and farm labor, especially in California.

The word euphemistically used to describe this effort to remove Mexicans and Mexican Americans from the United States was "repatriation." It was a misnomer. Repatriation suggested that individuals would return to their place of birth or residence to resume a life in Mexico after spending time in the United States. In fact, from the beginning of the repatriation movement, more than half of the individuals sent to Mexico had never lived there in the first place. Many did not speak Spanish, did not know the manners and customs of the country, and had no friends or relatives on which to rely. To many of these people, Mexico was a foreign country.

Repatriation involved no new emergency deportation law. Yet under the direction of the Hoover administration, officials of the Immigration and Naturalization Service began to launch increased efforts to deport those individuals who had actually committed crimes in the United States, whatever their severity. The word spread quickly to state and local governments; to businesses and charitable organizations; and to agencies designed to provide relief to the sick, elderly, and poor: Mexicans and Mexican Americans were not welcome in the United States. In buses, automobiles, trains, and even airplanes, Mexican Americans were dropped off in places where they had little or no relationship.

Relief rolls were purged. The threat of raids and deportation spread throughout the barrios, not only in towns and cities on the border but also in cities across the United States. The largest and most orchestrated efforts were launched in Los Angeles, the major city with the most densely population Hispanic communities. Los Angeles Country hired trains and transported thousands of Mexicans to the border. In one infamous case, an entire portion of a Mexican American community in Los Angeles was cordoned off, and banner headlines announced that deportation transportation would be provided. Hysteria and fear gripped the community as thousands were removed from the neighborhood.

The entire repatriation enterprise—unjust, demeaning, and cruel—reflected prevailing attitudes about race and culture that continually confronted Mexican Americans as they tried to make better lives for themselves and their children in the United States. Throughout the 1930s, repatriation raids terrorized communities; split families apart; humiliated men, women, and children; and generally created a climate of hysteria within Mexican American communities. Individuals were arrested as suspected aliens without warrant, held incommunicado without opportunity to seek counsel, and subsequently deported. Entire barrios virtually disappeared. Thousands of Mexican American immigrants were forced out and their property seized.

Esteban Torres, a former U.S. congressman, remembered the day when authorities raided his home in a mining camp in Arizona when he was three years old. They took away his father, sent him to Mexico, and Esteban Torres never saw his father again.

In California alone, nearly half a million individuals were forced from their homes. Most historians now believe that approximately 60 percent of the people sent across the border to Mexico were adults of Mexican descent who were born in America. Large numbers of those rounded up were farmworkers who had been so eagerly recruited years earlier by agribusiness interests who longed for cheap labor.

The repatriation enterprise often involved little advance preparation for the fate of those sent across the border. In November 1932 an internal memo from an immigration inspector reported that almost no food and other provisions had been made for nearly one hundred children who had been placed on a train and sent across the border. From 1929 to 1936 as many as 2 million Mexicans and Mexican Americans were forced to leave the United States.

They were scapegoats, falsely targeted as a major cause for an economic meltdown that had many more legitimate and profound causes. They were treated with little regard for their legal or human rights. Fear gripped communities as individuals left their homes to a country they did not know, most with little money and other resources, and without connections to necessary food and medical assistance and other needs. Once they arrived in Mexico, many children found themselves forced into menial work for survival, with school a secondary consideration. In some cases, families found themselves moved to remote areas where there were few opportunities for work or for the children to be educated.

Cruz Reynoso was one of the children caught up this societal maelstrom. Born to a family of farmworkers in Brea, California, he was less than two years old when he and his large family were sent across the border. When told of the move, he could only ask his parents, "What is Mexico?" Cruz Reynoso became a towering exception to the lamentable fates suffered by many "repatriates." He was able to return to the United States; earned a law degree from the University of California, Berkeley; worked with Cesar Chavez and Dolores Huerta in the farmworkers movement; and became an associate justice of the California Supreme Court. Later, as a professor, he continued to speak out about the treatment of his family and of those thousands of other families who endured unjust and cruel treatment in the 1930s.

So egregious were the violations of civil liberties and constitutional rights during the repatriation years that the state of California eventually apologized, passing the "Apology Act for the 1930s Mexican Repatriation Program." The apology was made in the year 2005. Acknowledging the suffering of thousands of families forced out of their homes, the statement read: "The State of California apologizes to those individuals . . . for the fundamental violations of their basic civil liberties and constitutional rights committed during the period of illegal deportation and coerced emigration. The State of California regrets the suffering and hardship those individuals and their families endured as a direct result of the government sponsored Repatriation Program of the 1930s."

THE BRACERO PROGRAM

As the United States entered World War II in 1941, the government increased mobilization in myriad industries, including agriculture. Government officials asked farmers to produce more vegetables, fruits, and other crops to support the war effort at a time when many U.S. men were being sent to war zones and other men and women were employed in industrial production. Growers in the West and Southwest thus needed additional workers. In an effort to combat this labor shortage, U.S. officials made an important request; it approached the Mexican government about a possible program to provide short-term contracts to Mexican laborers for the duration of the war. No longer were Mexicans the target of removal; they were again a needed commodity.

The bilateral agreement of 1942 was called the Bracero Program. The guest worker idea was not new. Indeed, in 1917, at the same time the United States was beginning to enact stricter immigration policies, U.S. officials negotiated with the Mexican government to provide temporary workers during the U.S. involvement in World War I. The guest worker program outlasted the war, ending in 1922.

The World War II Bracero Program allowed Mexican nationals to take temporary agricultural work in the United States. Over the twenty-two-year life of the program, more than 4.5 million Mexican nationals were legally contracted for work for limited periods in the United States. The workers had to be at least fourteen years old and from an area in Mexico that the Mexican government considered to be suffering serious unemployment. They had to meet certain health requirements and have previous experience working as an agricultural laborer.

Originally expected to last the duration of the war, as mentioned, the Bracero Program would comprise nearly 4.5 million contracts offered to nearly 2 million Mexican men. On paper, the agreement originally stipulated that the workers would

Mexican laborers apply for temporary employment in the United States at a recruiting center in Mexico City, 1942. The men were asked about their experience working in the fields and checked for outward appearances that would indicate such work, such as calloused hands. (Rosenberg, Howard R. "Snapshots in a Farm Labor Tradition," *Labor Management Decisions*, Winter-Spring, 1993)

be provided with sanitary housing, access to medical care, and be paid a wage typical of that paid to workers in the United States for the same type of labor.

Those rules were soon left to the individual states to administer. As many studies and investigations revealed during and after the program had ended, the system did not live up to any of those original guarantees.

Most braceros were experienced farm workers from regions such as Coahuila and other lush agricultural regions in Mexico. To secure a bracero contract, prospective workers had to travel to official recruitment centers in Mexico, often far from their homes. When they reached the centers, Mexican officials often demanded bribes to proceed with the recruitment process.

At the border towns, especially El Paso, Texas, the braceros were registered, given medical exams, fumigated, and shipped to farms mostly across the Southwest and especially to California. Contracts with the braceros were controlled by independent farmers' associations. Most braceros did not fully understand their conditions of employment. For example, braceros could return to their native towns in Mexico in case of emergencies only with written permission from the grower.

A boon to American growers, the system was fraught with harsh treatment of the migrant workers. Mexican nationals, eager for work, were willing to take jobs for meager pay, and many looked back on the experience as an opportunity they would not have otherwise had in Mexico. Yet many often felt as if they were treated like cattle. Cecilio Santillano, an ex-bracero, remembered the trip to the United States in a cattle car, packed like those very same cattle. One government official in the U.S. Department of Labor later referred to the Bracero Program as something akin to legalized slavery.

Once in the United States braceros faced humiliation at every turn. Signs such as "NO Dogs Negroes Mexicans" became common at businesses. Racism was so prevalent that many farmers and other citizens regarded braceros solely in terms of their labor, much as one would regard a farm implement.

They picked lettuce, cotton, tomatoes, asparagus, grapes, and other agriculture staples, enabling extraordinary growth in agribusiness. At first a wartime measure, the Bracero Program was codified into law and expanded, especially in California.

Celedonio Galaviz came to the United States as a bracero in 1951. Without money to make the trip to the border, his family sold their cow for eighty pesos. During his time in the United States, Galaviz had two contracts, the first in Texas and the second in California. His son later talked about the grinding physical demands his father faced, the harsh treatment, and the racial discrimination—using back entrances of establishments and water hoses for drinking water. In time, Galaviz became a U.S. citizen and brought seven family members to the country. For the Galaviz family, the Bracero Program, despite its rigors, had been a door for opportunity.

But at the time of the advent of the Bracero Program, labor conditions for Mexican American workers already in the United States were usually deplorable. In the harvest fields, men, women, and youngsters faced long hours picking crops for little pay and work conditions that shocked many observers. The men, women, and children in those fruit and vegetable fields faced stifling days in the heat, worked in contorted positions with inferior tools that made back injuries routine and lasting, made little in wages, had no benefits, and lived mostly in shacks. In the orchards and fields of the American Southwest and California, they worked a grueling routine, day after day, always without enough food and faced with constant danger of disease or accident. By the time most of the children were twelve years old, they joined their parents in the fields and attended school only when there was no work.

In the 1920s and 1930s some Mexican American leaders had attempted to form labor unions and to organize strikes to combat the power of the growers. In the 1930s they organized some forty agricultural unions in California alone, including El Confederación de Uniones de Campesinos y Obreros Mexicanos (CUCOM) that ultimately included some 5,000 members. These efforts at unionization nevertheless proved futile. In California, strikes by both field workers and those in canneries were quickly broken by the power of the growers, who often hired strikebreaking goons to batter the protestors into submission and by the use of scab labor. And yet, from towns across Mexico, individuals continued to make the trek to the border to find better work and living conditions.

And now, for many Mexican American field workers, the Bracero Program added even more burdens. Because of the financial advantages that the program afforded the growers, many of the local Mexican American workers and other migrant laborers frequently went without jobs. By the late 1950s Mexican American field workers had been replaced by the braceros to a large extent. Signs declaring "No Pickers Wanted" increasingly greeted those looking for work. And after the war ended, growers continued to lobby the federal government to continue the program, falsely claiming that there was still a labor shortage.

Not only were the braceros used by the growers as strikebreakers, but the low wages they received and the conditions under which they worked set a standard of wretchedness. The growers were treating these guest workers like the lowest peons, and it was all being undertaken under a government-sanctioned program.

The dilemma was extraordinary on both sides for the workers. Mexican American workers could not protest wages or working conditions for fear of losing jobs to braceros; the braceros, on the other hand, could not protest their treatment for fear of being returned immediately to Mexico.

Under the Bracero Program, agribusiness abuses continued. Growers used the proximity to the border as a tool for repressing attempts by Mexican immigrants and Mexican Americans to unionize by encouraging an influx of surplus labor to bust unions or by threatening to deport braceros asserting their bargaining rights. Out of such abuses came a renewal of activist energy.

Identifying the "Deportees" in Woody Guthrie's Famous Song

In late January 1948 singer-songwriter Woody Guthrie heard on the radio and read in the papers about a devastating plane crash in Las Gatos Canyon, southwest of Fresno, California, that killed thirty-two. It was the deadliest plane crash in the history of the state. The reporting over the air and in print named the crew members and an immigration official by name; the other twenty-eight individuals were merely referred to as "deportees." Touched by the tragedy and incensed by the coverage that gave no names of the workers, Guthrie wrote a song he called "Deportee (Plane Wreck at Los Gatos)." Aware of the backbreaking and crucial work of those hired under the Bracero Program, Guthrie wrote about their contributions and mocked their treatment not only in life but also in death: "And all they will call you will be deportees."

Guthrie's song became an iconic reminder of the toils of the agricultural laborers who worked the fields and has been recorded by numerous artists from Pete Seeger and Bruce Springsteen to Joan Baez and Woody's son, Arlo.

In 2010 Tim Hernandez, author, assistant professor at the University of Texas El Paso's MFA Program in Creative Writing at the University of Texas El Paso, and the son of a Mexican farm worker, read articles about the plane crash while researching a novel. Like Guthrie, he was outraged that no one had identified those workers, twenty-seven men and one woman, who had perished and who are buried in a mass grave at Holy Cross Catholic Cemetery in Fresno, California.

Hernandez decided to plunge into a painstaking research quest to track down the names of those workers who died and to attempt to trace their identities to their descendants in Mexico. He was able to not only find the names but also locate family members of seven of the workers.

In 2017 the University of Arizona Press published *All They Will Call You*, Hernandez's account of the tragedy and the lives of some of the workers who perished. There is now a new headstone at the grave that includes all thirty-two individuals who lost their lives. On the anniversary of the crash, the names of the victims were read on the floor of California's state capitol. Joan Baez gave a rendition of Woody Guthrie's song.

Activists, reformers, and the immigrant community itself would begin to fight back. They would make demands and seek ways to come together to force change against the kind of prejudice and dehumanization so prevalent in the lives of Mexican Americans. That reform energy and resistance would later manifest in the founding of the United Farm Workers by Cesar Chavez and Dolores Huerta.

The Bracero Program ended briefly in 1947 with approximately 200,000 contract workers having participated in twenty-one states, about half of them in California. In 1951 the program was resurrected because of labor shortages during the Korean War and continued until 1965.

The Bracero Program had a profound impact on migration patterns that would continue into the twenty-first century—Mexicans entering the United States to fill jobs, returning home for periods, and then arriving again in the United States to take on additional work, either legally or otherwise. Many braceros overstayed their work permits and remained in the United States.

The immigration tensions and politics surrounding the border during these years did not abate, but rather became even more intractable and resistant to compromise. The country awaited a fair, humane, and sensible resolution.

DOCUMENTS

President Wilson Vetoes Immigration Legislation, 1915

At the time Woodrow Wilson assumed the office of president in 1913, public opinion had swelled against unrestrained immigration. Not only prejudice against newcomers but also fears about competition for jobs had convinced legislators, both at the state and national level, that some kinds of limits had to be established on immigration policy. Petitions from states and labor groups flooded the offices of members of the U.S. House of Representatives, as well as the Senate, and Congress responded with a number of pieces of legislation. The two presidents who preceded Wilson had vetoed legislation because it had included literacy tests as a requirement for entry into the country. In 1915 Wilson also defied the Congress. His veto stalled the immigration legislation in 1915, but similar legislation was passed over another veto a year later. Wilson's message to Congress in 1915 stands as a reminder of the contributions made by individuals from countries across the world if given a fair opportunity.

To the House of Representatives:

It is with unaffected regret that I find myself constrained by clear conviction to return this bill (HR 6060), "An Act to Regulate the Immigration of Aliens to and the Residence of Aliens in the United States" without my signature. Not only do I feel it to be a very serious matter to exercise the power of the veto in any case because it involves the opposing the signal judgment of the President to the judgment of a majority of both the Houses of the Congress, a step which no man who realizes his own liability to error can take without great hesitation, but also because this particular bill is in so many important respects admirable, well conceived, and desirable. Its enactment into law would undoubtedly enhance the efficiency and improve the methods of handling the important branch of the public service to which it relates. But candor and a sense of duty with regard to the responsibility so clearly imposed upon me by the Constitution in matters of legislation leave me no choice but to dissent.

In two particulars of vital consequence this bill embodies a radical departure from the traditional and long-established policy of this country, a policy in which our people have conceived the very character of their Government to be expressed, the very mission and spirit of the Nation in respect of its relations to the peoples of the world outside their borders. It seeks to all but close entirely the gates of asylum which have always been open to those who could find nowhere else the right and opportunity of constitutional agitation for what they conceived to be the natural and inalienable rights of men; and it excludes those to whom the opportunities of elementary education have been denied, without regard to their character, their purposes, or their natural capacity.

Restrictions like these, adopted earlier in our history as a Nation, would very materially have altered the course and cooled the humane ardors of our politics. The right of political asylum has brought to this country many a man of noble character and elevated purpose who was marked as an outlaw in his own less fortunate land, and who has yet become an ornament to our citizenship and to our public councils. The children and the compatriots of these illustrious Americans must stand amazed to see the representatives of their Nation now resolved, in the fullness of our national strength and at the maturity of our great institutions, to risk turning such men back from our shores without test of quality or purpose. It is difficult for me to believe that the full effect of this feature of the bill was realized when it was framed and adopted, and it is impossible for me to assent to it in the form in which it is here cast.

The literacy test and the tests and restrictions which accompany it constitute an even more radical change in the policy of the Nation. Hitherto we have generously kept our doors open to all who were not unfitted by reason of disease or incapacity for self-support or such personal records and antecedents as were likely to make them a menace to our peace and order or to the wholesome and essential relationships of life. In this bill it is proposed to turn away from tests of character and of quality and impose tests which exclude and restrict; for the new tests here embodied are not tests of quality or of character or of personal fitness, but tests of opportunity. Those who come seeking opportunity are not to be admitted unless they have already had one of the chief of the opportunities they seek, the opportunity of education. The object of such provisions is restriction, not selection.

If the people of this country have made up their minds to limit the number of immigrants by arbitrary tests and so reverse the policy of all the generations of Americans that have gone before them, it is their right to do so. I am their servant and have no license to stand in their way. But I do not believe that they have. I respectfully submit that no one can quote their mandate to that effect. Has any political party ever avowed a policy of restriction in this fundamental matter, gone to the country on it, and been commissioned to control its legislation? Does this bill rest upon the conscious and universal assent and desire of the American people? I doubt it. It is because I doubt it that I make bold to dissent from it. I am willing to abide by the verdict, but not until it has been rendered. Let the platforms of parties speak out upon this policy and the people pronounce their wish. The matter is too fundamental to be settled otherwise.

I have no pride of opinion in this question. I am not foolish enough to profess to know the wishes and ideals of America better than the body of her chosen representatives know them. I only want instruction direct from those whose fortunes, with ours and all men's, are involved.

Woodrow Wilson
The White House
28 January, 1915

Source: Woodrow Wilson: "Veto Message," The White House, January 28, 1915. Printed in George McLean Harper, ed. *President Wilson's Addresses.* New York: Henry Holt & Company, 1918.

Report on Alien Smuggling at the Border, 1924

The practice of smuggling aliens across the U.S.-Mexican border is not a new phenomenon. Headlines in the twenty-first century mostly focus on the illegal entry into the United States by Mexicans or individuals and families from Central America. As an extract of a 1924 report of the Commissioner General of Immigration indicates, the problem a century ago involved large numbers of Europeans who, with the aid of smugglers, made their way to the border to evade immigration laws and quotas that would have excluded them from legal entry. Their journeys, as those of Latinos many years later, were fraught with danger and oftentimes driven by desperation.

In the nature of things the smuggling of Mexican aliens over this border constitutes a problem which will persist as long as there are immigration laws to be enforced . . . The principal alien smuggling problem with which we now have to deal has to do with Europeans seeking illegal entry by way of Mexico, most of whom are prevented by the terms of the restrictive immigration law from securing admission at American seaports.

There are thousands of aliens in Europe who previously resided in this country and who desire to return here, not only because of depressed industrial conditions abroad, but because they know from first-hand experience that labor conditions in this country are far superior to those in Europe, even in normal times. Thousands—perhaps millions—of others possessing general knowledge of the better labor and living conditions in the United States and tired of waging a losing fight with the economic situation existing in their respective countries, have fixed upon the United States as their goal. While the limitations created by the per centum limit act undoubtedly have had the effect of discouraging the majority of such aliens from translating desire into action, they have but intensified the desire as to thousands of others. These latter, upon being denied passport visas by American consuls because of exhausted quotas or for other good reasons, give ready heed to the suggestion of steamship and others that Mexico affords easy access to the United States. Reports received from time to time indicate that there are organized groups of smugglers, having agents throughout Mexico and Europe, who induce inadmissible aliens to take the "via Mexico" route to the United States, one agent forwarding them to another until the border is reached, all for a financial consideration, of course. The majority of the aliens are practically in destitute circumstances and the funds are supplied by friends and relatives in this country . . .

While there is reason to believe that the smugglers who actually bring the aliens across the international boundary line into the United States are operatives of one or more of the organizations whose ramifications extend through Mexico and Europe, this has not been verified by convincing evidence, as in nearly every instance the smuggler as well as the contraband aliens when arrested, claims to have been working independently or with local organizations. Sometimes the same smuggler takes the alien to the point of crossing, leads or carries him across the river at a shallow ford, or leads or conveys him by automobile across the land boundary, and either places him on a train or conveys him by automobile to an interior point. Generally, however, these several transactions are attended to by different persons working with a common understanding.

Some of the border smugglers—most all of whom are Mexican—are typical "Apaches," and when the international line is reached do not hesitate to rob the aliens and then abandon them. There have been unconfirmed reports to the effect that in some instances the smugglers murdered their victims when they had reason to believe that they were in possession large sums of money.

The contraband aliens depart from the border on foot, in automobiles, and in passenger and freight trains. Outgoing passenger trains are inspected by immigration officers at border points, and in numerous instances the contrabands have attempted to deceive the depot inspection officers as to their immigration status, hoping they will be permitted to proceed by train. Generally, however, those aliens who elect to journey to interior by passenger train are first conveyed by automobile beyond the border town, to the nearest point where trains stop, but if there is an inspection officer there, they are transported by automobile around and beyond that inspection point before being placed on the train. This service must then depend upon local peace officers and others, whose good will has been cultivate by immigration officers, to furnish telephonic or telegraphic information about the transaction, which information may result in the alien's apprehension at a station still farther in the interior . . .

It would require a large-sized army to effectively patrol the border line . . . as to prevent illegal entries of aliens, and it would be useless to station a handful of immigration officers on the line expecting them to prevent illegal sentries or even to apprehend aliens in the act of entering without inspection. In actual practice they are placed on the border line or river only when information is received from what is believed to be a reliable source that arrangements have been made by certain smugglers to cross a party of aliens at a given time and place. Generally this information is received from members of another smuggling outfit when competition is so close that one gang, in order to maintain its own profits, will use every means at hand to put another out of business.

It is apparent, therefore, that it is not hard for aliens to cross the international boundary line. The difficulty lies in getting away from the border towns on the American side, as the aliens must do sooner or later, since those places have little or no employment to offer them. In this desert country overland travel must follow certain well-defined routes, so that water, provisions, and gasoline may be procured, and it has been found that the best results in the matter of apprehending aliens after they effect illegal entry are obtained by stationing immigration officers at certain strategic points which must be passed by the aliens traveling overland. The work of the mounted or patrol inspectors is attended by considerable hardship and much danger, as it is often necessary for them to remain on duty long hours without opportunity for rest or sleep, in inclement weather, and the smugglers, who very frequently transport intoxicating liquor or narcotic drugs with the aliens, are desperate characters.

Source: *Annual Report of Commissioner General of Immigration to the Secretary of Labor,* June 30, 1924, Washington, D.C.: Government Printing Office, 1924, 17–19. https://babel.hathitrust.org/cgi/pt?id=uc1.l0054909940;view=1up;seq=13/

Interview with Immigrant Gerardo Chavez, 1979

Gerardo Chavez was born in 1942 in Guadalupe Victoria, Durango, in central Mexico to a farming family. He moved to the border town of Juárez in 1962 and was educated in both Mexican and U.S. schools, finally receiving a BS degree in education at the University of Texas, El Paso. He became a U.S. citizen and a high school teacher. Portions of an interview Chavez gave in 1979 provide a rich portrait of an immigrant's life journey.

Gerardo Chavez by Judy Ann Fuentes March 24, 1979

F: Give some details about your background, parents, where you grew up.

C: I was born in 1952 in Guadalupe Victoria, Durango, in central Mexico. Out of five children, I was the only one born in a hospital. My mother paid with two chickens and a sack of the harvest crop . . . My family remained in Guadalupe Victoria until I was eight or so, moved on to something better. Still, going back to explaining life in the village, when I was growing up we literally lived off the land. We grew our own vegetables, owned cows, a few chickens, and other types of animals. We would make a few dollars or pesos of the harvest. We would go to the city, about the size of Canutillo, Texas. The money from the harvest would last normally until the next harvest, in good years. Items like clothing, work tools, kitchen goods, would be bought during the sale of the harvest. Normally, the harvest provided money, a bit of money for food that could not be grown . . .

Life on the mountains was beautiful, by no means was it a job, it was an undertaking that had to be realized year after year —once again because in the mountains the grazing was better during that time of the year. It was normally very green, enough water for human and animals to live. Cows would daily be milked and the milk would be sent down to the nearby villages to be sold. In this way the people in the mountains would keep in touch with the people in the lower valley.

F: Would you tell us about where and when you attended school?

C: After leaving Guadalupe Victoria, we came to live in Juárez. I was enrolled in school while my family's papers were being handled or somehow being arranged so we could go to the U.S. After living in a rural area, Juárez seemed so different. We lived in a one-room house next to a couple of prostitutes, and on the other side a couple of homosexuals —the street which is called the Ferrocarril or Francisco Villa, which on this side properly known as Stanton Bridge or Santa Fe, one of the two. When we finally came to El Paso, I went to school for about 1 1/2 years and then moved to Odessa, Texas, about 300 miles east of El Paso. I finished high school and enrolled at UTEP, and at this point I have an Education degree.

F: Could you compare the school systems of the two countries?

C: The elementary school in Mexico seemed to be a little bit more advanced because of the simple fact that they obviously teach harder concepts at an earlier age. In the U.S. they were teaching the ABC's, while in Mexico I had been through a more advanced mathematical program and my vocabulary was advanced, in Spanish. The classrooms in Mexico were smaller, dirtier, not air-conditioned, and were fenced in. Textbooks were available, but made with cheaper type of paper, but the material seemed to be of high caliber. The content is what I am referring to. Basically, the concept I am trying to establish is that the Mexican elementary education program even though harder gave general students a better foundation in relation to the basic subjects. In coming to the U.S., I found this situation made the subject taught here a lot easier for me, once again because I had already had a more firm background, therefore I was a little bit more prepared than the other students here in the U.S. This is only a contrast and comparison, once again of elementary school standards. As far as secondary schools, the U.S. surpasses the Mexican type of education. For what reasons, I have not come to a conclusion.

We came to El Paso and I was enrolled in an all-white school. So starting out was very strange to be surrounded by an all-white community. I obviously stood out. These surroundings were strange and harsh. The culture, people and language were very hard to become accustomed to. However, as I said before, the material in school seemed to be easy. Once again the idea was very obvious because my foundation was firm enough to take anything being thrown at me. On the first day of school, I was sent home to take a bath. Hygiene was something I had yet much to learn. We were looked upon as immigrants. In general, they were curious and would come and ask questions we did not understand. Adjustments to the system were slow in as far as communication is concerned, so gradual in fact that I cannot even remember learning the language, the English language.

Everything on the U.S.A. was big, as they say in Texas, everything is big. Everything seemed to be new and fantasized. We kept old habits, like stealing, lack of cleanliness, and general prejudices of the white Anglo-Saxon. I try to keep as many of the traditions, concepts and ideologies as possible. A good example was my name, which was Gerardo, and it remained up to the end of grammar school, at which point I decided to change it to something much easier because so many people seemed to have trouble with it. My name eventually became Jerry, a very Americanized name. It seemed to be much easier for those who called on me. During this time before changing my name, I remember being taken to different classes hoping that someone, somebody, would be able to have the ability to pronounce my name correctly. Eventually, I gave up—Jerry was kept . . .

Eventually, I finished my high school years in Odessa, and because UTEP, university in El Paso was closest and also because it was so close to Mexico and would give me a chance to visit my relatives and visit my old culture, ultimately came and enrolled in El Paso. I graduated, earning my B.S. in Education. . . .

F: How did it feel to be sworn in as a U.S. citizen?

C: At the time of the proceedings when I was asked to reject all of my loyalties and allegiances to Mexico, my past life seemed to have literally flashed before me. It was hard to accept the fact that a decision had to be made to become a citizen of the United States, reject a whole country and nation, which was Mexico; yet, that decision had to be made. Even though I decided to become a U.S. citizen I still feel as if live never left Mexico, because logically, living in the border town or border area always so nearby it is hard to forget. The Southwest in the U.S. is almost like living in Mexico. The culture, language, religion, and philosophy seem to be about the same— not exactly, but it goes hand in hand. The technological advances are modern, in fact, maybe too advanced. However, the geography, the geographical aspects of Mexico and the Southwest are basically the same, which allows me an atmosphere of Mexican heritage.

Source: Interview with Gerardo Chávez by Judy Ann Fuentes, 1979, "Interview no. 641," Institute of Oral History, Special Collections, University of Texas at El Paso, http://digitalcommons.utep.edu/cgi/viewcontent.cgi?article=1658&context=interviews

Recollections of a Border Patrol Officer, David Blackwell, 1987

Born in 1922 in Altoona, Iowa, David Blackwell joined the U.S. Border Patrol in 1944. His career duties of over thirty years in the Border Patrol were largely in Texas in such towns as McAllen, Brownsville, and El Paso. The following is an excerpt of an interview in which he reflected on the role of the Border Patrol and his own impressions of the cross-border labor dilemmas faced by both workers and farmers.

. . . McAllen. I moved there in July of 1945. The principal activity there was farm and ranch check. There was some patrolling of towns and an occasional traffic check for short periods and there was line and river watch. The illegal aliens who both we and the aliens themselves referred to as "wets" were here in just huge numbers you couldn't imagine how many there must have been. At various times through the ensuing years the Sector was beefed up and they would push the population of the aliens down a little bit temporarily and then something would happen and it would bounce right back up and there would be more aliens than before.

The valley economy was largely agriculture and for that matter is still pretty much that way. The farmers welcomed the plentiful and cheap labor and the aliens who did virtually all the work on the farms in packing sheds and other agricultural product related fields did some of the more menial tasks for as little as a dollar a day. Skilled workers or the ones who had a little more on the ball like tractor drivers and irrigators and some of the other skills got up to about $5 per day. A lot of those days were 12 hours long. Wages for farm workers were really low. So low in fact that the local labor force just didn't have any choice but to board up their homes and follow the harvest north every year. About the only ones who could really afford to stay here year round were the crew bosses employed by many farmers and nearly all packing sheds and the harvest contractors who furnished crews of aliens to harvest the crops.

These people had their trucks and every able-bodied person they could find to cram on those trucks would be part of their crew. They kept books for them (the farmers) and took their cut off the top and paid the aliens on a piece meal basis because that's the way they were being paid by the farmers. Employers (again the farmers) liked the set-up because they were paying low wages and had no medical or unemployment insurance responsibilities and almost no responsibility to the alien other than to pay him whatever scale was agreed upon for the work actually produced. Yet they were able to sell their produce on markets away from this area where they were competing with prices based on different and a lot higher labor rates.

When minimum was laws were talked of particularly for farm workers the idea wasn't popular at all in the Valley. The farmers were always opposed and they'd have two or three fall-back positions in their arguments each time. They claimed that having to pay minimum wage even though low would put them out of business; and that the marginal quality of labor just wouldn't support that kind of expense. . . .

As more and more Valley people began benefiting from the illegal alien labor they resorted to ever increasing efforts to shield the aliens from apprehension. Wets were housed in every conceivable kind of shelter; ramshackled abandoned old houses, barns, sheds, chicken coops, abandoned automobile bodies, caves dug into canal banks, and tents. There were some farmers who built little one room houses for their laborers. The larger operators and some really not-so-large also provided a sort of commissary service. It was not unusual when we took aliens to collect their wages and belongings that they had little or no money coming. The wages would be tallied and also the provisions they had used would be tallied and the alien would get whatever the difference might be. Sometimes the difference wasn't very much particularly if we'd had inclement weather and they hadn't worked every day. Then too there was a mark-up on the items they were buying from the farmers. Prices were usually a little higher than regular retail prices in town. There were always a few employers though usually not farmers who would try to completely beat the aliens out of their wages.

Valley farmers had a system well not just the farmers everybody who had a wet whether it was a wet maid wet yardman or farm worker no matter what. Many employers kept these people in line by threatening to report them to La Patrulla or La Migra and back through the years the Mexicans particularly the less educated peon type person from deep in the interior was really frightened by the thought of the Border Patrol and being apprehended by them. One constable in Hidalgo County had a large crew of wets that he farmed out to work on various farms around the area. They were his employees they were his people and he had them in tents way back in deep brush concealed from view by some big canals. You just wouldn't notice them driving by on the road. Someone reported them and when the P.I.s raided the place and caught the wets the wets told us of having been forced to stay there and to work even though they had been abused and underpaid and wanted to go home wanted to quit wanted to leave and were not allowed to. This constable was charged and convicted of some state statute relating slavery. I don't remember just what it was . . .

Another time arrangements were made with Mexican Officials to remove the aliens from the border town by train. You have to realize that the Mexican border town officials didn't want these people any more than the Border Patrol did. The usual procedure was to send the aliens back to Mexico at the Ports of Entry. The numbers were so great that they simply overwhelmed the facilities of border towns like Matamoras, Reynosa and Rio Bravo. The local officials didn't want them there and I'm sure that had some bearing on the Mexican government's decision to allow their citizens to be transported inland from the border. That kind of removal benefited us too because it got the aliens back to the interior where some would stay and not re-enter illegally and it at least delayed those determined to come right back. Mexicans were moved literally by the hundreds and mostly in railway boxcars. The trains were loaded in Reynosa and every two or three cars there was a soldier. It was the soldier's job to keep the people being returned to the interior from getting off the train and walking right back to the border. Since it didn't take long for them to figure out their little . . . system and apply it to that the trains soon began reaching their destination all but empty.

It seems like an inhumane way of dealing with these people but it was not nearly as bad as it would appear. Back at that time most of the aliens we were catching (farm workers) were from interior towns ranches and farms and they had walked all the way from their homes to the border and from the border to wherever they were going in the Valley. For that matter they would go on north always just walking. They walked long distances and really they did it pretty fast and without ever appearing to hurry. They traveled single file and walked along the edge of highways or roads along railroads trails or even across open country and they just kept moving. It was surprising how far they would go in a day . . .

Source: Interview of David Blackwell, May 16, 1987; Courtesy of National Border Patrol Museum, El Paso, Texas, https://www.borderpatrolmuseum.com/interviews/david-v-blackwell.

California "Apology Act" for the 1930s Mexican Repatriation Program, 2005

In 2005 State Senator Joe Dunn successfully shepherded through the California state legislature a bill apologizing on behalf of the state for the unconstitutional removal and coerced emigration of U.S. citizens and legal residents of Mexican descent beginning in the 1930s. The legislation amounted to a remarkable admission of U.S. and state culpability of so-called "Mexican repatriation," a misnomer because a large percentage of those shipped across the border to Mexico had never lived in that country.

THE PEOPLE OF THE STATE OF CALIFORNIA
DO ENACT AS FOLLOWS:

SECTION 1. Chapter 8.5 (commencing with Section 8720) is added to Division 1 of Title 2 of the Government Code, to read:

CHAPTER 8.5. MEXICAN REPATRIATION

8720. This chapter may be cited as the "Apology Act for the 1930s Mexican Repatriation Program."

8721. The Legislature finds and declares all of the following:

(a) Beginning in 1929, government authorities and certain private sector entities in California and throughout the United States undertook an aggressive program to forcibly remove persons of Mexican ancestry from the United States.

(b) In California alone, approximately 400,000 American citizens and legal residents of Mexican ancestry were forced to go to Mexico.

(c) In total, it is estimated that two million people of Mexican ancestry were forcibly relocated to Mexico, approximately 1.2 million of whom had been born in the United States, including the State of California.

(d) Throughout California, massive raids were conducted on Mexican-American communities, resulting in the clandestine removal of thousands of people, many of whom were never able to return to the United States, their country of birth.

(e) These raids also had the effect of coercing thousands of people to leave the country in the face of threats and acts of violence.

(f) These raids targeted persons of Mexican ancestry, with authorities and others indiscriminately characterizing these persons as "illegal aliens" even when they were United States citizens or permanent legal residents.

(g) Authorities in California and other states instituted programs to wrongfully remove persons of Mexican ancestry and secure transportation arrangements with railroads, automobiles, ships, and airlines to effectuate the wholesale removal of persons out of the United States to Mexico.

(h) As a result of these illegal activities, families were forced to abandon, or were defrauded of, personal and real property, which often was sold by local authorities as "payment" for the transportation expenses incurred in their removal from the United States to Mexico.

(i) As a further result of these illegal activities, United States citizens and legal residents were separated from their families and country and were deprived of their livelihood and United States constitutional rights.

(j) As a further result of these illegal activities, United States citizens were deprived of the right to participate in the political process guaranteed to all citizens, thereby resulting in the tragic denial of due process and equal protection of the laws.

8722. The State of California apologizes to those individuals described in Section 8721 for the fundamental violations of their basic civil liberties and constitutional rights committed during the period of illegal deportation and coerced emigration. The State of California regrets the suffering and hardship those individuals and their families endured as a direct result of the government sponsored Repatriation Program of the 1930s.

8723. A plaque commemorating the individuals described in Section 8721 shall be installed and maintained by the Department of Parks and Recreation at an appropriate public place in Los Angeles. If the plaque is not located on state property, the department shall consult with the appropriate local jurisdiction to determine a site owned by the City or County of Los Angeles for location of the plaque.

Source: SB 670. United States Senate. http://www.leginfo.ca.gov/pub/05-06/bill/sen/sb_0651-0700/sb_670_bill_20051007_chaptered.html.

Reflections of Julian Hernandez, a Bracero Worker, 2010

Born to a farming family in the Mexican state of Tlaxcala in 1934, Julian Hernandez, at age twenty-six, joined thousands of young men who gathered at hiring centers in Sonora to sign up for the Bracero Program. In 2010 he sat down for an interview to recall those early days in his life when he crossed the border to work as a farm worker in the program. The following are excerpts from that interview.

When we arrived at the frontier, we were really dirty and once we crossed, they took us to some halls and we spent the night there, but again just on the floor. Well the floor wasn't cold because it was very warm there. But there were a lot of animals, like some kind of big grasshoppers. The floor was full of these animals and throughout the night they would crawl and jump all over us. After that we would go through an inspection where they would take off our clothes, fumigate and examine us. They checked our private parts, searched everything, and covered us with fumigating powder. It wasn't welcoming at all; we were rushed from one place to another. We didn't know that anything like that was going to happen to us, but I didn't like it, there was no need for any of that to happen . . . the longest a Bracero could be hired for was eighteen months and that's how long I lasted. Other than that I didn't know if there was any way of renewing the contract, all they told me was that, that a Bracero could last eighteen months here and no more . . . After that, in two occasions, I went to work in Sacramento in a town named Dixon, California. It's near the University of Davis. I was there for only two months, but I was here in Oxnard for eighteen. The truth is that we earned very little and they still took away money from us . . .

E: And when you got here, you arrived in Oxnard? They took you to a field to work? Or, how did they assign jobs to all those people that came in the train?

J: Well some are taken to northern California, others to Yuma, Arizona, and others to this part of California, all throughout Modesto. I came to Oxnard. Supposedly this area was great, had nice weather, and that's why when the Americans that fumigated us were doing the revisions, they would say rude comments to us. They said: "You guys are lucky; you're going to God's land." I didn't know why, but after I was legalized, I noticed what a great county Oxnard was to live in. The time I have living here I have lived well; I haven't had any serious illnesses or anything like that. I think this climate is great for the organism, this whole place is.

E: How were your experiences on the job?

J: I was used to working in the fields since I was a little kid. I didn't have any difficulties working here in the fields, and that is why they allowed me to work a full year and a half here. They never put up any obstacles and they never said I wasn't hard-working enough not to renew my contract. So in one word, I was tough. I put with any job, and once legalized, I was able to drive tractors and operate different kinds of machinery. It got better once I was legalized . . .

E: In what kind of job did you work in? Picking strawberries?

J: First picking strawberries and then I worked in a job called "con azadón al cortito" thinning-out lettuce, cabbage, and other crops you would find in the fields. When the plants grew we would pull off the petals, leaving just one at a time. That's a job where you have to be bent down the whole day. There were furrows that were almost a half of a mile long and I was only allowed to make two stops in the middle; I would get up and then wouldn't do it again until I finished. But many didn't even get up once; once they went into the furrow they would bend down and remain that way. Our bodies will get more use to being bent down than straight up. They were hard jobs but at the end we got used to them and were able to deal with them . . .

E: And was it easy the thing with the cortito? Or when you stood up in the middle of the furrow, did they scold you or told you off? Did the foreman get mad at you?

J: Well yea, what they want is for us to work from the time we go in until we get out. But I did a good job and, from what I can remember, they never reprimanded me. But yes, it was really tough, that and other things, such as cutting celery. It was hard but I was lucky, I was use to working hard and I had no trouble in that sense. I worked and worked hard, and I had strength and endurance to do so . . .

E: What was easier for you, picking lemons or lettuce?

J: Well picking lemons it's easier because it's done standing up and we don't have to bend down. What it's hard is filling up the big bags with lemons, and inside the gardens it gets really warm and we would sweat all the time. It has its good and bad things because we had to carry the big bag of lemons, because if we went back and forth with just a little at a time, we would fall behind and get nothing done. And it was contract-based there; they would pay us for the boxes we would fill.

E: How much would they pay you for each box?

J: Fourteen cents for each really big box, but everything was done based on the ranchers' own interests. If it was a rich orchard, it had good crops, they would pay us less and if the orchard wasn't so good, that's where they would pay us more. Where it was bad they would pay more and where it was good they would pay less.

E: And how many Braceros where with you? Because you lived in some kind of camp or, where did you live?

J: Yes, in Camp Buena Vista that's still there. There were ten thousand Braceros in three camps. One was called El Pacifico (The Pacific), which was for lemon pickers; another one called El Tres Eses (The Three S's), which was also for lemon pickers; and the last was where the Japanese stayed, but that one was apart from the others. . . . Because of the amount of people that had to go to the bathroom, we were never able to bathe with hot water. We came from work really tired and we had to bathe with cold water because so many people where there, there wasn't any hot water left. Now, go to the bathroom we also had to make line; we had to make line for everything. . . . When we were back home we thought we were going to come here and make money and everything was going to be nice and easy; that wasn't true. Everything that happened to us was all suffering.

E: And everyone always comes from Mexico thinking that they are going to make a lot of money, right?

J: Yes, that's right.

E: Well yea, it's really hard. . . .

J: Well people almost never slept. Some had to get up to get in line to go to the bathroom, others to go to the diner, but it was a continuous hustle almost all day and night . . .

E: What time did you get up to go to work? And at what time did your day end? Regarding your working hours, what was your schedule like?

J: Well before going to work we had to wake up, minimum, at six in the morning. But there were some that would wake up at two or three in the morning to get their lunch and so they wouldn't have to make much line, because they had to be aware of the trucks that arrived from everywhere, sent by ranchers, that would take them to work. The trucks that came for people would be there and ready to go, and the crew whose turn it was to go, had to be prepared; there were three hundred crews. So they had to wake up early but there wasn't a specific hour, some woke up at a certain time and other at another. It depended on the people picking them up, they had to be ready by then but there wasn't a set time to wake up. We had to find a way to wake up on time and not be late.

E: How many hours a day did you work?

J: We worked for ten hours almost always.

E: From dawn to dusk? . . .

E: Is there anything you want to tell me that may have caught your attention during your experience as a Bracero? I don't know, something you liked doing to help you remember your family? Or how did you communicate with your family?

J: Well I only had my dad, mom, and three sisters back in Mexico. It was hard leaving them, but I knew my life would be better here because I knew how to do many things in the fields. You know that when someone gets a job here they don't want you to be absent, and in order to keep that job we have to stay here and go to work. When we finally notice, years have passed and we are old, and that's what happened to me . . .

Source: Interview of Julian Hernandez, November 29, 2010, by Enrica Jimenez. Courtesy of the John Spoor Broome Library, California State University Channel Islands, http://repository.library.csuci.edu/bitstream/handle/10139/6396/HernandezJ_TranscriptEN~.pdf?sequence=2.

7

"Operation Wetback"

- On a day in Chicago in early 1954, a group of individuals of Mexican descent line up to board a U.S. Border Patrol plane at Midway Airport. Their destination: Brownsville, Texas, where they will be loaded onto a boat headed for Veracruz, Mexico.
- During a week in June 1954, the *Los Angeles Times* runs the following headlines:

  June 12, 1954: "Wetbacks' Detention Camp Slated: Elysian Park Will Be Focal Point in Alien Roundup"

  June 18, 1954: "500 Nabbed by L.S. Wetback Raiders: 200 Take Part in Dragnet"

  June 19, 1954: "1259 More Wetbacks Deported in Single Day: Yesterday's Returnees at Nogales Make Up Biggest Number in Current Crackdown"

  June 20, 1954: "Wetbacks Herded at Nogales Camp: 1187 Wait in Blistering Heat for Last Leg of Journey Home"
- Dolores Huerta, whose mother owned a motel in Stockton, California, remembers as a child seeing immigration agents raiding businesses, including a movie house across the street. Those without proper identification were herded off. The raids sowed paralyzing fear in the Mexican American community and helped inspire her later to join Cesar Chavez in founding the United Farm Workers.
- A major Mexican newspaper, *El Universal*, reports in June 1954 that 15,000 Mexican workers thrown out of the United States are living in huts in Tijuana built on the banks of the Tijuana River without basic means of survival.
- Over eighty deportees packed into a freight truck like cows die of heat exposure in Mexicali after crossing the border in 112-degree heat. More would have perished if the Red Cross had not intervened.
- One of the boats packed with deportees headed to Veracruz is described in a hearing in the U.S. Congress as something akin to a slave ship.

It was all part of "Operation Wetback," a major government-led action as degrading to an ethnic group as its name implied. Its complex origins stretch back into the war years of the 1940s, the operation of the Bracero Program, the conflicting needs of a stable work supply for farmers and ranchers, an ever-increasing number of undocumented immigrants, and a growing Cold War paranoia about Communist infiltration into the country through the U.S.-Mexican border. All of it culminated in a massive militarized drive by the administration of President Dwight Eisenhower to send unauthorized Mexicans back to Mexico and to institute a more orderly system to bring workers from Mexico into the United States.

THE RISE OF ILLEGAL IMMIGRATION

During the 1940s, especially during the period of World War II, the needs of farmers, ranchers, and other industries in the United States required the necessary labor to keep the country's economic system on course, and that need was filled by Mexicans crossing the border. Under the Bracero Program, a series of arrangements between the U.S. and Mexican governments, Mexican laborers were allowed to work in the United States under short-term contracts.

The system, at least on paper, guaranteed a minimum wage, essential housing, and food, as well as fair and humane treatment. Although the program was successful enough to last well beyond the war period, it produced a deeply concerning unintended consequence for both countries—an aggressive influx of laborers unable to find work under the Bracero Program who crossed the border illegally without proper authorization.

When word of the Bracero Program spread across Mexico, far more workers attempted to join the program than either Mexico or the United States had anticipated. When thousands of men, women, and children arrived at processing centers only to be told that the number of bracero contracts had been exhausted, large numbers decided to cross the border without authorization.

The problem was not only confined to the individuals seeking work but also to employers in the United States who exacerbated the problem by hiring the unauthorized laborers at cheaper wages and with less oversight and compliance regulations than dictated by the Bracero Program. After all, hiring such individuals reduced annoying paperwork and other overhead costs and allowed growers almost free rein in how they paid and housed the workers.

But the growing illegal immigration problem concerned a number of interest groups. U.S. labor unions complained that unauthorized laborers from Mexico would take jobs from members of their unions. Social service agencies were increasingly worried that growing numbers of Mexicans outside the Bracero Program would stretch the resources available to help the poor and destitute. Many U.S. members of Congress also worried that an open border invited not only a tide of illegal Mexican immigrants but also was an inviting target of entry for possible Communist infiltrators. And, as always, the influx of Mexicans sparked outrage by nativists and other xenophobic groups decrying a supposed coarsening of American culture by outsiders.

Undocumented migrants crossing the Rio Grande near El Paso, Texas, 1948. Because of the low water levels along many sections of the Rio Grande in Texas, those locations became favorite spots for migrants seeking to cross the border. (Bettmann/Getty Images)

Indeed, it was in the early 1940s that the term "wetback" became a popular slur on Mexicans who crossed the border illegally by swimming across the Rio Grande and were thus readily identifiable by their wet clothes. And with the derogatory term came the characterizations among many north of the border. Wetbacks were inclined to criminal behavior, the stereotype went; they carried disease, were ignorant, and even lazy (a charge reeking of lunacy, since Mexican laborers were far more productive in the harvest fields than Anglo workers). They were called "aliens," a term not unlike that applied to fictional creatures from outer space. Their influx into the country was seen by the press, in government, and in the public as an "invasion" by "hordes" or as a threatening "peril." Border Patrol agents simply called them "wets."

But the illegal immigration problem was not limited to U.S. interests; Mexican groups were also concerned about unsanctioned migration across the U.S.-Mexican border and pressured their government to do something about it. Mexican growers, especially near the border in the Mexicali Valley of Baja California and the Matamoros region in Tamaulipas, complained that cotton was dying in their fields because Mexican workers chose to seek better wages in the United States.

After extensive diplomatic negotiations, both through personal meetings of representatives from the two countries and in messages, U.S. and Mexican officials increased their efforts to patrol the border. In 1943 the U.S. Border Patrol launched an intensive effort to round up undocumented Mexican nationals. During the 1940s apprehension and deportation rates announced by the Immigration and Naturalization Service (INS) increased dramatically as the Border Patrol transferred much of its force to the southern border. Nevertheless, even though deportations increased, many of those dropped off across the border simply found ways to return again. With a Border Patrol force not equal to the task of preventing reentry, much of the roundup of aliens had little effect.

To counter the situation, in 1945 U.S. and Mexican officials agreed on a system of deportation that actively involved both countries. The Border Patrol was tasked with deporting Mexican nationals who were residents of the Mexican states of

Sonora, Sinaloa, and Jalisco through Nogales, Arizona. Residents of southern and eastern Mexican states were funneled through El Paso, Texas. At the deportation points, Mexican immigration officials then arranged for transportation of the deportees, usually by train, into the interior of Mexico. Although officials of both countries lauded the new cross-border collaboration, reports began to surface that the transport train trips into the Mexican interior were often scenes of misery and tragedy, as few of the trains were equipped with adequate food and medicine, and many of the deportees ended up in places totally unfamiliar to them.

Despite efforts to find an adequate solution to the illegal immigration problem, by 1946 the Mexican government made it clear that the system was still riddled with holes and that the U.S. Border Patrol was not living up to its role in locating large numbers of Mexican nationals outside the Bracero Program who were crossing the border and draining Mexican farmers and other businesses of needed laborers. U.S. leaders countered that the Mexican government had not provided a sufficient force to prevent their own people from illegally crossing the border.

Much of the continuing flow of illegal workers was the result of concerted efforts by U.S. agribusiness leaders and growers who continued to skirt the Bracero Program and hire undocumented workers at cheaper wages. Often, especially in Texas, growers would hide workers; some even set up elaborate radio systems to alert workers of Border Patrol officers approaching the fields.

In 1947 the INS reached a somewhat novel idea to deal with the illegal immigration problems. The process was essentially to "dry out," or legalize, the wetbacks and enter them into the Bracero Program. The arrangement required unauthorized immigrants to return to Mexico and then once again enter the United States, this time as braceros. In practice, however, the new system became almost comical. The so-called "illegals" would be brought to a process center at the border and then asked merely to touch a toe on Mexican soil. This action then officially fulfilled the obligation to return to Mexico, and they were allowed to become braceros.

When Mexican officials decried this obvious skirting of the Bracero Program's original agreements, U.S. officials dropped the experiment and turned to aggressive deportation sweeps. In the spring and summer of 1947, Border Patrol agents rounded up and deported thousands of Mexicans, especially in the states of California and Texas. In October 1948 an estimated 4,000 Mexicans were moved out of the country in a single sweep.

Despite the intensified efforts by a still-undermanned Border Patrol, the flow of immigrants continued to such an extent that the Mexican government, concerned about its depleting labor supply, declared a national emergency. The Mexican military then increased its own forces on the border. Mexican authorities built wire-enclosed detention facilities to hold the deportees until they could be herded onto trains and sent to Mexico's interior.

By 1951 both the Mexican and U.S. governments were using daily airplane transfers of Mexicans into the interior from airfields in Brownsville, Texas, and one near El Centro, California. Nevertheless, the INS reported in 1952 that the trend line for illegal immigration was continuing to climb, with new arrivals not only seeking work along the borderlands but also traveling in greater numbers across the country.

The border raids were particularly provocative to South Texas farmers and ranchers, who began to complain vociferously that Border Patrol agents were using what amounted to "Gestapo tactics" in apprehending Mexican workers, the lifeblood of the harvesting seasons in the region for the growers. The relationship between the Border Patrol and the South Texas agribusiness interests became extremely heated, especially in cases where agents raided fields and stopped and questioned individuals simply because of their racial characteristics, a practice, many argued, that violated the U.S. Constitution's Fourth Amendment protections against unreasonable searches and seizures. Some growers insisted that the Border Patrol, in its aggressive posture, was turning South Texas into something of a police state. Border Patrol officials, in response, threatened to station two-man teams on individual ranches if the grower refused to use braceros instead of unauthorized migrants. The teams would stay until the grower signed a pledge to use braceros instead of unauthorized workers.

In June 1950, pressured from all sides by the immigration issue, President Harry Truman signed an executive order establishing a President's Commission on Migratory Labor. Among its charges, the commission was asked to determine "whether sufficient numbers of local and migratory workers can be obtained from domestic sources to meet agricultural labor needs and, if not, the extent to which the temporary employment of foreign workers may be required to supplement the domestic labor supply" and "the extent of illegal migration of foreign workers into the United States and the problems created thereby, and whether, and in what respect, current law enforcement measures and the authority and means possessed by Federal, State, and local governments may be strengthened and improved to eliminate such illegal migration."

The commission interviewed a wide variety of individuals involved in border commerce, from ranchers and farmers, to law enforcement officials, to individuals who had actually migrated to the United States from Mexico either under the Bracero Program or as illegal entrants into the country.

The commission learned that since 1944, the magnitude of unauthorized immigration had reached new and concerning levels, what amounted to "an invasion," to quote several witnesses. It learned that the immigration labor force from various parts of Mexico was crucial not only to those agribusiness interests north of the border but also to those south of it. It learned that most of the migrants came in small groups without the aid of smugglers and that the desert areas near El Paso, Brownsville, and Calexico were major entry points. It learned that elements of fraud and deceit plagued the Bracero Program, from bribes and illegal fees paid by migrants to Mexican officials south of the border to improper treatment of workers and fraudulent withholding of portions of wages by growers to their workers north of border. It also learned that wages for field workers in the lower Rio Grande Valley were sometimes as low as fifteen cents an hour.

In its final report, the commission recommended a number of protections to domestic farm laborers as well as the reduction of the use of Mexican workers in the United States. Although the Truman administration tried to convince Congress of the efficacy of the changes recommended by the commission, the power of the growers' interest stalled legislation. In fact, the Bracero Program was extended.

After he assumed the presidency in 1953, Dwight Eisenhower sent Attorney General Herbert Brownell on a tour of the Southwest to ascertain, as best he could, the implications of undocumented immigration. Already armed with the report of the Migratory Commission, Brownell and his team talked to growers, government officials, law enforcement agents, and social service officers. He considered a report prepared by the Border Patrol and Southern California officials that argued that desperate individuals who had entered the United States without authorization were a threat in many ways: committing crimes simply to survive; contracting and spreading disease; and, in the case of destitute females, adding to the prostitution problem. Brownell reported back to the president that the immigration system was broken.

In late 1953 the chief of the U.S. Border Patrol proposed a fix. Harlon Carter, the son of a Border Patrol officer, brought a life history of dealing with Mexicans along the Texas border to his position. As a matter of fact, as a teenager he had hunted down a Mexican youth who had been loitering around the Carter property and shot him dead. Found guilty of murder, Carter spent two years in jail before being released after a court found a technicality in his murder trial. Following his father's lead, he later joined the Border Patrol, rose in the ranks, and in 1950 became the agency's chief.

In July 1953 Carter came up with a plan to rid the border of undocumented Mexican nationals. He even came up with a codename: "Operation Cloudburst." Essentially the plan involved sealing off the border, with thousands of U.S. military and National Guard troops building fences along the more porous areas of infiltration along the border, reinforcing the protection through the use of jeep patrols and radio-equipped towers, maintaining roadblocks on major roadways leading into the United States to inspect cars and trucks for illegal immigrants, and sending the deportees to the interior of Mexico by air and ship.

The plan had a major flaw. There was an 1878 law that prohibited the use of the U.S. Army as a tool for domestic law enforcement. Carter decided to overcome the obstacle by asking President Eisenhower to authorize such a plan through a presidential proclamation. Expecting the president to accede to the request, Carter sent a force of Border Patrol agents to California to prepare for the undertaking.

After weighing the possible proprieties of such a request, and despite the support of Attorney General Herbert Brownell, Eisenhower, one of the country's greatest military generals, refused to use the army for this purpose. He did not issue the proclamation.

Instead of Operation Cloudburst, the United States would embark on a different course. It would be called "Operation Wetback."

"OPERATION WETBACK" IN FORCE

In May 1954 General Joseph M. Swing was named by President Eisenhower to head the INS. Swing had been among Eisenhower's fellow classmates at graduation from the U.S. Military Academy at West Point in 1915. They had remained close friends.

The Curious Gun Career of Harlon Carter: From Prison to the Border Patrol to Operation Wetback and to the National Rifle Association

Harlon Carter and guns—it was as if he was born with a hand curled to carry one. The son of a Border Patrol agent in the border town of Laredo, Texas, Harlon lived in an area in which 90 percent of the residents were of Mexican heritage. Yet the Anglo leaders in Laredo, mostly veterans of the Texas Rangers, routinely intimidated, often brutalized, and, on occasion, lynched members of the Mexican population. One of those leaders was Harlon's father, Horace.

On March 3, 1931, at the age of seventeen, Harlon got into an altercation with three young Mexican boys between the ages of twelve and fifteen who were walking around the neighborhood. With harsh words escalating, Harlon hoisted his shotgun and blasted to death fifteen-year-old Ramón Casiano.

Sent to prison for the murder, Harlon spent only two years behind bars. He was later released by an appeals court judge who determined that his trial had been tainted because the trial judge's instructions to the jury had been incomplete and the jury had not been duly instructed on the meaning of "self-defense." In 1936 Carter followed his father's footsteps and became a member of the Border Patrol, where he rose quickly in its ranks. By 1950 he had become the organization's chief.

When President Eisenhower decided to take firm action against vastly increasing numbers of unauthorized migrant workers from Mexico crossing the border in the United States to find work opportunities, it was Carter, from his position as head of the Border Patrol, who vigorously promoted the idea of using the U.S. military to fend off what he saw as an alien invasion of the country. It was to be called "Operation Cloudburst," and it reflected Carter's militant stance against Mexican immigrants, a sentiment he had harbored from his earliest days.

When Eisenhower balked at allowing the U.S. military to run the operation using the U.S. Army, the plan to cleanse the border of illegal immigrants morphed into Operation Wetback and its heralded deportation of hundreds of thousands of Mexicans. Carter would later boast, with much bravado and lack of full understanding, that the immigration problem on the border had been solved.

Following his service with the Border Patrol, Carter became director of the southwestern region of the INS. But in his later years, his work would not be as a public servant. He began to work for a century-old organization founded by veterans of the Civil War and devoted to the mission of promoting and training individuals to safely use rifles for hunting as a sport. The emphasis was on safety, marksmanship, conservation, and the brotherhood between fellow hunters. The organization was the National Rifle Association (NRA).

First joining the national board of the NRA in 1961, Carter became the director of the organization's lobbying arm, the Institute for Legislative Action, in 1975. In 1977 Carter and a group of hardline activists allied with the Republican Party pulled off what amounted to a takeover of the NRA.

In the history of gun annals, it became known as the "Revolt at Cincinnati." At the 1977 NRA convention, a rump caucus of gun rights radicals took over the meeting and the organization. No longer would the focus of the NRA be on hunting, sport, marksmanship, and conservation; it would now be on a militant stance against any kind of gun control measures and any infringement on what the radicals saw as the meaning of the Second Amendment of the Constitution.

Carter, now known affectionately by his supporters as "Bullethead," became executive vice president of the NRA and its leading spokesman. The concept was simple, he affirmed: "No compromise. No gun legislation." For example, his answer to those who proposed background checks for gun purchasers to prevent weapons landing in the hands of violent criminals and the mentally ill was that any resulting danger was the "price we pay for freedom."

Carter led the NRA for four years. When the *Laredo Times* published an article detailing Carter's killing of fifteen-year-old Ramon Casiano years earlier, Bullethead first denied it, claiming that the name of the person who had committed the crime on the border was named Harlan and not Harlon. After further investigation by the press provided indisputable facts, Carter changed his story, admitting his crime and saying that he regretted it.

Carter was, in a sense, Wayne LaPierre, the later hardline leader of the NRA, before there was a Wayne LaPierre. When Carter died in 1991, LaPierre hailed him as a hero.

In 2016 the band Drive-By Truckers, an alternative country/Southern rock band, recorded an album called *American Band*. A song on the album memorializes, not Harlon Carter, but the teenager he killed, Ramon Casiano. Written by Mike Cooley, the song talks of the violence on the border, deportation, the injustices suffered by Mexicans, the life needlessly taken, and the continued hatred by some. "Someone killed Ramon Casiano," the song ends, "and Ramon still ain't dead enough."

Swing was no stranger to the U.S.-Mexican border. As a lieutenant under General John J. Pershing during the 1916 expedition into Mexico, he became familiar with much of the land south of the border and of Mexican-U.S. relations.

Later he served as a captain in the U.S. field artillery in France during World War I and was a major general of the 11th Airborne Division in the Southwest Pacific during World War II. Following the war he served as commandant of the Army War College.

Eisenhower felt confident that Swing could take on this enormous challenge with the kind of effective leadership he had demonstrated throughout his military career. Swing did not wait long to begin an operation that became more complex than it appeared on the surface.

The program aimed to reduce the flow of undocumented Mexican workers across the border with military-like precision and force, while, at the same time, actively attempting to persuade employers from hiring such laborers and to bolster the Bracero Program. His plan met fierce resistance from state and federal legislators representing districts where the demands of agricultural laborers was most intense.

Swing's strategy early on was to inform audiences along the border, especially farmers and ranchers, that the purpose of "Operation Wetback" was not to deny these business leaders access to labor but to make the labor process legal under U.S. law. Using undocumented labor, Swing reminded his listeners, was against the law. The Bracero Program, already in place, was the proper legal route, he insisted, for U.S. business leaders to attain their necessary workers from Mexico, not from what was, in a sense, a black market.

In the beginning Swing hoped to persuade many of the business leaders to adhere to the demands of the INS; he knew, however, that the process was going to be

U.S. officials explaining contract terms for new bracero workers, 1943. Launched in 1942, the farm labor Bracero Program lasted two decades and brought much needed Mexican guest workers to the United States. (Rosenberg, Howard R. "Snapshots in a Farm Labor Tradition," *Labor Management Decisions*, Winter-Spring, 1993)

anything but smooth. A large percentage of the farmers and ranchers disliked intensely the obligations imposed by the Bracero Program to provide proper wages, housing, and other necessities. Especially in Texas, Swing knew, persuasion would not be enough. However, the loss of undocumented labor, he believed, would force the business leaders reluctantly into compliance.

Swing announced that Operation Wetback, using the necessary paramilitary strategy without federal troops as proposed by Operation Cloudburst, would rid the country of the scourge of illegal immigration. The operation would proceed with the full knowledge and cooperation of the Mexican government. This would be an aggressive, full-throttle, all-out sweep nationwide using all the necessary resources that the INS and the Border Patrol could muster to send back to Mexico those who had crossed the border illegally. But it would also be an attempt to provide through the Bracero Program the immigrant labor necessary for U.S. growers and ranchers and other businesses to carry on their work without the use of undocumented "aliens."

The operation began with startling intensity. Swing had moved large numbers of Border Patrol agents from the Canadian border and from Florida's Gulf Coast to increase the force on the Mexican border. He assembled mobile task forces prepared to use trucks, jeeps, and even aircraft to round up unauthorized Mexican workers. This was not a novel approach—this kind of deportation drive had been used to some effect throughout the 1940s. This time, however, Swing advertised in advance the determination to drive the "illegals" out of the country through overwhelming force never before seen on the border.

Swing made major efforts to convince South Texas farmers and ranchers that their use of undocumented laborers was about to come to an end, despite their vociferous opposition. He assured them, nevertheless, that the Bracero Program, the legal guest worker alternative to using "wetbacks," could be modified to some extent to reduce the burdensome requirements and paperwork it entailed.

Swing and his deputies planned to launch Operation Wetback in California and Arizona, with the determination that Texas farmers and ranchers, seeing the widespread offensive against illegal immigration along the border and in other parts of the country, would gradually see the futility of further resistance and accept the inevitable—the use of braceros rather than "wetbacks."

By the time the deportation sweeps reached Texas, Swing anticipated that the INS would make sufficient modifications to the Bracero Program to placate the protests from South Texas. Reluctantly the Texas farmers and ranchers would see that the glory days of hiring near-slave labor without many restrictions was, at least for the time being, coming to an end.

As far as those in the Mexican communities in the Southwest were concerned, Operation Wetback brought vivid memories to workers and their families, either through personal experience or from the stories handed down, reminders of the terror inflicted on those communities in the infamous "repatriation" program of the 1930s. It did not take long for many in those communities to "self-deport," as Swing had hoped when he began to trumpet the call for a spectacular show of force, an all-out, warlike attack.

The exodus of those in Mexican communities in the first few days of the operation was especially noticeable as word circulated among residents that it might be the better of two evils for workers and their families to leave the United States on their own volition and decide where to relocate than to suffer this oncoming rabid deportation force that could drop them somewhere in central Mexico.

In mid-June agent patrols launched the actual raids in California and Arizona, using Nogales, Arizona, as the main portal through which the captured were herded. It was a time when public parks became detention centers; when fields were suddenly overrun with agents; when low-flying planes circled suspicious groups of brown people; when trucks on loan from the armed services filled with people about to leave the United States under duress; when even some Native Americans on reservations were paid $3.00 a head by the Border Patrol for any unauthorized immigrant they found hiding; when employees in hotels and restaurants and other establishments in cities and small towns were suddenly approached by INS officials for fingerprinting; when busboys and waiters and dishwashers were suspects; when factories lost workers who did not pass muster with regard to their legal status; when not only men were deported but also entire families; and when ships loaded with deportees sailed from Port Isabel, Texas, to Veracruz to unload their cargo of people totally unfamiliar with the area.

Some of those cargo ships, according to news reports, crowded as many as 500 Mexicans into boats that normally carried fewer than 100. And each of the ships had very few lifeboats, inadequate toilet facilities, and little food. Reports also circulated that a number of those passengers had either jumped to their death amidst such horrible conditions or had fallen into the waters.

In addition it became clear that the deportation sweeps in some areas were relatively indiscriminate in determining the legal status of residents. Many U.S. citizens, as well as their children who were born on U.S. soil, suddenly found themselves in a foreign country.

A number of Latino organizations, such as the League of United Latin American Citizens, and the American G.I. Forum had first supported a vigorous effort to halt unauthorized immigrants crossing the border. They not only feared that the influx of workers would hurt Mexican American workers already struggling in the United States but would also deprive Mexican industries the necessary labor to thrive. After some of the stories about overcrowded boats and family displacement and racial profiling that tore through and devastated Mexican American communities began to spread during Operation Wetback, those organizations began to air grievances against the cruelty and anti-Mexican hatred that had been spawned by the operation.

Later, Attorney General Herbert Brownell would declare that "Operation Wetback" was accomplished skillfully and quickly and at the same time every safeguard was employed to make certain the aliens were treated humanely and fairly. For thousands of Mexican workers stranded in places in Mexico where they had never been before with limited means of survival, the claim seemed ludicrous.

The whole unfolding scene became a bonanza for newspaper reporters and radio news broadcasts. At one point, Swing pronounced that Operation Wetback would drive at least 1 million undocumented Mexican nationals out of the United States. A Border Patrol spokesman boasted that the agency was capturing 2,000 undocumented immigrants a day.

The sweeps were in no way confined to the U.S. Southwest. In major cities such as St. Louis, San Francisco, Kansas City, and Spokane, large numbers of undocumented Mexicans were rounded up. Chicago was one of the focal points of the program in the Midwest. By the end of 1954, as many as three planeloads of Mexican workers were flown out of Midway Airport a day.

Civil rights protections were largely ignored in the frenzied movement of people. Hundreds of American citizens who could not readily produce documentation were swept up in the operation and sent to Mexico. In Nuevo Laredo, a labor leader from Mexico said that trucks were unloading "wetbacks" like cows about fifteen miles from the border and dropping them into the desert. Reports from Mexicali talked about thousands roaming the streets with little or no idea of what to do next.

Although the U.S. and Mexican governments had been communicating long before Operation Wetback about the immigration problem and had been attempting to find solutions acceptable to both sides, the excesses of the operation and the human misery inflicted stretched the bounds of cooperation. Soon, the massive military-style dragnet had run its course and the INS, with Swing leading the chorus, simply declared victory—that the operation had been an enormous success and that the border was now clear of illegal immigrants. In his recounting of the operation in the 1955 INS Annual Report, Swing boasted that the "wetback" problem no longer existed and that the border was secure.

Of course, the truth was not nearly so simple. In terms of the number of illegal immigrants that were in the United States and others who crossed the border illegally in the next few years, the positive assessment issued universally by Republicans, from Attorney General Brownell to General Swing to Harlon Carter, seemed on the mark.

And yet Operation Wetback had not merely been a magisterial deportation sweep that sent hundreds of thousands across the border; it had also been a drive to empower a Bracero Program that had lost the support of many ranchers and growers who had turned to illegal immigrants for a large part of the workforce. For a time, the bolstered Bracero Program did have the effect of limiting illegal immigration. Nevertheless, it was a part-time fix. The border was not secured for the long term. And as the support for a guest worker program gradually waned in the United States in the coming years, as the Bracero Program officially ended in the 1960s and guest worker opportunities were reduced, the incentives for increased illegal crossings by Mexicans seeking work opportunities increased. By then, the effects of Operation Wetback had long since vanished.

DOCUMENTS

Report on Use of Wetbacks by Texas Farmers and Ranchers Submitted as Evidence to Commission on Migratory Labor, November 1949

In June 1950 President Harry S. Truman signed an executive order establishing a Commission on Migratory Labor. Especially along the U.S.-Mexican border the problem surrounding the labor of Mexicans, both authorized and those who had entered the United States without authorization, was a burgeoning problem. Bringing together the views of various communities affected by the problem—ranchers, growers, Mexican American citizens, the Mexican government, and migratory workers—the committee, through hearings and much research, vividly illustrated in its work the confounding dilemmas surrounding the Bracero Program, the considerable influx of unauthorized laborers, and the mixed interests and loyalties held by the various groups. In its final report, the commission emphasized that the "wetback" phenomenon had become a national crisis and that intervention by the government was of paramount importance.

In gathering information about the migratory labor conditions in the Southwest, a variety of statements, depositions, and research papers passed through the hands of the commission members. One of those was a research paper authored by scholars at the University of Texas. The paper illustrated the complexity of the immigration issue. While condemning the influx of workers outside the Bracero Program, the work also illustrated the wretched poverty and near state of peonage suffered by the workers themselves once they became workers in the United States. The following is an excerpt.

Introduction

One of the most serious problems facing the people of Texas is the presence in the state of a very large, but as yet undetermined, number of wetbacks—illegal aliens who cross the border from Mexico mainly in search of agricultural employment, but who are to be found in many cities of the state, and in many non-agricultural jobs. The Spanish-speaking Texans are not the only ones affected. Every citizen of the state, Spanish and English-speaking alike, shares, to a greater or lesser extent, in the evil effects and devastating repercussions that derive from the presence in the state of from a hundred thousand to a half a million homeless wanderers—men, women, and children, without legal status, without skills, without knowledge of our ways and customs, without protection, and without opportunity for improving their condition. No citizen of the state, or of the other states into which many of the wetbacks eventually drift, can escape the consequences which appear in the form of poverty, disease, slums, ignorance, dependency, low wages, and social and personal disorganization, not only for the wetbacks themselves, but for the Spanish-speaking citizens whom they displace, and the English-speaking Texans in whose communities they, and the thousands of displaced persons, come to live.

No one knows how many wetbacks there are in Texas, but everyone who has given thought to the problem is aware that the number is almost unbelievably large. Low as are the wages which they can command for their services, these low wages are still several times greater than could be earned in Mexico. This economic differential becomes a powerful attractive force, drawing the laborers across the border in numbers which the Immigration Service and Border Patrol, with their present staffs, (approximately one patrol officer for each forty miles of border), could not control, even if they always wanted to . . .

With about 200,000 Mexican aliens being caught and deported to Mexico each year, it is evident that several times this number must cross the border during the course of any given year . . . The life of the wetback who escapes the attention of the Immigration Service is not pleasant. He has no rights and no privileges. He must stay off the highways and out of the towns. He must work for whatever is offered under whatever conditions the employer chooses to provide. His home is a shack or a brush shelter or a blanket thrown beside a ditch. He owns nothing except that which he carries. His wife and his children, when he has them, share his life.

Johanna Mertens, a social worker of the American Friends Service Committee, described a wetback camp which housed some thirty families who had lived for about five years in the brush a few miles this side of the border in Hidalgo County. The thatched shelters, she said, were similar. She states: "Each had one narrow bed built of two sawhorses and planks, covered with no more than a flannel sheet or blanket. The small babies slept in a suspended wooden box. The large families had nothing else but the hard wooden floor on which to sleep and eat . . . Most shelters had a makeshift bench, stool or chair. Each had an indoor fireplace with no chimney outlet. Thus the interior of the hut soon blackened darkening the already cave-like atmosphere. The two unprotected openings, serving as window and door, are the only source of light other than burning candles. . . . There are no cupboards . . . I saw no ice box nor even any food, with the exception of frijoles and tortillas. . . . A rain irrigation canal borders the camp on the East. This is the only source for washing, drinking, and cooking water . . ."

The condition of the wetback is incredibly bad, but his condition is only one aspect of the problem resulting from the uncontrolled importation of contraband labor. Much more important are the effects on the resident population and on their institutions in areas where the wetbacks are concentrated. No citizen, who wants to live in even a minimum of comfort and decency, can compete with the wetback wage scale. With an oversupply of cheap, unprotected labor always present, organization of workers is impossible, individual bargaining is futile. There are only two choices: work for what the wetback works for and live as he lives, or leave the area. Many accept the former alternative; those who can, choose the second and become displaced persons. Either choice results in undesirable conditions for the individual and social problems for the community. For those who stay and attempt to compete, there is poverty and all the evils that are associated with it: disease, ignorance, child labor, crime, and delinquency, lack of concern with civic affairs, slum conditions, and always there is the weight of a deadened, passive, apathetic population to be carried on the shoulders of the other elements of the community. For those who leave, there are similar problems of health, education, welfare, and housing—problems that affect both these migrating displaced families and those in the communities to which they go.

In every piece of fruit, every vegetable, every product of any kind that is produced in areas of wetback concentrations there is a hidden cost that never appears in the retail dealers' price tags. It is a cost that appears in the form of higher taxes for welfare and other community services; in illnesses and deaths from dysentery, tuberculosis, and, more recently, polio; in adult populations of citizens who cannot speak the language of the country in which they were born; in the labor of children and consequent denial to them of opportunities for education and mental and physical development; in the slums of San Antonio and Corpus Christi and El Paso; and in the maintenance in much of Texas of a permanent minority group, the majority of whom are citizens, who are denied many of the opportunities, rights, and privileges that their fellow citizens enjoy. One begins to wonder if grapefruit and cotton are worth it . . .

It is our opinion that the wetbacks constitute the outstanding issue facing the State of Texas today. It is true that there are other problems of a more spectacular nature, and which receive, or have received recently, more public attention—the tidelands question, the recent election of a US. Senator, the incidence of polio throughout the state. But there is no problem which occupies such a fundamental position in relation to other problems in the fields of health, housing, education, labor organization, politics, and social and economic relationships as does that of the wetback.

For the wetback is a major source of social and economic infection. He is a focal point from which flow social poisons that manifest themselves in symptoms of various kinds: disorganized, migratory populations; segregated schools; hostilities and tensions; political apathy; economic waste; peonage; and a divided citizenry.

A large part of the economy of central, western, and south Texas is being founded upon most dangerous ground: the shifting quicksand that is the wetback—contraband labor. The cotton and citrus industries, vegetable farming, and similar enterprises there, by the shortsighted dependence on wetback labor, are sowing the wind—and, as a result, the state and nation will long reap a whirlwind of social misery and unrest, of expensive remedial action, of international embarrassment. Those enterprises, by their very dependence on wetbacks and on modified peonage, are exposing themselves to economic disaster. The flow of contraband labor, like that of contraband goods, is subject to legal sanctions and to control; and a sudden turn of events could bring a sudden removal of this mainstay of a warped economy. . . .

Source: "The Problem of Migratory Farm Labor in the United States, 1948–1953," Excerpt of Report issued to the Commission on Migratory Labor, "Preliminary Report to the Advisory Committee, Study of Spanish Speaking People," The University of Texas, 1–4; The Harry S. Truman Library, Philleo Nash to David H. Stowe, with attachments, November 18, 1949. https://www.trumanlibrary.org/whistlestop/study_collections/migratorylabor.

Report of Attorney General Herbert Brownell to Congress on Operation Wetback, 1956

As secretary of state in the Eisenhower administration, Herbert Brownell held a vital position with regard to immigration policy and in facing the increasing realization that the U.S.-Mexican border was an uncontrolled sieve that allowed a veritable flood of unauthorized migrants into the United States. It was, he was convinced, a situation creating social, economic, and legal ramifications that had to be addressed. Born in Nebraska, a Yale University law graduate and prestigious New York lawyer, and a member of the New York State Assembly, Brownell was a long-time Republican insider. He managed Thomas Dewey's governor's race in New York and his presidential campaign in 1948, was national chairman of the Republican Party, and was an early and robust advocate on behalf of Dwight Eisenhower's rise to the party's nomination for president in 1952.

Given his close relationship to Eisenhower, Brownell's selection as attorney general was not a surprise. Later in the Eisenhower administration, Brownell became known as a strong advocate for civil rights legislation. Harboring little animus for the poor Mexican laborers crossing the border in search of work and help for their families, Brownell, nevertheless, realized early on that the administration had to take a strong position on the immigration issue. In addition, Brownell was unquestionably influenced by the increasing fears raised by anti-Communist politicians and pundits that the border was an open invitation for spies and nefarious infiltrators of all kinds to enter the increasingly vulnerable United States.

After traveling across the Southwest to assess the problem and consulting with numerous individuals affected by the border problems, Brownell agreed that Operation Wetback, an effort to rid the border of the influx of undocumented laborers as well as an effort to persuade and even force farmers and ranchers to hire bracero workers, was a sensible approach. In 1956 he reported to Congress that the operation had been a success. The following is an excerpt from his testimony.

Reorganization of Border Patrol

When General Swing came into office he found that the Border Patrol was under the administrative and operational direction of the district directors in charge of the several immigration districts along the borders. In the southwest area there were three districts along the Mexican Border alone. Each one was staffed separately, with separate supervision of the Border Patrol within each district. We found that the boundaries were really artificial and that by loose command the Border Patrol's effectiveness was impaired, at a time when the Mexican wetback problem was becoming increasingly serious. This has been changed. All field operations of the Border Patrol, including administration and personnel activities, have been centralized under the direction of a single officer in each of the four regional offices around the country. On the southern border all operations are vested in one command responsible for the entire border. Personnel and material can be moved where and when needed, immediately meeting the demands of any emergency.

Not only does the Patrol now perform the literal statutory function of the Attorney General to "guard the boundaries," but it makes searches in the interior. This ensures that the job is thorough, and discourages continued attempts to cross the border by dispelling the notion that if you once make it you're in.

Border Patrol officers have also been appointed Customs Officers with all the powers, duties and functions of such officers regularly serving under the Department of the Treasury. Those duties include the detection and apprehension of smugglers and narcotic law violators. During the last nineteen months Border Patrol officers have made sixty-one seizures of narcotics valued at $445,403.20. Prompt removal of Mexicans illegally in this country is now one of the functions of the Border Patrol air transport arm. Planes carry such illegal entrants from points in the interior to a border station where they are immediately placed on board vessels for Vera Cruz. We have thus been able to avoid unnecessary detention and to convert our former detention facilities into staging areas.

It will be recalled that "Operation Wetback" stemmed an actual invasion by illegal entrants from Mexico. It was a situation of such massive proportions that it had even been suggested that federal troops were the only solution. Indicative of the size of the task is the fact that in the month of June, 1953, in the Los Angeles area, there were over 50,000 apprehensions of illegally present aliens; in August there were 60,000; and in September there were almost 65,000. General Swing made an immediate inspection of the border and concluded that with proper disposition of personnel and material the border could be brought under control. "Operation

Wetback" was accomplished skillfully and quickly, and at the same time every safeguard was employed to make certain the aliens were treated humanely and fairly. The border areas and the large industrial centers where illegal entrants often made their way are now almost wholly relieved of the wetback problem.

The results have been gratifying. Whereas at the beginning of the reorganization the Border Patrol was faced with the problem of removing some 3,000 wetbacks daily, the numbers have been reduced to an average of less than 250 a day. The present monthly average compares to the daily average of a year ago.

The economic and social relief to affected communities has been noticeable. The Director of the California Department of Employment, at the request at the Governor, expressed his thanks for the Service's work in removing illegal aliens from California. It was stated that, as a result of the first month's operation alone, claims for unemployment benefits had dropped 10% resulting in a weekly saving to California taxpayers of $325,000. The Texas Employment Commission estimated that 30,000 Americans in South Texas, who in the past migrated north in the summer months to find seasonal work, stayed home because of higher wages and better working conditions. Reports are coming in from police and welfare agencies 1n many areas attesting to a decrease in crime and disease rates in their localities.

Correction of the Mexican border problem has had a beneficial impact also upon our farm labor program. While the number of illegal entries of farm laborers has been a matter of conjecture, we do know the number of legal entrants, commonly known as "braceros": in 1955 there were about 390,000; in 1954, 310,000; and in. 1953, 198,000. It is a fair assumption that this increase in legal hiring has resulted in large part from the control of the wetback problem.

I should like to stress, too, that the cooperation of farmers, ranchers and the Mexican Government has been invaluable. Following the extension of the Agricultural Act new laminated identification cards were issued to qualified braceros. This has made it possible for growers to be assured the return of workers who have been found dependable. There are presently some 150,000 braceros who possess such cards indicating their suitability and availability tor future employment.

Source: Statement of Honorable Herbert Brownell Jr., Attorney General of the United States. Prepared for Delivery before Subcommittee on Immigration of Committee on the Judiciary United States Senate, April 13, 1956; https://www.justice.gov/sites/default/files/ag/legacy/2011/ . . . /04-13-1956%20pro.pdf.

8

Chicano Spirit on the Border

The 1960s and early 1970s—a time of the burgeoning black civil rights movement, with its protest marches and its violent clashes in the streets but also with its steadily growing support for equal rights and the fight against discrimination; a time of great social and political divide over the escalating and deadly war in Vietnam; and a time rocked by assassinations. It was also a time that witnessed a drive to secure social and political justice on behalf of Mexican Americans. It was the Chicano movement.

When the Treaty of Guadalupe Hidalgo ending the Mexican War ceded to the United States vast territories of California, Arizona, and New Mexico, as well as portions of Colorado, Utah, and Nevada, the terms of the treaty offered a guarantee that Mexicans would be granted the same rights as U.S. citizens. Over the years, those guarantees withered away as economic, social, and political power was soon dominated by the onrush of newly arrived citizens from other U.S. states. That domination of and prejudice toward the Mexican population remained a constant through the years, as did extensive border violence committed by all sides.

During the early years of the Great Depression in the 1930s and, later, in the 1950s, U.S. leaders decided that one of the solutions to the problems plaguing the nation was to send out of the country as many in the "Mexican" communities as possible. Thus, using power granted under formal legislation enacted by the U.S. government, law enforcement agencies began to round up individuals of Mexican ancestry, many of them U.S. citizens, and force them to head to Mexico. The towering irony in all of this was that those same Mexican Americans had been recruited to work in the United States by businesses because they offered a source of cheap labor in railroad construction, ranching, mining, and, especially in California, farm labor.

Not only along the U.S.-Mexican border but in other areas of the country where Mexicans had found jobs, raised children, and attempted to lead normal lives, they inevitably faced racial and cultural denigration, much like the treatment meted out to African American citizens. Their schools were segregated and given inadequate facilities. Mexican Americans faced signs in front of certain businesses that read

"Whites Only—No Spanish or Mexicans." They could not use many of the public facilities available to whites, such as certain skating rinks and swimming pools. Often, Mexicans and blacks could only swim one day of the week, after which the pools would be cleaned. Some churches would not allow Mexican Americans to attend services or enter on certain days. Many cemeteries, even those publicly operated, reserved special sections specifically for Mexican Americans, thus separating them in death from Anglos just as they had been during life. Some theaters did allow Mexican Americans and Afro-Americans access but only on certain nights. "Mexican Night Every Wednesdays" and "Colored Night Every Thursday," read the advertisements.

Mexicans read stories in newspapers that called them "undesirables." They were accused by law enforcement officials and political leaders of being inclined to engage in criminal activities and were therefore a threat to law and order. When arrested for petty crimes, many were subjected to what was euphemistically called the "third degree"—from beatings with rubber hoses to "three-day hunger tests."

But activists, reformers, and the immigrant community itself began to fight back. They would make demands and seek ways to come together to force change against the kind of prejudice and dehumanization attacks against the lives of Mexican Americans.

Local and statewide groups organized to protest these abuses. Mutual aid societies, legal services groups, and other such organizations, some on a national level, also provided assistance. It was The League of United Latin American Citizens (LULAC), founded in 1929, for example, that sponsored legal actions that advanced the cause for Latino rights. It was the efforts of these early organizations and the fervent work of their founders and members that were the precursors to the later focused and fervent activism that would embody the Chicano movement.

CHICANO

Most scholarly studies trace the derivation of the word "Chicano" to the early 1900s when it was associated in the American public mind with poor, unskilled, uneducated immigrants from Mexico who were considered no more than tramps or bandits. In the 1960s the word took on a totally different aspect. It came to signify, especially to young Mexican Americans, a rejection of the discrimination meted out to their ancestors; it was now a word of cultural and ethnic pride; a badge of honor; a harkening back to their ancient Aztec past; and the determination to secure their rights, liberties, and equal opportunity in American society.

Throughout the late 1960s and early 1970s, the Chicano movement, inspired by its various groups, worked to increase ethnic pride and sought to remedy, through social and political action, the educational and community needs of this long-oppressed minority. This became a time when individuals in the Mexican American community increasingly talked about themselves collectively as "La Raza" (The People), referring to the historical mixture of Spaniards with the indigenous inhabitants of the Americas. Many began to talk about the concept of Aztlán, a place of origin of the Aztec people that included the portion of Mexico taken over by the United States in the Mexican War—a place of inherent cultural identity stolen by Anglos. The Chicano movement thus provided a foundation for a new identity, one that not only counteracted racist attacks and discrimination but also led to an increasing recognition of historical and cultural heritage.

In the coming years organizers would win two landmark cases in the courts that encouraged Mexican Americans that, despite the odds, they could successfully challenge some of the injustices with which they had so long been saddled. In 1947 a federal court in California ruled that segregation of Mexican Americans in public schools was illegal. *Mendez v. Westminster* set a precedent that helped the eminent African American Thurgood Marshall prepare his historic case in *Brown v. Board Education*, the 1954 U.S. Supreme Court decision that declared state laws establishing separate public schools based on race to be unconstitutional.

And in that same year—1954—the U.S. Supreme Court issued an opinion in the case of *Hernandez v. Texas*. The case began with a murder in a bar in the southeastern border town of Edna, Texas. In September 1951, Pete Hernandez, a twenty-one-year old Mexican American farm worker, shot and killed a man named Joe Espinosa. The guilt of Hernandez did not become the central issue in the case; he had committed the crime. Instead, the importance of the case involved the composition of the jury that tried Hernandez. In an area of the country with a high concentration of Mexican Americans, Hernandez was convicted by a jury composed entirely of whites.

A team of lawyers led by Gus Garcia, known for his work in fighting segregation of Mexican Americans in schools, seized on the Hernandez case to press an issue central to the civil rights of Latinos—that they had been systematically excluded from serving not only on juries but in other positions surrounding the legal process. Mexican Americans, Hernandez's lawyers argued, had been denied constitutional protections as a special class—neither white nor black. Indeed, in the small Texas courtroom, Mexican Americans, though legally white, could not use a bathroom labeled "Whites Only." Mexican Americans, the lawyers argued, had been denied equal constitutional rights simply because of their ethnicity.

In an arduous path from that lowly South Texas courtroom, through an appeals process, and finally to the U.S. Supreme Court, the case moved for three years. Finally, *Hernandez v. Texas* became a landmark case that gave Mexican Americans the "equal protection" guarantees granted by the Fourteenth Amendment to the U.S. Constitution.

Also in this period, a Latino civil rights organization would begin to make a profound difference. In 1947 community organizer Fred Ross and Ed Roybal, an executive with the California Tuberculosis Association and an aspiring political figure, formed the Community Service Organization (CSO). Established under the auspices and financial support of the Chicago-based Industrial Areas Foundation, headed by organizer Saul Alinsky, the CSO served the Mexican American community as a grassroots civil rights organization helping to fight discrimination in housing, employment, and education; promoting political involvement; setting up citizenship classes; and establishing self-help programs.

By the early 1950s the CSO had become an increasingly effective organization. It began to draw in thousands of men and women determined to change the lives of Mexican American citizens for the better, individuals who would hold house meetings to plan for political action, carry on voter registration drives, and bring to community groups the education and tools to battle for true citizenship through grassroots organizing. They would also seek ways to combat police brutality.

In the early 1950s Fred Ross met a young farm worker who had served in the armed forces and seemed to have a steely determination and drive to makes things right. His name was Cesar Chavez.

LA CAUSA

In the intense sun along the rows of crops, the migrants stooped from early morning until nearly dark. In the lettuce fields and the pea fields, in the grape orchards and cherry groves, they harvested—men and women alongside young boys and girls, day after day, their bodies contorted in painful routine. Many were forced to use the short-handled hoe, a tool that forced them to continue throughout the days bent over in such awkward postures that many of them, after a few years of such work, would suffer severely damaged backs.

At night, they returned to the housing camps—dirty, cramped, rundown shacks, converted chicken coops, and storage sheds, none with running water or electricity, almost all of them infested with mosquitoes. Dozens of families shared a single outhouse. Water came from nearby irrigation ditches. They never had enough food. Children went to school only when they were not needed in the fields. The average life expectancy of a farm worker was forty-nine years. One of those farm workers was Cesar Chavez.

César Chávez, cofounder of the organization that became the United Farm Workers and an inspirational figure in the Chicano civil rights movement. (Library of Congress)

Born in the borderlands town of Yuma, Arizona, on March 31, 1927, he was the second of six children. His grandfather, Cesario Chavez, had crossed the border from the Mexican state of Chihuahua in the 1880s. His father, Librado, and his mother, Juana, raised six children and worked the harvest fields along with their children.

In 1944 Chavez joined the U.S. Navy and then worked in the grape vineyards in California. It was there he began work with the CSO, organizing meetings to inform workers of their rights.

In 1962 he moved to Delano, California, to begin a quest that seemed entirely quixotic—he wanted to start a union of farm workers.

By the fall of 1962 Chavez had not only lined up workers who were interested in joining a union, he also had drawn to his side other loyal and talented lieutenants, especially Dolores Huerta, a dynamic leader who had also worked alongside Fred Ross at the CSO. Chavez and Huerta began to try to make U.S. labor history. On Sunday, September 30, 1962, in an abandoned theater in Fresno, California, nearly 300 workers gathered to celebrate a new organization, of which they were cofounders. They called it the National Farm Workers Association (NFWA).

By 1964 Chavez, Huerta, and other lieutenants had signed up over 1,000 families. They were able to create a credit union and begin to provide services such as immigration counseling and voter registration. The organization also began publishing its own newspaper called *El Malcriado* (The Unruly One).

As the summer of 1965 drew to a close near Delano, California, members of a mostly Filipino group called the Agricultural Workers Organizing Committee (AWOC) decided to go on strike, demanding higher wages. The Filipinos realized that any success they might have depended on an alliance with Chavez's new labor union. On Mexican Independence Day, September 16, 1965, Chavez rallied the men and woman to what he called "La Causa."

On September 20, 1965, NFWA workers wound in picket lines alongside a farm east of Delano, and for days on end they persisted, despite threats and intimidation by the growers. After absorbing the first round of volleys from the growers, in early December 1965 Chavez raised the level of the protest. He launched a boycott. He would try to convince citizens not to buy grapes until the industry instituted humane work practices and paid fair wages. The target was the large grape producer Schenley Industries.

Recruiting volunteers from churches, community and labor organizations, and universities, the union began to set up boycott centers in various cities across California. Soon, volunteers fanned out across the United States to such major cities as New York, Chicago, and St. Louis. The message: "Help Farmworkers—Do Not Buy Grapes."

In early 1966 Chavez announced a new tactic. The NFWA would begin a 300-mile pilgrimage, or peregrinación, from Delano to the state capital of Sacramento. On March 17, 1966, a line of sixty-eight chosen peregrinos began walking east onto Highway 99 toward Ducor, then Porterville, and other small towns through the rich agricultural areas in which they had worked. As they marched, some carried pictures and waved banners of the Virgin of Guadalupe, the patron and symbol of Mexico, representing the fusion of the Aztec and Spanish cultures. Covering about fifteen miles a day, they gathered additional marchers. By the time they reached Stockton, one of the FBI informants reported, their ranks had swelled to about 1,500.

As the marchers neared Sacramento, Chávez learned from a representative of Schenley that the company decided to enter into a contract to formally recognize the NFWA. This was the first time that a grassroots farm labor union had achieved recognition by a corporation.

On Easter Sunday, April 10, 1966, led by some supporters on horseback carrying the NFWA flag and many others wearing sombreros, to the sound of trumpets and the rhythm of guitars keeping the beat, marchers crossed the bridge into Sacramento and ascended the capitol steps. Chavez stood before the 10,000 supporters and told them that Schenley had bowed before the pressure of the union and before the will of the campesinos.

Although most of the work of the union was centered in California, there were major actions on the U.S.-Mexican border.

THE TEXAS MELON STRIKE OF 1966

In the cantaloupe fields near the borderlands town of Rio Grande City, Texas, growers paid their farm workers about forty cents an hour for laboring in the blazing sun. Sometimes children as young as five years old would join their parents and siblings in the fields to help the family get by in the most wretched conditions. Workers said later that no bathroom facilities were provided, and one laborer said that drinking water was a luxury. Often, he said, workers drank from puddles full of crickets and frogs.

In the spring of 1966 NFWA leaders on the Texas border organized a strike against the Starr County melon growers. One of the strikers later said it was like going to war. Demanding wages of $1.25 a hour, water breaks with nonfetid water, and access to bathrooms, the strikers faced an unsurprising response from the growers: they called in the Texas Rangers. Arrests and beatings did not stop the strike, so the growers decided to try another tactic; they began to bus in workers from across the border to act as scab laborers. Knowing that the only hope for success was to inflict economic damage on the growers, strikers tried to block the U.S.-Mexican bridge in Roma, Texas. They were dragged off the bridge and jailed.

With every local and state official and agency allied against the strikers and with the early momentum waning in the face of harsh retaliation, union leaders decided on another tactic, one that had gained such public attention in California—they organized a march, "La Marcha."

It would be a nearly 500-mile trek from the border to the state capital of Austin. On July 4, 1966, led by union organizers, members of the clergy, and a contingent of strikers, the marchers left Rio Grande City. When they reached Sullivan City a woman told organizers that she wanted to join the march but had no one to take care of her donkey. The organizers seized the moment: the woman joined the march and the donkey became the mascot. They named him "1.25," after their goal of a fair wage.

As the marchers slowly made their way north in the blazing hot Texas sun, local and national reporters began to join them. Nevertheless, state and local government authorities, most importantly Governor John Connelly, made it clear that they would do nothing in response to the strike or the march. When the marchers reached Austin on Labor Day with a contingent of more than 15,000, including Cesar Chavez who joined in the last several miles, Connelly was not even in the city.

Although the union's newsletter proclaimed that "La Marcha ended in triumph," the 1966 Texas Melon Strike did not result in any state action to raise the wages or any actions by the growers to bend to the will of the workers. There were still too many laborers available to pick the melons in their fields for the growers to yield to the efforts of the strike.

Despite the lack of immediate gains for the melon pickers along the border, the strike did lead to continued labor pressure that eventually succeeded in generating modest reforms. But most importantly, the strike shattered the notion that Mexican Americans in those fields would remain content to be mired in untenable work conditions. Looking back, some observers credit the strike with igniting the Chicano movement in Texas.

1974 YUMA LEMON STRIKE

South of Yuma, Arizona, to San Luis Rio, Colorado, lush lemon orchards defied the sweltering desert sun where temperatures sometimes reach 120 degrees. It was here in August 1974 that nearly 1,500 lemon workers, "limoneros," went on a labor strike that threatened the desert county's multimillion-dollar lemon industry and approximately 90 percent of the nation's lemon crop. Demanding wage increases from what was then about six dollars a day, a collective bargaining agreement, and recognition of the farm workers union founded by Cesar Chavez and Dolores Huerta, now called the United Farm Workers (UFW), the action became known as "The Strike in the Sun."

From the beginning of the strike, the union faced a dilemma: the geographical proximity of the lemon groves and the strike action to the U.S.-Mexican border—a border now undermanned by Border Patrol agents. Especially in the region around Yuma it was relatively easy for workers with no authorization to cross the border and take up work as scabs.

Heading the UFW drive in the Yuma area was Manuel Chavez, a cousin of Cesar. Manuel Chavez took a hardline stance against the illegal immigrants filling the orchards and threatening the strike and took surprisingly forceful action: he created a so-called "wet line" to patrol the border along with the Border Patrol in an attempt to stop the flow of strikebreakers.

The union men reinforcing the border area to stop the immigrants were often brutal. Numerous injuries followed, and the image of the UFW as a nonviolent cause promoted by Cesar Chavez—in the spirit of Martin Luther King Jr. and Gandhi—took a serious blow to its image. The UFW, in attempting to foster the growth of the union and the well-being of its members, had, many detractors claimed, betrayed its ideological underpinning in the Arizona desert.

Because of the ability of the lemon growers to find sufficient scab labor despite the UFW's "wet line," the "Strike in the Sun" was not one of the union's success stories. Nevertheless, despite the breaking of the strike, the action on behalf of the "limoneros" brought a new sense of determination and solidarity to large numbers of workers on the border and a sense that life could get better through common effort.

THE LEGACY OF LA CAUSA

Although the UFW never ultimately achieved great lasting gains as measured by traditional labor unions, it did for a time attract much international recognition for its struggle against agribusiness interests. It helped win the first state law in the country granting agricultural workers the right to organize. It taught organizational techniques and led many Latino voter registration drives and other actions to gain empowerment.

At its height, the UFW had over 50,000 members under contract and as many as 50,000 more affiliated farm workers. But in the late 1970s, at a time of the great ascendancy of the UFW, internal pressures began to crack its foundation, tensions that led to the loss of many of the union's top leaders. With its internal divisions and dissensions and its loss of organizational focus and drive, the UFW thus became less of a labor union and more of an advocacy group. Its influence declined.

In April 1993, back in the tiny southwest Arizona border town of San Luis, near Yuma, where his family settled a half-century earlier, Chavez arrived to help UFW attorneys defend the union against a lawsuit brought by Bruce Church, Inc., the giant Salinas, California–based lettuce producer. But on April 23, 1993, Chavez died at age sixty-six during the early morning hours. He was only thirty miles from the spot where the Immaculate Conception Church once stood where he had been baptized.

The UFW movement helped inspire a new generation of Mexican American youths to organize their communities and become active in social and political programs. La Causa proclaimed that the beginnings of progress to gain that dignity came in organizing, educating, and coalescing around common dreams and aspirations. Not only for farm workers but also for other Mexican Americans, the movement became an exciting struggle. People for the first time in their lives joined picket lines in front of grocery stores, passed out leaflets, registered others to vote, sang the songs and chants of protest, and gained a new awareness that they could actually make a difference. La Causa was a fight for empowerment and self-determination.

TO RECLAIM THE LANDS

About the same time that Cesar Chavez and Dolores Huerta were founding an infant union of farm workers in Delano, California, another leader in another state began his own seemingly impossible drive on behalf of Mexican Americans that had profound implications for disputes over borderlands that had simmered ever since the signing of the Treaty of Guadalupe Hidalgo. In New Mexico in 1963, Reies Lopez Tijerina, a former preacher and head of a commune, a man who could spellbind audiences with his oratory, a man driven to make change, founded the Alianza Federal de Mercedes Libres, a group dedicated to an improbable fight to reclaim Spanish land grants held before the Mexican War.

For years, many of the descendants of indigenous, pre-Columbian inhabitants who had been granted land had protested against the land seizures, had made claims, and sometimes had resorted to violent attempts to reclaim the land. Through fraud and manipulation by the legal and political systems, nearly all those attempts to reclaim the land had failed. When the fences first went up in what had been the Tierra Amarilla land grant early in the twentieth century, for example, a group that called itself La Mano Negra cut down many of those fences, burned down barns, and generally raised havoc in the area. In the late 1930s a group called La Corporacion de Abiquiu embarked on a decades-long battle, with little success, suing ranchers over property rights.

Tijerina was born in Fall City, Texas, in 1926 and raised by a family of Mexican cotton farmers. He dropped out of high school and attended the Assembly of God Bible Institute, where he was ordained as a Pentecostal minister. After a stint as a traveling evangelist, he landed in southern Arizona in the early 1950s where, along with a group of followers, he started a "Kingdom of God," a 160-acre spread where, with primitive shelters, his "los Bravos" could live a simple religious life. For several years he would have various skirmishes with the authorities and would spend time in jail.

This was hardly an auspicious beginning for a man who saw himself as destined to lead a movement. Yet in August 1962, while living in Albuquerque, New Mexico, Tijerina began making his first plans for what he called the Alianza Federal de Mercedes, or the Federal Alliance of Land Grants. On February 2, 1963, on the 115th anniversary of the signing of the Treaty of Guadalupe Hidalgo, the Alianza was incorporated. The organization included not only many of the Bravos who had been with him for some time but also many descendants of the original land grants. In Albuquerque the Spanish radio station KABQ gave the Alianza a weekly show, and the organization grew.

Tijerina zealously went on a quest. He traveled to Mexico to examine ancient archival materials and read any available literature on the subject. Through his new organization, the Alianza, he attempted to gain a foothold in making the case for those who had lost land by establishing a newspaper. He gave rousing speeches and organized marches, and he fired off letters to U.S. and Mexican government officials, pleading with them to examine the wealth of information he had gathered and the compelling facts surrounding the land grab in the borderlands.

He traveled to Spain in 1966 to examine additional documents in Spanish archives and returned with a plan to take even more aggressive measures to make his case. On the Fourth of July Tijerina, much like Cesar Chavez had done in the farm workers campaign, organized a march of supporters. The trek was from Albuquerque to Santa Fe. Beset by white opponents along the route, who screamed obscenities, Tijerina and his marchers managed to reach the New Mexico capital and deliver a message to the New Mexico governor, Jack Campbell, pleading for a formal state investigation into the land grievances. The state government did nothing.

In the fall of 1966, the undeterred Tijerina decided to take his quest to a greater level of civil disobedience. Alianza members occupied part of the Echo Amphitheater Park in the Carson National Forest, claiming that it had been part of one of the many land grants that had been stolen by Anglos. He defiantly announced that the area was now the "Republic of San Joaquín del Río de Chama." His supporters even "arrested" some U.S. Forest Rangers who demanded that the Alianza group leave the area. After a few days the show was over, and five Alianza members, including Tijerina, were arraigned and released on bond.

Meanwhile, tensions in New Mexico between Anglos and Mexican Americans simmered, especially along the border. Some feared a violent confrontation was in the works. By now, Tijerina had achieved one of his preeminent goals: he had gotten a great deal of attention. He was about to get much more.

On June 5, 1967, he and members of the organization charged into the Rio Arriba County courthouse in Tierra Amarilla, New Mexico, to free Alianza members. In the confusion and chaos that ensued, a prison guard was shot and a deputy injured. Taking two hostages, Tijerina and his force headed for the nearby mountains.

What followed was the largest manhunt in New Mexico history. Jeeps, police cars, even tanks headed into the Sangre de Cristo Mountains. Pursued by the National Guard as well as other law enforcement agencies, Tijerina and his followers finally surrendered a few days later. Tijerina himself faced charges that included kidnapping and armed assault. By this time, he had become something of a folk hero. As he awaited trial in prison, other Chicano leaders had taken notice. Eventually, the Alianza leader would be sentenced to two years for the now-infamous courthouse raid.

Finally, in the early 1970s, the crusade was broke and exhausted. Nevertheless, "King Tiger," as he became known, despite his inability to achieve the overall objectives of the Alianza to restore lands to rightful owners, had given the Chicano movement an issue that continued long after the demise of the organization. The land grant issue, through the work of the Alianza, gained much notice and support among many Mexicans and Mexican Americans across the Southwest, especially along the U.S.-Mexican border. And although the land grant movement achieved little tangible success, it did forcefully advance the feelings among Chicanos of self-identify and nationalism.

SEEKING POLITICAL POWER

José Ángel Gutiérrez, son of a medical doctor in a small borderlands town of Crystal City, Texas, seemed destined for serious activism in politics from an early age. In 1963, infuriated by the treatment of Latinos and the "Whites Only" signs he saw in various places, he worked canvassing door to door in local elections. Gutiérrez was still in high school.

In 1967, in San Antonio, Texas, Gutiérrez, while a student at St. Mary's University, cofounded with four other students the Mexican American Youth Organization (MAYO). An activist group dedicated to inspiring militant affirmation of the rights of Mexican Americans, it attacked discrimination in the schools and in local and state government and developed a political agenda. The group visited black civil rights leaders to gain perspective and other Chicano leaders in various states. They joined picket lines in California with Cesar Chavez and the farm workers, for example. Their philosophy amounted to a kind of cultural nationalism, one that rejected any kind of meek assimilation into mainstream society. It was a confrontational approach to polarize Mexicans from Gringo domination, and it led to an audacious attempt to take the fight to the political arena. They would try to throw off the control of the Democratic Party, which they deemed to be little better than the Republicans, and form their own political force.

In 1970 Gutiérrez and other MAYO members christened a new political party—La Raza Unida (The United People). The main target for a local organizing drive was the area around Crystal City. Most of the citizens in the area were farm laborers, who had never before been involved in any kind of political activity. Yet using intensive door-to-door canvassing techniques and grassroots organizing efforts, the infant party would make Crystal City a small political battlefield. In April 1970 the new party ran sixteen candidates in local elections in the towns of Crystal City, Cotulla, Carrizo Springs, and Robstown. Word spread quickly among the Mexican American families, who made up a large percentage of the population of those counties, that this was a serious effort to seize political power. The party won fifteen elections for city council and school boards in Crystal City and in a number of nearby towns. The first electoral foray by the party had been a heady success. Gutiérrez himself became a trustee and president of the Crystal City Independent School District. Within four years, he would become a Zavala County judge, elected on the ticket of the La Raza Unida As news of the elections in southern Texas spread, other chapters of La Raza party organized in a number of towns and cities in California, Colorado, New Mexico, and Arizona and even in some cities in the Midwest. In September 1972 the party organized a national convention in El Paso, Texas. Several hundred delegates from more than forty states attended the week-long convention. Gutiérrez was named party chairman.

Gutiérrez saw the early victories as the beginning of what he hoped would be a formidable national third party, one that could offer a degree of political sovereignty to a disenfranchised minority. He wanted Latinos to think beyond mere assimilation and integration to self-identity, assertion of rights, and political power.

Unfortunately for La Raza Unida Party, the high-water mark of electoral victories turned out to be the local elections in the Crystal City, Texas, area that had garnered so much enthusiasm and held out such promise. What leaders did not wish to admit or ignored was the fact that Crystal City, with its overwhelming Mexican American population, was the most fertile ground for electoral success that could be imagined. When the party tried to run statewide elections for U.S. senator and governor in Texas, its support barely dented the totals run up by the Democratic and Republican Parties. Other electoral attempts by the party in other states also proved disappointing—the typical fate of almost all third parties that have sought to break up the two-party domination in the United States.

Although the party itself never became a strong independent political institution, it did open the doors for increasing numbers of Latinos to enter the arena. It paved the way for political empowerment. Although still underrepresented at all levels of government, the percentage of Latinos in positions of political power continues to rise. In the U.S. Congress, in state legislatures, and in city and town governments, Latinos are increasingly taking more prominent positions of political influence. Many of those members are children and grandchildren of individuals who put their own lives and futures on the line in the Chicano movement.

FROM TEXAS TO CALIFORNIA: THE CHICANO SPIRIT IN ART

The political ferment of the 1960s and 1970s gave birth to Chicano art in its various forms: murals, paintings, sculpture, music, literature, and theater. Instead of fading after the political, civil rights, and economic battles of the Chicano movement itself, those art forms have continued to flourish. Some of the earliest works focused on such issues as the grape boycott, the Chicano revulsion against the Vietnam War, farm working conditions, struggles with the police and border agents, immigrants crossing the border and their mistreatment, and religious icons. New artists, inspired by the spirit of resistance and the striving for identity and recognition of the artists of earlier generations, have expressed in their own work the same intensity and cultural affirmation. Along the border, that art is especially revealing. The following are a few examples.

San Diego, California/Tijuana, Baja California

In 1997 at the border entry of San Ysidro, a district of San Diego, Tijuana artist Marcos Ramirez, known by the nickname ERRE, collaborated with several artists to install at a binational art event a majestic, two-headed wood and metal horse on wheels he named "Toy An-Horse," a work reminiscent of the Trojan horse from *The Iliad*. One head faced toward Mexico, the other to the United States. Placed directly on top of the border marker and clearly visible to the 50,000 people a day who crossed the border at that entry point, the work, according to the artist, was meant to symbolize not only the loss of land by Mexicans to Anglo encroachers but also the need for cultural exchange and reconciliation and an understanding of homeland in both countries.

Beneath the San Diego–Coronado Bridge in Barrio Logan is Chicano Park, one of the most recognized areas of Chicano art anywhere along the U.S.-Mexican border. Filled with a magnificent collection of outdoor murals and sculptures, Chicano Park, through its artwork as well as community spirit, is a celebration of the Chicano spirit.

There almost was no Chicano Park. In 1970 construction crews with a full array of equipment and bulldozers were clearing an area for a Highway Patrol station parking lot. It was then that a group of young Chicano activists, along with citizens of the area, from elderly men and women to children, organized a massive protest, evicted the construction crew, and seized the land. They occupied it for twelve days, clearing the area of debris and planting flowers. Chicano activists arrived from all over California, offering support. Eventually an agreement was reached in which the city of San Diego agreed to allow the land to be used as a community park.

Soon, Chicano artists began to create murals in the park, especially on the freeway abutments and pylons. Through the years the side of the San Diego–Coronado Bridge has become one of the great canvasses of Chicano muralists, a glorious mix of colors and themes marking the history and culture expressed in the Chicano movement.

Chicano Park is located in Logan Heights, San Diego, the oldest Mexican American barrio. The park originated in 1970 when residents protested plans to bulldoze much of the area to build a California Highway Patrol station. Led by a number of Chicano activists and artists who negotiated extensively with local government officials, the area instead became a park featuring the largest concentration of Chicano murals in the world and the site of an emerging arts district with galleries, boutiques, and playgrounds. (Ilan David/Dreamstime.com)

In 2018 a new mural appeared in Chicano Park. It features the iconic image of the Virgin of Guadalupe as an activist carrying water for migrants crossing the desert. Painted by Sal Barajas, one of the original artists who began work in Chicano Park in 1973, the mural pays tribute to the Border Angels, a group of volunteers who place water in the desert to help migrants survive. Across the top of the mural are the words "Amor, si se puede" (Love, yes we can).

In the northwest corner of Mexico, at the Playas de Tijuana, a border fence extends into the Pacific Ocean. It was here in 2011 that artist Ana Teresa Fernández used the actual border wall as a canvas for a work she called "Borrando la Frontera" (Erasing the Border). Using paint that matches the California blue sky as closely as possible, she created a work that from a distance, because of an optical illusion, makes it appear that a part of the border wall has disappeared. In December 2016 Fernández repainted the fence and extended the distance of the work to about seventy feet. She executed similar projects at other places along the border, such as Nogales, Ciudad Juárez, and Agua Prieta.

Since 2016 Mexican muralist Enrique Chiu, along with large numbers of community volunteers from Tijuana, have begun to cover the existing border wall on the Tijuana side of the border with a series of works they call "Mural de la Hermandad" (Mural of Brotherhood). Featuring images from Mexican folklore and

Chicano culture, the mural is a way, Chiu says, to help unite two divided nations. Born in Guadalajara, he first crossed the border with his mother when he was eight years old, returned to Mexico briefly, and came back to the United States on a student visa. Chiu, who has in eighteen years painted over eighty murals in cities across Mexico, Guatemala, and the United States, envisions a final work that could conceivably be many miles long and perhaps the longest mural in the world. His group of over 2,000 volunteers has already produced murals on the wall not only in Tijuana but in other areas all the way to Ciudad Juárez. Although it would be a monumental achievement, Chiu and his fellow artists carry on with the hope that eventually this artwork will become binational, fulfilling his vision of unity and a coming together of two countries and separate cultures.

Ambos Nogales

The twin cities of Nogales, Sonora, and Nogales, Arizona (still called by many "Ambos Nogales") have, since the 1800s, been a central passage between Mexico and the United States at the border halfway across Arizona. In 1898 the construction of The Southern Pacific of Mexico, a U.S.-owned railroad operating between Nogales and the Mexican city of Guadalajara, made Nogales a bustling border town, with extensive cross-border trade and cultural exchange. A major piece of art in Nogales, Sonora, a mural called "Paseo de la Humanidad," or "Parade of Humanity," reflects that history and the culture that ties together the two cities. Created by artists Alberto Morackis, Guadalupe Serrano, and Alfred Quiroz, it depicts the struggles and harsh realities of migrants traveling through the Sonoran desert. Especially considering the growing intensity, animosity, and political posturing surrounding the issue of immigration over the years, the mural has become something of an iconic reminder of the border struggles that have plagued both countries for generations.

El Paso, Texas/Ciudad Juárez, Chihuahua

Walking in El Segundo Barrio, the El Paso community directly across from Ciudad Juárez, is like a journey into the history of the U.S.-Mexican border. It is where revolutionaries plotted the overthrow of Mexican dictator Porfirio Diaz; it is where celebrated bandit leader Pancho Villa frequented an ice cream store; it was here that many began to call the "Ellis Island of the Southwest," a place where thousands of families migrated from Mexico; it was also here that some of the most colorful, reflective Chicano art appeared honoring the shared culture and heritage of the area. Chicano art works appear throughout various neighborhoods of the sister cities—new art collectives, galleries, and street art festivals.

In Juárez, artists David Flores and Juan Carlos Reyes established Colectivo REZIZTE, a multidisciplinary collective that showcases the work of artists from the two border towns. Featuring public art merging various genres, including graffiti and murals, the Colectivo is an artistic version of the Chicano spirit of empowering the people, of gaining an appreciation of culture covering hundreds of years, or what they called a "fronterizo identity." This is art with a powerful political voice. These artists, who call themselves fronterizos, see their work as a call against division and a bridge to common ground. "Ninguna ieza es illegal!" they say: "no work of art is illegal."

In 2014 artist El Mac painted sister murals in El Paso and Ciudad Juárez of people who have lost relatives and loved ones to border violence. His work is an assault on the lack of social and government control that has led to a breakdown of civility and has made being a resident of Juárez a dangerous proposition. The murals tell woeful stories of kidnapped children, murdered mothers, and the like, searing images that cry out for decency and justice. But they also tell of the heroism and fortitude of the survivors and those who have fought for the rights and for justice for the people, a theme familiar in the Chicano movement and in its artistic expression.

Jesus "Cimi" Alvarado has painted more than fifteen murals in the El Paso/Juárez area. He grew up in the El Segundo Barrio and was inspired to be an artist by his high school teacher and well-known Chicano artist, Gaspar Enriquez. Fittingly, many of Alvarado's works are prominent in El Segundo Barrio, but his work can be seen in many locations in the El Paso/Juárez area. Although much of his work focuses on everyday life and people in the area, he has also focused on such Latino icons as Ruben Salazar, the *Los Angeles Times* journalist killed by police during a Chicano march against the Vietnam War in 1970. Alvarado has remained active in the border area and has collaborated with many fellow artists in creating new artistic works with a Chicano theme.

Across the U.S.-Mexican border, the Chicano movement inspired a new world of cultural expression. It reflected powerful self-determination and a spirit of militant self-identity that emanated from the struggles for rights and social justice.

DOCUMENTS

Hernandez v. Texas, Summary, 1954

In the history of the U.S. Supreme Court, the year 1954 is most remembered for the monumental decision in the case of Brown v. Board of Education, *which marked the end of legal segregation in the nation's public schools. Two weeks before the* Brown *decision made national headlines, the court issued an opinion that had profound implications for the Chicano movement.* Hernandez v. Texas *was the first case the nation's highest court decided that extended constitutional protections to Latinos. The following are excerpts from the case summary.*

U.S. Supreme Court
Hernandez v. Texas, 347 U.S. 475 (1954)
Hernandez v. Texas
No. 406
Argued January 11, 1954
Decided May 3, 1954
347 U.S. 475

CERTIORARI TO THE COURT OF CRIMINAL APPEALS OF TEXAS

Syllabus

The systematic exclusion of persons of Mexican descent from service as jury commissioners, grand jurors, and petit jurors in the Texas county in which petitioner was indicted and tried for murder, although there were a substantial number of such persons in the county fully qualified to serve, deprived petitioner, a person of Mexican descent, of the equal protection of the laws guaranteed by the Fourteenth Amendment, and his conviction in a state court is reversed . . .

(a) The constitutional guarantee of equal protection of the laws is not directed solely against discrimination between whites and Negroes . . .

(b) When the existence of a distinct class is demonstrated, and it is shown that the laws, as written or as applied, single out that class for different treatment not based on some reasonable classification, the guarantees of the Constitution have been violated . . .

(c) The exclusion of otherwise eligible persons from jury service solely because of their ancestry or national origin is discrimination prohibited by the Fourteenth Amendment . . .

(d) The evidence in this case was sufficient to prove that, in the county in question, persons of Mexican descent constitute a separate class, distinct from "whites." . . .

(e) A *prima facie* case of denial of the equal protection of the laws was established in this case by evidence that there were in the county a substantial number of persons of Mexican descent with the qualifications required for jury service, but that none of them had served on a jury commission, grand jury or petit jury for 25 years . . .

(f) The testimony of five jury commissioners that they had not discriminated against persons of Mexican descent in selecting jurors, and that their only objective had been to select those whom they thought best qualified, was not enough to overcome petitioner's *prima facie* case of denial of the equal protection of the laws . . .

(g) Petitioner had the constitutional right to be indicted and tried by juries from which all members of his class were not systematically excluded . . .

MR. CHIEF JUSTICE WARREN delivered the opinion of the Court.

The petitioner, Pete Hernandez, was indicted for the murder of one Joe Espinosa by a grand jury in Jackson County, Texas. He was convicted and sentenced to life imprisonment. The Texas Court of Criminal Appeals affirmed the judgment of the trial court . . . Prior to the trial, the petitioner, by his counsel, offered timely motions to quash the indictment and the jury panel. He alleged that persons of Mexican descent were systematically excluded from service as jury commissioners . . .] grand jurors, and petit jurors, although there were such persons fully qualified to serve residing in Jackson County. The petitioner asserted that exclusion of this class deprived him, as a member of the class, of the equal protection of the laws guaranteed by the Fourteenth Amendment of the Constitution. After a hearing, the trial court denied the motions. At the trial, the motions were renewed, further evidence taken, and the motions again denied. An allegation that the trial court erred in denying the motions was the sole basis of petitioner's appeal. In affirming the judgment of the trial court, the Texas Court of Criminal Appeals considered and passed upon the substantial federal question raised by the petitioner. We granted a writ of certiorari to review that decision . . .

Throughout our history, differences in race and color have defined easily identifiable groups which have at times required the aid of the courts in securing equal treatment under the laws. But community prejudices are not static, and, from time to time, other differences from the community norm may define other groups which need the same protection. Whether such a group exists within a community is a question of fact. When the existence of a distinct class is demonstrated, and it is further shown that the laws, as written or as applied, single out that class for different treatment not based on some reasonable classification, the guarantees of the Constitution have been violated. The Fourteenth Amendment is not directed solely against discrimination due to a "two-class theory"—that is, based upon differences between "white" and Negro. As the petitioner acknowledges, the Texas system of selecting grand and petit jurors by the use of jury commissions is fair on its face and capable of being utilized without discrimination.] But, as this Court has held, the system is susceptible to abuse, and can be employed in a discriminatory manner . . .] The exclusion of otherwise eligible persons from jury service solely because of their ancestry or national origin is discrimination prohibited by the Fourteenth Amendment. The Texas statute makes no such discrimination, but the petitioner alleges that those administering the law do . . .

Circumstances or chance may well dictate that no persons in a certain class will serve on a particular jury or during some particular period. But it taxes our credulity to say that mere chance resulted in their being no members of this class among the over six thousand jurors called in the past 25 years. The result bespeaks discrimination, whether or not it was a conscious decision on the part of any individual jury commissioner. The judgment of conviction must be reversed.

To say that this decision revives the rejected contention that the Fourteenth Amendment requires proportional representation of all the component ethnic groups of the community on every jury.] ignores the facts. The petitioner did not seek proportional representation, nor did he claim a right to have persons of Mexican descent sit on the particular juries which he faced . . .] His only claim is the right to be indicted and tried by juries from which all members of his class are not systematically excluded—juries selected from among all qualified persons regardless of national origin or descent. To this much he is entitled by the Constitution.

Reversed.

Source: *Hernandez v. Texas* (347 U.S. 475) No. 406, Argued January 11, 1954; Decided May 3, 1954. Available at: https://supreme.justia.com/cases/federal/us/347/475/case.html.

Ruben Salazar's *Stranger in One's Land*, 1970

He was a pioneer, the first Mexican American journalist to cover the Latino community for a major newspaper in the United States. Born in Ciudad Juárez, Chihuahua, Mexico, in 1929, Ruben Salazar's parents immigrated to the United States when he was less than a year old, settling in El Paso, Texas. After serving in the U.S. Army, Salazar earned a journalism degree at Texas Western College and took a job as a cub reporter at the El Paso Herald Post. *It was at the* Herald Post *that he began to write about the brutal treatment of Mexican and Mexican American prisoners in Texas and also about police brutality. This focus on the plight of Latinos marked the beginning of a distinguished career that finally brought him to the West Coast as a writer for the* Los Angeles Times. *For Mexican Americans in Los Angeles, the appearance of Salazar as a reporter of consequence, one who was attuned to their cultural and social problems and challenges, was a vital signal that the* Times *was committed to fair news coverage of their community.*

In April 1970 Salazar made a critical career decision. He accepted an offer from KMEX, the Spanish-language television station in Los Angeles, to become news director. Although surprised by the offer, Salazar immediately saw the potential to reach new audiences with his work through Spanish-language media. He realized that much of the Spanish-speaking community did not receive their news through the print media but through radio and television. The KMEX job, he realized, would give him fresh opportunities to communicate directly, in their own language, to many of the people he had written about in his newspaper work.

At KMEX, with a staff of three reporters and one cameraman, Salazar sent his news team into the barrios to cover stories that the English-language media ignored. His crew covered the protest demonstrations held by Chicano activists. With his move to KMEX, Salazar did not sever his ties with the Times. *The paper asked him to write a weekly column on Chicano issues.*

On August 29, 1970, Salazar became a martyr, a symbol of the unjust treatment of Latino minorities by the police. He was covering the National Chicano Moratorium March, organized to protest the disproportionate number of Hispanic Americans killed in the Vietnam War. The peaceful march ended with a rally that was broken up by the Los Angeles police with such force that a riot ensued, during which Salazar was shot in the head at short range with a tear gas projectile while seated in a bar. A coroner's inquest ruled the shooting a homicide, but the policeman involved was never prosecuted. At the time many believed the homicide was a premeditated assassination of a very vocal member of the Los Angeles Hispanic community. His death has been commemorated in many ways, especially in songs, ballads, and murals.

Stranger in One's Land *is Salazar's account of the 1968 U.S. Commission on Civil Rights hearing on Mexican Americans and civil rights. It appeared as a commission publication in May 1970, a few months before the fateful and tragic day of August 29, and reveals much about Salazar's understanding of border issues. The following are excerpts from* Stranger in One's Land.

La Frontera

The marchers, followers of farm labor leader Cesar Chavez, finished their 100-mile trek across the blazing hot desert from Indio, California, to the border town of Calexico on Sunday, May 18, 1969. According to the plan, Chavez' people were supposed to hold a solidarity rally with Mexican national farm workers at the international line. But the rally never took place.

The official explanation was that the Mexican Government did not want its people to get involved in an American labor dispute, the California table grape strike-boycott. Actually, the Mexican workers who live in Mexico's border towns and work in American borderland farms and in American border cities are very much involved in a unique American labor controversy. As commuters, the Mexican workers are the unwitting pawns of an international labor dispute with precedence. The 1,800 mile United States-Mexican border stretches from the coast of California to the Gulf of Mexico in an irregular line which orators like to describe as the only such unfortified frontier in the world. This does not mean that "armies" do not crisscross this border every day.

Perhaps the most telling contrast between the two countries is that while an army of fun-seeking American tourists crosses the border into Mexico, another army of job-hungry Mexicans crosses the line into the United States.

The American tourists, for the most part, have a good effect on the Mexican economy and this army is welcomed with good will. The army of job-hungry Mexicans which commutes across the international line has an adverse effect on American labor. For many years this was passively taken for granted. But now, in the age of activism, a confrontation seems inevitable.

The situation is a highly complicated and sensitive one because it involves mostly Mexicans against Mexican-Americans. That is, the poorest of the poor Mexican nationals vying for jobs with Mexican Americans who are striving to attain U.S. economic standards. Result: Mexican nationals, because they're understandably willing to work for less, take jobs away from Mexican Americans.

Even in their resentment, Mexican Americans find it difficult to condemn these commuters. They, their parents, or grandparents were in the same boat not too long ago. The fact remains that Mexicans are pitted against Mexican Americans for the lowest paid jobs in America.

The problem is further complicated by the fact that U.S. borderland businessmen fear that any effort to terminate the commuter program would result in a retaliatory refusal by Mexico to allow its citizens to carry on their extensive trade in American border towns.

Cheap labor on the Mexican side of the border attracts industrialists as much as it does growers. A free industrial zone program in Mexican border towns was started in 1965, whereby American industrialists can set up factories there under a special program which exempts them for all import duties. Mexican workers reportedly earn as little as $2 a day in these American factories. The American labor movement, which helped kill the bracero [Mexican farm labor] program, claims that in effect under this new plan—since the braceros are no longer available in the United States—the work is now being taken to the braceros.

Former Secretary of State, Dean Rusk, in commenting on a court suit concerning the commuter program, voiced his concern over United States-Mexican diplomatic relations should the commuter system be stopped.

"[If] as a result of a substantial reduction in the commuter traffic across the border between Mexico and the United States, a significant number of Mexican nationals would be deprived of their earning power, the trade between the two countries would be substantially reduced," the Secretary said. "We would expect that this would have an immediate depressing effect on the economy of the region on both sides of the border. Moreover, the loss of gainful employment and dollar earnings by 30,000 to 50,000 Mexican nationals, estimated at over $50 million annually, might compel the Government of Mexico to consider compensating steps, which would further damage the economic life of the region." . . .

The commuter system will be much harder to abolish than the bracero program which, until its demise, was another burden on the backs of Mexican American farm and unskilled workers.

The bracero program, initiated during World War II when farm labor was genuinely scarce, was a formal program whereby two Governments, the United States and Mexico, made an agreement to bring Mexican farm laborers [braceros] to the United States until American farm workers were again available. Though farm workers feel the bracer program lasted too long after the war, the program was successfully phased out when unemployed farm workers in the United States were able to convince authorities that such an agreement between the two countries was having an adverse effect on them. The green card commuter, on the other hand, is a bracer, who, it might be said, made his contract individually with the U.S. Government by becoming an "immigrant" in name if not in fact.

Unlike the bracero, who came here under a special temporary arrangement, a commuter as an "immigrant" has virtually a permanent status, even though he has no intention of living permanently in the United States—as does the genuine immigrant.

One of the ideas behind the march to Calexico was to recruit commuters for Chavez' union. Commuters . . . have been used as strike-breakers notably in farm labor disputes in Delano, California, and in Starr County, Texas.

Knowing that the commuters are forced by poverty to be commuters, the union knew the system would continue. So Chavez extended an invitation to join the union so that commuters would not work for less than Mexican Americans along the border. Though it looks like a simple solution, it must be seen from the context of a rich economy [the United States] living next door to a poor one [Mexico].

To the Mexican commuter, joining the union is not as attractive as it looks on the surface. For one thing, he knows that besides his labor, it's his docility which the employer appreciates, and he is aware that joining the union will only alienate him from his employer . . .

Because the people involved in this commuter controversy are used to dealing with each other on a friendly basis for generations, and think of the border as an artificial line drawn by latecomers, the issue is one not only of great economic import but also of cultural significance.

Between the two countries writes J. Fred Rippy in his "The United States and Mexico," there have been no natural barriers, the two nations being separated by an imaginary line, a barbed wire fence, an easily forded river, an undergrowth of mesquite or chaparral. Citizens of both nations have passed back and forth with little difficulty or interruption, or have settled in neighboring states amidst natural surroundings which have not repelled them by their unfamiliar aspects . . ."

There's only one catch. On one side of the border, or *frontera,* is a rich Nation with the highest standard of living in history. On the other side is a poor Nation with a seemingly inexhaustible supply of cheap labor . . .

When talking about themselves or about each other, Mexicans and Mexican Americans refer to themselves simply as "Mexicanos." The commuter problem is beginning to cut a wedge into this traditional term. When poor Mexican Americans have to compete for low-paying jobs against very poor Mexican nationals only the poor suffer. But resentment builds up between the poor and the very poor.

And when that happens, the border becomes a real dividing line.

Source: Salazar, Ruben, *Stranger in One's Land.* U.S. Commission on Civil Rights Clearinghouse Publication No. 19, U.S. Government Printing Office, 1970, pp 1–3; 46–49.

Interview with Herman Baca of the Committee on Chicano Rights, 1980

It was a road that turned increasingly progressive that Herman Baca traveled in his political life—from a Republican block captain in Richard Nixon's successful run for the presidency in 1968 to one of the most ardent, devoted Chicano activists in California. Born in New Mexico, Baca moved to National City, California, in metropolitan San Diego with his family when he was eleven. He became a printer and opened his own business. Disillusioned with a political system that excluded Latino representation at all levels of government, Baca organized a local chapter of La Raza Unida in 1970.

Increasingly active politically, he established several community organizations on behalf of Chicanos and the Committee on Chicano Rights (CCR) in 1975, a small group that at first held meetings at his business, AZTEC Printers. Baca began to organize marches and protests to help farm workers and to protest police brutality against Chicanos. In 1975 he brought together over 10,000 people to protest the announced plans of the Ku Klux Klan to patrol the U.S.-Mexican border. In 1979 he organized a march of thousands of protestors from downtown San Diego to the U.S.-Mexican border to highlight immigration issues central to the Chicano community.

From the AZTEC Printers' location on Highland Avenue, a place that became known among Chicano leaders as "The Shop," Baca and his growing supporters in CCR became a hub of Chicano protest in San Diego. With a community-based volunteer membership, the group developed political awareness of Chicano needs and methods to fight for social justice. The CCR organized political campaigns, demonstrations, and even boycotts and produced newsletters and newspapers. On the office walls were portraits of Pancho Villa, Zapata, Martin Luther King Jr., and Malcolm X. Through Herman Baca's leadership, the CCR became a nationally visible force, and many of its members went on to become vigorous advocates in the Chicano movement.

In 1980 Baca looked back at the beginnings of the CCR..

The following are excerpts from an interview held on April 19, 1980, by the newspaper El Foro del Pueblo *at the offices of the CCR in National City, California.*

EL FORO: Herman, what is the history of the CCR? How did it get started and what issues has it involved itself with?

BACA: In the initial years we were an ad hoc confederation that dealt with everything from the Dixon-Arnett Bill, rape and violence by Border Patrolmen, the Rodino Bill, inland check points, local issues involving police brutality, the grand jury, etc.

In the process we finally launched a recall effort against the entire city council for their failure to deal with harassment of our community. This got people to join the ad hoc committee. That is when we gave up the confederation. So in, 1976 we organized' the Committee on Chicano Rights . . . Our independence rests on being independent from government monies. We are a-volunteer community organization which depends on community activities like tardeadas and dances for its financial support.

Most of the members of the Committee are from National City. We have three levels of membership which include: General members who come in and volunteer their work and time and make whatever concrete or regular contributions they can; Associate members contribute money as well as support our activities; and, lastly, there is general community support.

We have had several activities which we feel have had an impact on community awareness of the immigration issue. We organized a campaign against the Carter immigration plan and had a march of 3,000 persons at the border in October of 1977 against the presence of right-wing extremists like the KKK at the border.

We have especially focused on the question of violence at the U.S.-Mexican border. In 1979 we also the 3,000 persons march against Carter's "tortilla curtain" to denounce what we feel is the militarization of the border.

EL FORO: What would you identify as your most important victories since 1970?

BACA: I would say raising the political consciousness of the people here on the immigration issue. When we started out most Chicano activists could not see the relationship between the immigration issue and their own struggles. There was acceptance of right-wing beliefs that accused immigrants of stealing their jobs and so on. So our biggest victory has been in giving the immigration issue a different perspective.

EL FORO: Why do you feel immigration is the most crucial issue for us today?

BACA: It is the foremost issue of the Chicano Movement. But it is an issue being used to attack and destroy all the gains of the movement, all the efforts we have made to help the Chicano community. We, see it in Houston where there is an effort to deny immigrant Mexican children an education; we see it in California when bilingual-bicultural education is attacked; we see it in Phoenix when attempts to intimidate a whole community are initiated by going after its weakest sector, and we see it in Los Angeles and Orange County with the residential sweeps. Clearly, this is an effort to intimidate a whole community.

Source: "Interview: Herman Baca of the Comm. on Chicano Rights," *EL FORO DEL PUEBLO*, May 1980, Special Collections and Archives, University of California San Diego, http://library.ucsd.edu/dc/object/bb0649761n.

9

Fences, Walls, and Boundary Enforcement

When fences first appeared in the borderlands regions in the late nineteenth century, those fences had nothing to do with illegal immigration or the so-called "War on Drugs"; they had to do with farmers keeping their cattle on their property. As a result of decades of wars, immigration disputes, nativist impulse, security concerns, drug and human trafficking, and political attacks, assorted fences of various sizes and shapes now cover nearly 700 miles of the nearly 2,000-mile border, an assortment of corrugated steel, wire, and concrete barriers, much of it marred by age, patches damaged by weather, and various parts chopped apart by individuals in anger and desperation. Some of the fencing is fortified with infrared cameras, watchtowers, and floodlights patrolled by armed guards. Some of the fencing in the towns and cities now sits atop tunnels that have been secretly dug to smuggle both drugs and humans across the line. Long stretches of the border, particularly in Texas, are free of such constructions, especially across stretches of desert where many have died trying to cross without enough water or strength to endure.

And now, in the second decade of the twenty-first century, with the continually growing militarization of the border, there is debate over a proposed massive wall that would cover the border's entire length. But it's not just fences and walls that make border control seemingly an intractable and chaotic effort. It's more and more border agents, vehicles of all kinds both on the ground and in the air; it's the latest sophisticated surveillance equipment, some of it newly off the inventor's design. However, it's the image of the fence that has captured the imagination in recent years. Could there be such a construction, a panacea for the perceived ills of the border, or is the whole imagined enterprise a fanciful notion wrought with enormous costs and engineering nightmares? The debate over all of it rages.

FENCES ON THE BORDER: THE BEGINNING

Generations of citizens of Mexican descent harbored deep feelings about what they saw as a disgraceful appropriation of private lands by invading Anglos following the Mexican War. The signing of the Treaty of Guadalupe Hidalgo in 1848 had, after all, supposedly protected the rights and property of those Mexicans who decided to stay in the land ceded to the United States. Nevertheless, the offices and courts appointed to oversee the confirmation of the claims of those Mexicans who stayed in the United States following the war proved to be overwhelmingly biased. Only a small percentage of the ancestral land grant holdings claimed by those citizens were recognized, thus stripping most Mexicans of their rights to those lands.

The first fences along the borderlands were mostly built by Anglo ranchers and farmers to mark off their newly gained territory. On a few occasions, groups of peasant resisters, furious over the loss of their land, acted, tearing down some of the fences and destroying property. But mostly these were isolated, desperate, and futile acts. Anglo settlers took control and kept it.

The first fence erected along the U.S.-Mexican border by federal action was along the California–Baja California line. The work was undertaken in 1909 through the auspices of the U.S. Bureau of Animal Husbandry in an attempt to keep cattle in Mexico that had been infected by a tick-induced disease obtained when wandering into U.S. ranches and farms. Its main intention was not to keep out or separate people.

In 1918, however, as a result of military events during the latter part of the Mexican Revolution, the sister cities of Nogales, Sonora and Nogales, Arizona (Ambos Nogales) gained the distinction of erecting the first fence whose purpose was specifically to separate physically Mexican and U.S. citizens. Ambos Nogales had been the scene of two relatively insignificant skirmishes during the war, one in 1913 and the other in 1915. In 1918 the events of the revolution, along with the U.S. entry into World War I, caught up with the citizens of Ambos Nogales, and those events affected the history of the border.

Before, along dusty International Street that ran down the center of the two towns with its stores, saloons, and railroad depot straddling the border, citizens crossed from one side to the other without much thought that they were traveling from one country to another. Mostly they carried on life as if there were no border at all, enjoying friendly relations and some not so friendly. It is true that they were expected to cross the street at one of two entry points, either at the corner of Morley Avenue or at Grand Avenue. The requirements to abide by the rules of the entry points were sometimes not rigorously enforced.

Much changed after the president's announcement that the United States had entered World War I. Throughout the spring and into the later months of 1917, rumors, newspaper reports, military intelligence, and other sources infused such fear not only in the offices of U.S. government officials but also in the mind of the public that the U.S.-Mexican border was ripe for spies, sedition, and actual military invasion. Many concluded that the porous border was, in many ways, an open gateway to the enemy.

In May 1918 the U.S. government decided to close access across the boundary line as much as possible. The legislation was called the Wartime Measure Act or the Travel Control Act, and it required that all non-U.S. citizens obtain a visa or passport before being allowed to cross the border. For the local population the U.S.

Immigration Service initiated a program that issued border-crossing cards to those individuals who regularly crossed the border, but even these provisions made what had been routine activities much more difficult.

Soon, not only in Ambos Nogales but in other towns and cities along the border, the U.S. military began to station contingents of soldiers to monitor likely infiltration points, especially for trucks and railroad cars. Tensions at times along the border became scalding hot and, unfortunately on occasion, exploded.

On August 27, 1918, in Ambos Nogales, a Mexican carpenter was walking across the border from Arizona carrying what a U.S. Customs Inspector deemed to be a suspicious package and ordered him to stop. Apparently Mexican customs officials on the other side of the border motioned him to continue. The poor man, confused by the conflicting orders, hesitated, uncertain what to do. Suddenly, two U.S. infantrymen raised their rifles, ordering his return. In the next moments of confusion and chaos, U.S. and Mexican soldiers and customs officers began exchanging gunfire. What later became known as "The Third Battle of Nogales" was on.

Quickly, bullets whizzed across International Street from the guns of U.S. and Mexican soldiers, as well as other government officials and civilians on both sides. As U.S. 10th Cavalry soldiers crossed the border line and charged into the buildings in Nogales, Sonora, other U.S. troops gained a tactical advantage by scaling the heights east of the towns. From storefront buildings, houses, rooftops, and windows, for two hours, a hail of gunfire zinged throughout the two towns that only shortly before had been quiet.

Realizing that the Mexican military forces on the scene and the residents of Nogales, Sonora, were quite unable to defend themselves against a much heavier

A modest fence forms the boundary line between Nogales, Sonora, and Nogales, Arizona, ca. 1899. The fence was hardly a serious deterrent against crossing; indeed, at one time some commercial establishments straddled the line. (National Archives)

bombardment from the northern side, Felix B. Peñaloza, *Presidente Municipal* of his town, ran into the street carrying a white handkerchief tied to a cane attempting to stop the onslaught. He was gunned down.

When it was all over, twelve people lost their lives. Customs and military officials from both sides attempted to piece together as best they could what had triggered the deadly and senseless slaughter. One U.S. sentry said that he thought the carpenter was likely a German spy; others thought he was a smuggler. Various accounts from onlookers and those involved in the shooting lent little substance to what had actually occurred. In any event, both sides agreed that something had to be done to avert another such crazed occurrence.

The solution: U.S. and Mexican authorities decided to divide the two border communities with a fence. It became the first border wall put in place between the two countries that represented a formal effort to separate and identify the people in order to enforce border regulations more safely.

Within a few years, many other cities along the border had followed the lead of Ambos Nogales and had erected fences in the downtown areas. A whole new era in the history of the border had been opened—permanent barriers to control border crossings by individuals. In episodic periods over the years, this development would often be contentious, dangerous, and inimical to friendly relations between residents in both countries.

THE BORDER AND MORALITY CONCERNS

There have been many times in American history when governmental institutions have bended to the calls of anti-vice crusaders for moral healing, righteousness, and a break from the Devil's supposed grip. In 1873 such reformers managed to convince the U.S. Congress to pass the so-called Comstock Law, a piece of legislation whose main purpose was to close the mails to obscene material. Zealous reformers used the law to attack all kinds of individuals they deemed as contributing to unhealthy acts, even including owners of dress shops who displayed naked wax dummies, painters who worked from nude models, authors such as George Bernard Shaw who wrote about sexual acts, and any individual who passed out information about birth control. For example, Dr. Benjamin Reitman, anarchist and close confidant of Emma Goldman, spent six months in the Cleveland Workhouse in 1916 for distributing pamphlets on birth control, which the courts concluded were obscene.

Even horse racing came under attack from the righteous. "The sport of kings," was an elite American institution that dated to the colonial era, and gambling was an integral part of it. Opposition by evangelicals and social reformers made horse track gambling an illegal enterprise by the second decade of the twentieth century.

Another of society's victories over sin came in the form of legislation that took effect in June 1910 called the Mann Act. Named after Representative James Mann (R-IL), the law purportedly was designed to address "white slave traffic." But it went much further. The language made any individual a felon "who shall knowingly persuade, induce, entice, or coerce, or cause to be persuaded, induced, enticed, or coerced, or aid or assist in persuading, inducing, enticing or coercing any woman or girl to go from one place to another in interstate or foreign commerce, or in any

Territory or the District of Columbia, for the purpose of prostitution or debauchery, or for any other immoral purpose, or with the intent and purpose on the part of such person that such woman or girl shall engage in the practice of prostitution or debauchery." Other provisions of the law even effectively made prostitution itself a federal offense.

Over the years, the Mann Act was cleverly used by prosecutors in all kinds of cases, even for bringing women from one state to another in order to work as theater chorus girls. Even some wives brought cases before the courts to fight against their husbands running off with lovers across state lines.

In 1914 the U.S. government passed additional legislation to cleanse the country. It passed the Harrison Narcotic Act to regulate the production and distribution of opiate-containing substances. It was the first instance of the United States enacting a ban on the domestic distribution of drugs. By 1924 the United States, through the Heroin Act, had prohibited the manufacture, importation, and possession of heroin, even for medical reasons.

Nevertheless, the most spirited attacks against evil and sin came from numerous temperance organizations and hellfire preachers, especially the itinerant evangelist Billy Sunday, who saw America's most pronounced threat to human decency, purity, and God's will in the form of the liquor bottle, "ole John Barleycorn," as the reformers branded spirituous liquors. The decades-long crusade against drinking came to a tumultuous victory in the halls of the U.S. House of Representatives in December 1917, following a previous favorable vote in the U.S. Senate. It sent the issue of prohibition to the states for ratification. By January 1919 legislatures in the necessary three-fourths of the states had completed the process and ratified the Eighteenth Amendment to the U.S. Constitution. Prohibition officially began a year later.

Thus, as the war in Europe ended and the United States entered into a period ironically known in history as "The Roaring Twenties," much of the revelry and leisure acts in which citizens often engaged were illegal. The most notable result of this onslaught of puritanical legislation was, naturally, efforts to thwart it. Hence, the speakeasies, the bathtub gin, the hidden stills in the woods, and, most prominently, the growth and violence surrounding organized crime. If the public wanted to continue to use these products and institutions for recreation, the mob became its supplier.

But the war for morality also had profound implications for the history of the U.S.-Mexican border. If citizens could not find the vice of their choice on U.S. soil, what about Mexico?

By the early 1920s many of Mexico's border towns, especially Tijuana and Juárez, became the source of supply and demand. Now U.S. citizens, merely by crossing the border, could indulge in those activities that U.S. state, local, and federal governments, prodded by anti-vice crusaders, had deemed illegal. In 1931 a report written for the U.S. Department of Justice talked about the atmosphere in Juárez, with its cabarets, saloons, houses of ill repute, gambling halls, cockfights, drug dealing, racetracks, and other attractions that prospered from money brought into the town by the vice-deprived citizens of the United States. It was if Sodom and Gomorrah had arisen in the desert towns across the border.

Tijuana became an especially luring destination. Financed largely by U.S. businessmen, the number of saloons and honky-tonks in Tijuana doubled within a few years; racetracks opened in the early 1920s; and nighttime attractions, combining liquor with other assorted vices, opened with such names as the Mexicali Beer Hall and the Tivoli Bar. In many ways Tijuana became the heart of a vice industry for California, financed by businessmen who gained the moniker of "border barons."

In 1928 U.S. investors opened the elite Agua Caliente resort and casino, boasting an array of attractions, both vice related and otherwise, including both horse and dog racing, golf, a magnificent hotel with all the amenities, and even an airport. The opulence of Agua Caliente brought the stars of stage and screen and other entertainers to perform, from Charlie Chaplin and Jean Harlow to Bing Crosby and the Marx Brothers. Legend has it that mafia king Al Capone lost half a million dollars at the gambling tables at Agua Caliente in one night.

Throughout the 1920s and early 1930s both the U.S. and Mexican governments wrestled with the dilemma of what, if anything, to do about the burgeoning centers of morally challenged entertainment centers that had suddenly began to characterize the Mexican border towns. On the one hand, Mexican government officials at all levels worried about the issue of national identity and whether the proliferation of vice-related industry in the northern border cities would sully the reputation of the entire nation. On the other hand, U.S. reformers were appalled that the growth of and easy access immediately across the border to those vice-related activities, those debaucheries that had been declared illegal in the United States, were severely compromising the purpose of the morality laws.

In response, both countries, in halting and intermittent spasms of law enforcement, began to limit access across the border during nighttime hours, simply closing the border gates to traffic during the times in which the vice districts were most active. In 1924, for example, the U.S. government decided to institute a 9:00 p.m. curfew in Tijuana. Later, for a time, the gates were closed at 6:00 p.m.

By the end of the 1920s border cities from Texas to California instituted different closing hours at ports of entry at various times. Through those years, U.S. and Mexican officials quibbled over the desirability of shutting off late-night traffic with curfews. Eventually, with the end of Prohibition in the United States in the early 1930s and the ebbing of the voices of moral reform during the onset of the Great Depression, the lure of the vice districts in the border towns in Mexico waned to some extent. For example, by 1933 over one hundred saloons and liquor stores had opened in El Paso, eliminating the need for alcohol border runs by Prohibition-thirsted U.S. citizens.

In the decades following, places such as Tijuana and Juárez became accessible at all hours, and the frantic call for governmental action to thwart the ability of U.S. citizens to seek out forbidden pleasures diminished. There were efforts through those years by Mexican government officials to clean up the vice districts in the border towns. There also were periods in the United States where vice emporiums in major U.S. cities rivaled anything available south of the border. But what many saw as a moral crisis on the border in the 1920s gave way to other more pressing concerns through the decades. Nevertheless, the experience of the 1920s had given impetus to a major concern that has never waned—the issue of immigration control.

The Border Fence and the Tohono O'odham Tribe

Members of the Tohono O'odham Nation, descendants of the ancient Hohokam natives, live mostly in the Sonoran Desert of southcentral Arizona. The tribe has over 28,000 members, of whom about 2,000 live in Mexico. The U.S.-Mexican border splits the nation for about seventy miles.

With changes in immigration laws and the increase in border security over the years, life for tribal members traversing the line has adversely affected the O'odham in many ways, especially for those who must cross to visit family members, engage in traditional sacred rites, and even engage in commerce. Now, on their own reservation, they must produce passports and border identification cards. In this artificial division of O'odham society, U.S. Border Patrol agents have detained and even deported members who did not carry papers and have confiscated such items as pine leaves, bird feathers, and cultural religious items.

There is now a border fence with gates for those who travel back and forth. To members of the Tohono O'odham Nation, the proposal of a wall the size envisioned by Donald Trump is especially offensive—not only a physical barrier but also a metaphor of division that would further divide the tribe's people.

DRUGS AND BORDER CONTROL: OPERATION INTERCEPT

The issue of border control and immigration of course became a signal development in border relations in the 1950s with the advent of Operation Wetback. Although the Eisenhower administration publicly lauded its efforts to deport hundreds of thousands of so-called illegal immigrants back across the border, its militarization techniques, terrifying and demoralizing to Mexican Americans in the United States, many of whom were citizens deported for no reason whatsoever, left lasting feelings of distrust and betrayal between the two governments. In the days of Operation Wetback, the U.S. government's stated purpose was economic—to return jobs held by illegal Mexican immigrants to Anglos—but much of the impetus of the operation had been xenophobic and racial. Although almost every kind of military maneuver was applied in the 1950s to rid the country of as many Mexicans as possible or to turn illegal immigrants into legal ones through the Bracero Program, building fences was not a choice of action.

It was not until the growing concerns of the illegal importation of drugs into the United States that the creation of physical barriers of fences and walls and other militarization tactics became the preferred modes of border control. By the late 1960s recreational drug use in the United States had become so prevalent among the young, white, middle-class population and the supply of such drugs so plentiful that the situation became a potent political issue.

The major source of much of the drug importation was south of the border, and the reaction to the perceived burgeoning crisis was a military-type action. Just as politicians had responded to border concerns with Operation Wetback, in the coming years the attack against drug importation would bring such efforts as Operation Intercept, Operation Cooperation, Operation Hold the Line, Operation Gatekeeper, Operation Condor, and so on. And in keeping with the militarization effort, the whole enterprise, as coined by President Richard Nixon in 1971, would officially be called "The War on Drugs."

Much of the impetus for Nixon's response to the issue had been the advent of the 1960s counterculture movement. His own political campaign had been one against those pot-smoking hippies and antiwar demonstrators that had so derided the professional political class, especially during the 1968 election. Now in power, within two months Nixon had established a Special Presidential Task Force Relating to Narcotics, Marihuana, and Dangerous Drugs, headed up by tough-minded attorney general and later convicted felon John Mitchell. Unsurprisingly, the task force concluded that drug abuse was one of most serious challenges facing the United States and that the power to stop it was eliminating smuggling and the flow of drugs at the U.S.-Mexican border.

With these findings in order, Nixon now declared that the War on Drugs would be launched by what he called Operation Intercept. His administration, he pledged, would eradicate this illicit drug problem by attacking it at its source—the Mexican border.

Soon, in late September 1969, Operation Intercept employed thousands of additional Border, Customs, and Immigration agents to the border to carry out this vital mission. Nixon pushed through Congress such draconian measures as mandatory sentencing for drug offenders and no-knock warrants. He also created the Drug Enforcement Administration (DEA) in 1973.

Nixon's brazen actions, taken unilaterally without coordination with the Mexican government, strove to institute a policy that would interdict the flow of drugs through what amounted to a complete inspection of all who crossed the border, whether they were on foot, in cars, in trucks, in airplanes, or in whatever other mode of transportation. In other words, the agents were told to search anything human that attempted to cross the border.

The operation was a fiasco. There were simply not enough forces to carry out such a mission, and soon the border became nearly frozen in terms of movement. To the dismay of everyone involved, whether those engaged in commerce, simple day-to-day activities, or tourism, the enterprise virtually shut down the border.

Mexican officials were outraged. This kind of unilateral action on the part of the United States not only infuriated Mexican government officials, it signaled an intention by U.S. leaders to abandon any semblance of cooperation and coordination on matters concerning both nations regarding the border. It was a betrayal in their eyes. Mexican officials fired off communiqués to Nixon urging the president to correct the excesses of a move that not only had not resulted in any progress in stopping drug trafficking but had created economic and social chaos at cities along the border.

Beset not only by diplomatic concerns but also by derisive press coverage that highlighted the massive lines of vehicles and near-complete disruption of daily activity at the border, the administration finally relented after two weeks. In October the clumsy and embarrassing operation was called off. In its place, U.S. and Mexican officials, working together, employed a new effort they agreed should be called Operation Cooperation in which both countries agreed to collaborate on ways implementation to reduce the flow of narcotics across the border. Operation

Intercept did alert the world that the U.S. commitment to its "War on Drugs" would not be denied. This was only the beginning. That *war* would continue far beyond the Nixon administration.

THE 1970S AND "THE TORTILLA CURTAIN"

When Jimmy Carter took office as president in January 1977, there was increasing concern about the undocumented alien problem, especially among conservative, right-wing political forces. Under previous Republican administrations, the issue had been whipped into a powerful issue and vigorously supported by officials at the INS. A deep recession in the early 1970s occurred at the same time that the INS launched a surprisingly overt public relations campaign against the dangers of unauthorized immigration, a step that further inflamed political discourse and public fears that the country was facing a serious crisis.

When Carter appointed Lionel Castillo, a Chicano, to head the INS, it signaled a different approach that the president intended to implement. Although border security concerns remained high on the agenda, Carter also sought to introduce legislation that would make it possible for unauthorized individuals already in the country to gradually obtain legal status.

And on the issue of the drug problem, Carter also took a different path. In an address to Congress in August 1977, Carter acknowledged the serious social problems posed by narcotics trafficking and the devastating human toll it was taking on drug users and the daunting challenges it posed for law enforcement agencies and social service agencies at all levels. He was a strong proponent of U.S. government support for treatment programs and against the unjustly harsh laws punishing individuals who merely used drugs and were not involved in their distribution. He strongly urged President Lopez-Portillo of Mexico to institute a more vigorous eradication program against the cultivation of opium in Mexico. And he acknowledged that the federal government should be vigilant against the illegal importation and major trafficking of controlled substances.

Against this backdrop, it is somewhat ironic that Carter became a target of Chicano activists during his administration. It all had to do with fencing. In the press and in scathing attacks by the activists, the fence at the border became known as "The Tortilla Curtain." A proposal by the INS to build two 6-mile steel and barbed wire fences at El Paso, Texas, and at San Ysidro, California triggered strenuous objections from the Mexican government. To those detractors, such a plan was just further evidence of the racism and xenophobia so prevalent in U.S. society. In article after article in small pamphlets and newspapers, Chicano leaders railed against "The Tortilla Curtain." The issue had now become one of symbolic dimensions, a physical manifestation of tense cross-border feelings and issues.

The fence itself was of no practical consequence regarding the main issues of border security, drug trafficking, and the like. After all, the total length of the fence was miniscule in relation to the full length of the border. And yet, here was President Carter, whose instincts were undoubtedly far more conciliatory and geared toward mutual coordination of the border problems than his predecessors, faced with the issue of "The Tortilla Curtain," a culturally insensitive appellation that he would have never personally embraced or tolerated.

In Texas the issue became especially heated and resulted in what became known as "The Tortilla Curtain Incident." In El Paso, some fences had already been erected during the World War II era, along with watchtowers. The fences were erected not only to enforce immigration restrictions but also to limit the spread of livestock disease. Following the war, the watchtowers had been torn down but the fences remained. And in 1977 and 1978, when the U.S. Congress, under continued pressure from groups opposed to the number of immigrants crossing the border, ordered additional construction in El Paso and in San Diego, Mexican officials attacked the move with such vehemence that the Carter administration was concerned that other diplomatic negotiations would be compromised as a result of the uproar.

And in El Paso Chicano activist groups and other grassroots protest organizations such the Coalition against the Fence sprang into action. Especially egregious and dehumanizing, they insisted, was that the fence used razor wire to maim any individual attempting to climb across. Such a fence, they argued, was an affront to human dignity and just another example of the dehumanizing of Mexicans.

Protests at the El Paso/Juárez crossing became so intense that rumors spread that U.S. troops were heading there to break up the demonstrations. At one point, a group of Mexican women had their crossing cards confiscated by the Border Patrol. This action sparked a small riot in which protestors blocked traffic, tore down the U.S. flag, and threw it into the Rio Grande. With the escalating tensions over the "Tortilla Curtain" threatening to damage diplomatic negotiations between the two countries, the two sides compromised. The fence would be shorter than originally planned and there would be no razor wire.

THE ADVENT OF "AMERICA'S WALL": OPERATIONS GATEKEEPER, HOLD THE LINE, SAFEGUARD, AND RIO GRANDE

Ronald Reagan's presidency raised the stakes in the drug war to new levels. It was marked most notably by the rates of incarceration. The United States began imprisoning unprecedented numbers of individuals not only for importing and trafficking in narcotics but also for using relatively small amounts. In 1980 the U.S. government reported that 50,000 prisoners were behind bars for drug law offenses; by 1997 that number had exceeded 400,000.

These were days when illicit drug use, especially a smokable form of cocaine dubbed "crack" used extensively in major cities, became a deeply held public concern. These were the days when First Lady Nancy Reagan began a highly publicized, if sometimes mocked, campaign called "Just Say No."

In California, Los Angeles Police Chief Daryl Gates perhaps set the highest bar of zealotry on the issue when, during the years of the George H. W. Bush, presidency, he sat in 1990 before a hearing in the U.S. Senate and offered the suggestion that drug users be taken out and shot. After all, we were in a drug war.

All of this hysteria through these years was accompanied by well-meaning but often exceedingly ineffective and even counter-effective, drug laws. Congress, for example, opposed access programs to provide clean syringes and other efforts to reduce health damage, especially in reducing the spread of the dreaded disease of HIV/AIDS.

In addition to the War on Drugs, the issue of illegal immigration continued to ratchet up to great heights during the years of the Reagan and Bush Sr. presidencies. In 1986 Reagan signed the Immigration Reform and Control Act, a compromise legislation that was meant to fortify the border and ensure that an effective employer verification program would be in force so that only legal workers would be hired. The legislation also legalized close to 3 million undocumented immigrants, a provision that conservatives regretted almost from the moment the bill was signed, calling the action "amnesty."

For years afterward, as undocumented migrants continued to flaunt whatever efforts the government put forth to stem the tide across the border, the immigration fight raged, with right-wing politicians and their constituents demanding greater enforcement.

In 1990 President George H. W. Bush signed an immigration act that included a "Family Unity" provision, designed to keep family units intact while the immigration process in each case resulted in either in acceptance or deportation. The law increased family immigration visas and provided more families a more favorable path to citizenship. When Bush signed the act, he called the family "the essential unit of society."

Thus, conservative Republican administrations enacted immigration laws that did authorize more stringent actions to control border security, but also saw the issue in terms of the humanity of those desperate men, women, and children who looked for a better life in the United States. Nevertheless, the issue of illegal immigration remained a potent political force and weapon.

As a presidential candidate in 1992, Bill Clinton was a strong proponent for drug treatment policies as opposed to arrest and incarceration of drug offenders. Nevertheless, bending to public and political pressure, after the 1992 election the Clinton White House continued to carry on the drug war and lamented the growing illegal immigration at the border. The administration inaugurated, new measures to control the border. Indeed, Clinton, framing the border problem as an anti-crime initiative, decided to take aggressive action against what he deemed a totally uncontrollable flaunting of U.S. immigration laws and processes. He began several new operations, a multipronged strategy, to fortify the most heavily crossed points along the border, including El Paso and San Diego.

"Operation Hold the Line," initially called "Operation Blockade," began in the El Paso area in the fall of 1993. Suddenly, 400 agents in their Border Patrol SUVs began spacing every one hundred yards from one side of the city to the other along the border. Low-flying helicopter patrols radioed views of the operation from above, and bright lights illuminated the border line. This was fundamentally a new strategy. Before, the efforts of the Border Patrol had been to apprehend border crossers after they crossed the line; this new tactic, however, was a concentrated effort to intercept, not only with intimidation but also with actual manpower, any efforts to cross the border at all. The assemblage in some eyes resembled a war-zone front line.

The operation was hailed by the administration, the press, and advocates of fierce border enforcement as a rousing success. Reports indicated a drop in apprehensions of over 70 percent in areas fanning out from the El Paso area. Indeed, following the implementation of Operation Hold the Line, the administration launched an even more ambitious effort in California. It was called Operation Gatekeeper.

The advent of Operation Gatekeeper was inextricably tied up in the political furor in California unleashed when Governor Pete Wilson's administration inserted the infamous Proposition 187 into the general election ballot. The purpose of Proposition 187 was to make immigrants without legal authorization ineligible for public benefits. Although the voters of California approved the measure, it died in later court actions after federal lawsuits were filed by such groups as the Mexican American Legal Defense and Education Fund (MALDEF).

Nevertheless, the anti-immigration fervor in this key electoral state weighed heavily on the Clinton administration as it developed policies relating to the border. Also in 1994 the United States passed the Violent Crime Control and Law Enforcement Act that provided substantial increases in funding for the Border Patrol. With the administration under constant attack from right-wing groups about inattention to illegal immigration, Operation Gatekeeper became a logical, if overly aggressive, response.

Apprehensions of illegal immigrants across the entire length of the U.S.-Mexican border were greatest in the San Diego/Tijuana region. Across a patch of land known locally as "the soccer field" in Tijuana's Colonia Libertad neighborhood, large numbers of undocumented migrants waited on many nights until darkness to race across the border to avoid whatever Border Patrol agents lurked in waiting. In October 1994 "Operation Gatekeeper" was designed to eradicate this problem.

Beginning in October 1994 laborers erected two dozen miles of fences about fifteen feet high lit by high-intensity stadium lighting and fortified by heat sensors, helicopters, and infrared telescopes. In one notable perspective, the fencing was successful. By 2000 the administration could report that the apprehensions in the San Diego/Tijuana area had dropped significantly. On the other hand, to the east of the fence, apprehensions and illegal entries rose dramatically. It all had to do with unintended consequences.

As the human traffic shifted eastward away from the heavier patrols and the fences to more remote paths, more rugged terrain, through the punishing heat, with a lack of water, and vast distances to cover, the journeys for those attempting to cross the border became extraordinarily more dangerous. The deaths began rising precipitously. From 1998 to 2016 the Border Patrol reported nearly 4,000 deaths in California and Arizona. Because many lost bodies in the desert were undoubtedly never found, the numbers reported certainly vastly understated the horror of it all—a humanitarian disaster.

The third major operation launched by the Clinton administration to control the border was along the lonely desert stretch across Arizona known by the Border Patrol as the Tucson Sector. This was called Operation Safeguard, begun by the Border Patrol in the fall of 1994 and continued well beyond the years of the Clinton presidency.

The logic of the operation seemed simple enough. Fortify the urban port-of-entry areas such as Nogales and Douglas with such a massive increase of agents and equipment that would-be illegal crossers would be deterred from even attempting to penetrate the line at those points. Then, so the theory espoused, the border crossers would be easily spotted along the remaining parts of the border by roving patrols and helicopters.

The results of Operation Safeguard were very much the same as in Operation Gatekeeper. Driven from the more urban areas, border crossers faced a sweltering terrain that drove the death toll higher and higher. The tragedy of the enterprise was summed up by one retired Tucson Border Patrol sector chief who, looking back on the operation, said that mostly the only thing accomplished by the entire operation was killing people.

So horrendous were the consequences of the operation that some citizen groups formed to help reduce the hideous death toll. In Tucson, a group called Humane Borders, for example, organized over 2,000 volunteers, including some ranchers, to maintain water stations in the desert. Another group called Samaritan Patrol not only maintained water stations but also searched for migrants wandering in distress.

Eliy Ortiz, whose brother died in the Arizona desert, created an organization called Aguiulas del Desierto (Eagles of the Desert) who search for the dead or dying along the border. Ortiz has said that his group has rescued individuals who were walking on completely bare feet because the leather on their shoes had worn off in the unforgiving terrain.

In 1997 the Border Patrol launched yet another enforcement effort; it was called Operation Rio Grande and focused on the McAllen and Laredo areas of South Texas. Like the other operations before it, Operation Rio Grande used the familiar tactics of massing large numbers of agents, miles of lighting, and other technical equipment to shelter the urban areas from large numbers of border infiltrators. Like the other operations, it produced the same effects: dramatic decrease in the numbers of apprehensions in the protected areas and a significant rise in deaths in areas removed from those urban areas.

As in the previous operations, the Border Patrol trumpeted the success of reduced numbers of border crossers at the usual ports of entry, and once again it did not make much mention of the devastating loss of life in the desert regions far removed from the protected areas. In one incident in May 2003, in Victoria, Texas, thirty miles inland from the Gulf of Mexico, nineteen Latino migrants suffocated in a truck's sealed cargo trailer. Once again, it was another horrendous, unintended consequence.

POST-9/11 AND NATIONAL SECURITY

When hijacked planes hit the World Trade Center and the Pentagon on September 11, 2001, immense repercussions reached worldwide in innumerable forms. Life changed. For the U.S.-Mexican border the 9/11 attacks meant an immediate sense of urgency. Already plagued by problems of drug and human smuggling and grueling political debates over immigration policy, the border now became, as never before, a matter in the minds of U.S. leaders as a problem of national security.

Although those terrorists who flew those planes had no relation to Mexico or to the border and although the immediate attention focused on the Middle East and terrorist organizations, the border now seemed even more vulnerable, a place where U.S. ground could be invaded with relative impunity.

To policy makers, it seemed to make no difference that the Mexican border was now more patrolled than ever before. Some observers noted that the Canadian border, far more loosely secured than the Mexican border, would be a far more likely destination for any would-be terrorist to find his or her way into the United States. Yet it was the southern border, so long a source of contention and actual warfare, that drew the most attention with regard to national security following the 9/11 horror.

Soon rumors of plots and threats were reported to government officials. Soon, there were reports of sightings of al-Qaida terrorists. Soon, the U.S.-Mexican border was the focus of yet another concern, one that had to be met with even more fences, rangers, weapons, airplanes, and surveillance equipment. With islamophobia now at a fever pitch, it was therefore not surprising that all people of different cultures and colors were envisioned as possible terrorists or their accomplices.

Soon, the newly created Department of Homeland Security (DHS), a government agency created to combat terrorism, led by its Customs and Border Protection

Border wall between San Diego, California, and Tijuana, Baja California, 2017. As of 2019, slightly more than 700 miles of fences and walls divide the United States and Mexico along the nearly 2,000-mile length of the border. (Sherry V. Smith/Dreamstime.com)

branch, would now direct the further effort to secure the U.S.-Mexican border. The Canadian border still seemed to be of secondary concern.

In 2006 President George W. Bush signed into law the Secure Fence Act, legislation that called for the construction of hundreds of miles of "reinforced fencing" along with assorted vehicle barriers, checkpoints, and advanced technology, including satellites and "unmanned aerial devices." Although the Congress and the president had authorized this massive overhaul of security apparatus, the actual implementation ran into an array of funding difficulties when Congress set out to enact budget priorities.

The DHS realized, upon even cursory study, that "reinforced fencing" for the areas designated in the Secure Fence Act would not only be highly costly but would make little sense, given the various kinds of terrain encompassing the different areas of the border.

Led in the Congress by Senator Kay Bailey Hutchinson (R-TX), the act was amended to authorize DHS to abandon the idea that reinforced fencing was appropriate for all areas along the border and to implement whatever types of barriers were appropriate in the various locations to maintain operational control and the best use of technical resources to achieve border security. Thus, the idea of a single type of fence, a "one-size-fits-all" structure, was scrapped. It was, the DHS and Congress finally agreed, wasteful and merely symbolic and not the best approach to a more secure border.

Despite the complaints of hardline fence builders such as Senator Jim DeMint (R-SC) and Representative Duncan Hunter (R-CA), DHS did erect various kinds of fencing by 2011 that covered over 600 miles. It did not by any measure, however, meet the standards insisted on by the hard-liners.

Although the idea of a single type of reinforced fence was abandoned in favor of a more realistic and tactically appropriate approach, neither the administrations of George W. Bush nor Barack Obama backed away from supporting increased border security.

Bush did announce in a 2006 speech that he did not intend for the United States to militarize the border, arguing that such a move would compromise the goodwill and diplomatic cooperation between the two nations. Nevertheless, his administration did considerably enhance the physical buildup of forces and equipment to fortify the border, especially since the issue of national security was now so prominent. In fact, at one point, the administration deployed over 6,000 National Guard members in an operation called "Jump Start," designed to build roads and fences and to increase ground and air surveillance. As a matter of fact, the entire industry of predator drone-testing and high-tech surveillance infrastructure was supercharged in the years after 9/11 by the drumbeat of fear-mongering about terrorist infiltration of the border.

Congress facilitated the enhanced border security measures by passing a provision in an appropriations bill to fund the wars in Iraq and Afghanistan. That provision granted the secretary of homeland security the authority to waive any law necessary to ensure the expeditious construction of border barriers. That waiver included such laws as the Clean Air Act, the Endangered Species Act, the National Historic Preservation Act, and other mostly environmental historical measures.

The ecological consequences of these actions will be profound should a massive border wall be constructed. They will, for example, threaten the migration patterns of jaguars who need freedom of movement in their search for food and water. Not only will the lives of javelinas be threatened but also the ecosystems they foster. When a javelina eats and then excretes seeds, it nurtures the growth of such plant species as cacti and leguminous desert trees. The waiving of these laws along the border will threaten Mexican wolves, bighorn sheep, and ground-dwelling birds such as the Gambel's quail. The wall can be understood in myriad ways, and one of those is as an attack against the magnificence and natural order of the land.

Throughout the administrations of Bush and his successor Barack Obama, parts of the border were fenced. Almost 90 percent of the over 600 miles of fencing were built since 9/11. In a speech in El Paso in 2011, Obama declared that the fencing was "basically complete." He criticized hardline Republicans who demanded bigger and better fencing, at one point chiding his critics that some of them wouldn't be satisfied unless they built a moat filled with alligators. The point, he insisted, was that a uniform wall at all points along the border was not only unnecessary but also a wasteful expense. A much more sophisticated approach that applied appropriate technological apparatus that fit the circumstances of the areas involved would be far superior.

Defying the Fence: A Cross-Border Horse Race for the Ages, 1958

In Auga Prieta, Sonora, the sister city of Douglas, Arizona, the sport of horse racing has long been popular. In 1957 a horse called Relampago (Lightning) became the toast of not only the city of Agua Prieta but to horse race followers across Mexico. His speed, everyone said, was just like his name. Owned by Rafael Romero, proprietor of the Copacabana nightclub in Agua Prieta, the horse became so well-known both north and south of the border that many horse racing aficionados clamored for challenges by other well-known thoroughbreds. The most intriguing challenge came from the owner of a highly rated U.S. horse named Chiltepin (named after a fiery local wild chili), from a small village named Pirtleville on the U.S. side near Douglas. The owners of the horses agreed to a match race.

Scheduled for September 14, 1958, marking the 200th anniversary of the city of Douglas, the event was compromised by an outbreak of a hoof-and-mouth epidemic that forced government officials to close the border. Undeterred, the organizers of the event devised a unique solution—they constructed a track with the border fence in the middle. Although the horses would be running in separate countries, they would be matched side by side in the race separated by the fence.

With hundreds of people lining both sides, Relampago won the quarter-mile race. The horse became something of a hero.

In 2001 the cities of Agua Prieta and Douglas, in a genuine goodwill celebration not only of Cinco de Mayo but of the friendship of the people, decided to revive the 1959 event. The organizers in this case decided to temporarily tear down part of the fence. The Cinco De Mayo International Border Horse Race drew an estimated 20,000 people lining the border in grandstands on both sides. Ray Borane, the mayor of Douglas, said, "They say enemies build walls and friends build fences. Well, today we take down the fence to show that we are more than neighbors—we are friends and family."

It is not as if Obama abandoned the push for tighter security and implementation of the immigration laws. Indeed, his administration deported over 3 million people. Yet Obama continued to seek throughout his presidency a balanced policy toward immigration reform.

Like Bush before him, Obama vainly hoped that a greater commitment to fortify the border would help convince Republicans to work on negotiations leading to comprehensive immigration reform, including a path to citizenship for many of the estimated 11 million undocumented immigrants in the United States.

Meanwhile, at various locations across the length of the border, agents roam the line in recognizable vehicles; more sophisticated equipment is employed constantly—radar, drones, mobile ground sensors, helicopters, numerous barriers to prohibit vehicular crossing, and even blimps.

And the research goes on. For example, at the University of Arizona, scientists, under sponsorship of the U.S. government, are designing new autonomous border-surveillance systems that require less actual manpower, programs that can collect and act on data in real time, even deploying drones in increasingly more complex and effective ways. Using computer simulations and integrating data from multiple sources, engineers continue to find ways to solve the border security challenges without heavy militarization, the use of massive numbers of agents, or the construction of antiquated forms of walls.

TRUMP'S "WALL"

Following his election to the presidency, Donald Trump pressed for a massive wall that would extend from sea to sea along the border and insisted that Mexico would pay for it. It was, he declared, a campaign promise he would not abandon.

Into the months of his administration, however, it became clear that the idea of building a nearly impenetrable wall over the entire length of the U.S.-Mexican border stretched not only the limits of imagination but also of practicality. There were myriad problems. First, there was the insistence on who would pay for the construction. The response from the president of Mexico was immediate. He tweeted:

> Enrique Peña Nieto
>
> President @realDonaldTrump: NO. Mexico will NEVER pay for a wall. Not now, not ever.
>
> Sincerely, Mexico (all of us).
> 9:25 PM-May 29, 2018

In subsequent talks, it became clear that Mexico would never seriously consider paying for a project it considered not only worthless but also insulting. In press conferences and speeches, Trump continued to insist that Mexico would finally end up paying for the wall.

Following the Mexican presidential election in 2018, incoming president Manuel López Obrador was, if anything, even more dismissive and angered by the assertion that Mexico would even consider paying for such a wall. In a book published in 2017, Obrador had already attacked Trump's ideas on the issue of the border as insolent and demeaning. He had also said of Trump and his advisors that the new U.S. administration was speaking of Mexicans the way Hitler and the Nazis spoke of the Jews. Obrador had even filed a complaint with the United Nations' Office of the High Commissioner for Human Rights against Trump's planned border wall. Following his election, Obrador has not backed down.

Along with withering rebukes from Mexican leaders, Trump has been peppered with published studies, articles, and even advice from Republican stalwarts that a full-scale installation of a fortress-like construction along the entire length of the border would be budget shattering. At first, the administration asserted that the construction of 1,000 feet of a fifty-five-foot wall could be built for $18 billion even through mountainous terrain and desert alike. In contrast, a study published in *MIT Technology Review* estimates the cost would be $40 billion.

Other studies indicate that even these estimates are likely understated. One of the enormous problems, not only fiscally but also politically and socially, is the amount of privately held land that abuts the border. This is especially true in Texas.

A number of years ago officials, including mayors, judges, and business leaders on both sides of the border, formed the Texas Border Coalition. The organization insists that the wall would not only be an exorbitant waste of money but that it also would cut Texas off from the Rio Grande River because the wall would be built on Texas soil. And, most of all, says the coalition, it would not improve border security.

In addition, there is the problem of the government seizing private land through eminent domain laws. After the Secure Fence Act was passed in 2006, Customs and Border Protection used eminent domain to seize and pay for hundreds of pieces of land along the Rio Grande, and the political backlash was exceedingly hostile.

By the fall of 2018, there was talk of various unique types of construction that would fit special kinds of terrain. There was also a growing realization by the administration, although no spokesperson has admitted it, that Mexico was not going to bear the costs. Thus, Trump began to insist that costs for a wall be included in the U.S. budget, a demand that the U.S. Congress had, by the end of 2018, resisted.

Nevertheless, Trump ordered eight prototypes to be built in a desert spot outside San Diego. When he toured the area of the prototypes, Trump seemed satisfied that no one could get over any of them very easily. Subsequently, tactical teams testing the walls discovered that most of them could be breached without much difficulty.

Meanwhile, in the scorching summer sun of the Arizona desert, many migrants who crossed the border lacking sufficient water and food continued to perish. In the summer of 2017, four women brought water jugs and food to a place where they knew some of the migrants had died. In early 2018 the women, volunteers for a humanitarian aid group called No More Deaths, were convicted in a federal court in Tucson for operating a vehicle in a protected wilderness area. Outside the courtroom building, signs read "Humanitarian Aid Is Never a Crime."

And so the debate over the wall continues, as does the profound political and diplomatic discourse about the future of the border—its meaning, security, and the relationships of the individuals on both of its sides.

. . . .

Back in August 1971, First Lady Patricia Nixon was the featured guest at the inauguration of Border Field State Park in Imperial Beach, California. Located at the extreme southwest corner of the U.S. border, the park planners had envisioned free access to visitors from both sides. Yet at that park there was a fence. After a member of her security detail cut a section of the barbed wire, Mrs. Nixon walked into Mexico, embraced some children, and said "I hope there won't be a fence here too long."

DOCUMENTS

"Operation Intercept" Memorandum on Stopping Drug Trafficking, 1969

At the conclusion of Operation Intercept, one of the many unilateral attempts by the U.S. government to ward off border crossings, some in the State Department seemed surprised that the Mexican government and its people reacted with hostility. The following is a memo written by an official of the State Department's Office of Mexican Affairs to Deputy Attorney General Richard Kleindienst displaying concern that the U.S. actions in conducting Operation Intercept have strained U.S.-Mexican relations. It might be better, the memorandum advises, to take actions that do not indicate to the Mexicans that the United States considers them inferior.

Department of State
Washington, DC 20520
October 2, 1969

MEMORANDUM

TO: Honorable Richard Kleindienst

Deputy Attorney General

Department of Justice

FROM: Chris E. Petrow. County Director

Office of Mexican Affairs

SUBJECT: Operation Intercept

1. Purpose The purpose of this memorandum is to summarize the diplomatic aspects of Operation Intercept and well as the Mexican reaction to it.
2. Diplomatic Initiatives: The urgent U.S. concern about the drug abuse problem was transmitted to the Mexican President in July by Ambassador McBride and again on September 8 by President Nixon at the Amistad Dam meeting. In addition, briefings on the scope of Operation Intercept were given to the selected GOM officials, including the Secretary of Government, 10 days before the Operation began. Notification of

the start of "Intercept" was given one day in advance to the Acting Foreign Secretary by Ambassador McBride, and to the Mexican Ambassador here by officers of the Department of State.

We had hoped that advance notification of the purpose and scope of "Intercept" would not only impart to the Mexicans a sense of the seriousness of our determination to stop the drug traffic, but would also give them proof of our willingness to take them into our confidence. Our efforts in this respect were marred by press leaks—the first on August 28 in regard to placing Tijuana off-limits to military personnel, the second on September 8 to the New York Times, which gave some details on the proposed Operation Intercept. These leaks somewhat negated the benefits of advance private briefings and cast doubt on our willingness to take the Mexican authorizes into our confidence.

Finally, when "Intercept" began, the Department provided guidance to all Consuls in Mexico for handling inquiries and instructed Consuls to brief key Mexican local and state officials.

3. Mexican Reaction—As expected, "Intercept" has provoked strong hostility from commercial and civic organizations in the larger Mexican border cities where traffic delays have been severe. Revenue from tourism and retail sales has no doubt dropped.

Beyond the border areas, there is also strong discontent, although it is somewhat less intense. In reacting to "Intercept" the Mexicans are inclined to relate it to old and often unconnected grievances. Hence "Intercept" is not only judged on its own merits but is also considered as another harassment from the powerful northern neighbor. The problem not only stems from traffic delays and business losses, but perhaps even more fundamentally from a feeling of wounded dignity on the part of the Mexicans inspired by the intense personal search they are subjected to. Mexican sensitivity about their dignity, their suspicion that at heart Americans regard them as inferior beings, causes them to react at a high emotional pitch.

There has been a tendency for the Mexicans to consider retaliation by promoting a boycott of U.S. border cities. Some U.S. merchants and commercial groups have expressed concern over this possibility.

On the Governmental level, the Mexican response as initially noncommittal as they did not apparently fully comprehend what was involved. In recent days, however, under heavy press, commercial and other pressures, the Mexicans have taken several initiatives: 1) Foreign Secretary Carrillo Flores and Ambassador Margain have both informed us of Mexico's serious concern about repercussions of "Intercept" in the border area; 2) President Diaz Ordaz referred to "Intercept" in derogatory terms during a toast to the U.S. astronauts visiting Mexico City; 3) only one Mexican Cabinet Minister attended Ambassador McBride's reception for the astronauts although the entire Cabinet was invited; and 4) Carrillo Flores has sent a personal message to President Nixon on the subject of "Intercept." In addition, the Government-dominated press has shifted from an initially tolerant attitude on "Intercept" to an increasingly strident tone of hostility to it. It is clear that Operation Intercept as it is currently being carried out has damaged and is continuing to damage our relations with Mexico.

4. Proposed Bilateral Meeting on Intercept—In response to Carrillo Flores' appeal for some action to placate Mexican public opinion, Secretary Rogers, on September 27, advised Carrillo Flores of our readiness to meet with appropriate Mexican officials to discuss "Intercept." Action is under way to arrange such a meeting.
5. Comment—As noted above, the hostile reaction from Mexican border interests was anticipated. Although reports from our border posts in the past few days indicate that passions may be cooling somewhat, we believe Mexican anger will continue as long as the Mexicans do not receive what they consider courteous treatment as equals, the traffic tie-ups are not relieved and business losses are not alleviated. Mexican-organized "boycotts" may have some temporary success in certain cities but are very unlikely to prosper on a border-wide scale.

The negative reactions from the Mexican President and press are stronger than expected. We believe this is in part due to ire over discourteous treatment, dramatized by an unfortunate incident at El Paso in which the Mexican Consul General was subjected to a rigorous customs inspection, and in part to a persistent stream of U.S. press speculation that the "true" purpose of "Intercept" is to coerce Mexico into greater action on narcotics by willfully damaging border revenues.

We feel it is particularly important to act in a manner not offensive to the Mexican sense of dignity and to especially avoid recurrence of incidents like that in El Paso. We understand the Bureau of Customs has taken measures to this end.

The Mexican Government will probably attach much importance to the meeting of enforcement officials, and will give it much publicity, since participation in the meeting would constitute the "action" the Mexican border interests, and the country at large, are demanding of the GOM. We expect that the Mexicans will press for measures which will ease the main problems described above. Any measures which we can take without impairing the objectives of "Intercept" should be given careful consideration.

The Mexicans may also repeat their request for additional material for their own eradication programs.

In short, the official Mexican reaction to "Intercept" has been more hostile than anticipated and, if it continues may well affect U.S.-Mexican relations in areas unrelated to narcotics control. However, we believe that our acceptance of their proposal to hold bilateral talks will lead, at least temporarily, to abatement of the hostile reaction.

Source: State Department Memorandum on "Operation Intercept," October 2, 1969, Nixon Presidential Library, White House Special Files, Egil M. Krogh, available online at http://nsarchive.gwu.edu/NSAEBB/NSAEBB86.

Deaths in Border Crossings: A Report by the General Accounting Office, 2006

As the U.S. government increased its efforts to stem the flow of illegal immigration, it concentrated its resources around the ports of entry and urban city areas where the numbers of unauthorized crossings had traditionally occurred. The INS and Border Patrol efforts, along with increased enforcement after the Department of Homeland Security took control after 9/11, succeeded in reducing the numbers at those border locations such as San Diego, Nogales, and El Paso. Nevertheless, as men, women, and children skirted the more protected areas, they began to travel in areas along the border much more hostile because of searing heat, treacherous terrain, lack of water, and other dangers. Thus, alarming numbers of bodies lay strewn across lonely, desolate areas. A report by the General Accounting Office in 2006 provided statistical evidence of this ghastliness. Especially revealing in the report is the admission that methods of recording migrant deaths were severely limited in scope. Indeed, other later reports from other agencies revealed far greater numbers than reflected in this 2006 document. The following is an excerpt from the report sent to the U.S. Senate.

August 15, 2006
The Honorable Bill Frist
Majority Leader United States Senate

Dear Senator Frist: Reports by and others in recent years have indicated that increasing numbers of migrants attempting to illegally enter the United States die while crossing the southwest border in remote, desert areas or in other areas with particularly rugged and dangerous terrain. The U.S. Border Patrol implemented the Border Safety Initiative (BSI) in June 1998 with the intention of enforcing border security, educating and informing migrants of the dangers involved in crossing the border illegally, and carrying out search and rescue operations to help migrants in life-threatening situations. Additionally, the Border Patrol implemented the Arizona Border Control Initiative (ABCI) and the Interior Repatriation Program (IRP), efforts that also include components designed to reduce migrant deaths. As part of the BSI's mission, the Border Patrol established a methodology that outlines procedures to identify, track, and record data on migrant border-crossing deaths and rescues. The BSI methodology defines border-crossing deaths as those occurring in furtherance of an illegal entry and includes guidelines for recording those deaths occurring within its target zone—an area consisting of 45 counties on or near the southwest border with Mexico. These 45 counties are within an area that includes 9 of the 20 Border Patrol sectors responsible for enforcing U.S. borders and securing official ports of entry. According to BSI reports, since fiscal year 1998, there has been an upward trend in the number of migrant border-crossing deaths annually, from 266 in 1998 to 472 in 2005, with some fluctuations over time.

In light of concerns about reported increases in border-crossing deaths and interest in the BSI's approach to tracking and reducing these incidents, you asked us to analyze federal data on border-crossing deaths as well as available data on the Border Patrol's efforts to reduce such deaths. Specifically, for this report, we assessed: (1) How do the Border Patrol's data on trends in the numbers, locations, causes, and characteristics of border-crossing deaths compare to other sources of data on these types of deaths? (2) What differences, if any, are there in how the Border Patrol has implemented the BSI methodology across its sectors? (3) To what extent do existing data allow for an evaluation of the effectiveness of the BSI and other Border Patrol efforts to prevent border-crossing deaths?

You also asked us to compare deaths among migrants to deaths in the general U.S. population living within the BSI target zone. We compared each group's share of deaths for the causes of death most commonly associated with border-crossing. . . .

We conducted our work between August 2005 and June 2006 in accordance with generally accepted government auditing standards. Our analysis of the BSI and NCHS data shows that both datasets reflect similar trends in the numbers, locations, causes, and characteristics of migrant border-crossing deaths between 1990 and 2005. These trends are consistent with the trends identified in the studies by CIR that used state-level vital registry data to document migrant border-crossing deaths between 1985 and 1998. From the late 1980s through the early 1990s, the number of border-crossing deaths declined. Then, from the late 1990s through 2005, the number of deaths approximately doubled. For example, our analysis of the BSI data shows that the annual number of border-crossing deaths increased from 241 in 1999 to a total of 472 deaths recorded in 2005. Further, the majority of the increase in deaths during this period occurred within the Border Patrol's Tucson Sector—which includes much of the Arizona desert. Our analysis of the NCHS data indicates that, between 1990 and 2003, more than three-fourths of the rise in migrant border-crossing deaths along the southwest border can be attributed to an increase in deaths in the Tucson Sector. Over this period, deaths due to exposure, especially heat-related exposure, increased substantially, while deaths from traffic fatalities and homicide declined. This pattern represents a major shift in the causes of migrant border-crossing deaths, as traffic fatalities were the leading cause of migrant border-crossing deaths during the early 1990s, while from the late 1990s onward, heat exposure was the leading cause of death. The increase in deaths due to heat exposure over the last 15 years is consistent with our previous report that found evidence that migrant traffic shifted from urban areas like San Diego and El Paso into the desert following the implementation of the Southwest Border Strategy in 1994. Our analysis indicates little change over time in the ages of border-crossing decedents, and while the majority of decedents are male, the percentage of female decedents has more than doubled from 1998 to 2005.

Differences in the extent to which the Border Patrol's established methodology for tracking and recording deaths has been implemented consistently across its sectors may have led to the BSI data understating the total number of border-crossing deaths occurring within any given year. For example, although the BSI methodology instructs BSI sector coordinators—agents responsible for managing BSI operations within each of the nine Border Patrol sectors along the southwest border—to maintain regular contact with local officials such as county coroners and medical examiners in order to obtain information on any border-crossing deaths where the Border Patrol was not involved, we found differences among the sectors in the nature and frequency of the contacts made. Additionally, methods for coordinating with local officials have not yet been formalized in some sectors. These sectors are in locations in which relatively few border-crossing deaths occur, and as a result, the informal communication patterns may have had little impact on the total numbers of deaths recorded in the BSI data thus far. However, these trends have the potential to change in the future, as they did in the Tucson Sector between 1998 and 2005. According to our analysis of the BSI data, the number of deaths in the Tucson Sector increased from 11 in 1998 to 216 in 2005. Such incomplete data may in turn affect the Border Patrol's ability to understand the scale of the problem in each sector and affect the agency's ability to make key decisions about where and how to deploy BSI resources across the southwest border. . . .

Measurement challenges and data limitations inhibit a comprehensive evaluation of the BSI's efforts to prevent border-crossing deaths. Furthermore, there is insufficient evidence to support the Border Patrol's assertions that related efforts such as the ABCI and IRP reduced migrant deaths between 2003 and 2004. The effectiveness of the Border Patrol's efforts to prevent deaths cannot simply be measured by examining changes in the number of migrant deaths following the introduction of a prevention effort, as other factors may also affect the number of deaths. For example, changes in the number of migrants attempting to cross the border, variations in the locations where migrants attempt to cross, fluctuations in weather patterns, and changes in Border Patrol enforcement activities may all affect the number of border-crossing deaths in any given year. The effects of such factors on the number of migrant deaths need to be taken into account when assessing the impact of the BSI and related efforts. In addition, evaluating the BSI's efforts to prevent deaths is further limited by the extent to which the Border Patrol can accurately measure the hours and resources dedicated exclusively to the BSI and other prevention activities. . . . .

Source: ILLEGAL IMMIGRATION Border-Crossing Deaths Have Doubled Since 1995; Border Patrol's Efforts to Prevent Deaths Have Not Been Fully Evaluated, United States Government Accountability Office, Report to the Honorable Bill Frist, Majority Leader, U.S. Senate, August 2006, https://www.gao.gov/assets/260/251173.pdf.

A Trek to a New Life: Excerpt, 2016

The border-crossing odyssey of Rocio Mendez-Estrada mirrors that of hundreds of thousands other young children who arrived in the United States without legal documentation, were educated in U.S. schools, and have throughout their lives north of the border lived under the cloud of possible deportation. Like most of those children, she grew up in poverty with a family that sought a better life in the United States. From Piedras Anchas, Mexico, to life in Colorado and an educational experience that ended in her graduation from college, she became an activist for immigrant rights with MEChA (Movimiento Estudiantil Chicano de Aztlán). The following is an extract of an interview in 2016 with Rocio in which she details the harrowing trip with her family across the border.

CURTIN: Today is February 11th, 2016. My name is Tiffany Curtin, and today I am conducting an oral history interview with Rocio Mendez-Estrada, an immigrant activist and graduate of Castle View High School in Castle Rock. Ms. Mendez-Estrada immigrated to the United States in 2008. This interview is part of the Oral History, Our History Douglas County Immigrants Project. This oral history will be archived and made accessible through the Douglas County History Research Center with Douglas County Libraries. Rocio, welcome and please state your full name, when and where you were born and your native language.

MENDEZ-ESTRADA: Well, my name is Rocio Mendez and I was born in Piedras Anchas (Primera del Monte) in the State of Mexico [unclear] Sanchez. I was born in a really small town and my, my native language is Spanish and I came from a really big family.

CURTIN: And when your Dad came to the United States, your Mom stayed with you for a while? What, what was it like after your Dad left and came to the United States?

MENDEZ-ESTRADA: It was a little different because I always follow my Dad everywhere. He will have a lawn and he will have flowers, that, that was to support the family, and every time I would go with him, like around here and there just, I was always with my Dad. I was a daddy's girl. And when he left, it was different for me. I was "Why did he left? Why did he did left our family?" But after a while, it was kind of o.k. Then I got used to, to being with my Mom. My Mom became my Mom and my Dad.

CURTIN: And when your Dad came to the United States initially what was he doing to earn money? . . .

MENDEZ-ESTRADA: He would send money to us so we can go to school and have food, and he would paid rent here in the United States. But he was really hard for him because my Dad doesn't know how to write and read. He came alone and he will be walking everywhere, and he was just barely trying to find a way to give food to kids, to feed our kids. . . .

CURTIN: you mentioned that you came to the U.S. in 2008. Did you come to the U.S. with your Mom and your whole family at that time?

MENDEZ-ESTRADA: My Dad, back in 2001, we had a, life changed. My life change because one of my sisters suffered in a big accident, and my Dad had to sell everything that we had, and we left with nothing, just the life of my sister, so my Dad came back to the United States for the second time. He went back about that year, but he came back in the same year, and after that, he was so hard for us 'cause we were in debt at the hospital for my sister because my Dad took my sister to a private hospital because back in Mexico, it's hard when you don't have money. And then it was rather going to the private hospital and have my sister's life or just took her to a public and be dead. So we sell everything. We borrow money from other friends so it was really hard.

We didn't have any, so my Dad came to the United States, and when he came, he had an accident. He couldn't work probably for about six months, but he knew that he had people, a family to, to feed so he, after a week, he started working. It was a shock to us to see my Dad working that hard so we decide that we need to make a sacrifice so my Dad and my Mom took the decision that my Mom would come to the United States in 2002.

My Mom came in 2002, and I stayed in Mexico with my four siblings so it was 5 with me, I was about 11 years old, and so my Mom stayed here for two months. And then back December of 2004, my Grandmother died so Mom and my Dad decide to go back, and after a few months, my Dad came back to the United States, and I stayed with my Mom. And my Mom stayed with us, but after finished middle school around 2007, I want to go to school, and my Dad would say, "Yes," and my Mom would say, "Maybe." . . . And so then I asked my Dad, "Can I go with you? I want to go to school." And he would said, "I have to think about it because it's really dangerous. . . ."

Around January 2008, one of my uncles say, "Yes, I will go with you, but we need to walk, and we need to take a big risk." And all that time, I didn't think that it was a big risk. I said, like "Yes, I want to go." So in January 24th, that's when we decide to come to the United States. And it took us a week and a half to get here . . .

CURTIN: And with, in crossing, you said you . . .

MENDEZ-ESTRADA: And so we got to Sonalita. We eat something at a little restaurant, and we bought a lot of groceries. Backpacks around, probably seven backpacks, with food, canned food, water, bread, and candy for the kids. And after, probably about, around seven, I still remember, around seven, eight o'clock, a taxi got there, and we went in there, and he just went and drove us. But before getting to that, I remember seeing the signs saying, "Welcome to the United States." And after a few minutes, they drop us in a little stream so we went down to kind of a river and then we went up, and we just crossed the stream and we were in the United States. The only difference was just the stream. And on one side was Mexico and other one was United States. They told us you have to jump a fence and then just run so that's what we did. I thought it was kind of funny because there was other people crossing, too, but the US Border [Patrol] were looking for them, and they were like, we can hear them screaming like, "They're looking for us. They're looking for us."

So at that time, there was a helicopter looking for them so we run, and we went to hide. But it was hard to hide because there was nothing there. It was only dried bushes and we, we stayed there for about like two hours, and then we started walking all night. I remember being around like probably seven a.m., six a.m., and what I knew the time because we had a clock, and I was like, I was so tired. I told them, "I can't walk any more." And they were like, "We have to," so we sit down there, and I fell asleep, and after a while that was the first night we had under a few things, and we went into a trash bag because there was a few animals that they can bite you or they can eat you or they can do a few things to you. So we went into the trash bags and would sleep there the whole day, and probably around four, three, four p.m., we opened a few cans and eat some bread and beans and tuna, and I remember one of my little brothers crying. He saying like, "I want to go back. I don't want to go there." And that, it got us really hard because we were in the middle of nowhere. We can die. We can survive. We don't know what can happen to us so we continue walking and through the process we can see US Border Patrol, Patrol in cars and horses and helicopters and every single thing but for some thing, we were lucky, and I think God was with us because we got to be before them, after them or somewhere high from them so they never see us.

They never saw us, but we walk about days and nights and I remember really one night, it was raining so hard that I thought we weren't going make it any more because if you, if it rains then you get wet and if you walk too much, you can't walk anymore so you just have to go back to the stream and say, "I can't do it." I was going to the United States, but luckily, we find a little, I don't know, a little house or something was just [unclear] with cooper with a few things, and we got in there, and we stayed there for a few hours. And then we start walking again, but after that, there was nothing there. It was just different. You could barely see anything, and it was probably the second day, that we didn't have any water because there was so many kids and just drinking and drinking so we have to drink water from the [unclear] that was raining that we would drink water from the rain. And then we're still walking and walking and then we took a train, train trailers, kind of big like a, no, it's not train trailers, like the [unclear] train. I can't remember in English. Where the train goes?

CURTIN: Like the train tracks?

MENDEZ-ESTRADA: Yeah, the train tracks.

CURTIN: Are you walking on the train tracks?

MENDEZ-ESTRADA: Yes, we were walking. There was one, I think they were old train tracks, and that was our way to go was where we were supposed to be in the United States, but almost there, there was a big Border Patrol with a big, huge lamp, I guess. I don't know what they call it. But that came far away, like see you, so we stopped there, and said, "We need to find another way to go," so instead going just straight to the train tracks, we went around to the mountain. But I don't know what was there. I remember having my two little sisters in one hand and the others left and right, and I remember me falling asleep and not be able to walk and everything. But somehow it took us like so long to get out of the mountains, and then my Uncle said, "Keep walking," and we like, "Why, we're so tired . . ." And he said, "There was someone there."

And we didn't know if it's true or not, but there was a person there so we got scared, and we continued walking. Then they took us a little longer to get out of there. We were supposed to cross at I-25 and around probably one, and it was almost five p.m., so we crossed that. We were again in the train tracks and then there was a fabric close to it, and my Uncle came to United States before he knew English. And there was this guy called, talking on the phone, basically saying that there are these people walking, and you have to come and get them. They're Mexicans. They're coming to the United States. That's what he said, and then I asked my Uncle, "What, what should we do?" And he's like, "Just get down and run." That was the most scary thing we lived that day because after a few minutes, we saw three cops coming towards us, and then we run, and I remember me running and hiding in a little trash can, and I didn't know what's in it. I just went in there, and then the whole family was separated at the time, and it was separate for about like three, four hours. And they were looking for us with dogs, that was the U.S. Patrol Police, and we just stayed there. And the trees and the trash, and it took us like almost half of the day to be there, but luckily my Uncle came back and find us, me and my little brother and the other ones. My Mom was safe, and we stayed there for a few minutes. Everyone was so tired because we didn't have any food anymore. We didn't have any water anymore. We walked a few hours and we find another place, and luckily there was a big pot of water so we drink out of the water. But my little brother, he was around like four or five, he was there. "I want to see my Dad. I want a "torta," like a sandwich. He will said that, and like, so we sit down there and sleep for little while. Me and my Mom stay up to watch everyone, and somehow my little sister, Elizabeth, she got up and we saw her going to another space, a space where the sun was coming up, and I remember her seeing, laying down sleeping.

And I was so tired that I sleep for like probably a few minutes, and then when I wake up, my sister was gone. She went walking. I think she was like half asleep. She just went walking and at the moment, I saw my Mom. She didn't care if they were looking for us. We didn't care if they were looking for us. The only thing we cared was looking for my sister. So I stayed in the little place with my brothers, and my Mom, my Uncle and the person who was with us went looking for her. And after probably an hour, two hours, they find her, but I could never wish this to happen to a person. We almost lost my sister. We almost lost her. We didn't know where she was. If the Police took her or what happened to her? So that was the most scary thing we were leaving, crossing the desert, coming to the United States. And then there was no food. There was no water. And we were hungry because we were little kids, and my Uncle is my hero.

His name is Simbolo Mendez. He was with us all the time. He give me the strength to continue walking, and he would say, "I will find some food. You can eat," or why we just keep walking. And then we started walking again, and they were looking for us again. So we'd rather, there was the last chance to do it. There was only probably an hour away, two hours away from that hotel that we had to get. So we'd rather just, we decide to go and walk, but just don't look to anything. Just look to the floor, and we got behind a—We got there, and we got to, behind a business and close to the trash can so we decide to make two groups to cross the street because we knew that getting to the hotel, we would have to cross the street, and there was U.S. Patrol looking for people so we had take the risk again.

So the girls, me and my Mom, my two sisters and my little brother was the first, and everything was o.k., but my Uncle and my two brothers, they decide to stay, and they went after us, and they say, "We're going probably take a few minutes," but they got there after us. And we told them, "Why do that," so they were like because the Police saw us, and they were looking for us so we went to the hotel with no food. We took a shower and it was barely like our body was dead. Couldn't make any more, and everything was closed. We couldn't eat that day so basically we stayed there two days without us eating anything, and I remember watching that TV, and it was only about food, only about food! And we asked the person at that hotel, "Can you order something for us?" He says like, "No, everything is closed," so we couldn't eat. So we had to wait for the person that was going to pick us up, but another thing happened. The truck that we were going to take, it broke down in the middle, so they had to go back and get another car. But to be honest with you, it was a really indescribable story, and I'm not the only one. There's a lot of people. What I find, find on my story is that it came like five kids so it's mostly kids and three adults. So I find that, I was really lucky to be alive, and when I got to Phoenix, Arizona, a house, I was, I thank God and I thank my Uncle that he was my hero, and that's why I am here and I came so far because of him because he wanted me to have a better future.

Source: Douglas County History Research Center, Douglas County Libraries, Castle Rock, CO, http://douglascountyhistory.org/cdm/singleitem/collection/doh/id/528/rec/1.

10

Smuggling, Guns, Drugs, and Violence

As the U.S. government for decades attempted to control the border, there are those who have schemed, plotted, and devised various ways to thwart those control efforts. Drug smugglers have used tunnels, catapults, ultra-light aircraft, high-pressure cannons, and even go-carts to transport their cargo, along with the usual on-person delivery. In the case of the drug war the standoff at the border is, in simple terms, a phenomenon of guns crossing into Mexico to organized cartels and drugs crossing from the cartels into the United States—guns for drugs. Cartel violence has ravished several Mexican towns on the border, prompting the Mexican government to send troops to help quell the internecine battles. The territorial fights between rival cartels, using weapons mostly obtained from sources in the United States, have also had a deleterious effect on across-the-border trade and commerce in those cities, as well as increasing fear and intimidation on both sides.

The smuggling of drugs through cartel organizations is not the only major smuggling issue plaguing U.S.-Mexican relations on the border. There is also the smuggling of humans. Individuals and families trying to find a better life across the border often use organized networks of smugglers—"coyotes"—who escort clients. Many times those incursions over the border reach into treacherous desert areas and often lead to terrible human tragedy. There is also the hideous network of traffickers in young girls who are coerced or captured and led across the border into a life of prostitution.

For governments on both sides of border, the battle against the organized networks of smuggling enterprises of both drugs and people represents a daunting but profoundly paramount fight.

THE GROWTH OF MEXICAN DRUG CARTELS

For generations, contraband of various kinds has been streaming across the U.S.-Mexican border. During the 1920s and the Prohibition era in the United States, it was alcohol; later it was various kind of drugs that were outlawed in the United States that made their way through various surreptitious means across the border to fill a supply-and-demand need made more acute and lucrative for criminal enterprise by the laws prohibiting the distribution and use of everything from marijuana to cocaine to heroin as well as other substances.

The growth of the Mexican cartels was triggered by the opportunities opened up in the 1980s when the United States aggressively attacked the Caribbean networks that had dominated the drug trafficking business. When those networks weakened, the supply lines for illegal drugs shifted; the routes would now aim for the U.S.-Mexican border, and the drug trade would lead through cities such as Juárez, Nogales, Tijuana, and other northern Mexican cities to a waiting market in the United States.

In the 1970s the Columbian Medellin Cartel led by Pablo Emilio Escobar had supplied an estimated 80 percent of the cocaine smuggled into the United States. Some estimates suggest that Escobar and his cartel were sending some seventy to eighty tons of cocaine each month from Columbia to the United States. The notorious drug lord and his powerful, violent cartel dominated the cocaine trade and made its leader one of the wealthiest people in the world, whose lavish lifestyle made him a celebrity. Eventually the ruthless massacres of rival drug gangs and the murders of police officials, judges, and politicians made him one of the most sought-after fugitives. He was gunned down one day after his forty-fourth birthday in 1993 by Columbian government officials after a massive manhunt.

By the time of Escobar's death, the U.S. government, through task forces established by President Ronald Reagan in what became known as "The War on Drugs," had successfully shut down much of the Columbian cartels' pipelines to Florida. Now, the names of Mexican drug lords Félix Gallardo, Fonseca Carrillo, and Caro Quintero were in the crosshairs of the fight against drug trafficking. By 1984 the U.S. Drug Enforcement Agency (DEA) was focusing on what came to be called the Guadalajara Cartel, a loosely knit group of drug traffickers that eventually divided the Mexican border routes into territorial regions.

Nevertheless, just as Mafia mobs in the United States fought over territories in big cities such as New York and Chicago, the Mexican drug lords—ambitious, violent, addicted to their growing power, and increasingly jealous of other kingpins—began an increasingly vicious and deadly battle for supremacy. There would not be a single drug cartel in Mexico; there would be numerous cartels, with shifting loyalties, and power-hungry leaders who would wage savage warfare to increase their own control. There would be vast drug-growing regions in Mexico, especially in the Sinaloa region, and the cartel leaders would jockey for position, forge ever-changing alliances, invade the territories of rivals, and wage a constant struggle for power.

It did not take long for cartels to find the personnel necessary to carry on the drug trafficking trade and to fight off challenges to their control. An army of underemployed or destitute individuals gave the cartels a large pool from which to recruit soldiers and other forces to bolster their ranks. They became sophisticated profiteers, their business acumen matching their willingness to use every avenue to strengthen their enterprises.

A number of cartel leaders gained not only the muscle but also the footing within Mexican society to gain power. Much of the leverage came from simple bribery of police officials as well as government and political leaders. As the Mexican government over the years began to take forceful efforts to attempt to harness the searing violence and corruption of civil society infesting the country, especially in the cities at its northern border, it faced formidable obstacles. The Mexican government took extraordinary measures to burn large areas of drug fields, but the proliferation of new fields overwhelmed the efforts. Cartel dominance became a national disgrace.

From their early years of smuggling mostly marijuana and cocaine, the cartels branched out into heroin, methamphetamines, and synthetic opioids mostly to supply a market for individuals in the United States who had become addicted to painkillers. In the early twenty-first century, most of the heroin imported into the United States is transported by Mexican cartels, principally the Sinaloa, an organization with roots back to the 1970s.

Named after a state along the Pacific Coast, the Sinaloa cartel was founded by a group of farming families who trafficked in marijuana. Many of its leaders and members were related by blood or marriage and proudly gave the group the moniker "The Blood Alliance." Sinaloa eventually moved its operations to Guadalajara, where it established its connections with Colombian cocaine traffickers.

By the late 1980s the name of Joaquín Archivaldo Guzmán Loera became synonymous with the Sinaloa. Nicknamed El Chapo ("Shorty") because of his five-foot, six-inch height, his international stature as a drug lord would in time rival that of Columbia's Pablo Escobar. At an early age he and his brothers worked cutting and stacking opium poppy plants, and by the age of fifteen he had grown his own marijuana farm. In his early twenties he joined the Guadalajara Cartel, helping to ship drugs from the Sierra Madre range across the U.S.-Mexican border. El Chapo was a survivor—not hesitant about killing off rivals to gain increasing influence. He worked for a time coordinating shipments of drugs from Columbia to Mexico. Through the 1980s and 1990s, he began to wield increasingly ruthless control over the drug trafficking operations as the head of Sinaloa, the westernmost region that had been carved out by the drug lords.

By the early years of the twenty-first century, El Chapo became recognized as the most powerful drug trafficker in the world, directing Sinaola's operation worldwide, especially to large distribution centers in various cities in the United States. Like Escobar, he became a legendary, outsized, and feared figure, escaping from two separate prisons, one by loading himself in a laundry cart and the other one by famously digging a tunnel nearly a mile long. Many ballads tell of his criminal exploits.

El Chapo's drug empire made him a billionaire, and the international reach of his violent organization made him for a time the most wanted drug lord by U.S. federal authorities. He was finally captured again in Mexico after a shoot-out and extradited to the United States. He was tried and convicted in federal court in Brooklyn, New York, and in early 2019, faced life in prison. On February 13, 2019, El Chapo was found guilty on all ten federal criminal counts against him..

Over the years the Sinaloa cartel reigned over the Mexican drug empire, but other rivals arose to challenge its supremacy. A group that called itself the Jalisco cartel splintered from Sinaloa in 2010 and gained much territory, matching the ruthless bloodletting of its parent organization.

The arrest in Mexico City of Mexican drug trafficker Joaquín Guzmán Loera, nicknamed "El Chapo," February 22, 2014. Although the notorious drug king escaped from maximum-security prisons on two occasions, he was subsequently arrested again, extradited to the United States, convicted, and sentenced to life in prison in 2019. (Alfredo Estrella/AFP/Getty Images)

Other cartels fought for control, including the Juárez cartel that reigned in the state of Chihuahua and formed drug route connections across the border from New Mexico and Texas. The Gulf cartel held power in the northeastern state of Tamaulipas but lost a number of its leaders through violent death or arrest. The Arturo Beltran Leyva Organization, founded by four brothers, broke off from Sinaloa and, as it disintegrated, emerged as the Cartel Pacifico Sur with operations close to the northwestern Mexican border. The Arellano Félix Organization (AFO), also known as the Tijuana/AFO, traced its origins back to the Guadalajara cartel and was named after seven brothers who were nephews of Guadalajara's founder, Miguel Gallardo. La Familia Michoacana, based in the state of Michoacán, also had early ties with other cartels, including Gulf.

Perhaps the most feared cartel of all these iterations in recent years has been Los Zetas, an offshoot of the Gulf cartel, composed of a band of paramilitary thugs willing to instigate any type or degree of ruthlessness to wipe out other drug organizations or any law enforcement agency that tries to take them down. In addition to its notorious and vicious tactics, Los Zetas leaders gained enough brainpower among its leadership to develop a technologically sophisticated network of sex trafficking.

From its leadership on down to its foot soldiers, Los Zetas, based in the border city of Nuevo Laredo across from Laredo, Texas, gained the distinction of being perhaps the most barbaric of all of the cartels. In 2017, for example, a Zetas cartel leader named Marciano “Chano” Millan Vasques was jailed for killing twenty-nine people, one of whom, a child, he butchered in front of the parents.

Not to be intimidated by the levels of violence perpetrated by Los Zetas, Sinaloa at one point decided to send a warning to its rival. Sinaloa operatives dumped dismembered bodies in Zetas territory and decorated the scene with open letters referring to the Zetas as nothing but dishwashers and drunks. Each letter carried the signature, “Sincerely, El Chapo.”

In 2005 Mexico's president, Vicente Fox, began deploying troops to Tamaulipas and other states as part of what the government called Operation Safe Mexico. The soldiers and federal police sent to the border soon realized the extent of the criminal underworld they faced, its military might, and the corruption that existed among civic and government officials who protected the cartel's influence for hefty payoffs. The extraordinary violence in the northern Mexico cities did not permanently abate. Cartel leaders were now not only fighting each other; they were fighting government intervention. Nevertheless, through shifting alliances and tactics, the cartels not only survived but in some cases continued to thrive.

When Felipe Calderón assumed the presidency of Mexico in 2006, he made as one of his campaign promises an aggressive move against Mexican cartels. He immediately attempted to fulfill his promise, knowing well the sophistication and the extent of military power of the flourishing cartel enterprises. Just eleven days after assuming office, Calderón sent troops to the state of Michoacán, and in the following months to a number of other states, a total force of nearly 50,000. Yet the business operations of the cartels over the years made the success of any effort extraordinarily improbable. The cartel was bribing governors; mayors; prosecutors; local, state, and federal police officers; and senior officials in the army and navy, as well as other government agencies. Indeed, Calderón's own drug czar was on the take.

The increased military force of the government did succeed in damaging the operations of several cartels, especially Beltran-Leyva Organization and the Tijuana cartel. Also the offensive disrupted the command-and-control operations of several other cartels. The United States aided the effort by providing Black Hawk helicopters and training police and other law enforcement personnel. The operation was especially successful in apprehending a number of high-level cartel leaders and associates.

Yet by the end of his presidency, Calderón admitted that the war against the cartels remained one of the country's most daunting challenges. His successor, Enrique Peña Nieto, continued to ratchet up the government's efforts to combat violence on the border, mostly using the same operational strategy as Calderón.

In 2014, however, the government unveiled Plan Tamaulipas, specifically aimed at attacking the area along the border in northwest Mexico that had suffered a spike in violence. The plan was to try to close smuggling routes and, especially, to strengthen public security. As did a number of plans put into operation by the Mexican government on the border, Plan Tamaulipas had only limited success. Indeed, in the town of Reynosa, across from McAllen, Texas, thugs of the Gulf cartel resorted to attacking not only the military forces arrayed against them but also resorted to inflicting attacks against businesses and private citizens. For a time, the town of Reynosa became something of a minor war zone; even journalists were reluctant to venture into the town.

As some of the major cartels lost some of their leaders in the ongoing campaign, smaller drug smuggling groups emerged. With struggles over succession and territorial rivalries, the killings intensified. Some of cartels turned to kidnapping and extortion to keep their organizations together. Between 2006 and 2016, almost one hundred mayors and former mayors of Mexican cities and towns were killed along with other civic and political leaders. One Mexican journalist likened the narco trafficking enterprises to weeds spreading throughout society.

The corruption became so widespread on both sides of the border that the tiny town of Columbus, New Mexico, mostly known for the raid of Pancho Villa during the Mexican Revolution, became a haven for cartel drug trafficking. In 2011 the mayor, police chief, and well-known civic officials were arrested by U.S. marshals for smuggling arms and ammunition to one Mexican cartel. The police chief received a regular payoff from the cartel and even allowed some of his associates to use official police vehicles in the smuggling activity. Columbus is located across the border from Puerto Palomas, Chihuahua, where street violence had reached such horrendous, barbaric levels that on one occasion three severed heads were found in a gazebo in the town plaza.

Through all of these years of turmoil and bloodshed in many of northern Mexico towns and cities, it is true that almost all of it has remained south of the border. At the same time that Juárez, Chihuahua, was experiencing the horrors of cartel violence that drove the murder rate to fearsome levels, for example, El Paso, Texas, across the border remained relatively free of violent crime. Nevertheless, sometimes the violence does spill over to the U.S. side, and mayors and civic officials of those towns and cities are always wary about grim possibilities that it could spread.

Meanwhile, the cartels carry on business, and Mexican government authorities, helped on occasion by U.S. assistance, explore ways to eradicate the seemingly intractable problems of the cartel enterprises and their gruesome, horrific bloodletting.

ARMING THE CARTELS FROM ACROSS THE BORDER

Where do Mexican drug cartels get their guns and other armaments? They get them mostly from sellers in the United States. One typical smuggler told an interviewer, "One day, I took firearms to Mexico in several trips. Nuñez went with me. I bought nine thousand large-bore bullets, 9mm and 22mm. Then, I took twelve thousand more. I also took 25 automatic rifles. I made space on the car, because I could fit in it lying down. I put all the firearms inside the car, covered everything, and painted the car. That time, I got out that deal like 15 million pesos—that's when the dollar was worth 60 pesos. That was in '81 or '82. Here you don't have trouble getting firearms. I get them daily."

According to a report by the U.S. Government Accountability Office (GAO), by 2018, more than 200,000 firearms crossed the border every year, fueling the Mexican violent crime rate and keeping cartel warriors and thugs well-armed. Most of the firearms are purchased in the Southwest border states in gun shops and gun shows, and over 50 percent are high-caliber rifles.

The state of Texas has over 5,600 licensed gun retailers as well as a plethora of private dealers not authorized by the government; the entire country of Mexico has one gun store. Although Mexico is one of the few countries that allow citizens to purchase guns, the restrictions the government places on those purchases are about as daunting to would-be buyers as any gun control system could possibly be. To enter the Directorate of Arms and Munitions Sales, run by the Mexican army in a fortress-like structure in Mexico City, gun buyers must have undergone extensive background checks. Sales in the government-run facility run about thirty-eight weapons a day; at the same time, nearly 600 guns of various calibers and deadly force are smuggled into the country from the United States daily.

U.S. gun policy, it is clear, has helped enable Mexican drug cartels to assemble arsenals. Cartels use buyers in the United States, especially in Texas, to purchase weapons and smuggle them across the border with relative ease. In one typical case, the Gulf cartel hired a young machinist to buy weapons in Rio Grande, Texas. He walked out of the gun shop carrying three assault weapons similar to the M-16. A few days later he bought five similar weapons at a Houston gun store. Before crossing the border into Mexico at an isolated area, he had a haul of fourteen assault rifles along with additional guns and ammunition. One of those guns was later traced to his smuggling efforts after the killing of a number of Mexican police officers.

Often, vehicles crossing into Mexico carrying guns and other weapons from the United States are the same vehicles that are used to smuggle drugs in the opposite direction. During the U.S. presidential administration of Bill Clinton, Congress in

The Queen of Smuggling—Rosa Emma Caravel Ontiveros, "La Guera Polvos" (Blonde Powder Woman)

If there were a Hall of Infamy for border smugglers, she would be a prominent member. Her name was Rosa Emma Carvajal Ontiversos, and she became something of a legend in the Mexican town of Palomas as well as across the border in New Mexico. They called her "La Guera Polvos," or "The Blonde Powder Woman." She ran an operation that included not only dope smuggling but also undocumented Mexican and Central American migrants. In her storied career, Carvajal once led a group of loyalists who stormed and sacked the Palomas Police station. She once shot a woman in a jealous rage over a lover's straying habits. Carvajal's life, a woman jockeying for position of power in a world of gangland men, exemplifies the lives of numerous other women "coyotes" who managed to gain influence among machismo cartel operations. Not surprisingly, "La Guera Polvos" was gunned down gangland style while in her car in Palomas in 2007.

1994 banned the manufacture of semiautomatic assault rifles. Although public opinion in the United States overwhelmingly approved of the ban, intense lobbying efforts by the National Rifle Association persuaded Congress to allow the ban to die. The Mexican cartels were grateful.

AK-47 Kalashnikov assault rifles, AR-15 assault rifles, Barrett .50-caliber armor-piercing sniper rifles, fragmentation grenades, machine guns, armor-piercing handguns—all of it is a death stream of armaments crossing the border into the hands of cartels, firepower to take on rival gangs, Mexican military and police, and any others who dare challenge the smuggling operations.

TUNNELS, TRAINS, TRUCKS, AND PLANES

In addition to his reputation and that of his cartel thugs as psychopathic killers, El Chapo Guzmán was known for his innovative methods of border smuggling. Among the creative innovations devised by the leader of Sinaloa was mixing apparently innocuous business ventures with smuggling operations. There was, for example, the chili pepper racket. He opened a factory in Guadalajara that produced a product he called "Comadre Jalapeños" and shipped the cans to Mexican-owned grocery stores in California run by some of the cartel's operatives. They contained cocaine.

Cartels have used shipments of other foodstuffs as a favorite mode of smuggling. There have been shipments of carrots stuffed with drugs along with watermelons, plantains, cucumbers, and pineapples. In early 2015 Mexican soldiers were able to confiscate packages of donuts that had been sprinkled not with sugar but with cocaine. In another case, authorities found frozen sharks stuffed with packets of cocaine.

As early as the 1980s El Chapo also pioneered the use of tunnels in drug-running operations. He hired an engineer to design a passageway from a house close to the border in Agua Prieta, Sonora, to a warehouse owned by the cartel in Douglas, Arizona. The opening of the tunnel was operated by a lever disguised as a water facet that triggered a hydraulic system to open a hidden trapdoor in one of the rooms of the house. Although the tunnel was only 200 feet long, it launched a whole new area of development in the constantly evolving schemes to transport drugs.

There would now be "super tunnels"—lighted, with motorized carts, reinforced to prevent collapse, air ventilation systems, and even small elevators, all designed by skilled engineers.

The manufacturing of tunnels continued apace even as government authorities on either side of the border worked to find and destroy them. Not surprisingly, tunnel building increased with the erection of fences. During the George W. Bush administration, nearly 300 miles of fencing was erected along the border; at the same time more than three times as many tunnels were uncovered by Border Patrol and other law enforcement officers than had been found during the entire decade of the 1990s.

In 2013 at a point along the border near Tijuana and San Diego, authorities found what amounted to an evolutionary masterpiece in cartel tunneling. This underground piece of work was the length of nearly six football fields and linked warehouses in Tijuana to the Otay Mesa industrial area in San Diego. The tunnel was equipped with an electric rail system.

In the sister cities of Nogales, Sonora, and Nogales, Arizona, tunnels became so numerous that some city officials worried that the unstable ground above might result in possible cave-ins. Mexican federal agents became so alarmed by the tunneling that they have inspected and sometimes seized houses close to the border. The entrance to one of the tunnels began inside a graveyard tomb. City and federal authorities have devoted much time and resources to locating and filling up underground passageways linking the two towns.

Most of the drug smuggling is still accomplished with motor vehicles of various kinds, specially designed to defy even the most aggressive searches by border control agents. Cartel workshops design so-called "trap cars" with secret compartments attached underneath, on top, and anywhere clever designers can figure out places to stash packets of drugs. In some cases they build hiding places inside gas tanks and disguise containers as engine parts. In other cases customs agents have to use blowtorches to cut open some of the drug-holding cubicles. Some of the trap cars are designed so that stash compartments can be opened only with complex mechanisms. One type of car, for example, has a specially designed system in which the compartments can be opened only with the driver seated, with all doors closed, and the car's defroster turned on.

Cartels have also used planes. From ultra-light aircraft to 747s, in which they can load as much as thirteen tons of cocaine, drug traffickers have been able to find landing spots and elude U.S. law enforcement. They continue to use advancing technology. A number of shipments of drugs flown by drones have been found by drug officers.

The Border Crossing Odyssey of a Major Leaguer

Born in a tiny sugar-cane mill town about 150 miles from Havana, Yasiel Puig, from his earliest years, was a baseball prodigy. Muscular, strong, and fast, he moved into Cuba's highest amateur ranks swiftly, debuting with the Cienfuegos Elefantes. To the dismay of his coaches, however, he was full of mischief that bordered on insubordination. Suspicions surfaced that the youngster had his sights on something higher than amateur baseball. As many Cuban ballplayers, Puig harbored dreams of playing in the major leagues in the United States.

Aided by friends and smugglers, he began in the summer of 2012 what became an odyssey in traveling from Cuba through Mexico and crossing the U.S.-Mexican border. After a harrowing journey on a boat piloted by cartel thugs, after narrowly escaping not only authorities but also a near collision at sea when the boat ran out of fuel, after spending many days held captive in a rundown hole of a hotel, after hearing threats that he might be attacked with a machete, after escaping from the cartel thugs to be rescued by other unsavory characters, and after spending some additional anxiety-filled days in Mexico, Puig walked across the international bridge spanning the Rio Bravo/Rio Grande between Reynosa, Mexico, and Hidalgo, Texas, entered the Immigration and Customs patrol station on the U.S. side, and with only his Cuban national ID card to prove his citizenship, declared for asylum. He began his career with the Los Angeles Dodgers.

They continue to use freight trains. So many trains cross the U.S.-Mexican border every day that it is impossible for border security agents to search all of them with any confidence of finding a large percentage of the hidden drug cargoes. Additionally, cartels have often been able to pay off train workers to aid the drug transports.

One of the simpler yet inventive methods of drug transporting has its roots in centuries past. A Border Patrol agent in Douglas, Arizona, reported that a catapult had lobbed about fifty pounds of marijuana into the United States. He lamented that the fence in Douglas had met its match. Border authorities had erected the best fence money could buy, he said, and the drug traffickers had countered with technology that was over 2,000 years old.

HUMAN AND MIGRANT SMUGGLING AND CONTINUING VIOLENCE

For generations, individuals and families have sought opportunity and refuge crossing the U.S.-Mexican border. For some, the journeys have led to new lives and hope for those mired in poverty and in danger from violence. Others have failed; many have died. Over the years, through changing circumstances and political struggles, the nature of migration has changed dramatically. Not only is it now much more difficult to cross the border than it was many decades ago, but the risks in making those efforts are increasingly perilous.

In recent years, the drug cartels have achieved such extraordinary power and sophistication in their drug operations that they have branched out into a new area—migrant smuggling and human trafficking. There are important differences in the terminology of the two activities.

Migrant smuggling occurs when an individual or family hires a smuggler (often called a "coyote") as a guide and escort to cross the border. The agreement with smuggling often involves not only providing transportation but also procuring fraudulent documents. Sometimes it includes the smuggler locating and harboring the migrants for a time in the United States. The agreement between the migrant and the smuggler is consensual.

Unlike migrant smuggling, human trafficking is a heinous crime that is not consensual and involves the exploitation of an individual for the purposes of compelled labor or commercial sex. Unfortunately, people who are smuggled can be extremely vulnerable to human trafficking, and tragic stories abound of youngsters as well as adults being forced into prostitution and a life of something akin to human slavery. Some youngsters have been captured by cartels not only for sexual exploitation but also to be used as child soldiers in the drug wars.

Just as they have done over the years with drug trafficking, cartels organized the business of the smuggling of people into an enormously profitable enterprise. Some migrants pay smugglers as much as $5,000 for their journey north.

In recent years, most of the families apprehended crossing the border are from Central American countries such as Honduras, El Salvador, and Guatemala. These are countries suffering from pitiful economic conditions, wrenching poverty,

Led by a human smuggler, or "coyote," undocumented migrants seek a safe route across the border near Nogales, Arizona, 2006. At that time, smugglers charged $1,000 to $3,000 for passage; by 2018 that price had tripled in some cases. (Kevin G. Hall/MCT/MCT via Getty Images)

escalating violence, and deepening misery among their people. Desperate, fearing for their lives, and seeking any bit of hope for a better life, individuals abandon their communities, familial roots, and any remaining sense of belonging and head north. They are refugees.

At the southern border of Mexico, most are vulnerable to cartel exploitation, either through increasingly high prices for migration north to the U.S. border or, for some, the horrors of capture and victimization in the trafficking for sex or labor. The dangers to women for abuse are so grant that some smugglers give women contraceptive injections in case of rape. And at Mexico's southern border a perilous journey of some 2,000 miles lies ahead to the United States.

As the Mexican government makes periodic efforts to police its southern border, the migrants from Central America continue to make the journey. Also, many Mexicans continue to attempt to travel to the United States. Some make many border crossings only to be turned back; others successfully outmaneuver the Border Patrol agents and other law enforcement officials and find a place in the United States. Many others suffer great pain and death. One of many examples involved a tractor trailer parked in a Walmart parking lot in San Antonio. Inside were immigrants packed together; ten died and more than thirty sustained various degrees of injuries and dehydration.

Meanwhile, at the border towns, the violence of the cartels defies any attempts by the Mexican government to contain it. In some cases, small towns are now without any law enforcement officers. They have either been killed or were so intimidated that they moved on.

In the early years of the twenty-first century, one of the deadly centers of cartel fighting was in the fifty-five-mile Valley of Juárez, in the state of Chihuahua, an area that for many years had been a relatively prosperous cotton-growing region dotted with towns such as Práxedis G. Guerrero, Porvenir, Esperanza, and Guadalupe. When cartel traffickers, drawn by easy access to the United States across the Rio Grande, moved into the area, a number of cartels unleashed a war against each other for control. Mostly a battle between the Sinaloa and La Linea organizations, the ensuing violence over the years turned the valley in a veritable battleground, a deadly onslaught of terror that killed off not only rival cartel fighters but also local police, mayors, business leaders, and other residents. It also, for a time, turned the major city of Juárez, the sister city of El Paso, Texas, into one of the deadliest metropolitan areas in the world.

The major crime syndicate in the valley since the 1980s had been the Juárez cartel, an organization that had paid out millions in bribes for protection not only to Mexican army leaders but also to state and law enforcement officials. In 2008 El Chapo's Sinaloa cartel had gained so much strength in military power and organizational savvy that it decided to move against the Juárez cartel in the region. The result brought near-total mayhem to normal civic life. When Mexico's federal government attempted to intervene in the cartel war, the bloodshed and atrocities in and around Juárez made international news.

In the small town of Guadalupe, the town government and its police had been wiped out by the end of 2010. Juárez newspapers began calling the farming areas the "Valley of Death." So many small towns in the region had suffered such horror that residents fled, many to Texas. The Juárez Valley became populated mostly by cartels and soldiers in their seemingly endless struggle for supremacy. The crime rate in Juárez continues to be high as of 2019.

Meanwhile, life continues in Juárez and, across the Rio Grande, in El Paso. Thousands of commuters cross the river every day at the Paso del Norte bridge. Commerce continues even as the drug wars drag on. Many of Juárez's richest citizens have managed to take their money across the border and have formed what amounts to a middle- and upper-class community in exile, El Paso, however, remains a safe city as the turmoil across the river continues.

Another area wracked by violence along the U.S. -Mexican border is in the state of Tamaulipas in Mexico's northeast corner, adjacent to the Gulf of Mexico. Long in control of the Gulf cartel, the area has also become a major smuggling haven of the Zetas cartel as well as a few other smaller organizations. Such cities as Matamoros, across from Brownsville, Texas, and Reynosa, across from McAllen, Texas, have witnessed scenes of terror, assassination, and murderous raids that have left the area in social and economic upheaval. Thousands of people have been reported killed or missing since 2010.

Throughout the turmoil on the Mexican side of the border, the drug and human smuggling carried on by the warring cartels continues. The drugs continue to get through to a waiting market in the United States; migrants continue to hire cartel coyotes to attempt to make it across the border; cartels continue warring with each other, jockeying for control and committing atrocities and using gruesome methods in those clashes; young women continue to be captured and forced into prostitution rings; and a terrifying flow of high-powered weapons continues to flow across the border from U.S. gun suppliers to keep alive the vicious cycle of tragedy.

DOCUMENTS

Reflections of a Smuggler, 1991

Francisco Villa attended high school in the western Mexican town of Tepic and went to college for a year in Guadalajara. In 1975, at age twenty, he decided, as many others had done, that his future would not be in Mexico but in El Norte. He would attempt to make his way to the United States. After numerous crossings and subsequent detentions and deportations, Villa decided to use his own experiences and failures as something akin to job training—he decided to become a smuggler. Using Tijuana as a base of operations, he began his career. In 1991 he was interviewed by the Mexican Migration Project at Princeton University. This is an excerpt of that interview.

I started having problems with my father because I liked to go out everywhere and have fun; I remember one day, my father got drunk, went to my mother's home—they were separated, and asked me what I was planning to do, to work, or if I was thinking that my mother would continue supporting me. That's when I said to my mom that I wanted to go to the North . . .

When a friend knew that I was leaving to the North, he said that he wanted to go as well, but didn't have any money. He also said that he had an aunt in Tijuana and that we could stay with her. So, I told him that I had enough money for both of us. For me it was better to go with him, since I was doing this just for adventure. We got to Tijuana with his aunt; she knew some smugglers, who only crossed my friend, I stayed back with nothing. I lived at my friend's aunt's home for one more month, and during that time, I knew all Tijuana. I spent all day long in the streets, and tried daily to cross by my own, but I was deported daily. The first couple of days, I tried to cross, just to see how far I could get. I got all the way to San Diego, but I didn't have any money for transportation. Since I was always deported, I learned all the ways in the mountain, besides, I met a lot of people, mostly a lot who did dirty business.

One day, one of them said to me that he could take me all the way to Los Angeles, only if I could help him to cross six people to San Diego. I took them to where he had a parked car. Once he got the people in, he came back and I stayed in Los Angeles without knowing anyone. I was in the North, but didn't know what to do . . .

I returned to Tijuana. Since I knew how to cross, I started crossing people . . . The people I crossed was people that I met in the border. Since I knew how to cross, everything was a lot easier. I stayed for four years crossing people. I did get people myself in the bars, on the streets, on terminals. I crossed them myself. I had my car parked on one spot on the other side. I could never get my car to Mexico because it didn't have documents. So, it always stayed on the other side; I had two set of keys . . .

I moved to Los Angeles. I contacted a friend with the forging business and told him: "You know, give me the machines that I'm going to start crossing people." Thus, I started crossing people. I go to Tijuana for them. They are people I know, and who usually do not have money to pay. I just tell them to pay for gas and I'll cross them.

You have to be conscious of what you're getting into and the problems all that brings. It's not easy to raise $50 or $60 dollars without doing anything. You have to work to get them. This job is both easy and difficult. It's difficult because today you'll have people, but tomorrow you may not. As you see me right now here crossing people, you may not see me tomorrow.

But, what can I do? Instead of robbing, I have to do something. . . . I don't get caught too often. One time, I got caught with 15 forged green cards and 15 social security cards in Arizona. They confiscated my car and I was in jail. The border patrol detained me.

Here, you have to work doing anything. One day, I took fire arms to Mexico in several trips. Nuñez went with me. I bought nine thousand large-bore bullets, 9mm and 22mm. Then, I took twelve thousand more. I also took 25 automatic rifles. I made space on the car, because I could fit in it lying down. I put all the firearms inside the car, covered everything, and painted the car. That time, I got out that deal like 15 million pesos—that's when the dollar was worth 60 pesos. That was on 81 or 82. Here you don't have trouble getting firearms. I get them daily. So, there's an exposition the first and the 15th day of the month, where you can buy arms . . .

I came here due to family problems. I didn't like the agriculture, and in my town, that was the only type of work. During those years, the North was the good option. One could come here and make money because there were only a few people. There were good salaries and good jobs. Seventeen years ago, I worked for $5 dollars an hour. Today, there wage continues to be $5 dollars an hour. It keeps going down because now we are many workers here.

The one that crosses the line is not the boss. The one that crosses you is someone who works with someone else. The smuggler crosses you; that guy knows the way and has people looking for you on the back. The boss is the one who picks you up, the one who gets all the money. The smuggler is just the guide who crosses about 10 people. The smuggler gets paid $75 to $100 each time. I used to work alone all the time. The danger is when there are people waiting for the group. Only one time I was attacked; they took away a ring, a watch and $100 dollars. The robbers were drug dealers from Tecate and they were robbing everyone on the line. I couldn't do anything because I was crossing two kids, a lady, and a cousin—my Uncle Pedro's son. One of the robbers put the knife on Pedrito, and I didn't want to do anything because they could kill him.

"I'll give you everything I've got, but leave him alone," I said.

About ten minutes later, a friend of mine picked me up and looked for the robbers. I obtained the lady's watch back, but not mine because they had sold it already . . .

The North is like a battle. If you're now with your own, it's very difficult. Most of the people come with no money. Sometimes, your own family is the last ones to help out. I don't understand how people get so conceited once they get to the North and have money. Whenever a river grows, it looks for a path. When you come to the North, you have to do whatever to survive. You don't care about the laws, because you have to work somehow to feed your family.

Source: Interview of Francisco Villa, August 1991, Mexican Migration Project, Princeton University, http://mmp.opr.princeton.edu/expressions/life_histories/hdvda11-en.aspx.

Carlos Morales: Immigrant Journey from El Salvador through Tijuana, Mexico

With growing economic and political instability plaguing a number of Central American countries along with increasing violence, many migrants who attempt to travel to the United States to find refuge and a new life come from countries such as El Salvador. The following is an excerpt of an interview conducted by the University of Maryland with an immigrant from El Salvador named Carlos Morales who made his way to the United States in 1980. His account exemplifies the harrowing challenges and perils facing such migrants in their journeys through Mexico and across the U.S. border.

. . . I immigrated in January of 1980.

And from the border with Guatemala, to another, until to the capital of Guatemala, it was already night time almost, it was getting dark. From there I took a bus that took us to the border with Mexico. But we got there in the middle of the night, we got to the border, like around one in the morning, so we couldn't pass, we had to stay in the pueblo at the edge of the border there. Tecun Aman it seems like it is called, we stayed there, we were there until the morning with other people who came on the same bus. Some people from Honduras and from El Salvador that were coming. There in a park walking and talking until it was morning because well, there weren't any hotels or anything to stay at for . . . for the next day at first hour to be able to cross the border. But since those Mexicans are some thieves, see I had a visa, for Mexico right, because in those times no, since it was different not too many people emigrated then, they gave visas. They gave me a visa. But when I cross the border they tell me that I can't pass because they wanted me to give them money "una mordida" like they called it. And I tell him, "But I have a visa." The scoundrels said no, ah, because I didn't bring enough luggage they told me because I only had one small bag with a . . . two outfits no more . . .

From Guadalajara to Tijuana?

. . . So I was going and they were taking and taking money. Well at, at the end I had about ten or eleven dollars, I think, but maybe it was what is convenient. A man came on, a man that was Mexican. Because there are good people in Mexico too. And he came with this big hat and sat next to me and I sat next to him. And since I was a teenager I was only seventeen years old, I looked young, so I . . . I . . . and I told him the story of what they had been doing to me and that I didn't have any more money. "Ah, don't worry son" he told me, "I will help you and you will see . . ." and the man was coming sipping on some tequila and he gave me some, right, and because I was used to those things, right, I took a shot. But look, I, look, when we got to ______there in Mexicali like they call it . . . he told me "You fake like you're sleeping and I'm going to tell them you're my son and that's it" right, and when they come, because those guys come like this—with a flashlight, they stop the bus and since its nighttime, no, they are shining face by face, right, and if they see something suspicious, be it by the clothes or the appearance there are questions or if they hear you talk . . .

They detect you. Well I did like this . . . I even got down in the seat, right, so I could look smaller. And the man, "No my son is sleeping" and that was it. What a difference! See the difference that the word of someone does, right.

So they didn't take me off. I got to Tijuana . . . and well when I got to Tijuana it was, it was difficult because I didn't even have money and I didn't even know where to go. But when I got to Tijuana, there was a taxi driver there and I told him the story and he told me, "Ah I'll take you to a hotel that's there, near here" he told me. And see he charged me a lot, right, because what I, what I had he took it he said "Give me that and I will take you to a hotel there". But he helped me because the woman of the hotel that was right, well the hotel was here and you see the line and on the other side is the United States. Especially that I was on the second level I saw well from there. Well he already, those guys already know those people right.

He took me to the hotel and the women . . . he left me there. Ah and she attended to me well. She said to me "There's no problem stay here" because she knew that I responded, right, physically for . . . for the money. I didn't have money but someone was going to send me money.

So she gave me a room, she even gave me cigarettes because I smoked, she gave me food, and that's it. I went to . . . I went to take a shower because I hadn't showered. The hard thing was that I had never known what hot water was, well, and the water fell on me, and the hot water fell on me and I got burned "How does this work?" I was saying to myself, in El Salvador I had never seen hot water (laughing). Only the water that came from the mountains that came out burning. And I asked the woman and she came to regulate it and told me how to shower, right, and that . . . but being in that hotel . . . she let me borrow the telephone so I could call my brother. Ah so my brother, since he didn't have papers either, right, but he had a friend who was Mexican and he sent him to bring me money, to be able to pay the hotel and buy food while they got a coyote that would take me to the other side.

So he came a day later . . . he came the next day . . . this guy came and he took me in his car to eat tacos, right, and he bought me some beers there and he even left me with cigarettes. And well the woman gave me the food and see the difference it makes . . .

I could see the river that divided, no, but the rover was on the side of the United States, even the . . . the fence, like that at night I could see the helicopters that were around. Well the day that . . . that they were going to pass me, the person came, the coyote, to pick me up . . . and I thought that he would pass me directly but it wasn't like that. Instead he took me to another house and I was there, I was there all afternoon. There I stayed refuged like waiting for nighttime to come. And he went to look for others . . . other people right, because I wasn't the only one to cross. The fun thing was that since they had their holes, right, I crosses the, the bar and I went in and that's it we were on the side of the United States, but the river was there. Only a shallow river that was there. That, that . . . and right there is Tijua . . . no San Diego that they call it . . . there in Tijuana, there isn't much there. There's no desert or anything, none of that, instead there are some bushes . . . if you cross the river . . . there . . . but the river was almost dry . . . some got in the water, others over rocks. There are some bushes and there are highways right there, the streets and the hotels and that. So those guys already know everything.

But what I want to tell you is that we were there, and the helicopters were around. And the big helicopter with the big lights and shining them on you and we were there. Because they know, they were waiting for them to switch turns. They waited until the middle of the night when they change of personnel, it's like the helicopter rests and in that time you go. When the helicopter comes back we already passed and are in the bushes. And then we crossed, right, running, it was exciting.

And because one is stealthy, right, and young, no, one is astute. And what, what is going to scare you in those situations, for me it was like excited like they say in English. (Laughing) well, yea. So . . . well we crossed and we stayed there and we got to the highway looking there . . . and without anyone noticing we crossed the street near there and we walked and there was a hotel and well there, we went inside. There we stayed in a room. There were four of us in a room . . . but the next day they came to pick us up in a car, a man that was going to take me. But he, he was looking . . . he, for another person and he left me for the time being . . . and went to go pick up the other person and he dropped me off at a park that was near the airport of San Diego, right, already seeing those . . . but well I felt strange because I was by myself there . . . and I just watched the planes how they came down and how . . . next to the . . . there . . . I was astonished by how fast they dropped and went up . . . I saw the plane that passed one day and in the air. "The Lunch One" we would say in El Cobano where I . . . until the man came to pick me up in the afternoon. And then I came with the other guy that he was going to take. And we went in the car but over there he got off the highway before crossing the clearing there before Chula Vista I think they call it, where immigration is. He opened the trunk and told us to get into the trunk, right, in the back part of the car. And the other guy didn't want to get in and said he wouldn't get in. that it was dangerous and that I don't know what, he didn't want to and he went into the woods and he stayed. So I got in and . . . I got in and he closed the trunk and he went. Well I don't know how long he drove, but it was some, some, twenty minutes maybe, the thing is that we got through fast, and he got off the highway on the, he got on the side and opened the trunk for me and then I got in . . . so then he told me we were going to Los Angeles then. And I was looking at the highways and I saw all that beauty, right. Well because I hadn't, never seen something so immense . . .

Source: Archive of Immigrant Voices, Carlos Morales, 2014, University of Maryland, College Park; https://archiveofimmigrantvoices.omeka.net/items/show/2.

Texas Department of Public Safety Threat Overview, 2017

In 2017 the Texas Department of Public Safety collaborated with state and local law enforcement, the U.S. Department of Homeland Security, and other government agencies across Texas and the United States to produce an overview of the safety threats facing the state. The following is an excerpt from that report relating to the cartels.

Mexican Cartels

Mexican cartels constitute the greatest organized crime threat to Texas. These powerful and ruthless criminal organizations use military and terrorist tactics to battle each other and the government of Mexico for control over the lucrative US drug and human smuggling markets. They dominate the wholesale trafficking of illegal drugs along the Texas-Mexico border, producing or smuggling most of the illegal drugs to the US. The cartels also engage in other criminal activities beyond drug smuggling, including profiting from human smuggling, weapons and ammunition smuggling, extortion, kidnapping for ransom and robbery.

All eight of the major cartels operate in the state, moving drugs and people into the US, and transporting cash, weapons, and stolen vehicles back to Mexico. These include the Gulf Cartel (CDG), Los Zetas, Juárez Cartel, Sinaloa Cartel, Knights Templar, La Familia Michoacana, Cartel Jalisco Nueva Generacion and the Beltran Leyva Organization. Of these, the Gulf Cartel, Los Zetas, the Sinaloa Cartel, and the Juárez Cartel have the most extensive presence and influence throughout Texas. . . . The threat from Mexican cartels is particularly high due to their wide range of criminal activity in Mexico and in Texas. Cartel members and associates are involved in the cross-border smuggling of people, weapons, drugs, and currency. Their operations are either run directly by cartel members, or indirectly through affiliated criminal organizations that pay fees to transit across cartel territory.

Approximate Areas of Operation of the Top Four Mexican Cartels Operating in Texas

Cartel operatives and associates have engaged in home invasions and other acts of violence in Texas. These crimes are often aimed at recovering lost drug loads, intimidating or silencing rivals and witnesses, and retaliating against enemies. For example, in May 2016, two Mexican citizens were convicted of conspiracy to commit murder for hire and interstate stalking, while a third pled guilty before trial, for their roles in the 2013 murder of a Southlake, Texas attorney they shot and killed in his SUV. The victim was also a Mexican national and reportedly a former attorney for a leader of the Gulf Cartel. From 2011 through 2013, the three defendants traveled from Mexico to Southlake with the intent to kill the victim. They purchased and placed surveillance cameras around the victim's neighborhood to track him and his family, in addition to placing tracking devices on their vehicles. While in the area, the defendants continually bought and rented new vehicles in order to avoid detection.

Drug Trafficking

Mexican cartels directly supply illicit drugs to cities throughout the US and rely on US-based gangs to further distribute drugs. Mexican drug traffickers have increased production of heroin significantly and have probably increased methamphetamine production for the US market, according to the Worldwide Threat Assessment of the US Intelligence Community.

Marijuana remains the most commonly used and most widely available illicit drug in the US. Marijuana continues to be smuggled from Mexico in large volumes, even though domestic production has increased

The majority of cocaine available in the US is produced in South America and smuggled across the Southwest Border. Despite the overall reported decrease in supply, cocaine remains widely available in US markets.

Mexico-produced methamphetamine also is available in the US due to sustained production in Mexico. Large shipments are regularly seized at the Southwest Border. Heroin availability is increasing throughout the country, with National Seizure System data showing an 80 percent increase in seizures in the past five years.

Seizures at the Southwest Border are also rising as Mexican cartels increase heroin production and transportation.

Texas Department of Public Safety Highway Patrol seizures

The cartels take advantage of the large volume of legitimate travel and trade between Texas and Mexico to camouflage their criminal activities. They use many kinds of vehicles, including stolen commercial vehicles, as well as legally registered commercial vehicles, for transporting contraband. And as drugs flow into the United States, cash flows out, with Mexican cartels laundering billions of dollars a year in associated proceeds.

Gang members associated with the Mexican cartels in the Rio Grande Valley use various tactics to evade law enforcement. For example, the Mexican cartels have deployed a substantial number of scouts to conduct around-the-clock surveillance of law enforcement at hotels, airports, restaurants, observation posts and on the river. More concerning is their willingness to use violence against law enforcement officers, as well as to engage in other evasion tactics—such as the deployment of spiked, tire-puncturing caltrops on public roads—which place officers and the public at risk, as in these instances:

- In March 2016, the Texas Highway Patrol, US Border Patrol, and Escobares (Texas) Police Department were pursuing a vehicle transporting narcotics near Rio Grande City, Texas. During the pursuit, the suspect rammed the Escobares Police Department vehicle in an attempt to evade arrest. The driver was arrested, and the narcotics in the vehicle were seized.
- In October 2015, US Border Patrol agents followed a vehicle suspected of containing narcotics near the Rio Grande River in Brownsville, Texas when a passenger inside the vehicle threw caltrops onto the roadway in an attempt to disable the Border Patrol vehicle. The suspect vehicle was later found abandoned with several hundred pounds of marijuana.
- In July 2014, in Anzalduas, Texas, eight to 12 subjects from the Mexican side of the river threw rocks at a DPS shallow water boat that had been conducting deterrence operations along the Rio Grande River. One subject on a Jet Ski rammed the DPS boat as its crew was attempting to arrest another suspect in the river. Both subjects returned to Mexico, abandoning the Jet Ski.

Source: Texas Department of Safety Threat Overview, January 2017, http://www.dps.texas.gov/director_staff/media_and_communications/2017/threatOverview20170115.pdf.

11

NAFTA, Maquiladoras, and Border Economics

The North American Free Trade Agreement (NAFTA), signed on January 1, 1994, by Canada, Mexico, and the United States, established a free-trade zone in North America. The agreement lifted tariffs on most goods produced by the three nations and called for the gradual elimination, over a period of fifteen years, of most remaining barriers to cross-border investment and to the movement of goods and services among the three countries.

Along the U.S.-Mexican border, much of the cross-border economic development and exchange, in addition to the long-standing commuter workers who travel daily between the two countries, is rooted in the maquiladora industry and that industry was vitally affected by NAFTA.

THE ORIGINS OF MAQUILADORAS

The term "maquiladora" is derived from the Spanish word "maquila" that, according to etymologists, was first used in reference to millers grinding wheat brought by farmers to be converted into flour. In modern usage it has come to mean processing and assembly plants used by transnational companies located in low-wage, tax-favorable countries that convert raw materials and parts into final products for export. Along the U.S.-Mexican border, northern Mexican cities have become a haven for such industries.

In cities and towns along the border, maquiladoras, owned by U.S. investors, produce everything from electronic equipment and clothing to automotive parts and appliances. For many working-class and poor, unskilled laborers in Mexico's rural interior, the growth of the plants along the border in towns such as Tijuana, Juárez, Nogales, Matamoros, and Reynosa became havens of opportunity. The wages offered in the plants, although appreciably lower than similar plants in the United States, drew increasing numbers of workers, a large percentage of them women, to the border.

Although what became known as "The Maquiladora Program" was not launched by the Mexican government until the 1960s, its antecedents reach back decades earlier. Mexico's northern border region, racked with conflict and violence from the early days after the Treaty of Guadalupe Hidalgo, had not been the focus of economic development for the country's government until the 1930s.

Following the end of the Prohibition movement in the United States in 1933, it became clear to Mexico's leaders that the country's border cities would not have the same kind of allure to U.S. visitors; thirsty seekers of "demon rum" would no longer have to cross the border. In addition, the economic devastation wrought by the Great Depression continued to affect merchants of all kinds in the Mexican border cities as well as those in the United States.

In the summer of 1933, the Mexican government enacted the Ley de Perimeters Libres (Free Zone Law) that established the areas of Ensenada and Tijuana into free-trade zones; no longer would businesses in those districts have to pay import duties on foreign goods. The move, the government believed, would begin to convert local economies along the border into areas of broader economic development beyond the vice districts that had dominated cross-border traffic for so long.

Soon other areas were designated as free-zone areas and the number of businesses in the region began slowly to increase. Although the northern Mexican towns along the border still did not have manufacturing industries, the new business activity served to increase cross-border consumer interaction, and the populations in the regions gradually increased.

It was World War II, however, that sparked a marked rise in population in the Mexican border towns and cities as the demand for Mexican goods and factory workers in the United States rose markedly. Nevertheless, it was not until 1961 that the Mexican government took an aggressive effort to promote economic development in the border region. Through a plan called Programa Nacional Fronterizo (PRONAF) the government began to encourage various mayors and other city and town officials not only to promote the border regions as desirable destinations for foreign tourists but also to help link, both economically and socially, the northern regions of the country with the rest of Mexico.

With limited funds, some of the cities, especially Juárez and Tijuana, did respond with a number of cultural centers and events. New schools, libraries, hotels, and convention centers appeared in several cities, along with other civic improvements. In addition, a few border industries were founded, such as an olive packing company in Tijuana and a pasteurization plant in Nogales.

Although the border program did not radically change the economic and cultural makeup of Mexican border towns, it did set the stage. The triggering event that would result in radical change was the end of the Bracero Program in 1964. Since the early 1940s, through that guest worker, cooperative program between the Mexican and U.S. governments, Mexican workers had filled vital temporary and seasonal employment needs in the United States, mostly for agricultural work but also for railroad companies and other industries. It ended because of illegal immigration concerns in the United States and political pressure from labor unions that began to organize domestic farm workers.

The end of the Bracero Program created an unemployment crisis in many northern Mexican cities. Instead of attempting to return to their homes in various parts of the country, many former braceros stayed on the border, many hoping to return again to the United States and others hoping to find employment in Mexican border towns. Soon in the larger cities such as Juárez, Mexicali, and Tijuana up to 50 percent of the population was unemployed.

To counter this consequence of the demise of the Bracero Program, the Mexican government established a program that reversed the long-standing prohibition against the ownership of factories by foreign businessmen. And so began the advent of the maquiladora industry along the border.

U.S. business leaders could now establish companies in Mexico; bring in raw materials, building equipment, and other factory necessities across the border duty-free; and hire Mexican workers to assemble the parts into products that would be sent back to the United States for sale.

Companies in the United States were attracted not only by the cheaper labor costs available in Mexico but also by the location on the border. U.S. companies soon began to appear. The first cross-border plants in such cities as Juárez, Matamoros, Nuevo Laredo, and Tijuana began assembling at the end of 1966. Within the next few years, over fifty plants employing more than 4,000 workers dotted the northern Mexico border.

By the mid-1980s Juárez had become a vibrant, bustling major city with nearly 1 million people, a number that dwarfed its sister city across the Rio Grande: El Paso. Such U.S. companies as RCA and Proctor-Silex made up over 150 maquiladoras in Juárez, and an estimated 700 had been established along the length of the U.S.-Mexican border, as well as some in other parts of Mexico.

Although the Mexican government had anticipated that the growth of the maquila industries along the border would reduce overall unemployment in the country, the arrival of the new processing plants produced a new workforce phenomenon—a very large percentage of the workers taking new jobs in the plants were young women, most of whom had not been employed before. The appearance of women in an industrial workplace in Mexico was an unusual development that would over the years affect not only work environments but also social etiquette and interaction.

The preference shown toward women workers early on in the history of the maquiladoras unquestionably reflected gender stereotypes: they could be asked to perform some of the least rewarding jobs in the factories without the expectation of rising in status or from the low-wage brackets in which they were hired; they were thought of as supplementary income-earners who would not stay in the jobs for extended years; they represented a rich source of previously untapped labor in which only the best candidates could be selected; they were often in unsettled personal positions in which they were willing to put forth maximum effort to keep what heretofore had been unavailable employment; they would also be willing to keep up a rigorous work schedule and pace because of the chance to get guaranteed medical care; and, perhaps, most significantly, many of them for the first time in their lives could gain a degree of self-regard and independence that they had for so long lacked.

Workers at a maquiladora in Ciudad Juárez, 2010. Typically in maquiladoras, many of the employees are women. (Jesus Alcazar/AFP/Getty Images)

When the maquiladoras had been in operation for a few years, merchants in the Mexican towns along the border, especially those in retail clothing, realized a new source of buyers—young women with some money to spend on themselves. The introduction of so many new young women in the factories did impinge on the traditional patterns of male authority and machismo so culturally present in Mexican society. Because of such concerns, some companies began to offer courses to reaffirm the values of a stable family life, home economics, and other traditional cultural norms intended to combat serious culture shock. Yet various social studies over the years have concluded that women's work in the factories had not resulted in major social and familial changes. Many young women, for example, turned over or shared their earnings with their mothers or husbands. Most continued to be responsible for household chores, cooking, and the like. In short, women workers in the factories generally did not upend the established norms of Mexican society. One maquiladora worker told an interviewer, for example, that women remained in a bind. Either as husbands or managers, men continued to exert power over women.

If the Mexican government had assumed that the maquiladora industries would alleviate the employment distress among former male bracero workers who had settled along the border, that assumption proved generally faulty. Those former braceros who continued to look for employment in northern Mexico remained mostly unemployed and desperate.

The first assembly plants established under the new program were largely in the electronics industry. By 1973 over 160 electronic assembly plants had been established. Motorola, for example, moved its assembly plant from Phoenix, Arizona, to Nogales, Sonora. The move saved the company an estimated $4 million a year. The average wage of an employee in the Phoenix plant had been over $5,000 a year; a Mexican worker received wages of slightly more than $1,000 per year.

In the course of two decades, the cross-border industry had transformed border economics in a number of ways. It allowed for increased financial exchange, reduced Mexican unemployment, opened up opportunities for Mexican communities to benefit from new technologies introduced with the industries, and made the northern Mexican economy more central to the overall growth of the country.

By the 1980s management of the maquiladoras, led by auto parts industries, had introduced new automation and computer-controlled machinery that made production more flexible. Some estimates by economists and labor experts indicated that labor productivity in the plants along the border was three times greater than in the previous decade.

By the early 1980s the Mexican government had concluded that the growth of the maquiladora industry had become a vital part of the economy of the borderlands. Future economic well-being of the region, Mexico's leaders believed, would depend on the nurturing and cultivating of that industry through whatever legislative and diplomatic negotiations were deemed necessary.

The Killed and Missing Women of Juárez

Since 1993 over 1,000 young women have been found murdered or have disappeared in the city of Juárez, Chihuahua. A large number of them have been teenagers who worked in the city's many maquiladoras. Most were abducted on their way home from work in the factories. More than 60 percent of maquiladora workers are women and girls, many as young as thirteen or fourteen. Many mutilated bodies have been found in the desert surrounding the city of over a million and a half people.

Over the years, anguished parents and concerned citizens have formed groups to demand more vigorous investigations by local police and the federal government. And yet the horror continued. Most of the families and their supporters believe that the women have been victims of the local drug cartels and that the police and local authorities have been bribed to help cover up the gruesome and heartbreaking femicide.

Women's rights marchers have demanded more aggressive investigations. Holding vigils, erecting crosses throughout the city, and searching in the fields for more victims, the protesters have mounted something of a crusade to stop the shameful abomination. Hundreds of posters are placed around the town. Pink crosses, with the message "Not One More," mark the spots where several bodies were found.

In Juárez's sister city, El Paso, in a demonstration of binational solidarity, labor leaders, legislators, and students formed a group called the Coalition on Violence against Women and Families on the Border that held demonstrations along the bridges connecting the cities. One of the founders of the group said that 80 percent of the factories in Juárez are owned by U.S. business interests and those employees must be considered fellow workers.

In 2015 five men connected with the La Linea cartel were convicted of the death of eleven women. Their prosecution represents only a fraction of the crimes inflicted on this vulnerable segment of the population of Juárez. The merciless terror continues. In 2017 over 300 women were reported missing.

For U.S. businessmen, ever-changing Mexican laws and requirements for establishing new plants across the border remained difficult to understand and to process. Nevertheless, hundreds of firms joined the potentially lucrative maquiladora development that began to gain increasing momentum. Lured by labor costs that could be reduced by 50 percent or more and the logistical benefit of cross-border interaction as opposed to other offshore locations, American business leaders in increasing numbers joined the new growing economic force along the border.

THE ADVENT OF NAFTA

On December 8, 1993, President Bill Clinton signed NAFTA. The agreement between the United States, Mexico, and Canada established a free-trade zone in North America, immediately lifting tariffs on the majority of goods produced by the three nations and calling for the gradual elimination, within fifteen years of the life of the agreement, of most remaining economic obstacles to investment opportunities and for the promotion of greater cross-border movement of goods and services.

NAFTA was a bipartisan creation. As early as 1980 Ronald Reagan, in his presidential campaign, proposed a free-trade agreement between the United States and Mexico. The concept of free trade had long been embraced by conservative economists, believing that such policies would stimulate economic growth in the United States.

Soon after he took office, President George H. W. Bush, President Reagan's successor, began negotiations with young Mexican President Carlos Salinas de Gortari, and in June 1990 the two endorsed a comprehensive free-trade pact between the two countries. Canada joined the talks in 1991, paving the way for three-way negotiations and the final deal on NAFTA. In 1992 at a meeting in San Antonio, Salinas, Bush, and Canadian Prime Minister Brian Mulroney gathered for the signing of the agreement. It still had not been approved by the U.S. Congress and the president, but the basic framework had been worked out.

Behind the scenes, powerful bankers, politicians, and businessmen of the United States, such as Henry Kissinger and David Rockefeller, worked to secure agreement. For the United States, the hopes were that NAFTA would provide factory owners with Mexican labor and open up markets by eliminating trade barriers. For Mexico, the agreement promised greater job opportunities for its many unemployed, especially in the borderlands, and new trading privileges that would strengthen its economy.

A number of groups opposed the NAFTA agreements as drawn up by the representatives of the three countries who had labored over its provisions. U.S. labor unions were particularly concerned that the agreement would result in the loss of thousands of jobs for U.S. workers. Environmentalists were concerned that the agreement did not include sufficient protections against air pollution and water contamination. During the presidential campaign in 1992, Ross Perot, a Texas billionaire running as an independent candidate, famously railed against the NAFTA

President Bill Clinton signs the North American Free Trade Agreement (NAFTA), December 8, 1993. Although many politicians disagree on the efficacy of this major trade deal, most economists agree that NAFTA generated significant cross-border economic growth. (Jeffrey Markowitz/Sygma via Getty Images)

agreement by predicting that U.S. job losses to Mexico under NAFTA would be "a giant sucking sound going south."

When Democrat Bill Clinton was elected in November 1992, one of the first major decisions looming in his administration concerned the ratification of NAFTA. Pressured by labor unions and environmental groups, both traditionally staunch Democratic supporters, Clinton decided to reopen the NAFTA negotiations. An alarmed President Salinas soon requested a meeting with the president-elect. At a meeting in Austin hosted by Governor Ann Richards of Texas, Clinton and Salinas worked out a final deal that included more protection for workers. The agreement moved through the U.S. Congress, Clinton signed it, and NAFTA went into force on January 1, 1994.

Both Clinton and Salinas extolled the promise of economic growth not only for the United States but also for Mexico. Clinton believed that increased cross-border economic cooperation would create additional jobs for U.S. and Mexican workers alike. He also anticipated that the growth of industries on the border would lessen the pressure on unemployed Mexican workers to attempt to cross the border illegally.

Meanwhile, the cross-border interaction and business and tourist activity continued under NAFTA. For example, approximately three-fourths of people who cross the border between Mexico and Arizona are there to shop. Close to the border fences, merchants on both sides make the most-sought-after goods easy to find—prescription drugs, beer, and curios on the Mexican side and clothes and household items on the American side.

Along the entirety of the border, most of the sister cities are not uniform in size. In almost every case, the population in the Mexican cities is greater than the population on the U.S. side. For example, Nogales, Sonora, has nearly ten times the population than Nogales, Arizona. Thus, the towns on the American side depend much more heavily on their economic well-being on border-crossing shoppers than those on the Mexican side. The city of El Paso, Texas, for example, relies predominately on cross-border traffic from Juárez, Chihuahua, for its economic base. McAllen, Texas, relies so heavily on such commuter trade for its economic stability that its chamber of commerce spends nearly a quarter million dollars a year advertising in Mexican cities, especially in the large city of Monterrey.

GAUGING THE NAFTA EFFECT

Ever since the inauguration of NAFTA, economists have jostled over the agreement's effects. In the years immediately following its ratification, foreign direct investment in Mexico surged, as did its total exports, especially into the United States. The maquiladora industry, bolstered by the agreement, also continued to surge. Within six years of the implementation of NAFTA, maquiladora employment grew over 100 percent. In the years since NAFTA, U.S. trade with its border neighbors has more than tripled, and Mexico and Canada account for more than a third of the total U.S. exports.

Nevertheless, it is true that thousands of U.S. jobs disappeared as new factories across the border opened in the aftermath of the NAFTA agreement. Many economists, however, argue that NAFTA actually mitigated the total number of manufacturing jobs that were lost because the agreement encouraged business owners to invest in Mexican plants rather than in China and other worldwide locations. The proximity of the border-city plants and the cross-border economic interaction, they argue, had less of an insidious effect on job numbers than has been assumed by many of NAFTA's detractors.

The four U.S. states that form the borderlands region with Mexico—Texas, New Mexico, Arizona, and California—are vitally affected by the economic forces at play between the two countries. Mexico is the top export market for each of the four states, and those states sell over 50 percent of all U.S. exports to Mexico. Indeed, in Texas border towns especially, an enormous percent of all U.S.-Mexican trade passed across the border benefiting local economies. McAllen, Texas, for example, saw its unemployment rate plunge from nearly 25 percent in a few years down to less than 8 percent with the boost of economic and business activity.

The increased interaction over the years along the border between working families—from those employees in the factories to merchants and to those working for businesses that depend on cross-border cooperation—has brought many common interests and needs together to form increasing familiarity and often friendships, despite the fears and frustrations elicited by cartel violence and racial tensions. The two nations worked together to cement positive relationships.

They have worked together, for example, to combat the violence perpetrated by the warring cartel organizations along the border. They have joined forces in attempting to slow down the illicit drug trade and to enhance border security.

In 2007 the two countries created the Mérida Initiative, which has become the centerpiece of bilateral efforts to fight transnational crime and its nefarious impact. In March 2007, at the request of Mexican President Felipe Calderón, the U.S. government, under the presidency of George W. Bush, launched this effort of counter-drug and anti-crime assistance, with an emphasis on shared responsibility. The bilateral security arrangement pressed for the eradication of trafficking in persons, drugs, and weapons through financial and technical assistance to the Mexican police, army, and other agencies responsible for security.

The Mexican government pledged to fight more vigorously the crime and corruption so rampant along the northern Mexican border cities. The United States, in return, promised to tackle drug demand and the illicit trafficking of firearms, the perplexing problems that fueled the cartel violence.

During the first phase of the Mérida Initiative, Congress appropriated funds to enable the purchase of military equipment to support Mexico's security forces, with an emphasis on border security. The initiative also was aimed at supporting increased intelligence gathering and the sharing of information regarding border security threats. The United States also provided funds for modernizing Mexican judicial practices along the border. The Mérida Initiative opened the door to a partnership on security cooperation that grew during the eight years that U.S. President Barack Obama held office.

The two countries have worked together on a number of important border infrastructure projects. For example, the first railway bridge between the two countries in one hundred years opened in 2016, connecting the Brownsville-Matamoros port of entry. Mexican and U.S. officials created a Border Bilateral Executive Steering Committee, which became the primary forum for policy makers from both countries to coordinate infrastructure projects by aligning the interests of state and local governments, as well as business enterprises, on both sides of the border.

Other U.S.-Mexican initiatives such as the Border Enforcement Security Task Force, which integrated the work of Mexican officers with the U.S. Immigration and Customs activities, further enhanced coordination between the two countries. Through these various initiatives, the leaders of both countries have come to realize that the searing violence, security threats, and other lingering problems along the border extend beyond national boundaries and defy the ability of either of the two nations to combat them alone.

Since NAFTA, Mexico and the United States have engaged in an extensive exchange of information relating to drug trafficking and migration, both legal and illegal. Such cooperation has been necessary because of the mutual and cooperative economic interests of the two countries. The increase of trading partnerships reinforced cooperation and helped assuage some of the tensions that have long plagued the borderlands.

The great paradox of the U.S.-Mexican border today is that the economic riches of goods and services and the regional integrated industrial climate fostered at the various sister cities needs as easy access across the border as possible. It is a striking

The Nava Brewery, Coahuila Mexico

On the shelves of grocery stores and in bars and other establishments across the United States is a product of one of Mexico's major maquiladoras. The product is beer, especially Corona, and the maquiladora is the Nava Brewery near Piedras Negras, Coahuila/Eagle Pass, Texas.

Built by Grupo Modelo in 2010 and sold to Constellation Brands in 2013, Nava Brewery employs about 2,000 employees. Nava's production offers a vivid portrait of the supply chain network in operation under NAFTA. Getting a bottle of Corona brewed and transported from the Mexican borderlands to stores and bars across the United States involves a complex cross-border system.

Nearly half of the costs to Nava of brewing its beer are tied to supplies, ingredients, and transport that originate in the United States. Hops, barley, freight costs, and a portion of the bottles used in the Mexican plant all come from the United States. All of this benefits U.S. workers and business interests. As the countries consider the renegotiation of NAFTA, the economic ramifications of extensive changes, such as the introduction of new tariffs, must be weighed heavily in those negotiations.

irony that an economy based on cross-border connection is being increasingly created at the same time that the border is being, in a real sense, barricaded. The security requirements and growing consciousness about illegal immigration have resulted in far more stringent efforts to patrol border crossings. Thus, regional integrated economic activity is hampered by new border fences, additional Border Patrol agents, and other measures designed to slow down access between the two countries.

NEGOTIATING A NEW TRADE DEAL

Throughout the presidential campaign of 2016, one of the principal targets of candidate Donald Trump was NAFTA. Although free trade had traditionally been Republican Party orthodoxy and although NAFTA was built on the support of Republican members of the Senate and House of Representatives, along with business interests, Trump insisted that the deal was one of the worst trade deals in the history of the republic. He railed that the deal had cost thousands of jobs, hurt the United States in a number of economic ways, and must be severely renegotiated or killed. As an experienced businessman known for his deal-making acumen, Trump argued, he would be the right president to wipe clean the failed NAFTA trade policies. Unlike the free-trade boondoggle under which the United States had suffered for so long, he would consider, for example, enacting tariff protections for U.S. goods and services.

At one point early in his presidency, Trump ordered his staff to draft an executive order officially withdrawing the United States from NAFTA. His staff managed to stall and to distract Trump and eventually maneuvered the administration into renegotiations.

In August 2017 the administration set about to dismantle and replace NAFTA with an agreement more advantageous to the United States. Led by Trump's principal negotiator, U.S. Trade Representative Robert Lighthizer, the administration began a long, wrangling negotiating process that lasted until October 2018 when the U.S., Mexican, and Canadian representatives in the talks finally reached an agreement. Although the agreement was subject to ratification by the U.S. Congress and the governments of the other principals to the agreement, and although its provisions would not take effect until 2020, the outlines of a new NAFTA had been drawn up.

First of all, the agreement would not be called NAFTA; it would be called the United States–Mexico–Canada Agreement, or USMCA. The main goal for the United States under the agreement is to have a greater share of car and truck parts made in North America. An additional rule requires that a percentage of workers in auto manufacturing in Mexico must earn at least $16 an hour, an extraordinary increase from current wages drawn by such workers. It is unclear how such wage increases in Mexico could be enforced.

The new agreement also stipulates that Mexican workers have more ability to organize into unions, that Mexican trucks that cross the border into the United States must meet higher safety requirements, and that U.S. automobile companies that assemble cars in Mexico's maquiladoras need to use more U.S.-made parts to avoid tariffs.

On November 30, 2018, Trump, Canadian Prime Minister Justin Trudeau, and outgoing Mexican President Enrique Pena Nieto signed the agreement at a meeting in Buenos Aires, Argentina. Meanwhile, as the countries await the decisions on ratifying the new agreement, the cross-border economic engines continue to run. Thousands of commuters and shoppers and trucks and trains cross the border in both directions to carry on trade. Factories in Mexico, owned by U.S. business interests, continue to manufacture a variety of products free of tariff restrictions. And despite the tensions and divisions among people along the border, there is also a continuing sense of common interests and hopes. And commerce rolls on as the fate of NAFTA or its replacement remains under negotiation.

DOCUMENTS

State Department on U.S. Relations with Mexico, 2017

As the administration of President Donald Trump took office in 2017, the State Department's Bureau of Western Hemisphere Affairs issued a report on the state of relations between the United States and Mexico. The following excerpts deal with the border and various cooperative working arrangements between the two countries, especially relating to security, education, and economic interdependence.

U.S. Relations With Mexico
BUREAU OF WESTERN HEMISPHERE AFFAIRS
January 25, 2017

U.S.-Mexico Relations

U.S. relations with Mexico are strong and vital. The two countries share a 2,000-mile border, and bilateral relations between the two have a direct impact on the lives and livelihoods of millions of Americans, whether the issue is trade and economic reform, education exchange, citizen security, drug control, migration, entrepreneurship and innovation, or the environment. The scope of U.S.-Mexican relations is broad and goes beyond diplomatic and official relations. It entails extensive commercial, cultural, and educational ties, with some 1.4 billion dollars of two-way trade and hundreds of thousands of legal border crossings each day. In addition, a million American citizens live in Mexico. U.S. tourists to Mexico numbered over 20 million in 2013 making Mexico the top destination of U.S. travelers. Mexican tourists to the U.S. were over 14 million in 2013, and they spent an estimated $10.5 billion.

Bilateral Economic Issues

In September 2013, Vice President Biden and his Mexican government counterparts launched the High Level Economic Dialogue (HLED) to further elevate and strengthen the U.S.-Mexico bilateral commercial and economic relationship. The HLED, which is led at the cabinet level by the Secretaries of State and Commerce and the U.S. Trade Representative, is envisioned as a flexible platform intended to advance strategic economic and commercial priorities central to promoting mutual economic growth, job creation, and competitiveness. It serves to facilitate dialogue and joint initiatives and to promote shared approaches to regional and global economic leadership. It will build on, but not duplicate, a range of existing successful bilateral dialogues and working groups. The HLED had its first meeting in September 2013 chaired by the Vice President, and will meet again at that level in late 2014. Cabinet and sub-cabinet level meetings throughout 2014 have been driving forward the HLED's priorities.

Mexico is the United States' second-largest export market (after Canada) and third-largest trading partner (after Canada and China). In 2013, two-way trade in goods and services was more than $550 billion. Mexico's exports rely heavily on supplying the U.S. market, but the country has also sought to diversify its export destinations. Nearly 80 percent of Mexico's exports in 2013 went to the United States. In 2013, Mexico was the third-largest supplier of foreign crude oil to the United States, as well as the largest export market for U.S. refined petroleum products and a growing market for U.S. natural gas. Top U.S. exports to Mexico include electrical machinery, nuclear equipment, motor vehicle parts, mineral fuels and oils, and plastics. Stock foreign direct investment by U.S. companies in Mexico stands at $101 billion, while Mexican investment is $17.6 billion, and has grown by over 35 percent the past five years. It is the seventh fastest growing investor country in the United States.

Through the North American Leaders' Summits, the United States, Canada, and Mexico cooperate to improve North American competitiveness, ensure the safety of their citizens, and promote clean energy and a healthy environment. The three nations also cooperate on hemispheric and global challenges, such as managing transborder infectious diseases and seeking greater integration to respond to challenges of transnational organized crime.

The U.S. and Mexico, along with Canada, are partners in the North American Free Trade Agreement (NAFTA) and enjoy a broad and expanding trade relationship.

Mexico is currently President Pro Tempore of the Pacific Alliance, a regional economic integration effort spearheaded also by Chile, Colombia, and Peru. Mexico is a champion of free trade, having more free trade agreements than any other country in the world, including pacts with Japan, the EU, and many Latin American partners. In 2012, Mexico joined Chile, Colombia, and Peru to launch an ambitious regional economic integration effort, the Pacific Alliance, focused on liberalizing trade and investment, as well as facilitating the movement of citizens.

Mexico is a major recipient of remittances, sent mostly from Mexicans in the United States, totaling over $22.4 billion in 2012. Most remittances are used for immediate consumption—food, housing, health care, education—but some collective remittances, sent from Mexican migrants in the U.S. to their community of origin, are used for shared projects and infrastructure improvements under Mexico's "3 for 1" program that matches contributions with federal, state, and local funds. Protection and enforcement of intellectual property rights (IPR) is essential to foster economic growth and innovation. Mexico has seen moderate success and continued challenges on the IPR front, particularly on enforcement of IPR. The 2014 U.S. Trade Representative Special 301 Report, a yearly evaluation of IPR and market access conditions that exist with U.S. trading partners, designated Mexico as a "Watch List" country. The 2014 report noted the widespread availability of pirated and counterfeit goods in Mexico and the lack of coordination between authorities responsible for enforcing IPR. The U.S. continues to support and urge Mexico to take the necessary steps to improve the IPR protection and enforcement environment in Mexico.

U.S. Mexico Border

The border region, defined as the ten U.S. and Mexican border states, represents a combined population of nearly 100 million people and the world's fourth largest economy. Cooperation between the United States and Mexico along our border includes state and local problem-solving mechanisms; transportation planning; and collaboration in institutions that address resource, environment, and health issues. In 2010, a high level Executive Steering Committee for 21st Century Border Management was created to spur advancements in creating a modern, secure, and efficient border. The multi-agency U.S.-Mexico Binational Group on Bridges and Border Crossings meets three times a year to improve the efficiency of existing crossings and coordinate planning for new ones. The ten U.S. and Mexican border states are active participants in these meetings. Chaired by U.S. and Mexican consuls, Border Liaison Mechanisms operate in "sister city" pairs and have proven to be an effective means of dealing with a variety of local issues including border infrastructure, accidental violation of sovereignty by law enforcement officials, charges of mistreatment of foreign nationals, and cooperation in public health matters. We have many other mechanisms involving out border region, including Border Master Plans to coordinate infrastructure and development, and close collaboration on transportation and customs issues.

The United States and Mexico have a long history of cooperation on environmental and natural resource issues, particularly in the border area, where there are serious environmental problems caused by rapid population growth, urbanization, and industrialization. Cooperative activities between the U.S. and Mexico take place under a number of arrangements such as the U.S.-Mexico Border 2012/2020 Program; the North American Development Bank and the Border Environment Cooperation Commission; the North American Commission for Environmental Cooperation; the Border Health Commission; and a variety of other agreements that address border health, wildlife and migratory birds, national parks, forests, and marine and atmospheric resources. The International Boundary and Water Commission, created by a treaty between the United States and Mexico, is an international organization responsible for managing a wide variety of water resource and boundary preservation issues.

The two countries also have cooperated on telecommunications services in the border area for more than 50 years. Recent border agreements cover mobile broadband services, including smartphones, and similar devices. The High Level Consultative Commission on Telecommunications continues to serve as the primary bilateral arena for both governments to promote growth in the sector and to ensure compatible services in the border area. The United States and Mexico are implementing an agreement to improve cross-border public security communications in the border area.

Education Exchange

In May 2013, President Obama and President Peña Nieto announced the U.S.-Mexico Bilateral Forum on Higher Education, Innovation and Research (herein referred to as the Bilateral Forum) to expand opportunities for educational exchanges, scientific research partnerships, and cross-border innovation to help both countries develop a 21st century workforce for both our mutual economic prosperity and sustainable social development. The Bilateral Forum complements President Obama's 100,000 Strong in the Americas initiative, which seeks to increase student mobility between the United States and the countries of the Western Hemisphere, including Mexico. It also complements Mexico's program Proyecta 100,000 that aims to send 100,000 Mexican students to the United States and to bring 50, 000 US students to Mexico by 2018.

Entrepreneurship and Innovation

Another related effort is the Mexico-U.S. Entrepreneurship and Innovation Council (MUSEIC) which seeks to enhance regional competitiveness by strengthening the North American high-impact entrepreneurship ecosystem. MUSEIC is made up of public and private sector representatives from both countries who are working to develop new initiatives along with public policies to promote entrepreneurship and innovation. This work through the Bilateral Forum and MUSEIC builds upon and augments the many existing productive educational and research linkages between U.S. and Mexican academic institutions, civil society, and the private sector.

U.S. Security Cooperation with Mexico

The Merida Initiative is an unprecedented partnership between the United States and Mexico to address violence and criminality while strengthening the rule of law and the respect for human rights. Since 2010, our Merida Initiative cooperation has been organized under four strategic pillars. The first pillar aims to disrupt the capacity of organized crime to operate and the second pillar focuses on enhancing the capacity of Mexico's government and institutions to sustain the rule of law. The Merida Initiative's third pillar aims to improve border management to facilitate legitimate trade and movement of people while thwarting the flow of drugs, arms, and cash. Finally, the fourth pillar seeks to build strong and resilient communities.

U.S. cooperation with Mexico under the Merida Initiative directly supports programs to help Mexico train and equip its law enforcement agencies, promote a culture of lawfulness, implement key justice reforms, and modernize Mexico's borders. Through fiscal year 2013, the U.S. Congress has appropriated $2.15 billion for the Merida Initiative. U.S. Agency for International Development (USAID) programs under the Merida Initiative support Mexican efforts to address key challenges to improving citizen security and well-being, developing and testing models to mitigate the community-level impact of crime and violence, and support Mexico's implementation of criminal justice constitutional reforms that protect citizens' rights.

In addition to the Merida Initiative, the U.S. and Mexico collaborate on security policy through high-level exchanges to develop strategies for work on security matters that affect both countries. Through this process, the U.S and Mexico develop joint approaches to combat transnational organized crime, enhance law enforcement cooperation, and stem the flow of illicit money and arms across our common border.

Mexico's Membership in International Organizations

Mexico is a strong supporter of the United Nations (UN) and Organization of American States (OAS) systems, and hosted the G-20 Leaders' Summit in 2012. Mexico and the United States belong to a number of the same international organizations, including the Asia-Pacific Economic Cooperation (APEC) forum, Organization for Economic Cooperation and Development (OECD), International Monetary Fund (IMF), World Bank (WB), and World Trade Organization (WTO). In 2012, Mexico became a member of the Wassenaar Arrangement, a multilateral export control regime for conventional arms and dual-use goods. Mexico was elected in late 2013 to a three-year tour on the UN Human Rights Council. In 2013, Mexico joined the Australia Group, an informal forum of countries which, through the harmonization of export controls, seeks to ensure that exports do not contribute to the development of chemical or biological weapons.

Source: U.S. Department of State, Bureau of Western Hemisphere Affairs, January 25, 2017, https://www.state.gov/r/pa/ei/bgn/35749.htm.

Trump Administration Objectives for NAFTA Renegotiation, 2017

From early on in his presidential campaign and after his election, Donald Trump was highly critical of NAFTA and other foreign trade deals, which he saw as unfair to the United States. Determined to renegotiate such deals from a position of national strength and benefit for the United States or to end them altogether, Trump and his foreign policy advisors soon focused on NAFTA. In July 2017 the Trump administration's Office of United States Trade Representative issued a summary of objectives for a renegotiation of the NAFTA agreement. The following is an excerpt of that summary.

The North American Free Trade Agreement (NAFTA) entered into force over 23 years ago, and since that time, the U.S. economy and global trading relationships have undergone substantial changes.

The America that existed when NAFTA was signed is not the America that we see today. Some Americans have benefited from new market access provided by the Agreement. It contributed to the linking of the continent through trade, while at the same time NAFTA provided much needed market access for American farmers and ranchers.

But NAFTA also created new problems for many American workers. Since the deal came into force in 1994, trade deficits have exploded, thousands of factories have closed, and millions of Americans have found themselves stranded, no longer able to utilize the skills for which they had been trained. For years, politicians promising to renegotiate the deal gave American workers hope that they would stop the bleeding. But none followed up.

In June 2016, then-candidate Donald J. Trump made a promise to the American people: he would renegotiate NAFTA or take us out of the agreement. As President, he immediately started work to fulfill that promise. The first NAFTA consultations began just a few weeks after the President took office.

On May 18th, President Trump became the first American president to begin renegotiating a comprehensive free trade agreement like NAFTA. At the direction of the President, and following more than three months of Administration consultations with Congress, U.S. Trade Representative Robert E. Lighthizer announced the Administration's intention to renegotiate the deal.

Since Ambassador Lighthizer notified Congress of the renegotiation, USTR has been conducting extensive consultations with Congress, stakeholders, and the public at large. President Trump is listening.

The Trump Administration has held dozens of meetings to solicit advice and input. In addition, USTR sought public comments and received more than 12,000 responses. Finally, USTR held three days of public hearings on the negotiations and heard from more than 140 witnesses, who provided testimony on a wide range of sectors, including agriculture, manufacturing, services, and digital trade. During this process, the Administration received valuable advice which has directly impacted the development of the negotiating objectives.

Now, in accordance with section 105(a)(1)(D) of the Bipartisan Congressional Trade Priorities and Accountability Act of 2015, the Administration is providing this summary of specific objectives with respect to the NAFTA negotiations. These objectives reflect the valuable input 3 received during the preceding consultation period from Congress, advisory committees, other agencies, and members of the public. USTR will continue to consult with Congress and stakeholders and we will update these objectives as we advance our work on these important negotiations.

Once negotiations begin, the Administration intends to ensure truly fair trade by seeking the highest standards covering the broadest possible range of goods and services. A successful renegotiation of NAFTA will further the negotiating objectives of the United States, as described in this document, and will benefit the economies and populations of the United States and of our trading partners. The result will be a much better agreement for Americans.

The new NAFTA must continue to break down barriers to American exports. This includes the elimination of unfair subsidies, market-distorting practices by state owned enterprises, and burdensome restrictions of intellectual property. The new NAFTA will be modernized to reflect 21st century standards and will reflect a fairer deal, addressing America's persistent trade imbalances in North America. It will ensure that the United States obtains more open, equitable, secure, and reciprocal market access, and that our trade agreement with our two largest export markets is effectively implemented and enforced.

Under these objectives, a new NAFTA will give our farmers, ranchers, service providers, and other businesses new opportunities to grow their exports and reclaim American prosperity. But most importantly, the new NAFTA will promote a market system that functions more efficiently, leading to reciprocal and balanced trade among the parties.

If we succeed in achieving these objectives—maintaining and improving market access for American agriculture, manufacturing, and services—then we look forward to a seamless transition to the new NAFTA.

Source: Summary of Objectives for the NAFTA Renegotiation, Office of the United States Trade Representative, July 17, 1017, Introduction, https://ustr.gov/sites/default/files/files/Press/Releases/NAFTAObjectives.pdf.

12

Dreamers and the Politics of the Border

Carlos Martinez and his brother were brought to the United States in 1991 when Carlos was only nine years old. His father emphasized the importance of studying, and Carlos took his father's advice to heart. He graduated ninth in his class at Cholla High School in Tucson, Arizona.

Carlos enrolled at the University of Arizona. Even though he had never owned a computer, Carlos loved math and dreamed of being a computer engineer. Four years later in 2003, Carlos graduated with a bachelor's of science in Computer Engineering with minors in Computer Science, Electrical Engineering, Mathematics, and Spanish. He was named the top Hispanic graduate in his class.

After Carlos graduated, reality set in. He received job officers from top tech companies but couldn't work because he was undocumented. But Carlos did not give up on his dream. He enrolled in a master's program at the University of Arizona. He completed the two-and-a-half-year program in just a year and a half. He was also nominated for the University of Arizona Graduate School Centennial Award, given to the school's top graduate student.

Thanks to Deferred Action for Childhood Arrivals (DACA), President Obama's new policy, Carlos will finally be able to work in his field. He was one of the first people to receive deferred action. As soon as he received that notification, he went to a career fair at his alma mater and handed out resumes to the tech companies that first tried to hire him years ago.

In a letter Carlos wrote to Senator Durbin, he said, "It was the best news [of] my life. Finally I would be able to work as a software engineer or own [a] business and create jobs."

(Dreamers' Stories, https://www.durbin.senate.gov/issues/immigration-and-the-dream-act/dreamers-stories.)

DREAMERS AND THE DREAM ACT

Carlos Martinez is one of millions of undocumented immigrants now living in the United States who arrived in the country under the age of eighteen. That number is estimated to be as high as 3.6 million, about one-third of the total undocumented population. Carlos and the others are known as Dreamers (or, as frequently spelled with the first five letters capitalized—DREAMers). The word is derived from the first version of the Development, Relief, and Education for Alien Minors (DREAM) Act, introduced in 2001.

When that act failed to pass Congress during the next decade, President Barack Obama in 2012 began a temporary program to help individuals such as Carlos avoid deportation. It was called Deferred Action for Childhood Arrivals (DACA). For several hundred thousand individuals who signed up for the program. DACA was, at least for a time, a safety valve policy that relieved the threat of deportation so that they could further acculturate into American society and follow their hopes of a successful life and career.

In 2014 Carlos Martinez was one of the first ninety-nine individuals who received a work permit under DACA. He soon began working for IBM as a technical sales specialist in San Francisco. It is the story of individuals such as Carlos that has hung over U.S. immigration policy for nearly two decades and has remained a contentious, racially and culturally charged issue that continues to defy reasonable, bipartisan solution.

During the 1980s, at a time when the United States was more aggressively controlling the flow of migrants at the border, the pattern of migration development changed with it. Before the more stringent patrol of the border, it was common for Mexican men to risk crossing, take periods of work, and then return to their families. Rather than permanently settling in the United States, they would lead a life of what became known in academic circles as "circular migration."

Many Mexican families preferred to raise their children in their homeland rather than make the massive cultural shift to the United States. Now, with more rigorous control of the border by the U.S. Immigration and Naturalization Service, the crossings for Mexican men became more difficult, injuries and deaths became more common, the prices charged by smugglers became greater, and the chances of successful crossings became more tenuous. Thus, as the border became more difficult for Mexican men routinely to cross and then return, the families resorted to more drastic means. As circular migration was deterred, many families decided to pull up roots and move, if possible, as a unit. Now, they would cross, find permanent work if possible, and settle with their children in the United States. One successful crossing, after all, could make such a move possible.

As entire families forded streams and climbed through hills and valleys and risked desert heat, many managed to make it to the United States despite the danger and risks. Their settlement in the United States meant that thousands of children, including many infants, grew up in the United States, in states across the country, without papers. It is these children that today are the "Dreamers." It is a staggering irony that policies meant to fortify the border and to keep out as many illegal immigrants as possible actually led to more illegal migrations of entire families and increased the number of Dreamers.

In 2001–2002, led by the bipartisan sponsorship of Senator Richard Durbin (D-IL) and Senator Orrin Hatch (R-UT) in the U.S. Senate and by Representative Lucille Roybal-Allard (D-CA) and Representative Ileana Ros-Lehtinen (R-FL) in the U.S. House, the DREAM Act was first introduced. Under the language of the act reported to the Senate in June 2002, the U.S. attorney general would be authorized ". . . to cancel the removal of, and adjust to permanent resident status, an alien who: (1) has attained the age of 12 prior to enactment of this Act; (2) files an application before reaching the age of 21; (3) has earned a high school or equivalent diploma; (4) has been physically present in the United States for at least five years immediately preceding the date of enactment of this Act (with certain exceptions); (5) is a person of good moral character; and (6) is not inadmissible or deportable under specified criminal or security grounds of the Immigration and Nationality Act." In addition the attorney general could "take similar steps with respect to an alien who: (1) would have met such requirements during the four-year period immediately preceding the enactment of this Act; and (2) is enrolled in, or has graduated from, an institution of higher education."

Various versions of the bill appeared over the years seeking relief for youngsters from possible deportation and a path for eventual citizenship. Nevertheless, despite bipartisan support of the bill, it failed to become law in 2002 and also failed in the several subsequent attempts to pass the legislation with modifications of its specific provisions.

Over the years the most determined sponsor of the bill has been Senator Durbin. First elected to the Senate from Illinois in 1996, Durbin became deeply involved in the plight of the Dreamers when he met Tereza Lee, a teenage piano prodigy who had been brought to the United States from Brazil when she was two years old. At the age of seven, she was told by her father about the uncertainty of their lives and the possibility of being uprooted. Her father and mother had fled South Korea after the Korean War, moved to Brazil when Tereza was two, crossed the border into the United States on tourist visas shortly thereafter, and moved to Chicago. After the visas expired, the family stayed in Chicago, her father becoming a pastor at a church on the city's north side and her mother taking work in a dry-cleaner's store.

At her father's church, Tereza learned to play the piano. She became such a young, budding virtuoso, even with little training, that a wealthy member of the congregation bought her a piano and she began to win competitions. She earned a scholarship to attend the Merit School of Music in Chicago.

When Durbin contacted federal immigration officials about Tereza's possible path to citizenship, his overtures were rebuffed. She would have to be deported back to her native country, wait ten years, and then petition for re-entry.

The realization that hundreds of thousands of youngsters such as Lee were living in this nightmare of immigration law in which they constantly feared their lives would be uprooted spurred Durbin to seek allies in both the Senate and House to repair what he and many others regarded as a broken system. Tereza Lee became a centerpiece of the drive to pass the DREAM Act.

When he first proposed the bill, Durbin believed it would be a commonsense and humane solution to a perplexing and confounding legal dilemma facing youngsters who, through no fault of their own, had known the United States as their home, the place where they would strive for their life dreams. From the time the DREAM Act first met resistance from many Republican lawmakers who saw the porous border as a dire threat, whose instincts were to reduce the increase of non-Anglo citizens, and who saw the issue as a political wedge, Durbin never backed down. He began to make speeches on the floor of the Senate where he told personal stories of Dreamers such as Tereza Lee who came forward and agreed to make their own struggles public. He featured the stories and pictures of Dreamers on his congressional website.

The DREAM Act came very close to passing in 2010, clearing the House of Representatives and falling five votes short of the sixty members of the Senate needed to proceed to a vote. As Senator Durbin and others continued to fight for passage, President Barack Obama decided in 2012 to temporarily break the impasse in order to provide protections to youngsters.

In June 2012 the Obama administration announced a program allowing Dreamers to come forward, pass a background check, and apply for work permits. It was called DACA.

THE ORIGINS OF DACA

While he was a U.S. senator, Barack Obama held strong views about the border and the debate over immigration. In 2005 he made it clear that he agreed that the border needed better security, that employers who chose to hire illegal immigrants needed to be sanctioned, and that the rule of law must be respected regarding those who cross into the United States without proper authorization, unchecked and undetected.

At the same time, he pressed for a guest worker program, an interim legal status, and a path for citizenship for the millions of undocumented immigrants already living in the United States and bipartisan legislation that would both enhance border security and, at the same time, offer fair and reasonable standards for legal immigration that would ensure that the United States remain a country that was welcoming to newcomers from all parts of the world.

When he became president, Obama faced fierce opposition to the immigration reform he proposed. Thus, in 2012, he initiated the DACA policy, much to the vociferous opposition of most Republicans. In November 2014 he addressed the nation about the debate over immigration and new steps he was taking to clear a path toward reconciling the impasse.

In a speech to the nation, Obama declared, "Our history and the facts show that immigrants are a net plus for our economy and our society. And I believe it's important that all of us have this debate without impugning each other's character. Because for all the back and forth of Washington, we have to remember that this debate is about something bigger. It's about who we are as a country, and who we want to be for future generations."

To qualify for DACA, Dreamers had to show that they arrived in the United States before they were sixteen years old, that they were thirty years old or younger, and that they were attending school or were in the military. They had to pass careful background checks and had to show that they had not committed a felony or serious misdemeanors. DACA provided temporary work permits, exemption from possible deportation for two years, and the possibility of renewal. It did not provide a path toward citizenship.

Nevertheless, the ability to work gave DACA recipients a path toward pursuing a higher education through in-state tuition grants, the benefits in many instances of obtaining health insurance from their employers, and, most of all, the sense of dignity and purpose that has guided many of their lives. By 2017 approximately 800,000 individuals were part of the program. At the time of DACA's inception, public opinion polls reported that about two-thirds of U.S. citizens favored allowing Dreamers to stay in the country.

At the same time Obama initiated DACA, he continued to hope for bipartisan legislation that would provide a concrete, lasting solution to the fierce political debate over immigration policy. In laying the groundwork for such a comprehensive, two-party resolution, he did not, despite DACA, back off a stern policy of border enforcement that resulted in an increasing number of deportations in his administration. So vigorous were the arrests and deportations by his administration's Immigration and Customs Enforcement (ICE) that many immigration activists began calling him "The Deporter in Chief."

Nevertheless, Obama's orders to ICE adhered to policies of previous administrations; he did not, for example, consider breaking families apart in deportation proceedings. He emphasized to the nation's law enforcement and legal agencies involved in border security that they should use sensible prosecutorial discretion in acting in as humane a way as possible while, at the same time, strengthening border security. He declared that deportation actions should not be blindly enforced without regard to the individual circumstances. He emphasized that many of the young people, the Dreamers, had already contributed to the country in significant ways.

In November 2014 Obama took further action. He announced an executive action to prevent the deportation of some 4.7 million of the 11 million undocumented immigrants in the United States. The action allowed undocumented parents of U.S. citizens to remain in the country temporarily. Under the executive action, those undocumented residents could apply legally for jobs but could not vote or qualify for health insurance under the national healthcare law. The action applied to those parents who had been in the country for at least five years.

The executive order further enraged anti-immigrant hawks in the Congress and prompted opponents to take action in the courts. After a string of court decisions the measure reached the U.S. Supreme Court, and in June 2016 the court deadlocked on the challenge to the president's action. The split vote allowed a lower court ruling to remain in place. The Obama administration had survived a vigorous challenge to its immigration policies. Those policies would come under severe attack by an incoming presidential administration.

NEGOTIATING THE FUTURE OF DREAMERS

When Donald Trump took over the presidency in 2017, it was clear to most Dreamers that the DACA program was in jeopardy. After all, Trump had focused much of his presidential campaign on the dangers of illegal immigration, the need for a massive wall that would stretch across the entire length of the border, and the threat to the country of undocumented aliens who threatened the safety and security of the nation.

It came as no surprise when Trump, in late January 2017, signed two executive orders directing the construction of the wall and increasing Border Patrol agents

Protestors rally in Ann Arbor, Michigan, in support of renewal of the Deferred Action for Childhood Arrivals (DACA) program, September 8, 2017. Established in 2012, DACA protected approximately 800,000 young undocumented immigrants from deportation. When the Trump administration announced it was ending the program in 2017, its renewal became a political battle tied up in Congress, the White House, and the courts. (Smontgom65/Dreamstime.com)

and immigration officials to carry out arrests and deportations of those illegally crossing the border and of those who had already made their way into the United States.

Trump also called for the government to strip certain metropolitan areas of federal grant funding if they were engaged in protecting illegal immigrants from deportation. Those so-called "sanctuary cities" had raised the ire of Republican immigration hawks for many years. Nearly 300 states and localities had sanctuary policies of varying proportions. Some mayors and governors across the country had aligned themselves and their political fortunes with immigrant rights groups, church organizations, and other activists who had pressed for a more lenient approach to those individuals already living in the country and making a positive contribution to their cities and counties. They had directed their law enforcement officials and other city officers to limit their cooperation with ICE agents and federal officials in searching for and uprooting undocumented individuals who had committed no crimes and who had successfully integrated into U.S. society.

Trump had promised a harsh new day and now had taken his first steps in attempting to deliver it. Across the country, government officials, community leaders, and legal services attorneys rallied to the defense of this new assault on the undocumented. Many activists lamented that Trump would unleash ICE agents in a kind of police-state operation to fulfill his political agenda and promises.

Soon those activist fears became prescient, at least in some states and localities. ICE arrests in Texas began to rise sharply, for example. Given nearly free rein by the administration to pursue, detain, and deport, ICE agents began to target employers, opening new investigations and audits to uncover those living in the shadows. Suddenly, ICE agents began making arrests in schools, courthouses, and other sensitive locations that heretofore had been limited. And they began to apprehend individuals who had no criminal backgrounds.

The fear in many communities became palpable. The new policy even had the unintended consequence of discouraging some immigrants from reporting crime for fear that they themselves would become targeted.

It was no surprise, then, when in September 2017 Trump attempted to rescind the DACA policy. Trump justified his action on the assertion that President Obama had illegally overreached his executive authority that should have come only from Congress. Although the administration declared that no current beneficiaries would be affected before March 2018, it announced that no new requests would be processed. Trump pressed Congress to "do your job" and pass an immigration bill that would include funds for a border wall and other measures the administration deemed necessary.

On December 6, 2017, pro-immigration activists rallied in Washington, D.C., in support of the Dreamers and DACA. At the U.S. Capitol 200 protestors were arrested for civil disobedience. A few weeks later, other protestors were also taken into custody for attempting to block congressional passageways and tunnels. Across the country, supporters of DACA staged demonstrations at the offices of U.S. members of Congress.

Meanwhile, a number of federal judicial decisions delayed the attempts by the administration to end DACA. Beginning in January 2018, courts in California, New York, and the District of Columbia issued injunctions delaying the implementation of the presidential executive order.

Later, on the other side of the issue, a ten-state coalition led by the Texas attorney general began a campaign to encourage the Supreme Court to take up the immigration case and to overrule the lower federal courts. Trump, they argued, must be allowed to end the DACA program unilaterally.

In mid-January 2019 the U.S. Supreme Court decided to take no action regarding lower-court rulings on the DACA program despite President Trump's wish for a resolution of the impasse. The decision by the court thus preserved the program for the immediate future.

As the pressure and rhetoric on both sides of the debate continued to rise, efforts in Congress to find some kind of bipartisan, sensible immigration that Trump would sign continued.

Dreamers awaited their fate.

In 2018 jazz artist, composer, bandleader, and teacher John Daversa began a project to help raise awareness about the Dreamers and DACA recipients. He worked with fifty-three young men and women musicians and singers who had received DACA awards and produced an album titled *American Dreamers: Voices of Hope,*

Music of Freedom. Several of the performers said the project was life-changing, and a number of them, in agreeing to participate, revealed their Dreamer status for the first time. Recorded at the University of Miami's Frost School of Music, the album received three 2019 Grammy Award nominations. The producer of the album, Kabir Sehgal, said that the team had to stop the recording sessions on a number of occasions because they were in tears.

DOCUMENTS

Senator Richard Durbin (D-IL) Testimony before Senate on DACA, January 13, 2015

From early in the twenty-first century, Senator Richard Durbin of Illinois has been the most vocal supporter of legislation that would protect children living in the United States who had been brought across the border by their parents without legal authorization. For many of these individuals, the United States was the only home that they had known and for which they had any personal and cultural identification. And now they faced possible deportation. From the time he and others introduced legislation to protect so-called Dreamers, Durbin made numerous speeches in Congress telling the stories of these young people. In a speech in January 2015, he talked about Oscar Vasquez who helped organize a high school robotics team that beat MIT in a national robotics competition and whose story became the focus of a movie.

Senator Dick Durbin

"Spare Parts" Screening and Funding for the Department of Homeland Security

Remarks as Prepared for Delivery

January 13, 2015

Mr./Mme. President, this evening I am joining with the Center for American Progress to host a screening of "Spare Parts," a new movie that tells the true story of four students at Carl Hayden High School in Phoenix Arizona.

These students were undocumented immigrants who were brought to the United States as children. And they started a robotics team at their high school that went on to great success.

The movie was produced by actor and comedian George Lopez and stars Lopez, as the coach of the robotics team; Jamie Lee Curtis, as the high school principal; Marisa Tomei, as a high-school teacher; Carlos Pena, as Oscar Vazquez, one of the students; and Alexa Vega, as Oscar's girlfriend Karla.

I'm especially excited about seeing this movie because I have known one of these students, Oscar Vazquez, for some time.

Six years ago, I told Oscar's story here on the floor of the Senate for the first time.

Let me briefly summarize it now. Oscar was brought to Phoenix, AZ, by his parents when he was a child. He dreamed of enlisting in the military, and he spent his high school years in Junior ROTC.

At the end of his junior year, a recruiting officer told Oscar he was ineligible to serve in our military because he was undocumented. So Oscar found another outlet for his talent. He helped to start the robotics club at Carl Hayden High School.

Oscar and his three teammates entered a college-level robot competition sponsored by NASA. They worked for months in a storage room in their high school. They were competing against students from MIT and other top universities. The Carl Hayden High School team won first place.

After high school, Oscar went on to Arizona State University, and in 2009, he graduated with a degree in mechanical engineering. He was one of the top three students in his class.

Following his graduation, Oscar took a brave step. He voluntarily returned to Mexico, a country where he had not lived since he was a child. He said: "I decided to take a gamble and do the right thing."

In 2010, the Obama administration granted Oscar a waiver to reenter the United States. Without this waiver, Oscar would have been barred from returning to the United States for at least 10 years. He would have been separated from his wife Karla and their daughter Samantha, both of whom are American citizens.

When Oscar returned to the United States, he did two things. He applied for citizenship, and he enlisted in the U.S. Army.

Oscar served as a cavalry scout in the war in Afghanistan, fulfilling the dream that he had as a child. He also became a citizen of the country he was willing to die for.

Last year, Oscar testified at a hearing that I held on the benefits of allowing immigrants to enlist in our military.

The Falcon Robotics team, which Oscar and his friends started, is now a fixture at Carl Hayden High School.

I've told the stories of two other members of the Falcon Robotics team here on the Senate floor.

Dulce Matuz graduated from Arizona State University with a bachelor's degree in Electrical Engineering. As a senior, Dulce received an internship to work on the NASA Space Station.

After graduation, Dulce couldn't work as an engineer, so she co-founded the Arizona DREAM Act Coalition. As a result of her activism, Dulce was named one of the 100 most influential people in the world by Time Magazine.

Angelica Hernandez served in Junior R.O.T.C. and was President of the National Honors Society. Angelica graduated from high school with a 4.5 GPA. She graduated from Arizona State University as the outstanding senior in the Mechanical Engineering Department, with a 4.1 GPA.

Why am I telling you about the movie "Spare Parts" and the Carl Hayden robotics team? Because it puts a human face on legislation that will be debated in the House of Representatives later this week.

The House Republicans are preparing to pass a bill that would defund the President's immigration policies, including the Deferred Action for Childhood Arrivals program—also known as DACA.

The DACA program puts on hold the deportations of immigrant students who grew up in this country and allows these young people to live and work legally in America on a temporary basis.

These young people—immigrants like Oscar Vazquez, Dulce Matuz, and Angelica Hernandez—are known as Dreamers. They were brought to the United States as children. They grew up in this country and have overcome great obstacles to succeed. They are the future doctors, engineers, teachers, and soldiers who will make this country stronger.

In the last two years, more than 600,000 Dreamers have received DACA. DACA has unleashed the potential of these Dreamers to contribute more fully to our country.

Many DACA recipients are already contributing to our country. For example, Angelica Hernandez, a former member of the Carl Hayden robotics team, is now working as an engineer at Nexant Corporation, where she specializes in renewable energy.

The Center for American Progress and the Partnership for a New American Economy has found that giving legal status to Dreamers will add $329 billion to our economy and create 1.4 million new jobs by 2030.

But the Republicans in the House of Representatives want to end DACA. They want these young people to be deported to countries that they barely remember.

And what bill are the Republicans using to eliminate DACA? It's the legislation to fund the Homeland Security Department, a government agency that is responsible for protecting Americans from the threat of terrorism.

In the aftermath of the horrible terrorist attack in France, it is surprising—to say the least—that the House of Representatives is considering a bill that threatens to shut down the Homeland Security Department.

We shouldn't even be debating funding for the Homeland Security Department at this time. Every other government agency is funded through the end of the fiscal year—September 30th—which is the normal schedule for government funding.

But Republicans insisted that DHS only be funded through the end of February. Why did they demand that we put Homeland Security funding at risk?

Because they wanted an opportunity—early this year—to take a stand against President Obama's immigration policy.

And the House Republicans feel so strongly about deporting Dreamers that they are willing to hold our homeland security funding hostage to force Democrats to agree.

Well let me be clear: Democrats will not be swayed by this kind of blackmail. We will insist that the Department of Homeland Security be funded and that the President have the authority—which every President has had—to establish his own immigration policies.

This is just a continuation of Republican obstructionism on immigration.

More than a year and a half ago, on June 27, 2013, the Senate passed comprehensive immigration reform legislation on a strong bipartisan 68–32 vote. This bill would strengthen border security, crack down on illegal immigration, protect American workers, and, in a fair and humane manner, address the situation of 11 million undocumented workers who are currently living in our country.

But for the last year and a half, the House of Representatives has refused to allow a vote on the Senate's immigration reform bill. If Speaker Boehner had brought our bill to the floor, it would pass with a strong bipartisan majority and the President would sign it into law.

For the past decade, I've been involved in several efforts to pass bipartisan immigration reform legislation. But every time, we've been stopped by Republican opposition. The House Republicans have left President Obama with no choice. For the good of the American people, the President was forced to use his authority under current law to do what he can to fix our broken immigration system.

So the President has put a temporary hold on the deportations of individuals who are the parents of U.S. citizens or legal permanent residents, who have lived in our country for years, and who do not pose any threat to our safety.

This is not an amnesty. It simply puts a hold on the deportations of qualified immigrants—so American citizen children won't be separated from their parents—and allows these parents to live and work legally in America on a temporary basis. Individuals who receive this "deferred action" are not granted permanent legal status or citizenship—only Congress can do that.

The President's executive action will make us safer by bringing millions of immigrants out of the shadows to register with the government and undergo rigorous law enforcement and national security background checks.

The President's executive action will also help our economy and American workers. The reality is that these immigrants are already part of the workforce. But they are working illegally, which undercuts wages and working conditions for American workers.

By bringing undocumented workers into the legal workforce, we will eliminate the unfair competition of the underground economy. And all of these workers will be paying payroll taxes, which will increase tax revenues by billions of dollars every year.

The President's executive action is also a smart and realistic approach to enforcing our immigration laws. It is not humanly possible to deport all of the undocumented immigrants in this country. So every Administration has to set priorities about who to deport.

The government should not waste its limited resources to deport immigrants who have lived and worked here for years, who have children who are American citizens or lawful permanent residents, and who don't pose a threat to our safety. Instead, this Administration has made it the top priority to deport those who have committed serious crimes or are a threat to public safety.

Executive action on deportations is clearly lawful. Every President since Dwight Eisenhower has used his executive authority to improve our immigration system. And the Supreme Court has repeatedly affirmed that the federal government has broad authority to decide who to deport. President Obama is acting well within his legal authority when he establishes policies about who will be deported by his Administration.

The American people want their government to solve problems. Because the House Republican leadership has failed to reform our immigration system, the President had no choice but to use his authority under the law to improve our economy and security and keep families together.

But however you feel about the President's immigration policies, it is hypocritical and counterproductive to take out your frustration by putting at risk critical homeland security funding.

Source: Senator Richard Durbin Senate Testimony, January 13, 2015, https://www.durbin.senate.gov/newsroom/press-releases/durbin-we-are-a-nation-of-immigrants.

Testimony of a Dreamer, Marie Nazareth Gonzalez, May 2007

As Congress wrestled with various bills introduced relating to Dreamers since 2002, many young people have volunteered to come forward to tell their stories. One of those individuals was Marie Nazareth Gonzalez. A migrant from Costa Rica in 1991, Marie graduated with honors from Helias High School, one of the top high schools in Missouri. In 2005 both of her parents were deported from the United States, but she was granted permission to continue her studies at Westminster College in Fulton, Missouri. She became a leader in the movement to pass the DREAM Act and garnered national attention in print publications and on television promoting the legislation. On May 18 she appeared before the U.S. House Judiciary Committee Subcommittee to tell her story.

Good morning. My name is Marie Nazareth Gonzalez. I am a 21-year-old junior from Jefferson City, Missouri currently attending Westminster College in Fulton,

Missouri. I'm majoring in Political Science and International Business with a focus on communication and leadership.

My family is originally from Costa Rica. I was born in Alajuela, Costa Rica but have been living in the United States since the age of five. My parents Marina and Marvin, brought me to the United States in November of 1991. Having come over legally, their plan was to become US citizens so we could one day all benefit from living in the land of the free. We sought to live the "American Dream"—the promise of a better education, a better life, and all together a better future—what any parent would for their child.

Strong values and good morals have been instilled in me from a very young age. As long as I can remember my parents have worked very hard for every dollar they've earned, and in the process have taught me that life is not easy and that I must work hard and honorably for what I want in life. That is exactly what they did. When they came to the US they had no intention of breaking the law, or of making an exception for themselves. Unfortunately, the law is very difficult and complex. I am not making excuses for what happened, just trying to clear my family's name. Throughout all our years in the United States we worked very hard for what we had, thinking that one day soon we would be citizens.

On April of 2002 our family's dream of becoming citizens was halted by a phone call. My father had been working for the state as a courier for the Governor's Office. The job was not prestigious in any way, but my father was very devoted to his job and was loved and respected by his co-workers. On one occasion the governor even publicly stated his appreciation for my dad while he was making opening remarks at an event for Missouri high school sophomores that I attended.

All of that ended after an anonymous person called the governor's office requesting that our immigration status be confirmed. From that day forward, my life became a haze of meetings with attorneys, hearings, and rallies.

When they heard that we were facing deportation, the community that knew us in Jefferson City rallied behind my family and me to an overwhelming degree. They knew we were hardworking, honorable, taxpaying people, and they fought to allow us to stay in the US. Members of our Catholic Parish—where my mom worked as a volunteer Spanish teacher and after school care director—joined with other community members to form the "The Gonzalez Group" to rally support by collecting signatures for petitions and organizing phone calls. My classmates, teachers and others also got involved because they considered me an important part of their community.

I was in high school at the time, with graduation quickly approaching. I was in my class's homecoming court. When it came out in the newspaper that I was being deported to a country I had not known since the age of five, people all across the country responded. They started a "We Are Marie" campaign, and tens of thousands called and wrote letters on my behalf. When I was a high school senior and our family's deportation date was looming very close, they brought me to Washington, DC.

I got involved in advocacy for the DREAM Act. Unlike thousands of others like me who would benefit from the DREAM Act, I had little to fear from speaking out since I was already facing deportation. When I gave the "valedictorian" speech at a mock graduation in front of the Capitol, I became a national symbol of the DREAM Act.

Eventually all of the work of so many people on my behalf began to pay off. My Representative, Ike Skelton, and both of my Senators, Jim Talent and Kit Bond, responded to the support from the community and got involved in the effort to keep me here. Eventually, though, all of our appeals were exhausted and a final date was set for our family to leave the US for good.

I remember that the weeks before that date were surreal. I was overwhelmed by the support I received. I appeared on national television, once with Senator Richard Durbin at my side, and was contacted by the media so often that I got tired of it. I thought, "even if it is too late for me, at least it might help the DREAM Act to pass so that others like me won't have to face this ordeal." Then, on July 1, 2005, I got word that the Department of Homeland Security had relented and would allow me to defer my departure for one year.

When I got that news I cried—simultaneously with happiness and grief. Even though I would be able to stay, my parents would have to leave in just three days. The Gonzalez Group had made shirts and organized a float for the Fourth of July parade. So, the day before their departure, my parents and I rode in the parade with other members of the group that had been such a huge part of our family. Hundreds cheered us on and voiced their support and sorrow.

My life since April of 2002 can be easily compared to a roller coaster. There have been times when I have felt like I was on top of the world, living out mine and my parent's dream of being a successful young woman in her college career, only to be brought down by the realization that at any moment it can be taken away. The deferral of my deportation has been renewed twice, each time for a year. Last month, when they gave me until June of 2008, they told me it would be the last renewal. If the DREAM Act does not pass by then, I will have to leave.

I recognize that I am lucky to have been allowed to stay as long as I have. Others in my same situation have not had nearly the support that I have. Even so, it is hard not knowing if I will be able to remain in school at Westminster long enough to graduate.

I am only one student and one story. In the course of fighting to remain here, I have been lucky to meet many other students who would benefit from the DREAM Act, and one of the reasons I wanted to come here and testify is to speak to you on their behalf. Unlike them, I can speak about this issue in public without risking deportation. I share with them in their pain, fear, and uncertainty. Their stories are heartbreaking and similar. In my experiences and my travels I have come to the realization that they would only be an asset to the country if only given the chance to prove themselves. The DREAM Act has the potential to not only impact the thousands of students who would qualify but also this great nation by allowing these students to pursue their education and their dreams of success.

I can personally attest to how life in limbo is no way to live. Having been torn apart from my parents for almost two years and struggling to make it on my own, I know what it is like to face difficulty and how hard it is to fight for your dreams. No matter what, I will always consider the United States of America my home. I love this country. Only in America would a person like me have the opportunity to tell my story to people like you.

Many may argue that because I have a Costa Rican birth certificate I am Costa Rican and should be sent back to that country. If I am sent back there, sure I'd be with my mom and dad, but I'd be torn away from loved ones that are my family here, and from everything I have known since I was a child.

I hope one day not only to be a US citizen, but to go to law school at Mizzou, to live in DC, and to continue advocating for others who can't speak for themselves. Whether that will happen, though, is up to you—our nation's leaders—and to God.

Source: Written Statement: House Judiciary Committee Subcommittee on Immigration, Citizenship, Refugees, Border Security and International Law Hearing on Comprehensive Immigration Reform: The Future of Undocumented Immigrant Students May 18, 2007, https://www.nilc.org/wp-content/uploads/2015/11/marie-gonzalez-2007–05-16.pdf.

Response to President Trump's Congressional Joint Address by Dreamer Astrid Silva, February 28, 2017

In 1989 Astrid Silva's father crossed the border and worked at a golf course for three years. He then asked his wife to cross with their daughter, four-year old Astrid. Through arrangements with smugglers, they navigated the Rio Grande on a tire raft. All Astrid had in her possession was a small doll, a cross, and the clothes she wore. Raised in Nevada, she became an outstanding student and earned two degrees at a community college and an associate degree at Nevada State College. Nevertheless, Astrid couldn't get a driver's license and lived in fear, along with her parents, of being deported. During a political rally for Democratic Senator Harry Reid, Astrid, now twenty-one years old, slipped him a handwritten note expressing the fears and sadness that enveloped her family as they lived in a kind of shadow existence. The note touched Reid and led to a friendship that inspired Silva not only to volunteer for his reelection bid but to begin speaking publicly at his campaign events.

In 2014 President Obama used Astrid's story in his remarks to the nation on immigration reform. She soon became such a vocal advocate for the DREAM Act that she was asked to deliver a speech at the Democratic National Convention in Philadelphia in 2016. She also became a founder of a group called Dream Big Vegas that fights for immigration reform.

Following an address by President Trump to a joint session of Congress in February 2017, Silva was asked to deliver a Democratic response. The following are excerpts from her remarks.

Good evening, my name is Astrid Silva and I'm a DREAMer and activist from the great state of Nevada. My family came to this country when I was 4 years old, looking for a better life. And like many of you, this is the only home I know.

It is an honor for me to be here today to give the Democratic response to President Trump's first joint address to Congress.

I'm here representing Democrats, Latinos, and the 11 million undocumented immigrants who are an integral part of this country and who embody the values and the promise of America. The same ones that President Trump is threatening with his mass deportation plan.

The speech we heard moments ago from President Trump was divisive and aims to cause fear in communities across the country. It serves as evidence and reminder that President Trump and Republicans' vision and plan for the United States, go completely against our values as Democrats, as Americans, and as human beings.

The United States is not a country guided by hatred, fear, and division, as Trump makes it seem. Our country is guided by respect, hard work, sacrifice, opportunity, and hope.

In this country there is no space for discrimination, racial profiling, or persecution. But sadly, this is what the Trump Administration has brought forth for Latinos and immigrants.

During his first weeks as President, Trump signed executive orders that endanger our entire community. He took actions that focus specifically on hurting immigrants and refugees. He is spending resources on targeting working immigrant families for deportation, he wants to spend billions of dollars to build an unnecessary border wall, and he's looking for ways to deny entry to our Muslim brothers and sisters.

He made it very clear during his presidential campaign that he wanted his supporters to believe that all immigrants are criminals and refugees are terrorists.

And recently, he directed immigration enforcement agents to arrest and deport any undocumented person they find, essentially legalizing racial profiling and setting in motion his mass deportation plan.

Among the people that ICE arrested, are mothers, fathers, DREAMers with DACA, a victim of domestic violence, and many more.

As a matter of fact, tonight in the gallery listening to President Trump's speech were Guadalupe Garcia de Rayos' children, a working mother from Arizona who went to her appointment with ICE only to be arrested and deported without reason. Today Guadalupe is far from her children who are U.S. citizens and who are an example of the great impact that Trump's actions have over the American people in general, not just on the undocumented community.

These people should not be ICE's target or priority. This is not who we are as a country.

President Trump is taking us back to some of the darkest times in our history: criminalizing anyone who is different, pitting us against each other, and sending the wrong message to the rest of the world, helping to breed anger and hate from terrorist groups to our country.

But we must remember that this is a kind country that is full of hope, where freedom of expression rules, and the people are powerful.

Instead of mass deportations, President Trump should focus on creating jobs and growing our economy. He should recognize immigrants' great contributions to our country, of which he has benefited as well.

Instead of separating families, President Trump should pass comprehensive immigration reform that honors our country's tradition of welcoming immigrants . . .

Source: Transcript and Video: Astrid Silva's Full Response to Trump's Congressional Joint Address (English & Spanish); https://americasvoice.org/blog/astrid-silva-full-response-to-trump.

13

Cross-Border Spirit and Cooperation

Along the border, cultures come together; they blend. Friendships and camaraderie overcome native differences. Food, language, forms of artistic creativity from theater, art, and sculpture to literature, music, and cinema all find common ground. The borderlands reflect a collective spirit and a unique sense of place and time.

- Nuevo Laredo, Tamaulipas/Laredo, Texas—2018

  At Uni-Trade Stadium in Laredo, the Tecolotes de los Dos Laredos (the Owls of the Two Laredos) take the field as fans respectfully stand for the playing of the national anthems of both the United States and Mexico. For one of the oldest teams in Mexican baseball, this game in Texas is not considered a "road game." For this team, the border is not a dividing line; the team plays "home games" in stadiums on both sides of the border. The mayor of Nuevo Laredo, Enrique Rivas, declares that the team lives in a reality different from the perspective of what leaders in Washington, D.C., and Mexico City think. This team, he says, tries to unite what politics seems unable to do.

  The owner of the Tecolotes, a team that is part of the Liga Mexicana de Béisbol, or the Mexican Baseball League, takes pride in emphasizing the close ties of the two cities and how they represent one of the busiest land ports in the United States. Nearly 40,000 folks cross the border every day here. The Owls logo is designed to represent the binational and cultural ties of the two cities, and the Tecolotes' slogan appears on signs around the parks here in Laredo and in the park in Nuevo Laredo: "Dos Naciones, Un Equipo," or "Two Nations, One Team."

  Fans crossing the border from Nuevo Laredo to see this game have their $3.50 border crossing fee waived with a game ticket stub, a gesture approved by the U.S. city to encourage attendance from the Mexican side.

  Many of the players understand and appreciate the efforts of the team's management to make the Owls a symbol of mutual friendship and respect and a bridge to solidarity. One of the players remarks that many of the Border

Patrol agents follow the games and have come to know the players themselves. This, they know, is a good thing.

- Palomas, Chihuahua/Columbus and Deming, New Mexico—2018

Lugging their backpacks over their shoulders, high school students in Palomas gather at the border to board a bus that will take them about thirty-five miles to Deming, New Mexico. Younger children await a bus ride that will take them a much shorter distance across the border to Columbus, New Mexico. Past the barbed wire fence and the Mexican border agents on one side through to the U.S. port of entry on the other, the students begin their daily round-trip excursion to public schools. This is a routing that many of their parents had taken when they were youngsters, a phenomenon that dates back for over six decades and one that has helped maintain cross-border community, family, and friendship ties between the sister cities for generations.

The majority of students who attend Columbus Elementary School and Deming High School live in Palomas, and most were born at the nearest hospital thirty miles north of the border in Deming. Indeed, over half of the residents of Luna County, New Mexico, are Latinos who were once schoolchildren from Palomas.

Most of the over 800 students from Palomas who attend schools in New Mexico are U.S. citizens whose parents are migrant workers living in homes with dirt floors and without indoor bathrooms. Many have, at one time or another, been deported from the United States after crossing the border without authorization. According to some of the grade school teachers at Columbus Elementary, some of the children have never used a pencil.

Because most of the parents are not legally allowed to enter the United States, they cannot have normal parent-teacher meetings with the teachers or even see the schools in which the children are educated. Both Columbus and Deming schools have begun using an online videoconferencing tool that enables parents in Palomas to talk via computer in a local internet café to the teachers in New Mexico.

The access to superior educational opportunities became an escape road out of poverty for many youngsters in Palomas. The owner of the Hacienda De Villa Motel in Columbus, for example, received an education in New Mexico, as did her four adult children, all of whom are now living and working in the United States.

Although some of the residents in Columbus and Deming resent the idea of U.S. tax dollars being spent for the education of children living in Mexico, most have not only accepted the arrangement but appreciate and value the attachments in commerce, culture, and community between the towns on opposite sides of the border.

With the raging debate about border walls and border security in the United States, one of the school superintendents who has observed the effects of the system in place says that everyone in the United States should spend a morning at the school bus stop and watch five-year-olds walk through the gates on their way to school with their futures ahead.

- Nogales, Sonora/Nogales, Arizona, 2018

  One hundred years ago, in 1918, after a skirmish during the Mexican Revolution, authorities on both sides of Nogales, Sonora, and Nogales, Arizona, or "Ambos Nogales," agreed to erect what they believed would be a permanent chain link fence down International Street where the border divides the United States and Mexico. Soon the fence became something of a joke in some people's eyes. After the war, during the U.S. Prohibition era, for example, Mexican businessmen built saloons along International Avenue that actually straddled the border. Thirsty patrons from both sides could enter the bar but only if they agreed to stay in their own country inside the establishments. The odds that those restrictions were strictly enforced are long indeed.

  Now, in 2018, the sister cities are beset by border security concerns, the revelations of numerous tunnels dug by drug traffickers to avoid detection, and the increased border security force in both men and equipment put in place by the U.S. government. Nevertheless, citizens on both sides remain closely attached in numerous ways by cultural, family, and business ties.

  To retain those close ties, however, citizens today have to deal with yet another fence, this one erected in 2011 that consists of rust-colored steel rods encased in cement four inches apart and the fact that, unlike decades earlier, border crossers into Nogales need official papers. What in past days could be a simple walk by U.S. citizens across the border into Nogales, Sonora, to go to restaurants or to shop now involves having a passport or other official documents allowing the crossing.

  Now, as in Friendship Park in California and in other ports of entry, the sight of family members holding up newborn babies to show to relatives on the other side is common. To separated family members and friends, those steel rods are indeed personal barriers.

  Here on both sides of the border, almost everything seems binational, from the language to the food to the curios on sale along the streets, to clothing and shoe stores catering to men and women, many of them of mixed heritage, that feature classic Western styles.

  Nogales, Sonora, has a population of approximately 450,000 people and dwarfs the size of its U.S. sister city. Nogales, Arizona, depends heavily on commerce from across the border and the transportation industry that services the maquiladoras and the importation of Mexican fruits and vegetables. It also relies on Mexican consumers crossing the border to shop, something that has, because of the more stringent security measures, reduced the cross-border traffic.

  But despite the increasing barriers both physical and emotional, the binational spirit and emotional attachment still pulsate, especially in events such as the cross-border celebration of Veterans Day. On this day, citizens from both sides are reminded of the squadron of Mexican Eagles who flew U.S. Air Force planes with the Mexican Air Force insignia on the tails during World War II. They are reminded of how the armed services and diplomats of both countries worked together following the 9/11 attacks. They are reminded that not only in matters during such periods of crisis but also in abiding matters of respect—ancestral, cultural, and personal—the ties between people on both sides of those rust-colored rods remain strong.

A SENSE OF COMMUNITY

There is a sense of shared identity common to people living on both sides of the border.

Although each border community has its own particular character across the 2,000 miles of the line—whether in Tijuana/San Diego or Matamoros/Brownsville—each of these communities have formed interrelationships that depend on shared economic interests and common purpose.

They are hubs of all kinds of activity—from sports to music to commerce—that nurture shared interests and goals. Here, in these communities, millions of people live and work, find leisure activities, and gradually absorb cultural features and traditions handed down from past generations. For these people in the borderlands, the territory is the foundation for their way of life. Some even describe themselves as fellow "transborder" citizens. All of this interaction between citizens on both sides of the line creates shared outlooks and a kind of integration that transcends boundary. There is a road sign someone erected in New Mexico that says simply "*Es una frontera, no una barrera.*" (It is a border, not a barrier).

There is no question that the cartel violence in the cities, the increased border security apparatus and requirements, and the political maelstrom involving immigration issues have fractured the everyday lives of large numbers of border residents. Legal border crossers find their commutes more difficult. Many agricultural workers from Mexicali, for example, leave at 4 a.m. to reach the farms and orchards in the Imperial Valley. At the San Diego/Tijuana port, 70,000 passengers in vehicles traveling north daily across the border from Mexico and thousands who walk across find the lines increasingly long and the waiting time much longer.

In 2016 Cronkite News, Univision News, and the *Dallas Morning News* conducted a poll among residents in the borderlands about their views of life in the sister cities; their sense of community, opportunity, and binational and bicultural influences; their views on border security; and other matters affecting their lives and dreams. On both sides of the border, citizens overwhelmingly affirmed their sense that in myriad ways they were living in an integrated society, one that gave them a strong sense of connection to those on the other side of the line. One respondent from Arizona described the Mexican town across the border as a "lifeline."

Reflecting the attitudes of about 1,500 respondents in fourteen sister cities along the length of the border, the poll reported that 72 percent of citizens on the U.S. side and 86 percent on the Mexican side were opposed to the building of a wall. Also, the poll found that 86 percent of residents in the U.S. towns and cities on the

The Advent of Spanglish

Cross the border in any direction at any point along its winding 2,000 miles and you will hear from both Latinos and Anglos words and phrases that evolved over many decades from the interaction of people in the borderlands. So intertwined did the vocabulary and grammar of English and Spanish become that it gained its own definition as a hybrid dialect—Spanglish.

Spanglish has evolved from the bilingual culture along the U.S.-Mexican border and is so common now that it has spread to cities and communities across the country with expanding Latino populations. Especially in the borderlands, conversations between bilingual individuals will often alternate between English and Spanish words. But the most notable distinction of Spanglish is the actual structural merging of the two languages into new words and phrases.

For example, some Spanglish words emanate simply from adding endings to English words. "To park" thus becomes "parquear." The following are a few examples of Spanglish words and terms:

- Frizado: frozen
- Ehsteen: steam
- Parree: party
- Chequear: to check something
- Jamberger: hamburger
- El ticket: a ticket
- Cojelo con: take it easy (a phrase meaning to relax and stop worrying)
- Conflei: cornflakes and other cereals
- ¿Estás ready?: Are you ready?

border and 79 percent of Mexicans had high regard for those on the other side and that over 80 percent of respondents on both sides favored a path to citizenship for unauthorized immigrants who live in the United States. The poll echoed the sentiment that the two interwoven cultures, languages, heritages, and commerce on which they depend have made them, in a large sense, one community.

BINATIONAL COOPERATION

Most Mexicans are not aware that the United States works with Mexican government authorities in training and equipping law enforcement agencies south of the border or that the U.S. Bureau of Alcohol, Tobacco, Firearms, and Explosives (ATF) helps those authorities trace confiscated illegal weapons.

Most U.S. citizens have no knowledge that Mexican authorities helped prevent a massive electricity blackout in San Diego or that experts from Baja traveled north to help contain a disease outbreak among poultry stocks in California.

The U.S.-Mexican border, with its diverse inhabited regions and land characteristics, faces many formidable challenges that call for mutual cooperative efforts by governments on both sides. Although much additional coordination and personal interaction need to occur to make the border regions safer and more productive and its living conditions more accommodating for the needs of the vast majority of its citizens, there has been surprising cooperation between the two countries over the years.

Water Resources and Environmental Protection

One of the most enduring organizations between the two countries established to deal with the border traces its origins back to the nineteenth century: the International Boundary and Water Commission (IBWC)/Comisión Internacional de Límites y Aguas (CILA).

The IBWC/CILA, originally created to determine the location of and to settle disputes relating to the international boundary, has continued, through various treaties and cooperative works, not only to carry out its original mission but also to engage in other actions and studies relating to border interests. Now headquartered in El Paso/Juárez, the IBWC/CILA, administered through the U.S. Department of State and the Mexican Ministry of Foreign Affairs, took on responsibilities for issues relating to water resources and allocation.

One of the most significant evolutions in the work of the IBWC/CILA was the binational 1944 Treaty between Mexico and the United States for the Utilization of Waters of the Colorado and Tijuana Rivers and of the Rio Grande. The treaty has been one of the most influential steps in allocating and shaping water resources and developing water policy between the two nations.

Responsibilities under the treaty have included not only the allocation of water from the Rio Grande, Colorado River, and other smaller rivers but also overseeing the salinity levels of the Colorado River as it enters Mexico; levee projects to protect lands along the rivers from floods; the joint construction and operation of dams, reservoirs, and hydroelectric generation plants; and steps to solve water quality problems caused by issues such as hazardous waste and water pollution.

In August 1983 at the Baja California port city of La Paz, Presidents Ronald Reagan and Miguel de la Madrid signed the United States–Mexico Agreement on Cooperation for the Protection and Improvement of the Environment in the Border Area. It became known as the La Paz Agreement and has remained a milestone for bilateral cooperation on the protection of the environment in the borderlands regions.

The agreement outlined responsibilities of both countries to work together in preventing water and air pollution as well as other environmental hazards that became a threat to the land. Although La Paz did not pledge specific monetary responsibilities, it became an umbrella collaboration under which representatives from both the United States and Mexico could exchange information, monitor environmental impact and change, and cooperatively launch scientific programs with the aim of protecting land, air, and water in the borderlands region. It formed a national coordinating group for each country that held regular meetings and working groups.

Soon after the La Paz agreement was signed, it served as a diplomatic platform to launch a number of specific efforts to combat environmental decline, including a serious wastewater sanitation problem at the port of Tijuana/San Diego (a problem that continues to plague the area), a program to restrict air pollution in the smelter regions along the Arizona-Sonora border, an effort through cross-border regulation to deal with the shipment of hazardous wastes, and the beginnings of negotiations to regulate and manage air quality in the urban regions along the border, especially Juárez/El Paso.

Although environmental groups decried the lack of enforcement responsibilities provided by La Paz, the agreement at least provided a diplomatic platform under which future advancements could be undertaken. La Paz moved the issues of what had formally been considered local (sanitation, air quality, sewage) to an international level. It has become, even with its limitations, a visionary agreement that some legal scholars have defined as "preventive diplomacy."

When the North American Free Trade Agreement (NAFTA) was implemented in 1994, La Paz had already provided an impetus for the United States and Mexico to act regarding the effects on the border of industrial development and the extensive population growth that increasingly taxed the natural resources of the border regions. After the advent of NAFTA, the two countries created entities to deal with these increasing pressures: the North American Development Bank (NADB) and the Border Environment Cooperation Commission (BECC).

In the decades that followed, the NADB contracted loans for hundreds of BECC-certified infrastructure projects that addressed the problems of safe drinking water, clean energy, treatment of wastewater, and water distribution. The projects ranged from a wastewater system rehabilitation project in Piedras Negras, Coahuila, to a water conservation project in Yuma, Arizona.

In Texas BECC-NADB support has launched many projects focusing on water and wastewater problems. Wastewater treatment in Juárez was introduced through these projects and has greatly enhanced the water quality for citizens on both sides of the border.

Security Cooperation

Following his victory in the Mexican presidential election of 2006, President-elect Felipe Calderón decided that a central focus of his administration would be to address the spreading violence and rupture of order and stability in many cities at the hands of the cartels and other criminal enterprises that had heretofore repulsed Mexican national efforts to provide peace and stability to the nation's citizens. In the first meeting between Calderón and U.S. President George W. Bush, the two agreed on forging greater collaboration and support between the two nations in suppressing violence and criminal enterprise.

The agreement that eventually emerged from those discussions became known as the Mérida Initiative, named after the capital of the Mexican state of Yucatán where the early discussions originated. The initiative called for the Mexican government to increase national anti-crime and corruption efforts, especially along the U.S.-Mexican border; the United States pledged to engage in efforts to reduce drug demand in the United States and the illicit trafficking of guns and weapons that fortified the warring cartels and gangs that caused such violent mayhem in Mexico.

In the early years of the Mérida Initiative, the U.S. Congress appropriated funds to supply aircraft and helicopters to support Mexico's military and police. The two countries increased their cooperative efforts to share intelligence in reducing the flow of illegal narcotics; in increasing training and establishing standards for police, prosecutors, and judges in handling an increasing assault against cartel operations; and in a number of other areas related to border security and operational standards. Under the Mérida Initiative, the U.S. Agency for International Development (USAID) undertook efforts to increase civilian safety in the border regions and to support criminal justice reforms in Mexico to protect citizens' rights.

Although many U.S. government officials feared that, despite the cooperative undertakings through the Mérida Initiative, there would be considerable cartel-led trafficking violence that would spill over from major Mexican cities into areas across the border, as well as possible terrorist infiltration, these concerns proved to be relatively unfounded. Major U.S. border cities well into the twenty-first century remain some of the safest cities in the nation, and no terrorist infiltration has been uncovered by U.S. national security agencies.

The continuing cooperative efforts between the two countries will undoubtedly change as such major issues as border security, illegal immigration, illicit gun and drug trafficking, and the U.S. debate over a possible wall across the entirety of the border continue to challenge diplomatic negotiations. It remains clear, nevertheless, that a coordinated and closely allied approach will benefit both nations, and they maintain their close commercial and diplomatic ties as neighboring countries.

Education Exchange

In 2014 President Obama and President Peña Nieto launched the U.S.-Mexico Bilateral Forum on Higher Education, Innovation and Research, or the "Bilateral Forum." Its main purpose is to increase scientific research partnerships and educational exchanges.

Through the program, the two governments have brought together representatives from the higher education communities and the private sector to encourage broader access to post-secondary education, especially for young people who do not have the financial resources or other means to receive such education and especially in such areas as engineering, mathematics, and science. Leaders in the initiative have engaged in scholar and teacher exchanges across the border, conducting joint research and sharing discoveries and innovative techniques.

The U.S. side in the Bilateral Forum is led by the Department of State with participation from other agencies such as the National Science Foundation and the U.S. Department of Education. The Mexican side is co-chaired by the Ministries of Public Education and Foreign Relations and involves other agencies such as the Ministries of Economy and Energy.

Community Spirit and Pathos at Friendship Park

For over a decade every spring at Friendship Park's wall separating Tijuana and San Diego, hundreds gather at a celebration called the Fandango Fronterizo. Filling the air are the sounds of the *jarama*, an eight-string instrument patterned after a sixteenth-century baroque Spanish guitar. From both sides of the border fence, the music of the *jaramas* along with harps and percussion instruments rhythmically mix with songs into a declaration of solidarity.

Amidst the presence of Border Patrol agents and surveillance cameras, the festival is a testament to cultural and familial ties that, at least for this time and place, overwhelm the anxieties and turmoil that haunt aspects of border life. The Fandango Fronterizo is one of a number of events organized each year at Friendship Park. On many weekends the gates are opened to at least allow individuals from both sides to enter the enforcement zone and approach the primary steel fence. Through the barrier's mesh, friends, family, and loved ones meet to talk and touch fingers. Many on the Tijuana side have been deported with their loved ones remaining in the United States. Some individuals talk about seeing grandparents meeting their newborn grandchildren for the first time through the fence.

Various local groups continue to press for greater access for the families. In December 2018 The Border Church announced the opening of its second site (the first is located near the border in San Diego). This second site is in the "El Chaparral" neighborhood of Tijuana near the pedestrian crossing at the San Ysidro port of entry. Since 2011 The Border Church has celebrated communion at Friendship Park as a symbolic stance to promote integration of people, spiritual unity, and binational common ground on the borderlands.

CULTURAL MELDING

Among the most important legacies of the Chicano movement was the cultural flowering that it inspired, one that encompassed many forms—theater, art, sculpture, literature in many forms, music, and cinema. This expressive culture has endured well into the twenty-first century and reflects the collective spirit that exemplified the fight for self-identity, a sense of belonging, and the will to demand rights and justice so strong in the "Movemiento" and so strong on the border. Cultural expression and aesthetic have always been deep in the character of the border and its people.

McAllen, Texas, located on the border about seventy miles from the Gulf of Mexico, has a long history dating from the turn of the twentieth century. From a farming community to a tourist attraction as a gateway to Mexico and, later, as an oil-producing area, McAllen became one of the growing centers across the Rio Grande bolstered by trade and growth of the maquiladora industries in its sister city of Reynosa. As many other cities on the border, it has in recent years been not only a hub of commerce between the two countries but also a source of tension as the violence from warring cartels became increasingly dangerous in Reynosa and a significant issue of concern for residents of McAllen, worried that the violence would spread.

But deep cultural ties have grown between the sister cities over a century, enduring bonds that unite people from both sides of the border through traditions, language, family and friendships, religion, work, and commerce.

The annual McAllen "Dreams" festival held in the spring has sought to inculcate that sense of cultural sharing with such performers as the pop-punk band Fantástico, the Chicano musician Cuco, and Piñata Protest, an accordion-powered Tex-Mex band from San Antonio.

As visitors to the event wander around the venue, the cultural mix is more than evident; it is invigorating. It is especially notable in the mix of conversations between young people, most using Spanglish. It is evident in the bonds that they have forged across the border as many have worked and gone to school on both sides. It is evident in the music on stage with its progressive blend of sounds and instruments and lyrics melding Mexican roots with country and rock. It is evident when the rock band Downtown Boys chants brown pride lyrics or when some of the English lyrics are translated into Spanish. Here in McAllen and at the Dreams event, from the musicians to their fans and to most everyone mingling and having a good time, the political battles over immigration and walls and all the rest can take a minor role to the cultural interplay. After all, it is likely that most of those at the festival do not have to look too far or too distant in time to find their connections to those across the border.

About 1,000 miles from McAllen northwest along the border, residents of the sister cities of Agua Prieta, Sonora/Douglas, Arizona, held their own cultural festival in early 2018. They called it "Shared Spaces: An Evening of Dance, Music and Poetry at the US/Mex Border."

Performers and participants gathered on both sides of the border near the Douglas port of entry. The dancers, musicians, and artists, some from Sonora and some from Arizona, were there, emphasized the organizers, to promote cultural awareness, social justice, and the close ties between people on both sides. There were young dancers, some in traditional Mexican outfits; there were singers and musicians performing everything from Mexican folk to modern jazz; and there were artists from both sides who brought paint and canvases and other materials and invited youngsters to participate.

Before their performance youngsters from the dance groups Ballet Folclórico Aztlán and Angeles de Agua Prieta held hands through the border fence. Nearby a poster read, "At the border everything is possible."

Alejandro Escovedoa, a Texas-born songwriter and musician and the son of Mexican immigrants, is familiar with the kind of feelings expressed by those who attended the festivals in McAllen and Agua Prieta/Douglas. He has had a long and distinguished career that has taken him and musicians with whom he has worked who into various genres known variously as punk rock, Chicano rock, alternative rock, heartland rock, and others. In 2018, working with an Italian musician and former journalist named Antonio Gramentieri and his band known as Don Antonio, Escovedoa released the most personal album of his career. It is called *The Crossing.*

One of the songs is called "Texas Is My Mother." It was inspired by a conversation the artists had with a Dreamer in a Dallas restaurant who had carried his aunt across the Rio Grande. The chorus of the song is: "I would carry you on my shoulders, across the muddy river / Texas feels like Mexico. It reminds me of my mother." On the one hand, the river and the border symbolize migration; they also symbolize connection.

DOCUMENTS

Interview with Chicano Artist David Avalos, 1988

Muralist, painter, and art administrator, David Avalos is one of the prominent artists whose work flowered in the early years of the Chicano movement. Educated at the University of California at San Diego, deeply engaged with the San Diego Chicano muralist movement, the formation of the Border Workshop, and various collaborations between artists and art administrators, Avalos is not only an innovative artist but also an eloquent proponent of understanding the cultural development of the U.S.-Mexican border and how that development has manifested itself in a wide spectrum of artistic expression. A forceful spokesman for social justice, he has mentored generations of artists and activists. In 1988 he discussed various issues relating to border culture and artistic expression in an extended interview in San Diego that is now part of the Archives of American Art at the Smithsonian Institution. These are excerpts from that interview.

DAVID AVALOS: I was born in San Diego at what was then called the county Hospital in 1947 on September 12th. My mother is Maria Torres Avalos. She was born in Guadalajara, Mexico, in 1911 on June 8th. My father is Santos Urquizo Avalos, and he was born in Durango on November 1, 1911, also. They traveled . . . my mother's family brought her to the United States as a child—as a small infant actually. I think she probably crossed over within a couple of years after her birth, and eventually her family made its way to National City, California. My father left Mexico when he was about eight or nine years old, and his father, Gregorio Avalos, my grandfather, followed the railroads, crossed in El Paso, went to Kansas City with the railroads, then was in Arizona for a while and finally settled in National City where there was a railroad-tie curing yard . . . .

MARGARITA NIETO: Did you ever go to Mexico with your parents as a child?

DAVID AVALOS: Well, my mother's sister, my tia Rosie, lived in Tijuana, so I would visit them with the family on any number of occasions when I was growing up, and I still, still see her once in a while. Like we have, we saw her last year for example and we took her out to Rosarito's for some fish, tacos. And my grandfather, Papa Goyo [nickname for Gregorio Avalos—DA], lived in Tijuana for a time as well, had property there, and my father used to visit him regularly and take me along with him. so Tijuana being Mexico, I visited Mexico constantly throughout my childhood, but beyond that never ventured into the interior.

MARGARITA NIETO: That's an interesting point, though. Did you see Tijuana as Mexico or did you think of a difference? Or was it all part of the same landscape, part of the same world? . . .

DAVID AVALOS: No, I think my inclination in answering the question was to say first of all, "No, I've never been to Mexico; I used to go to Tijuana," so there is, there is a kind of separation, on my part, of being a difference when you talk about Mexico that Tijuana's not representative of that. There's a separation between this idea of what Mexico is and what Tijuana, what Mexico is as a myth and what Tijuana is as a reality . . .

I had a conscience, because my mother was very devout and strict. She was a very devout Catholic and a very strict disciplinarian, and I had a sense of right and wrong, and I also—which was also pretty clearly articulated —I also had a sense of what it was to be around people who cared about you, because in my family everybody cared about everybody else. [It] was not articulated, and it was only until years later, after having been in the drug culture, that I realized that there was something in my upbringing that I hadn't found within that drug culture and that was people who cared about you in the way that your family cares about you. Not in a honey-dripping way, abut in a real way where there's real concerns as well as real disagreements and annoyances and so forth.

But I didn't have a consciousness, and I think that that consciousness came only with my involvement with the civil rights organization in my home town, National City, the Committee on Chicano Rights . . . the real driving force behind the committee was Herman Baca, and he had a tremendous sense of understanding when it came to the media, so that in 1977 there was an announcement by the Ku Klux Klan that, that they were going to patrol the border, and they were going to stop so-called illegal aliens at the border. And Herman . . . . At that time, I had graduated from UCSD and was at Stanford in their PhD. program in communications. Herman and the committee began organizing a march to protest the announcement of the Klan and essentially to protest the immigration plan . . .

it was a youth culture that transcended the border. Looking at, at all these, looking at all these kinds of things, we began thinking at the Centro Cultural about what does it mean, now? What does it mean . . . ? Do we embrace the idea of bicultural exchange in terms of San Diego takes down the symphony? Mexico brings up the Ballet Folkorico Nacional. Or is there something else happening here? And that something else, as we formulated it back in the late Seventies and early Eighties, was this idea that we do not have two distinct cultural entities, separated by this line of political demarcation. It's one thing. It's interlinked, it's cross-pollinating, it's constantly being influenced. I came up, years later I came up with this . . . . Well, not that many years later, I guess. During this period I came up with this metaphor that the San Diego/Tijuana border region is like a plantation society. Now within a plantation society you have the field hand as well as a master on his horse, the southern belle waving a handkerchief from the second story window. Everybody has their place; everybody has their role. But it's one thing. Okay? It's one thing. It's one world view—both good, bad, and ugly. So I began seeing the border that way, and in fact that thinking in terms of plantation emerged in the phrase, 'Welcome to America's Finest Tourist Plantation," the bus poster that happened earlier this year.

MARGARITA NIETO: That was funny; I was thinking that that was a perfect lead-in to that. That created quite a commotion at the LACE [Los Angeles Contemporary Exhibition gallery—MN], you know.

DAVID AVALOS: Yeah, and I'd like to get into that, but before that, I just want to talk about this development of the idea that, you know . . . . This goes back to the idea that culture is not a static, monolithic thing that exists in its artifacts. It's a living thing. It's a constantly unfolding thing that lives in the attitudes, ideas, and feelings of the people. Back in 1982, 1983, it might have been . . . I think it was 1982, there was a, there's this commission, the U.S.-Mexico Border Governor's Conference, the four American border states and the six Mexican border states . . . I was co-chairman of the steering committee of this whole project, and people delivered papers—not artists so much as academicians, social scientists, although there were artists involved such as myself. And the consequence of it was they issued a statement that there was something unique to the border, culturally, that was different from the national cultures of both Mexico and the United States. And prior to this, when they talked about border culture, they always in terms of, when they talked about the border they always talked about it in terms of, "It's a great place to communicate, for the two national cultures to communicate." It was never discussed in terms of "Hey, there's something here that's happening that's different."

MARGARITA NIETO: As an entity unto itself.

DAVID AVALOS: In 1984 Rene [Yanes, Yanez] at the Galeria de la Raza asked me if I would put together a Chicano exhibit of Chicano artists. He said he was very impressed with what was happening in San Diego. The Chicano artists seemed to be coming alive, so to speak. And I, of course, I went to Victor Ochoa first of all and talked to him about it, and then we set up a meeting with some of the veterans here in San Diego. And what was amazing was that they were more interested in what could be done to get them into galleries, to get them commercial sales—with that aspect of the art world, which is just as legitimate as any other aspect. We were more interested as a nonprofit organization in putting together a show that was about defining cultural parameters. And as a consequence, I made the decision to put the show together not with, exclusively with Chicano artists but around the theme of the border. And I invited, after Victor Ochoa I invited Michael Schnorr, who's a teacher at Southwestern College, which has an enormous number of Spanish-speaking students from Mexico that go there. . . .

So we had this group. And it was difficult for me, because there's a lot of the cultural nationalist in me. And it was difficult for me to justify in my mind how a Chicano cultural organization and a Chicano artist could be putting together a show that included non-Chicanos. . . . But at the same time I felt that it was absolutely the right thing to do. I just didn't have a conceptual framework for it. The group included Mexican citizens as well as U.S. citizens, Chicano and non-Chicano. And the way I came to grips with it was by saying "Well, the border is not a Chicano issue. It's not a Mexican issue. It affects everyone who lives here in this region. If you believe that it's one region then everybody in the region is about making that culture and that we shouldn't be making it in isolation.

The border is something central to U.S. culture. You can see it in the idea of our being a nation of immigrants, people who cross from outside that border to inside.

As I said earlier, the only people who believe in the American dream are immigrants. Americans don't believe in it anymore. That's what fuels some of the greatest myths. That's the price that you have to pay to enter this country. You've got to announce as soon as you cross that border, "Hey, I believe in the American dream." The other, the other aspect of our culture is this idea of the frontier, the constantly expanding frontier, the idea of a border constantly changing, constantly moving outward.

Source: Oral History Interview with David Avalos, 1988 June 16–July 5. Archives of American Art, Smithsonian Institution; https://www.aaa.si.edu/collections/interviews/oral-history-interview-david-avalos-5428.

State Department Report on Mexican Government Cooperation in Attacking Drug Smuggling, 2016

The State Department's Bureau of International Narcotics and Law Enforcement Affairs (INL) develops programs to combat narcotics trafficking and international crime. In carrying out its mission of minimizing the impact of the illegal entry of narcotics and the influence of crime syndicates into the United States, the INL partners with Mexico in training and promoting modern law enforcement operations. A 2016 report by the INL on drug smuggling and other criminal activities affecting the U.S.-Mexican border demonstrates the close cooperative efforts between the United States and Mexico to fight cartel violence and other criminal enterprises.

Bureau of International Narcotics and Law Enforcement Affairs
2016 International Narcotics Control Strategy Report (INCSR)
Report

A. Introduction

Mexico remains a major transit country for cocaine and heroin and a source country for heroin, marijuana, and methamphetamine destined for the United States. Narcotics trafficking and related violence in Mexico continue to pose significant problems to citizen security and economic development.

According to the most recently available statistics, published by Mexico's statistics agency (INEGI) in September 2015, reported homicides decreased by nearly 15 percent and kidnappings decreased by 22 percent from 2013 to 2014. However, an estimated 93 percent of all crimes went either unreported or uninvestigated in 2014.

Mexico actively combats drug trafficking organizations and U.S.-Mexico cooperation in this area is substantial. The Merida Initiative is a major component of these efforts; since 2008, nearly \$1.5 billion in training, equipment, and technical assistance has been delivered to help strengthen Mexico's judicial and security institutions. U.S. and Mexican law enforcement counterparts cooperate on investigations and other criminal justice issues related to transnational criminal organizations. Such cooperation boosted efforts to capture leaders of these groups.

These successes, however, have resulted in smaller, fractured groups that violently compete for power, terrain, and market share.

Mexican consumption of illicit drugs is lower than U.S. levels, although insufficient data exists to determine current consumption trends.

B. Drug Control Accomplishments, Policies, and Trends

1. Institutional Development

Mexico continues to strengthen federal and state institutional capacity to confront organized crime. Since 2006, the Government of Mexico restructured and tripled the size of its Federal Police. Many states are reforming their police forces to reduce corruption, including establishing internal affairs units and implementing a single command structure, known as "mando único."

Mexico's 2016 budget for public security and national security increased by 3.6 percent to $15.4 billion. Funding is used to combat organized crime, expand crime prevention programs, improve interagency coordination, consolidate police forces, support justice reforms, and encourage citizen participation in crime control.

Impunity levels in Mexico remain high and Mexico's transition to an accusatorial criminal justice system remains uneven ahead of the country's June 2016 constitutional deadline for implementation. Six states are now fully operating under the new criminal justice system. Other states have thus far adopted partial accusatorial systems, utilizing the new system in certain municipalities or for certain types of crimes. States are also using hybrid systems, trying cases grandfathered under the old inquisitorial system and new cases under the accusatorial system. The Mexican government seeks to increase transparency and decrease corruption in criminal cases through the adoption of the accusatory system. Early results from states implementing the reforms are encouraging. However, the learning curve moving forward will be steep as the Mexican public and justice operators adjust to it and a new criminal procedure code.

Multilaterally, Mexico participates in the Inter-American Convention on Mutual Assistance in Criminal Matters, and subscribes to the 1996 Anti-Drug Strategy in the Hemisphere and the 1990 Declaration and Program of Action of Ixtapa. Likewise, Mexico is a regional observer in the Central American Integration System and collaborates with Central American countries to improve regional security.

Mexico participates with Canada and the United States in the North American Maritime Security Initiative, in which naval authorities meet regularly to share information, improve response to transnational threats, and develop and refine protocols for maritime interdictions. In addition, Mexico hosted a trilateral police chief meeting with Canada and the United States in March 2015.

The current U.S.-Mexico extradition treaty has been in force since 1980, and Mexico remains a strong extradition partners. A bilateral mutual legal assistance treaty in force since 1991 fosters a broad range of cooperation in criminal matters.

Collaboration between the United States and Mexico has been promising since new Attorney General Arely Gomez was appointed in March.

2. Supply Reduction

Mexico cooperates with the United States on supply reduction. Maritime and land corridors through Central America and Mexico continue to be the most significant transit routes for cocaine from South America bound for the United States. While the United States remains the primary destination for illicit drugs trafficked via Mexico, trafficking routes through Mexico are diversifying to accommodate growing markets around the world.

Mexico is a major producer of heroin, marijuana, and methamphetamine destined for the United States. Full calendar year 2015 figures were not available at the time of this report. The Government of Mexico reported eradicating 21,425 hectares (ha) of opium poppy in 2014, a significant increase from the 14,419 ha eradicated in 2013. The Government of Mexico also reported eradicating 5,679 ha of cannabis in 2014, a slight increase over the 5,096 ha eradicated in 2013.

The United State estimates that opium poppy cultivation increased 59 percent in 2014, to 17,000 ha from 11,000 ha in 2013, which could potentially produce 42 metric tons (MT) of pure heroin, compared with 26 MT in 2013. Also, in 2014, the United States estimated that Mexico cannabis cultivation decreased 15 percent to 11,000 ha compared with 13,000 ha in 2014.

The Office of the Attorney General reported Mexico seized 929.4 MT of marijuana in 2014, a decrease of 3.0 percent from 2013. Mexico seized 3.6 MT of cocaine, a 41.5 percent decrease, and 1.4 MT of opium gum in 2014, an increase of over 400 percent. U.S. law enforcement seizures of heroin along the U.S.-Mexico border have also increased significantly over the past several years.

With respect to synthetic drugs, Mexican seizures of methamphetamine, which totaled 19.8 MT in 2014, increased 35.9 percent when compared to 2013. Seizures of clandestine drug labs rose slightly. The Mexican government seized 143 labs in 2014, an 11.7 percent increase compared to 2013. Mexican officials participate in regular meetings with U.S. experts to identify and target the latest trends in synthetic drug production.

3. Public Information, Prevention, and Treatment

Official statistics indicate illegal drug use in Mexico is lower than U.S. levels. According to the most recent official study conducted in 2011, prevalence of illegal drug use showed a statistically insignificant increase from 1.4 percent in 2008 to 1.5 percent in 2011. Marijuana remains the most commonly used illegal drug. The 2011 national survey does not include a category for new or designer drugs, known as new psychoactive substances. Regionally, northern Mexico is the area with highest prevalence of illegal drug use (2.3 percent versus 1.5 percent nationally). Mexico plans to conduct a new national survey in 2016.

The National Commission against Addictions (CONADIC) coordinates and implements national drug policy. The Secretariat of Government has included demand reduction as a component of its National Program on Crime and Violence Prevention. The National Institute of Psychiatry leads addiction research. These offices liaise with the United States, the Organization of American States (OAS), and the United Nations Office on Drugs and Crime.

Funding for public information initiatives, prevention, and treatment largely comes from the federal budget. In 2015, the budget for demand and treatment-related initiatives increased by 3.4 percent ($83.7 million), though this increase was mitigated by currency depreciation affecting the Mexican peso.

Mexico has made significant efforts to establish drug treatment courts (DTCs) throughout the country. The first DTC was established in Guadalupe, Nuevo León in 2009. Currently, there are 15 DTCs operating in the country, two of which are juvenile courts. The United States continues to fund training and technical assistance by the Inter-American Drug Control Policy Commission of the OAS to establish DTCs in Mexico.

The United States supports the Organization of American States' Inter-American Drug Abuse Control Commission in their technical support to the government's drug treatment and prevention systems, including training and support to treatment facilities.

Additionally, the Government of Mexico is promoting the establishment of anti-drug coalitions on the model developed by the Community Anti-Drug Coalitions of America (CADCA). CADCA supports the formation and/or enhancement of effective drug-free community coalition programs, which assist civil society organizations in reducing drug use. There are now 22 coalitions in Mexico, implemented through a U.S.-funded grant.

CONADIC began a drug counselor certification program in 2015 with U.S. Government support. Previously, drug counselors were not required to be certified, often resulting in inadequate treatment for drug users. Training, evaluation, and certification will continue through 2016, resulting in the certification of roughly 1,500 drug counselors.

4. Corruption

As a matter of government policy, the Government of Mexico does not encourage or facilitate illicit drug production or distribution, nor is it involved in laundering the proceeds of the sale of illicit drugs. Although federal anticorruption standards are improving, corruption continues to impede Mexican counternarcotics efforts. The Mexican government has taken steps to reduce corruption in law enforcement and has designated the National System for Public Security as the agency responsible for overseeing stronger vetting for law enforcement personnel.

In February 2015, President Peña Nieto announced an eight-point anti-corruption plan to enhance the government's commitment to eliminating corruption and increasing transparency. He appointed Virgilio Andrade as the head of the revived Secretariat of Public Administration, which will lead the government's anti-corruption efforts. In April, Mexican Congress passed legislation to create a new anti-corruption system; however, implementing legislation has not yet been passed.

Mexican law enforcement officials remain poorly compensated, under-resourced, inadequately trained, and vulnerable to corruption. Each state and the Federal District have established centers responsible for vetting law enforcement officers. Progress has been uneven, but the centers have had some success identifying corrupt individuals, prompting the removal of officers, and the rejection of police recruits. The Mexican government and some state governors have conducted large-scale dismissals of corrupt police, but work remains to ensure only fully vetted officials remain in the ranks. Some Mexican law enforcement entities have also established, restructured, or augmented their internal affairs offices.

C. National Goals, Bilateral Cooperation, and U.S. Policy Initiatives

U.S. assistance aims to help Mexico develop more effective and transparent security and rule of law institutions and to foster cooperation with international partners to reduce threats from transnational and domestic crime, improve border security, and protect human rights.

Since 2008, the United States has delivered approximately $1.4 billion in assistance through the Merida Initiative. A government-wide effort involving numerous U.S. agencies, Merida has contributed to better law enforcement training, criminal justice reforms, crime prevention efforts, programs for at-risk youth, human rights initiatives, drug demand reduction projects, alternatives to incarceration, and border security programs. Merida trained joint intelligence task forces have led to more efficient and effective intelligence operations, canine unit and non-intrusive inspection programs have resulted in increased interdictions of illicit funds and narcotics, and prison accreditation assistance has resulted in decreased violent prison deaths and outbreaks of violence. Merida has initiated a nation-wide training program to help prepare police for their changing roles in the new justice system and continues to advance a full spectrum of police professionalization activities, including the application of international standards regarding training and accreditation, the implementation of minimum employment standards throughout the career of a police officer, basic policing training, instructor development, continuing education opportunities, and leadership training.

D. Conclusion

Mexico continues its efforts to disrupt or dismantle transnational criminal organizations, reform its judiciary and prisons, improve its police, and address money laundering. These efforts have strengthened Mexico's public institutions while helping to weaken organized crime. Available supply reduction data indicate that interdiction remains a major challenge for Mexico. Only a small portion of the cocaine, marijuana, methamphetamine, and heroin originating in or transiting Mexico is interdicted inside the country. Cultivation also remains a challenge, with data trends suggesting illicit opium poppy cultivation is increasing and will continue to increase, especially without the presence of a holistic alternative development program. With respect to drug demand, the limited official statistics indicate that illegal drug use among Mexicans remains low and stable.

Under the Peña Nieto administration's security strategy, future bilateral efforts will emphasize strengthening Mexican institutions, building capacity for all criminal justice actors to carry out their new roles under an accusatorial justice system; professionalizing police, investigators, intelligence analysts, and forensic specialists; and interdicting illicit goods, all with the goal of achieving security goals shared by both nations. The United States will also continue programs to curb its own domestic drug demand and inhibit the illegal flow of arms and cash into Mexico.

Source: U.S. State Department, Bureau of International Narcotics and Law Enforcement Affairs, 2016 International Narcotics Control Strategy Report, https://www.state.gov/j/inl/rls/nrcrpt/2016/vol1/253288.htm.

Postscript

On June 1, 2015, real estate mogul and television celebrity Donald Trump descended in an escalator in opulent Trump Tower in New York accompanied by his wife, Melania, an immigrant from Slovenia, and announced that he was running for president. In his announcement he proceeded to attack immigrants: "When Mexico sends its people," he declared, "they're not sending their best. They're not sending you. They're not sending you. They're sending people that have lots of problems and they're bringing those problems with us. They're bringing drugs, they're bringing crime, they're rapists, and some, I assume, are good people." This was not some general allusion to the threat of terrorism; this was an unveiled, dehumanizing characterization of a people and reflected an unabashed nativist impulse that had driven the arguments about the U.S.-Mexican border over the decades. This was xenophobic invective used as a political bludgeon.

In a rally in August 2016, candidate Trump, speaking about the need to prevent illegal immigration, declared, "We will build a great wall along the southern border. And Mexico will pay for the wall. One hundred percent. They don't know it yet, but they're going to pay for it." He envisioned the edifice as a "physical, tall, powerful, beautiful southern border wall."

When Trump launched into his campaign, illegal immigration into the United States across the Mexican border had nearly reached its lowest level in fifty years. The number of apprehensions at the border had declined from more than 1 million in 2005 to fewer than 400,000 in 2017, according to U.S. Customs and Border Protection data.

Yet Trump's appeal to the fears of an immigrant and terrorist invasion appealed to a large enough segment of the Republican Party that it helped him unexpectedly sweep through a bitter primary contest against a host of opponents and secure the nomination. In his acceptance speech at the Republican Convention, Trump continued to stoke dread about crime and disease and a loss of American values that a porous U.S.-Mexican border portended.

In his first year as president, Trump continued to insist on the urgent need to erect a monumental wall along the entire length of the border, one for which, in some way, through some kind of persuasion, Mexico would foot the bill. Meanwhile, illegal border crossings declined even further during that year.

Nevertheless, as his political fortunes tottered under intense scrutiny by a major investigation involving illegal conduct by his campaign during the 2016 election aided by the Russian government and other inquiries regarding his business dealings, Trump wildly focused with even more ferocity on the imminent dangers lurking behind the southern border. But even with the Republican Party in control of the White House as well as both houses of the U.S. Congress, Trump's political clout was not enough to generate legislation to fulfill his most sought-after campaign promise—the wall.

Both during the campaign and after he assumed office, Trump continued his attacks on immigrants, in some cases using the word "infestations" in referring to their migration into the country. Dehumanization and degradation had become common parlance in the war over the border. It was as if rhetoric was harkening back to the days of such signs as "No Mexicans or Dogs Allowed."

CRUELTY AS POLICY

In April 2018 Trump seized upon events in Mexico that he believed could bring the border and his wall front and center in political discourse. In this he succeeded.

The issue involved migrants fleeing from countries in Central America wracked by poverty, gang violence, and political warring. Most were from Honduras but also included families from El Salvador, Guatemala, and Nicaragua. Numbering over 4,000 individuals, they crossed Mexico's southern border determined to make their way to the southern border of the United States to ask for asylum from the dangers to their lives and to the lives of their children. The act of crossing the border, surrendering to authorities, and requesting asylum is protected by the United Nations refugee protocol signed by the United States.

Along the way, many migrants managed to find refuge and jobs in Mexico; others continued their journey. As the remnants of what the administration called the "caravan" neared the border, the Trump administration directed attorneys in the border states to vigorously prosecute all cases of illegal crossings and to handle with great suspicion all petitioners who asked for asylum. Trump called it a "zero-tolerance policy."

In the spring, it became clear what "zero tolerance" meant. In June a large tent city suddenly appeared in the border town of Tornillo in West Texas to house over 2,000 minors and children who had been taken from their parents after crossing. The policy now involved separating children from their parents, placing them in detention centers, and treating the administrative cases of the children and the parents separately.

It was a policy designed as a threat to other families thinking of attempting to illegally enter the United States. The scene of young, weeping children taken from the arms of their parents and hustled off to detention pens shocked many on the border as well as investigative reporters, social and immigrant rights groups, and others on the scene. Medical organizations protested that such child detention increased risks of depression, post-traumatic stress, and other disorders. After it was cited for health and safety concerns, the camp in Tornillo was slated to close. Scores of others, however, operated at other points on the border.

With reports of many children falling ill and at least two deaths, a federal judge ordered that youngsters be reunited with their families immediately. After extensive public outcry over stories about the family separation policy emerged, Trump backed down and signed an executive order in late June ending the barbaric practice.

Even if the administration had been inclined to adhere to the court order as quickly as possible, which it did not, the task was complicated. It soon became evident that the government agents at the border had not kept accurate enough information to match many of the children with their parents. The Border Patrol did not use adequate methods either through fingerprinting or taking photographs during processing to ensure that the youngsters could be easily traced to their parents. Indeed, some of the parents of the children still in detention were immediately sent back to their home countries without their children.

Immigration judges on the border were soon faced with situations that seemed impossible. Unaccompanied children, some under the age of six, were brought into courts to answer questions regarding their lack of papers. In one case, an immigration official reported, a two-year-old girl was lifted onto a chair to face a judge.

In addition to Trump's refusal to extend the protection afforded young people under the DACA program initiated by President Obama, the administration refused to extend the program known as Temporary Protected Status (TPS). A temporary legal authority granted to individuals from countries facing the dangers of warfare, natural disasters, or other circumstances threatening their lives, TPS enables refugees to live and work for a limited time in the United States. A high proportion of those individuals already living in the country under TPS are from Honduras and El Salvador, the very countries that largely made up the refugees from Central America. Just as Trump was temporarily blocked from ending the DACA program, his attempted action on TPS was also halted by federal courts in October, pending further legal action.

With the elections of 2018 looming and additional Central American refugees headed to the U.S.-Mexican border, Trump took to the political stage to claim that the group represented a looming crisis at the border; he even claimed that many in the group were likely terrorists. Shortly before the election, Trump ordered federal troops to the border to protect against what he called "an invasion." It was an obvious political ploy, but it did little to help Republican fortunes. Trump's party suffered a loss in the form of control of the House of Representatives. It was clear to almost everyone that the U.S. military was not needed on the border to protect the country from an imminent invasion.

In late November, following an incident in which Border Patrol agents used tear gas on migrants at the border, Trump took to his usual morning Twitter practice by declaring that he might temporarily close entry of all traffic to the United States from Mexico along the entire border. "Mexico should move the flag waving Migrants, many of whom are stone cold criminals, back to their countries," he declared. "Do it by plane, do it by bus, do it anyway you want, but they are NOT coming into the U.S.A."

BUILD THE WALL OR CLOSE THE GOVERNMENT

In late December 2018 the debate over Trump's proposed wall took on an even more threatening turn. With a number of U.S. government agencies still not funded through the regular appropriations process, Trump insisted that over $5 billion be included by Congress to begin construction of the wall or he would not sign appropriations bills for those agencies. With Democrats united in opposing any federal funds for the wall, Trump told incoming Speaker of the House Nancy Pelosi and Democratic minority leader Charles Schumer in a meeting on December 11 that without money for the wall, he would close down the government. On December 22 he followed through on the threat.

Through the holiday season and into the new year, approximately 800,000 federal workers from such agencies as the Department of Homeland Security and the National Park Service were without work, as were over 1 million federal contract workers. In early January Trump told congressional leaders that the shutdown could last for "months or even years" if no money for the wall was allocated. He rejected all pleas to sign a continuing resolution to fund the government while debate over border security could be undertaken.

He continued to declare that the border was a chaotic scene that threatened national security. At one point he said that border rangers had found prayer rugs in the southwest desert left by terrorists after they had crossed the border. Reporters checking this story found that in one of the claims the so-called prayer rug had turned out to be a soccer jersey. They turned up no credible evidence of actual prayer rugs being left in the desert.

As the partial government shutdown ground into a third week with no agreement at hand, its effects soon began to have a demoralizing effect not only on those government employees and contractors waiting at home for the impasse to be resolved but also on public services—from drastic slowdowns in the workings of the IRS, to national park closures, and, most importantly, to a gradual slowdown in air travel. Finally, after thirty-five days, a period that represented the longest government shutdown in history, Trump relented on January 25. He opened the government for three weeks but promised the nation that his border wall would be built. Administration spokespersons threatened another government shutdown or a declaration of a national emergency to secure funds for the wall. In addition, in late January Trump ordered additional troops to the border.

On February 4, 2019, in a State of the Union Address Trump again warned of the lawless southern border and the "onslaught" of migrants, gang members, drug cartels, and other ominous dangers threatening the country. Of the wall he said, "I will get it built."

Meanwhile, on the same day, New Mexico's Governor Michelle Lujan Grisham ordered the withdrawal of the majority of National Guard troops deployed to the state's southern border. Rejecting Trump's claims of a security crisis, the governor pointed out that the border towns in New Mexico were some of the safest in the state. She wanted no part of Trump's "charade of border fear-mongering by misusing our diligent National Guard troops."

Trump and his supporters continued to claim that rampant crime along the border demanded immediate action and that lawlessness and violence plagued cities and towns from San Diego to Brownsville. In fact, the FBI Uniform Crime Report 2017 showed that border counties from California to Texas had far less crime per capita than American counties in other parts of the country. Several members of the U.S. Congress representing border communities angrily charged the administration with spreading malicious and false narratives about life on the border.

And so the fierce contention and debate over the U.S.-Mexican border and the proposed wall continue. In September 1964 Rev. Martin Luther King Jr. visited the Berlin Wall that had been erected three years earlier dividing the city. "For here on either side of the wall," he declared, "are God's children and no man-made barrier can obliterate that fact—men and women search for meaning, hope for fulfillment, yearn for something beyond themselves, and cry desperately for love and community to support them in this pilgrim journey." Although King a half-century earlier was not speaking about the U.S.-Mexican border, today his words resonate as the United States faces critical decisions about immigration and the future of border relations.

Bibliography

Arreola, Daniel and James Curtis. *The Mexican Border Cities: Landscape Anatomy and Place Personality.* Tucson: The University of Arizona Press, 1993.

Bacon, David. *The Children of NAFTA: Labor Wars on the U.S./Mexico Border.* Berkeley: University of California Press, 2004.

Balderrama, Francisco and Raymond Rodríguez. *Decade of Betrayal: Mexican Repatriation in the 1930s.* Albuquerque: University of New Mexico Press, 2006.

Ball, Larry. *The United States Marshals of New Mexico & Arizona Territories, 1846–1912.* Albuquerque: University of New Mexico Press, 1978.

Balli, Celilia. "Two Cities, Two Countries, Common Ground." *New York Times,* February 5, 2018. https://www.nytimes.com/2018/02/05/travel/nogales-arizona-mexico-border.html.

Bender, Steven. *Run for the Border: Vice and Virtue in U.S.-Mexican Border Crossings.* New York: New York University Press, 2012.

Benton-Cohen, Katherine. *Borderland Americans: Racial Divisions and Labor War in the Arizona Borderlands.* Cambridge, MA: Harvard University Press, 2009.

Bilker, Mollie. "New Poll of Cronkite News, Univision News and the Dallas Morning News Shows Strong Sense of Community on Both Sides of the U.S.-Mexico Border." *Cronkite News*, July 17, 2016. https://cronkitenews.azpbs.org/2016/07/17/border-poll-overview.

Blust, Kendall. "Hundreds Celebrate Binational Mass in Douglas-Agua Prieta." *Arizona Daily Star*, February 21, 2016. http://tucson.com/news/hundreds-celebrate-binational-mass-in-douglas-agua-prieta/article_bc9921e0-d90a-11e5-9515-c316ff2ce1ff.html.

Bruns, Roger. *Documents of the Chicano Movement.* Santa Barbara, CA: ABC-CLIO, 2018.

Bruns, Roger. *Encyclopedia of Cesar Chavez: The Farm Workers' Fight for Rights and Justice*. Santa Barbara, CA: Greenwood, 2013.

Cantú, Francisco. *The Line Becomes a River: Dispatches from the Border.* New York: Riverhead Books, 2018.

Chatfield, Leroy, comp. *Farmworker Movement Documentation Project*. http://www.farmworkermovement.org.

Chávez, Ernesto. *"Mi Raza Primero!": Nationalism, Identity, and Insurgency in the Chicano Movement, 1966–1978*. Berkeley: University of California Press, 2002.

Davidson, Miriam. *Lives on the Line: Dispatches from the U.S.-Mexican Border*. Tucson: University of Arizona Press, 2000.

Dear, Michael. "Monuments, Manifest Destiny, and Mexico." *Prologue,* Summer 2005. https://www.archives.gov/publications/prologue/2005/summer/mexico-1.html.

Dibble, Sandra. "Cross-Border Percussion Concert Unites U.S., Mexico Musicians at Friendship Park," *San Diego Union Tribune*, January 27, 2018. https://www.sandiegouniontribune.com/news/border-baja-california/sd-me-percussion-friendship-park-20180127-story.html.

Doyle, Kate. "Operation Intercept: The Perils of Unilateralism." *Proceso and National Security Archives*, 2003. https://nsarchive2.gwu.edu/NSAEBB/NSAEBB86.

Ganster, Paul with David Lorey. *The U.S.-Mexican Border Today: Conflict and Cooperation in Historical Perspective*. Lanham, MD: Rowman & Littlefield, 2016.

Ganz, Marshall. *Why David Sometimes Wins: Leadership, Organization, and Strategy in the California Farm Worker Movement*. New York: Oxford University Press, 2009.

Garcia, Ignacio. *United We Win: The Rise and Fall of La Raza Unida Party*. Tucson: University of Arizona Press, 1989.

Garcia, Mario T., ed. *Border Correspondent: Selected Writings, 1955–1970: Ruben Salazar*. Berkeley: University of California Press, 1998.

Gonzales, Richard. "What Is DACA and What Happens Next?" *NPR*, September 5, 2017. https://www.npr.org/2017/09/05/548754723/5-things-you-should-know-about-daca.

Grillo, Loan. *El Narco: Inside Mexico's Criminal Insurgency*. London: Bloomsbury, 2012.

Griswold del Castillo, Richard. *The Treaty of Guadalupe Hidalgo: A Legacy of Conflict*. Norman: University of Oklahoma Press, 1990.

Griswold del Castillo, Richard and Richard A. Garcia. *Cesar Chavez: A Triumph of Spirit*. Norman: University of Oklahoma Press, 1995.

Grossman, Ron. "The 1954 Deportation of Mexican Migrants and the 'Wetback Airlift' in Chicago," *Chicago Tribune,* March 4, 2017. https://www.chicagotribune.com/news/opinion/commentary/ct-flash-deportation-migrant-mexican-0305-20170303-story.html.

Guardino, Peter. *The Dead March: A History of the Mexican-American War*. Cambridge, MA: Harvard University Press, 2017.

Gutiérrez, José Angel. *The Making of a Chicano Militant: Lessons from Cristal*. Madison: The University of Wisconsin Press, 1998.

Heer, Jeet. "Operation Wetback Revisited," *New Republic,* April 25, 2016. https://newrepublic.com/article/132988/operation-wetback-revisited.

Herman Baca Collection, University of California San Diego, Digital Resources, http://library.ucsd.edu/dc/collection/bb03768122.

Hernández, Kelly Lytle. *Migra! A History of the U.S. Border Patrol.* Berkeley: University of California Press, 2010.

Hinckley, Story. "A Border, a Bus, and Then School Begins in New Mexico." *Christian Science Monitor,* November 6, 2018, 24–30.

Hing, Bill Ong. *NAFTA, Globalization, and Mexican Migration.* Philadelphia: Temple University Press, 2010.

Hogan, Andrew. *Hunting El Chapo: Taking Down the World's Most-Wanted Drug-Lord.* New York: HarperCollins, 2018.

Hurst, James. *Pancho Villa and Black Jack Pershing: The Punitive Expedition in Mexico.* Santa Barbara, CA: Praeger, 2007.

Hutton, Paul. *The Apache Wars: The Hunt for Geronimo, the Apache Kid, and the Captive Boy Who Started the Longest War in American History.* New York: Broadway Books, 2017.

Hutton, Paul. *Phil Sheridan and His Army.* Norman: University of Oklahoma Press, 1999.

Johnson, Kevin and Bernard Trujillo. *Immigration Law and the US.-Mexican Border.* Tucson: University of Arizona Press, 2011.

Kang, S. Deborah. *The INS on the Line: Making Immigration Law on the U.S.-Mexican Border, 1917–1954.* New York: Oxford University Press, 2017.

Katz, Friedrich. *The Life and Times of Pancho Villa.* Stanford, CA: Stanford University Press, 1998.

Kelly, Patrick. "Lincoln Looks South of the Border." *New York Times,* November 22, 2013. https://opinionator.blogs.nytimes.com/2013/11/22/lincoln-looks-south-of-the-border.

Krasner, Caitlin. "History of the Border Fence." *National Border, National Park: A History of Organ Pipe Cactus National Monument.* https://organpipehistory.com/border/history-of-th-border-fence.

Martínez, Oscar. *Border Boom Town: Ciudad Juárez since 1848.* Austin: University of Texas Press, 1978.

Martínez, Oscar. *Border People: Life and Society in the U.S.–Mexico Borderlands.* Tucson: University of Arizona Press, 1998.

Martínez, Oscar. *Troublesome Border.* Tucson: University of Arizona Press, 2006.

Matthews, Matt. *The US Army on the Mexican Border: A Historical Perspective.* Fort Leavenworth, KS: Combat Studies Institute Press, 2007. https://www.armyupress.army.mil/Portals/7/combat-studies-institute/csi-books/Matthews_op22.pdf.

McLynn, Frank. *Villa and Zapata: A History of the Mexican Revolution.* New York: Basic Books, 2002.

Medrano, Lourdes. "Bullets Across the Border: The Trial of a U.S. Border Patrol Agent Raises Legal, Foreign-Policy Issues." *The Christian Science Monitor Weekly,* March 19, 2018. https://www.csmonitor.com/World/Americas/Bullets-across-the-border-Trial-of-US-Border-Patrol-agent-raises-legal-foreign-policy-issues.

Meier, Matt and Feliciano Ribera. *Mexican Americans/American Mexicans: From Conquistadors to Chicanos.* New York: Hill and Wang, 1993.

"Mendez v. Westminster: Paving the Way to School Desegregation," *Constitutional Rights Foundation*, Summer 2007. http://www.crf-usa.org/bill-of-rights-in-action/bria-23-2-c-mendez-v-westminster-paving-the-way-to-school-desegregation.

Miller, Tom. "Thornton Wilder's Desert Oasis," *Smithsonian Magazine*, July 2009. https://www.smithsonianmag.com/travel/thornton-wilders-desert-oasis-30864552.

Monroy, Douglas. *The Borders Within: Encounters between Mexico and the U.S.* Tucson: The University of Arizona Press, 2008.

Mora-Torres. Juan. *The Making of the Mexican Border: The State, Capitalism, and Society in Nuevo León, 1848–1910.* Austin: University of Texas Press, 2010.

Morgan, Brandon. "Villa and the Raid on Columbus, New Mexico 1916." *Office of the State Historian, State Records Center & Archives, Santa Fe, NM.* http://newmexicohistory.org/events/pancho-villa-and-the-raid-on-columbus-new-mexico-1916.

Navarro, Armando. *La Raza Unida Party: A Chicano Challenge to the U.S. Two-Party Dictatorship.* Philadelphia: Temple University Press, 2000.

Nevins, Joseph. *Operation Gatekeeper and Beyond: The War on "Illegals" and the Remaking of the U.S.-Mexican Boundary.* London: Routledge, 2010.

Ngai, Mae M. *Impossible Subjects: Illegal Aliens and the Making of Modern America.* Princeton, NJ: Princeton University Press, 2004.

Olivas, Michael. *Colored Men and Hombres Aquí: Hernandez v. Texas and the Emergence of Mexican American Lawyering.* Houston: Arte Público Press, 2006.

Orozco, Cynthia E. *No Mexicans, Women, or Dogs Allowed: The Rise of the Mexican American Civil Rights Movement.* Austin: University of Texas Press, 2009.

Ortiz, Laura Velasco and Oscar Contreras. *Mexican Voices of the Border Region: Mexicans and Mexican Americans Speak about Living along the Wall.* Philadelphia: Temple University Press, 2011.

Pawel, Miriam. *The Crusades of Cesar Chavez: A Biography.* New York: Bloomsbury Press, 2015.

Pawel, Miriam. *The Union of Their Dreams: Power, Hope, and Struggle in Cesar Chavez's Farm Worker Movement.* New York: Bloomsbury Press, 2009.

Payan, Tony. *The Three U.S.-Mexico Border Wars: Drugs, Immigration, and Homeland Security.* Santa Barbara, CA: Praeger, 2016.

Report of the Boundary Commission upon the Survey and Re-marking of the Boundary Between the United States and Mexico West of the Rio Grande, 1891–1896. Washington, D.C.: U.S. Government Printing Office, 1898.

Rios, Pedro. "Friendship Park: A Demonstration of Humanity Between the Border Walls." *American Friends Service Committee*, June 8, 2016. https://www.afsc.org/blogs/friendship-park.

Ruiz, Matthew Ismael. "City of Dreams: Music and Politics Meet in the Border Community of McAllen, Texas." *Pitchfork,* May 25, 2017. https://pitchfork.com/features/article/10083-city-of-dreams-music-and-politics-meet-in-the-border-community-of-mcallen-texas.

Salas, Miguel Tinker. "Sonora. The Making of a Border Society, 1880–1910." *Journal of the Southwest* Winter 1992, 429–456. http://www.jstor.org/stable/40170040.

Shuchart, Scott. "Careless Cruelty." *The Washington Post: Outlook,* October 28, 2018, B1, B4.

Soennichsen, John. *The Chinese Exclusion Act of 1882.* Santa Barbara, CA: Greenwood, 2011.

Soldatenko, Michael. *Chicano Studies: The Genesis of a Discipline*: Tucson: University of Arizona Press, 2011.

Sorkin, Amy Davidson. "Political Borders." *The New Yorker,* December 10, 2018, 19–20.

Stavans, Ilan. *Spanglish: The Making of a New American Language.* New York: Harper Perennial, 2004.

Strum, Philippa. *Mendez v. Westminster: School Desegregation and Mexican American Rights.* Lawrence: University of Kansas Press, 2010.

Tejano Voices Interviews, University of Texas at Arlington, Center for Mexican American Studies, http://library.uta.edu/tejanovoices.

Theroux, Paul. "Myth and Reason on the Mexican Border." *Smithsonian Magazine,* September 21, 2016. https://www.smithsonianmag.com/travel/myth-reason-mexican-border-180960357.

Thompson, Jerry, ed. *Juan Cortina and the Texas-Mexico Frontier 1859–1877.* El Paso: Texas Western Press, 1994.

Tijerina, Reies. *They Called Me King Tiger: My Struggle for the Land and Our Rights*. Houston: Arte Publico Press, 2000.

Truett, Samuel. *Fugitive Landscapes: The Forgotten History of the U.S.-Mexican Borderlands.* New Haven, CT: Yale University Press, 2006.

Valdez, Luis. *Zoot Suit and Other Plays.* Houston: Arte Publico Press, 1992.

Wagner, James. "A Mexican Baseball Team Plays in Texas. It's a Home Game." *New York Times*. September 21, 2018. https://www.nytimes.com/2018/09/21/sports/baseball/mexico-baseball-laredo.html.

Walters, Joanna. "What Is DACA and Who Are the Dreamers?" *The Guardian,* September 14, 2017. https://www.theguardian.com/us-news/2017/sep/04/donald-trump-what-is-daca-dreamers.

Index

An italicized *f* following a page number indicates a figure.

About the Author

Roger Bruns is a historian and former deputy executive director of the National Historical Publications and Records Commission at the National Archives and Records Administration in Washington, D.C. He is the author of many books, including *Documents of the Chicano Movement*; *Encyclopedia of Cesar Chavez: The Farm Workers' Fight for Rights and Justice*; *Icons of Latino America: Latino Contributions to American Culture*; *Knights of the Road: A Hobo History*; *Preacher: Billy Sunday and Big-Time American Evangelism*; and *Almost History: Close Calls, Plan B's, and Twists of Fate in America's Past*. He has written several biographies for young readers on such figures as Cesar Chavez and Martin Luther King Jr.